Pocosin Lakes National Wildlife Refuge

Comprehensive Conservation Plan

U.S. Department of the Interior
Fish and Wildlife Service
Southeast Region

September 2007

Submitted by: _____ Date: 8/24/07
Howard Phillips, Refuge Manager
Pocosin Lakes NWR

Concur: _____ Date: 8/25/07
Mike Bryant, Project Leader
North Carolina Coastal Plains Complex

Concur: _____ Date: 9/26/07
Pete Jerome, Refuge Supervisor
Southeast Region

Concur: _____ Date: 9/27/07
Jon Andrew, Regional Chief
Southeast Region

Approved by: _____ Date: 9/28/07
Sam Hamilton, Regional Director
Southeast Region

COMPREHENSIVE CONSERVATION PLAN

POCOSIN LAKES NATIONAL WILDLIFE REFUGE

**U.S. Department of the Interior
Fish and Wildlife Service**

Southeast Region
Atlanta, Georgia 30345

November 2007

TABLE OF CONTENTS

COMPREHENSIVE CONSERVATION PLAN

EXECUTIVE SUMMARY 1

I. BACKGROUND 1
    Introduction 1
    Purpose and Need For The Plan 1
    U.S. Fish and Wildlife Service 2
    National Wildlife Refuge System 2
    Legal Policy Context 3
    National Conservation Plans and Initiatives 3
    Relationship To State Partners 4

II. REFUGE OVERVIEW 5
    Introduction 5
        Location 5
        Establishment 5
    Refuge History and Purposes 5
        History 5
        Purposes 7
    Special Designations 8
    Ecosystem Context 9
    Regional Conservation Plans and Initiatives 9
    Ecological Threats and Problems 11
        Forest and Fragmentation 11
        Alterations To Hydrology 13
        Siltation of Aquatic Ecosystems 14
        Proliferation of Invasive Aquatic Plants 14
        Conservation Priorities 14
    Physical Resources 16
        Climate 16
        Geology 16
        Subsurface Resources 17
        Soils 17
        Hydrology 21
        Water Quality 22
        Air Quality 22
    Biological Resources 25
        Habitat 25
        Wildlife 36
        Invasive and/or Exotic Species 43
    Cultural Resources 44
    Socioeconomic Environment 44
        History of the Area 44
        Land Use in the Area 46
        Demographics In The Area 47
        Employment In The Area 51
        Forestry In The Area 53

Comprehensive Conservation Plan

    Outdoor Recreation In The Area 54
    Outdoor Recreation Economics 54
    Tourism In The Area 55
    Transportation 56
    Cultural Environment 56
  Refuge Administration and Management 57
    Land Protection and Conservation 57
    Personnel, Operations, and Maintenance 63

III. PLAN DEVELOPMENT 65

  Public Involvement and the Planning Process 65
  Summary Of Issues, Concerns, and Opportunities 66
    Hydrology 66
    Fish and Wildlife Populations 66
    Habitats 67
    Wilderness Review 68
    Public Use 68
    Resource Protection 69

IV. MANAGEMENT DIRECTION 71

  Introduction 71
  Vision 71
  Goals 72
  Objectives and Strategies 72
    Fish and Wildlife Populations 72
    Habitat Management 76
    Public Use 82
    Resource Protection 88
    Refuge Administration 91

V. PLAN IMPLEMENTATION 95

  Introduction 95
  Proposed Projects 95
  Volunteers 101
  Partnership Opportunities 101
  Step-Down Management Plans 101
  Monitoring and Adaptive Management 103

APPENDICES

APPENDIX I. GLOSSARY 105

APPENDIX II. REFERENCES AND LITERATURE CITED 111

APPENDIX III. RELEVANT LEGAL MANDATES 117

APPENDIX IV. PUBLIC INVOLVEMENT **125**
    Summary of Public Scoping 125
    Draft Plan Comments and Service Responses 125

APPENDIX V. DECISIONS AND APPROVALS **159**
    INTRA-SERVICE SECTION 7 BIOLOGICAL EVALUATION 159
    APPROPRIATE USE DETERMINATIONS... 162
    COMPATIBILITY DETERMINATIONS.. 177

APPENDIX VI. REFUGE BIOTA **201**

APPENDIX VII. PRIORITY BIRD SPECIES AND SPECIES SUITES..**227**

APPENDIX VIII. BUDGET REQUESTS **229**

APPENDIX IX. WILDERNESS REVIEW **257**

APPENDIX X. CONSULTATION AND COORDINATION **265**

APPENDIX XI. FINDING OF NO SIGNIFICANT IMPACT **269**

List of Figures

Figure 1. The location of Pocosin Lakes National Wildlife Refuge in Tyrrell, Washington, and Hyde Counties, North Carolina 6
Figure 2. Pocosin Lakes National Wildlife Refuge in the South Atlantic Coastal Plain Physiographic Area. 10
Figure 3. Characteristics of soils of Pocosin Lakes National Wildlife Refuge 20
Figure 4. Vegetative Habitat Types of Pocosin Lakes NWR. 27
Figure 5. Existing boundary of the Pocosin Lakes National Wildlife Refuge 58
Figure 6. Current visitor facilities at Pocosin Lakes National Wildlife Refuge 60
Figure 7. Proposed Visitor Facilities of the Pocosin Lakes National Wildlife Refuge. 83
Figure 8. Wilderness inventory units of Pocosin Lakes National Wildlife Refuge 258
Figure 9. Potential wilderness study areas of the Pocosin Lakes National Wildlife Refuge 262

List of Tables

Table 1. Pocosin Lakes National Wildlife Refuge acquisition history 6
Table 2. The Nature Conservancy ranking of vegetative communities of Pocosin Lakes National Wildlife Refuge 8
Table 3. Federally threatened and endangered animal species that occur on the South Atlantic 11
Table 4. Characteristics of soils of Pocosin Lakes National Wildlife Refuge 18
Table 5. Active National Pollution Discharge Elimination System (NPDES) permits in Tyrrell, Washington, and Hyde Counties, North Carolina 23
Table 6. Classifications of water bodies and streams surrounding the Pocosin Lakes National Wildlife Refuge 24
Table 7. Habitat types by approximate acreage for Pocosin Lakes National Wildlife Refuge 26
Table 8. 1999-2000 Monthly peak waterfowl use on Pocosin Lakes National Wildlife Refuge 38
Table 9. 1999-2000 Monthly waterfowl use days on Pocosin Lakes National Wildlife Refuge 39
Table 10. 1988-2005 annual peak waterfowl use on Pungo Unit 40
Table 11. 1988-2005 annual waterfowl use days on Pungo Unit 41
Table 12. 2002-2005 (aerial survey only) annual peak waterfowl use on Pocosin Lakes National Wildlife Refuge (including the Pungo Unit) 42
Table 13. 2002-2005 (aerial survey only) annual waterfowl use days on Pocosin Lakes National Wildlife Refuge (including the Pungo Unit) 42
Table 14. Tyrrell County agricultural statistics from the 2002 USDA Census 48
Table 15. Commodity production in Tyrrell County in 2002 and 1997 from the 2002 and 1997 48
Table 16. Hyde County agricultural statistics from the 2002 USDA Census 49
Table 17. Commodity production in Hyde County in 2002 and 1997 from the 2002 and 1997 49
Table 18. Washington County agricultural statistics from the 2002 USDA Census 50
Table 19. Commodity production in Washington County in 2002 and 1997 from the 2002 and 50
Table 20. Economic and population data for northeastern North Carolina Counties 52
Table 21. Protected lands in Tyrrell, Washington, and Hyde Counties 57
Table 22. Staff of the Pocosin Lakes National Wildlife Refuge 63
Table 23. Projects supporting fish and wildlife population strategies 95
Table 24. Projects supporting habitat strategies 96
Table 25. Projects supporting public use strategies 97
Table 26. Projects supporting resource protection strategies 98
Table 27. Projects supporting refuge administration strategies 99
Table 28. Proposed staff for the Pocosin Lakes National Wildlife Refuge 100

Executive Summary

The Fish and Wildlife Service has prepared this Comprehensive Conservation Plan to guide the management of Pocosin Lakes National Wildlife Refuge (Pocosin Lakes NWR) in Hyde, Tyrrrell, and Washington Counties, North Carolina. The plan outlines programs and corresponding resource needs for the next 15 years, as mandated by the National Wildlife Refuge System Improvement Act of 1997.

Before the Service began planning, it conducted a biological review of the refuge's wildlife and habitat management program and conducted public scoping meetings to solicit public opinion of the issues the plan should address. The biological review team was composed of biologists from Federal and State agencies and non-governmental organizations that have an interest in the refuge. The refuge staff held six public scoping meetings and two public meetings to solicit public reaction to the proposed alternatives. Also, a 30-day public review and comment period of the draft comprehensive conservation plan and environmental assessment was provided. In addition, two open house type public meetings were held during the 30-day public comment period to answer questions and take comments on the plan.

The Service developed and analyzed four alternatives. Alternative 1 was a proposal to maintain the status quo. The refuge currently manages its impoundments very intensively by controlling water levels and vegetation to create optimum habitat for migrating waterfowl. It also manages pine forests and marshes with prescribed fire. Waterfowl are surveyed on a routine basis. The refuge has a visitor center, which includes an auditorium and indoor and outdoor classrooms, but depends on volunteers and cooperating agency personnel to staff and maintain the center. With regard to public use, each of the priority public uses as defined in the National Wildlife Refuge System Improvement Act of 1997 (e.g., hunting, fishing, wildlife observation, wildlife photography, and environmental education and interpretation) is encouraged. The staff conducts a limited number of environmental education and interpretation programs. Under this alternative, eight staff members (7.5 full-time equivalents) are dedicated to refuge management and eight staff members (7.5 full-time equivalents) are dedicated to fire management, as was the case when the plan was started. Because of budget constraints, two of the refuge management positions have been held vacant for the last several years.

Alternative 2, the preferred alternative, proposed moderate program increases to address the refuge priorities. The refuge would manage its impoundments very intensively by controlling water levels and vegetation to create optimum habitat for migrating waterfowl. It would also manage pine forests and marshes with prescribed fire and would manage the vegetative composition of habitats in selected areas. Waterfowl would be surveyed on a routine basis. The staff would develop inventory plans for all species and implement them in selected habitats. The staff would develop and implement a black bear management plan. The staff would maintain the visitor center with volunteers and cooperating agency personnel supplementing refuge personnel. There would be eighteen staff members (17.5 full-time equivalents) dedicated to refuge management and eight staff members (7.5 full-time equivalents) dedicated to fire management. The volunteer program would be expanded to recruit volunteers to contribute 4,000 hours of service. Two workamper pads would be built to attract volunteers with recreational vehicles. The six priority public uses would be allowed and the staff would conduct environmental education and interpretation programs to meet local needs.

Alternative 3 proposed substantial program increases. The refuge would manage its impoundments very intensively by controlling water levels and vegetation to create optimum habitat for migrating waterfowl. It would also manage pine forests and marshes with prescribed fire and would manage the vegetative composition of habitats on the entire refuge. Waterfowl would be surveyed on a routine basis. The staff would develop inventory plans for all species and implement them over the entire refuge. The staff would develop and implement a black bear management plan. The staff would maintain the visitor center with volunteers and cooperating agency personnel supplementing refuge personnel. There would be twenty-five staff members (25 full-time equivalents) dedicated to refuge management and seven staff members (7 full-time equivalents) dedicated to fire management. The refuge would conduct forest management and hydrology restoration by contract. The volunteer program would be expanded to recruit volunteers to contribute 10,000 hours of service. Eight workamper pads would be built to attract volunteers with recreational vehicles. The six priority public uses would be allowed and the staff would conduct environmental education and interpretation programs to meet local needs and expand outreach to the communities.

Alternative 4 proposed maintaining the refuge in caretaker status. The refuge would manage its impoundments very intensively by controlling water levels and vegetation to create optimum habitat for migrating waterfowl. It would manage pine forests and marshes with prescribed fire. Waterfowl would be surveyed on a routine basis. The visitor center would depend on volunteers and cooperating agency personnel to staff and maintain it. There would be four staff members (3.5 full-time equivalents) dedicated to refuge management and eight staff members (7.5 full-time equivalents) dedicated to fire management. The six priority public uses would be allowed; however, the staff would not conduct any environmental education and interpretation programs.

The Service selected Alternative 2 as its preferred alternative and is reflected in this comprehensive conservation plan. Alternative 2 advances the refuge program considerably, and is more realistic than Alternative 3 in terms of expected staffing levels to conduct the proposed program.

COMPREHENSIVE CONSERVATION PLAN

I. Background

INTRODUCTION

This Comprehensive Conservation Plan (CCP) for Pocosin Lakes NWR was prepared to guide management actions and direction for the refuge. Fish and wildlife conservation will receive first priority in refuge management; wildlife-dependent recreation will be allowed and encouraged as long as it is compatible with, and does not detract from, the mission of the refuge or the purposes for which it ws established.

A planning team developed a range of alternatives that best met the goals and objectives of the refuge and that could be implemented within the 15-year planning period. The draft of this plan was made available to State and Federal government agencies, conservation partners, and the general public for review and comment. The comments from each entity were considered in the development of this CCP, describing the Fish and Wildlife Service's preferred plan.

PURPOSE AND NEED FOR THE PLAN

The purpose of this CCP is to identify the role that Pocosin Lakes NWR will play in support of the mission of the National Wildlife Refuge System, and to provide long-term guidance to the refuge's management programs and activities for the next 15 years.

The plan will:

- provide a clear statement of the desired future conditions when refuge purposes and goals are accomplished;
- provide refuge neighbors and visitors with a clear understanding of the management actions on the refuge;
- ensure management of the refuge reflects policies and goals of the Refuge System;
- ensure refuge management is consistent with Federal, State, and local plans;
- provide long-term continuity in refuge management; and
- provide a basis for operation, maintenance, and capital improvement budget requests.

Perhaps the greatest need of the Service is to communicate with the public and include public participation in its efforts to carry out the mission of the National Wildlife Refuge System. Many agencies, organizations, institutions, businesses, and private citizens have developed relationships with the Service to advance the goals of the Refuge System. This CCP supports the following: Partners in Flight Initiative, South Atlantic Coastal Plain Migratory Bird Conservation Plan, North American Waterfowl Management Plan, Western Hemisphere Shorebird Reserve Network, and National Wetlands Priority Conservation Plan.

U.S. FISH AND WILDLIFE SERVICE

The U.S. Fish and Wildlife Service is the primary Federal agency responsible for the conservation, protection, and enhancement of the Nation's fish and wildlife populations and their habitats. Although the Service shares some conservation responsibilities with other Federal, State, Tribal, and local and private entities, it has specific trustee obligations for migratory birds, threatened and endangered species, anadromous fish, and certain marine mammals. In addition, the Service administers a national network of lands and waters for the management and protection of these resources.

As part of its mission, the Service manages more than 540 national wildlife refuges covering over 93 million acres. These areas comprise the National Wildlife Refuge System, the world's largest collection of lands and waters specifically managed for fish and wildlife. The majority of these lands (77 million acres) is in Alaska. The remaining 16 million acres are spread across the other 49 states and several island territories.

NATIONAL WILDLIFE REFUGE SYSTEM

The mission of the Refuge System, as defined by the National Wildlife Refuge System Improvement Act of 1997, is:

> *... to administer a national network of lands and waters for the conservation, management, and where appropriate, restoration of the fish, wildlife and plant resources and their habitats within the United States for the benefit of present and future generations of Americans.*

The National Wildlife Refuge System Improvement Act of 1997 established, for the first time, a clear mission of wildlife conservation for the Refuge System. The Act states that the Service shall manage each refuge to:

- Fulfill the mission of the Refuge System;
- Fulfill the individual purposes of each refuge;
- Consider the needs of fish and wildlife first;
- Fulfill the requirement of developing a comprehensive conservation plan for each unit of the Refuge System, and fully involve the public in the preparation of these plans;
- Maintain the biological integrity, diversity, and environmental health of the Refuge System;
- Recognize that wildlife-dependent recreation activities, including hunting, fishing, wildlife observation, wildlife photography, and environmental education and interpretation, are legitimate and priority public uses; and
- Retain the authority of refuge managers to determine compatible public uses.

Following the passage of the Act in 1997, the Service immediately began efforts to carry out the direction of the new legislation, including the preparation of comprehensive conservation plans for all refuges. The development of these plans is now ongoing nationally. Consistent with the Act, all refuge comprehensive conservation plans are being prepared in conjunction with public involvement, and each refuge must complete its own plan within a 15-year schedule.

Approximately 36.7 million people visited the country's national wildlife refuges in 2004, mostly to observe wildlife in their natural habitats. As this visitation continues to grow, substantial economic benefits are being generated to the local communities that surround the refuges. Economists have reported that national wildlife refuge visitors contribute more than $1.37 billion annually to the regional economies (U.S. Fish and Wildlife Service 2005). In addition, the National Survey of Fishing, Hunting, and Wildlife Associated Recreation reports that nearly 40 percent of the country's adults spent $108 billion on wildlife-related recreational pursuits in 2001 (U.S. Fish and Wildlife Service 2001).

Volunteerism continues to be a major contributor to the successes of the Refuge System. In 1998, volunteers contributed more than 1.5 million person-hours on the refuges nationwide, a service valued at more than $20.6 million.

The wildlife and habitat vision for national wildlife refuges stresses that wildlife comes first; that ecosystems, biodiversity, and wilderness are vital concepts in refuge management; that refuges must be healthy and growth must be strategic; and that the Refuge System serves as a model for habitat management with broad participation from others.

LEGAL POLICY CONTEXT

A variety of international treaties, Federal laws and regulations, Department and Service Policies, and Presidential executive orders guide the administration of Pocosin Lakes NWR. The documents and acts listed in Appendix III contain management options under the refuge's establishing authority and the National Wildlife Refuge System Administration Act of 1966 and National Wildlife Refuge System Improvement Act of 1997 (the legal and policy guidance for the operation of national wildlife refuges).

NATIONAL CONSERVATION PLANS AND INITIATIVES

Along with the Service's legal mandates and initiatives, other planning activities directly influence the development of the comprehensive conservation plan. Various groups and agencies develop and coordinate planning initiatives involving Federal, State, and local agencies; local communities, non-governmental organizations, and private individuals to help restore habitats for fish and wildlife on and off public lands.

The Service is initiating cooperative partnerships in an effort to reduce the declining trend in biological diversity. Biological planning for species groups targeted in this plan reflects the North American Waterfowl Management Plan. The North American Waterfowl Management Plan of 1986 brings together international teams of biologists from private and government organizations from Canada and the United States. The partnerships, called joint ventures, are working to restore waterfowl and other migratory bird populations to the levels of the early 1970s by protecting about 6 million acres of priority wetland habitats from the Gulf of Mexico to the Canadian Arctic.

The United States Shorebird Conservation Plan and Waterbirds for the Americas outline approaches to conserving those species groups. Restoration of migratory songbird populations is a high priority of the Partners in Flight Plan. It also provides strategies for conserving and managing wintering, breeding, and migration habitat for mid-continental wood duck and colonial bird populations.

The Partners in Flight Plan emphasizes land bird species as a priority for conservation. Habitat loss, population trends, and the vulnerability of species and habitats to threats are all factors used in the priority ranking of species. Further, biologists have identified priority species for each habitat type from which they will determine population and habitat objectives and conservation actions. This list of priority species, objectives, and conservation actions will aid migratory bird management on the refuge.

The Farm Bill programs administered by the United States Department of Agriculture provide cost-share funding and technical assistance to private landowners to install and manage conservation practices on working farms and forests, restoring cropland to natural habitats. The programs provide opportunities for landowners in the vicinity of national wildlife refuges to manage their land better as wildlife habitat or protect it with easements.

RELATIONSHIP TO STATE PARTNERS

A provision of the National Wildlife Refuge System Improvement Act of 1997, and subsequent agency policy, is that the Service shall ensure timely and effective cooperation and collaboration with other Federal agencies and State fish and wildlife agencies during the course of acquiring and managing refuges. This cooperation is essential in providing the foundation for the protection and management of fish and wildlife throughout the United States.

The North Carolina Wildlife Resources Commission is a State-partnering agency with the Service, charged with enforcement responsibilities for migratory birds and endangered species, as well as managing the State's natural resources. The Commission also manages approximately 1.8 million acres of game lands in North Carolina.

The Commission coordinates the State's wildlife conservation program and provides public recreation opportunities, including an extensive hunting and fishing program, on several game lands and from several boat ramps located near Pocosin Lakes NWR. The agency's participation and contribution throughout this comprehensive conservation planning process has been valuable, and it is continuing its work with the Service to provide ongoing opportunities for an open dialogue with the public to improve the condition of fish and wildlife populations in North Carolina. Not only has the agency participated in biological reviews, stakeholder meetings, and field reviews as part of the planning process, it is also an active partner in annual hunt coordination planning and various wildlife and habitat surveys. A key part of the comprehensive conservation planning process is the integration of common mission objectives between the Service and the North Carolina Wildlife Resources Commission, where appropriate.

II. Refuge Overview

INTRODUCTION

LOCATION

Pocosin Lakes NWR is in Tyrrell, Washington, and Hyde Counties, North Carolina (Figure 1). The Service named the refuge for the pocosin habitat that dominates the landscape and for the lakes that occur within the pocosin. A pocosin is a swamp on a hill dominated by a dense, shrubby plant community and deep organic soil. The eastern edge of the refuge is on the Alligator River, just west of the Alligator River National Wildlife Refuge, and 47 miles west of the Atlantic Ocean. The northern edge of the refuge is U.S. Highway 64, four miles south of Albemarle Sound. The western edge of the refuge is just east of North Carolina Highway 45. The southern edge of the refuge is on the Intracoastal Waterway, four miles north of Mattamuskeet National Wildlife Refuge. This region is part of the physiographic area known as the South Atlantic Coastal Plain and the Fish and Wildlife Service administrative ecosystem known as the Roanoke-Tar-Neuse-Cape Fear Ecosystem.

The population of Tyrrell County is 4,419; the population of Washington County is 13,723; and the population of Hyde County is 5,826.

ESTABLISHMENT

Congress established the 12,000-acre Pungo NWR in 1963 by the authorities of the Migratory Bird Conservation Act of 1929 and the Fish and Wildlife Act of 1956. The Service established the Pocosin Lakes NWR in 1990 and made the Pungo NWR a unit of the refuge. The refuge now includes 110,106 acres.

REFUGE HISTORY AND PURPOSES

HISTORY

The 12,350.35-acre Pungo Unit of Pocosin Lakes NWR was established in 1963 as the Pungo NWR. In 1990, adjacent lands were donated to the Fish and Wildlife Service, establishing the Pocosin Lakes NWR. In 1991, Pungo NWR was abolished and the acreage transferred to Pocosin Lakes NWR. It is now known as the Pungo Unit of Pocosin Lakes NWR. Also in 1991, 5,707 acres in the Frying Pan area were transferred from Alligator River NWR to Pocosin Lakes NWR due to its proximity.

The refuge's complete acquisition history is in Table 1.

Figure 1. The location of Pocosin Lakes NWR in Tyrrell, Washington, and Hyde Counties, North Carolina

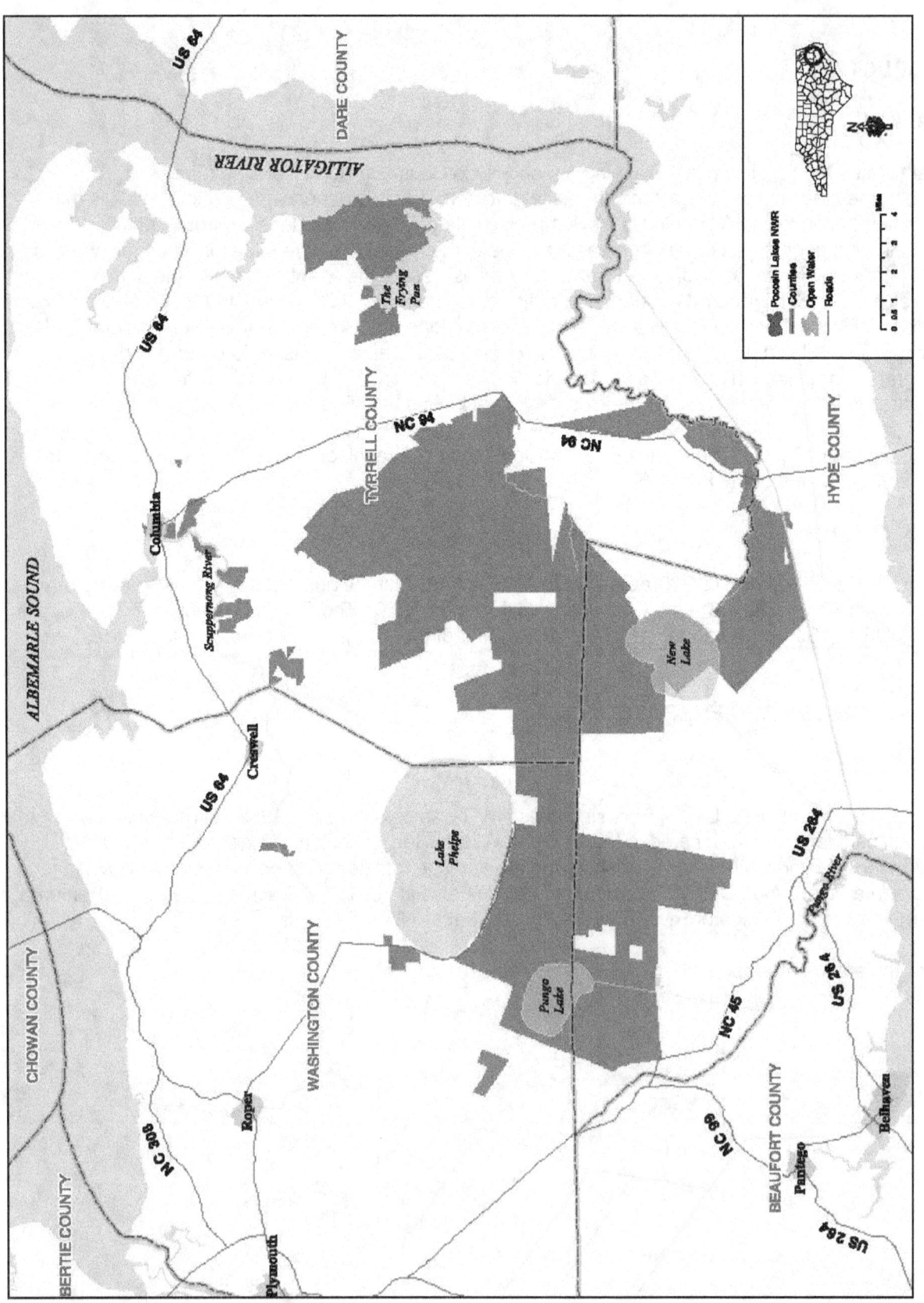

Table 1. Pocosin Lakes NWR acquisition history

DATE	TRACTS	ACRES	COST	COST ACRE	TOTAL ACREAGE	TOTAL COST
1990	1	89,658.00	$0	$0	89,658.00	$0
1991	3	19,465.37	$1,682,158	$93.14	109,123.37	$1,682,158
1993	1	55.53	$0	$0	109,178.90	$1,682,158
1994	1	879.32	$0	$0	110,058.22	$1,682,158
1999	2	48.32	$0	$0	110,106.54	$1,682,158
Total	8	110,106.54	$1,682,158	$15.27		

PURPOSES

The purpose of Pocosin Lakes NWR, as reflected in the legislation under which Congress authorized the refuge and the refuge has acquired land, is to protect and conserve migratory birds and other wildlife resources through the protection of wetlands, in accordance with the following laws:

...for use as an inviolate sanctuary, or for any other management purpose, for migratory birds... 16 U.S.C. Sec. 664 (Migratory Bird Conservation Act of 1929);

...for the conservation of the wetlands of the Nation in order to maintain the public benefits they provide and to help fulfill international obligations contained in various migratory bird treaties and conventions... 16 U.S.C. Sec 3901 (b) 100 Stat. 3583 (Emergency Wetland Resources Act of 1986)

...for the development, advancement, management, conservation, and protection of fish and wildlife resources... 16 U.S.C. Sec 742f(a)(4) (Fish and Wildlife Act of 1956)

...for the benefit of the United States Fish and Wildlife Service in performing its activities and services. Such acceptance may be subject to the terms of any restriction or affirmative covenant or condition of servitude... 16 U.S.C. Sec 742f(a)(4) (Fish and Wildlife Act of 1956)

The following objectives for the refuge were established in the Interim Management Plan completed soon after the establishment of Pocosin Lakes NWR:

1. To protect and enhance habitat for those species which are classified as threatened, endangered, or of special concern;

2. To protect and restore wetlands which will contribute to the Presidential Initiative of "No Net Loss of Wetlands;"

3. To protect the watershed of nearby lakes, rivers, and estuaries which support recreational and commercial fisheries and which provide wintering habitat for Canada geese, snow geese, tundra swans, and a variety of ducks;

4. To protect organic soils and pocosin wetlands from wildfires;

5. To protect and enhance production habitat for wood ducks and songbirds and winter habitat for other waterfowl; and

6. To provide opportunities for wildlife-dependent interpretation, outdoor recreation, and environmental education.

The North American Waterfowl Management Plan's Atlantic Coast Joint Venture office, working through a collaborative effort with private, State, and Federal agencies, has established certain habitat objectives for the physiographic area.

SPECIAL DESIGNATIONS

The North Carolina Natural Heritage Program has designated most of the refuge, with the exception of cropland, moist-soil areas, and the shop area, as a "Significant Natural Heritage Area." The Nature Conservancy ranks certain vegetative communities as imperiled or rare (Table 2).

The North Carolina Division of Water Quality has designated several water bodies in the vicinity of Pocosin Lakes NWR as outstanding resource waters or high-quality waters (Table 2). The North Carolina Division of Marine Fisheries has designated several streams and water bodies within and off the eastern border of the refuge as anadromous fish spawning habitats.

Table 2. The Nature Conservancy ranking of vegetative communities of Pocosin Lakes NWR

Vegetative Community	State Rank	Global Rank
Nonriverine Wet Hardwood Forest	S1	G1
Peatland Atlantic White Cedar Forest	S2	G2
Nonriverine Swamp Forest	S2, S3	G2, G3
Low Pocosin	S2	G3

S1 = Critically imperiled in North Carolina because of extreme rarity or otherwise very vulnerable to extirpation in the state.
S2 = Imperiled in North Carolina because of rarity or otherwise very vulnerable to extirpation in the state.
S3 = Rare or uncommon in North Carolina.
G1 = Critically imperiled globally because of extreme rarity or otherwise very vulnerable to extinction throughout its range.
G2 = Imperiled globally because of rarity or otherwise very vulnerable to extinction throughout its range.
G3 = Either very rare or local throughout its range, or found locally in a restricted area.

ECOSYSTEM CONTEXT

Pocosin Lakes NWR lies within a physiographic area known as the South Atlantic Coastal Plain (Figure 2). The South Atlantic Coastal Plain was once a 25-million-hectare (62-million-acre) complex of forested wetlands and uplands, dunes, and marshes that extended from Florida to North Carolina. Historically, the extent and duration of seasonal flooding along the ecosystem's rivers fluctuated annually, recharging the South Atlantic Coastal Plain's aquatic systems, creating a rich diversity of dynamic habitats that supported a vast array of fish and wildlife resources. The natural hydrology of nonriverine wetlands maintained saturated conditions in mineral and organic soils. Precipitation in excess of the soil's storage capacity ran off of the surface in sheet flow to area streams and water bodies.

The refuge is one of the ten national wildlife refuges in eastern North Carolina. Those ten national wildlife refuges – Alligator River, Pea Island, Cedar Island, Currituck, Great Dismal Swamp, Mackay Island, Mattamuskeet, Roanoke River, Pocosin Lakes, Swanquarter – and the Back Bay National Wildlife Refuge in Virginia are all located in the watersheds of the Roanoke, Tar, Neuse, and Cape Fear Rivers, which has been designated as Ecosystem Unit # 34, the Roanoke-Tar-Neuse- Cape Fear Ecosystem, by the Fish and Wildlife Service.

REGIONAL CONSERVATION PLANS AND INITIATIVES

Along with the Service's legal mandates and initiatives, other planning activities directly influence the development of the comprehensive conservation plan. Various groups and agencies develop and coordinate planning initiatives involving regional, state, and local agencies; local communities; non-governmental organizations; and private individuals to help restore habitats for fish and wildlife on and off public lands.

The Service is initiating cooperative partnerships in an effort to reduce the declining trend in biological diversity. Biological planning for species groups targeted in this plan reflect the North American Waterfowl Management Plan, which includes the Atlantic Coast Joint Venture, the Joint Venture between North Carolina Wildlife Resources Commission and Fish and Wildlife Service, Partners in Flight Plan, and the South Atlantic Migratory Bird Initiative.

The Atlantic Coast Joint Venture focus is that of the middle and upper Atlantic coast. Within the Atlantic Coast Joint Venture is the joint venture formed between the North Carolina Wildlife Resources Commission, the Fish and Wildlife Service, and private conservation organizations.

The South Atlantic Coastal Plain serves as a primary migration habitat for migratory songbirds returning from Central and South America. It also provides wintering, breeding, and migration habitat for mid-continental wood duck and colonial bird populations. Restoration of migratory songbird populations is a high priority of the Partners in Flight Plan for the South Atlantic Physiographic Region.

The Partners in Flight Plan emphasizes land bird species as a priority for conservation. Habitat loss, population trends, and the vulnerability of species and habitats to threats are all factors used in the priority ranking of species. Further, biologists from local offices of the Service; the North Carolina Wildlife Resources Commission; and conservation organizations, such as Audubon Society and the Nature Conservancy, have identified priority species for each habitat type from which they will determine population and habitat objectives and conservation actions. This list of priority species, objectives, and conservation actions will aid migratory bird management on the refuge.

Figure 2. Pocosin Lakes NWR in the South Atlantic Coastal Plain Physiographic Area

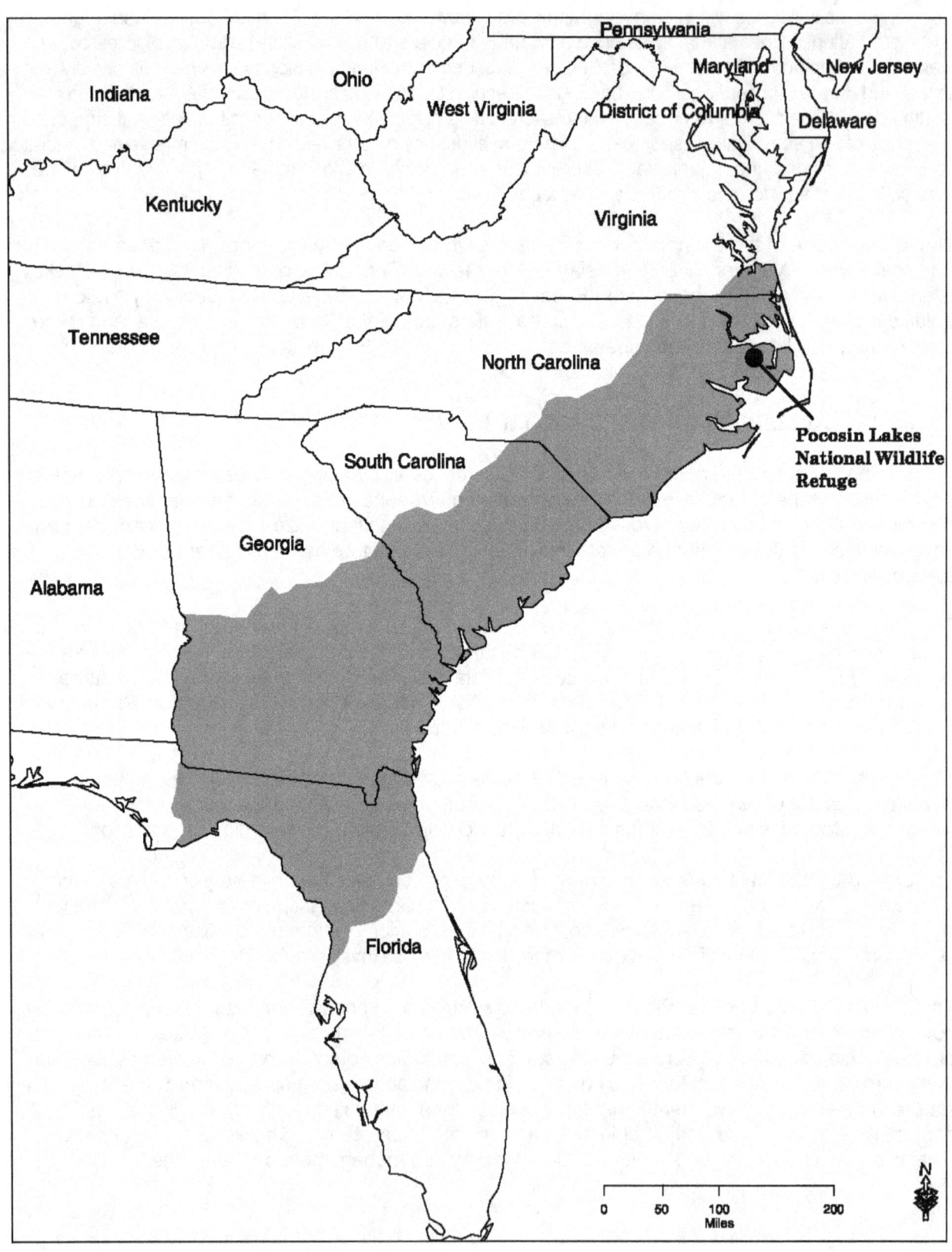

The Farm Bill programs administered by the U.S. Department of Agriculture each has State level plans and priority ranking systems in which the Service has input. The Service also utilizes those programs to assist private landowners in the vicinity of national wildlife refuges to manage habitat for wildlife or protect their land with easements.

The North Carolina Wildlife Resources Commission has its own Comprehensive Wildlife Conservation Strategy to help direct the State's allocation of funds from the federally funded State Working Grants Program. The Service has provided input to the development and execution of the strategy.

ECOLOGICAL THREATS AND PROBLEMS

FOREST AND FRAGMENTATION

The South Atlantic Coastal Plain has changed markedly over the last 100 years as civilization spread throughout the area. It has been estimated that 40 percent of the natural vegetation has been lost to land conversion. The greatest changes to the landscape have been in the form of land clearing for agriculture and urban development (Hunter et al., 2001).

Although these changes have allowed people to settle and earn a living in the area, they have had a tremendous effect on biological diversity, biological integrity, and environmental health of the South Atlantic Coastal Plain. Development has reduced vast areas of bottomland hardwood forests to forest fragments, ranging in size from very small tracts of limited functional value to a few large areas that have maintained many of the original functions and values of forested habitats. Severe fragmentation has resulted in a substantial decline in biological diversity and integrity. Animal species endemic to the South Atlantic Coastal Plain that have become extinct, threatened, or endangered include the red wolf and Bachman's sparrow (Table 3).

Table 3. Federally threatened and endangered animal species that occur on the South Atlantic Coastal Plain in North Carolina

Region	Status	Common Name	Scientific Name
Coastal Plain	Endangered	Manatee, West Indian	*Trichechus manatus*
Coastal Plain	Endangered	Sea Turtle, Hawksbill	*Eretmochelys imbricata*
Coastal Plain	Endangered	Sea Turtle, Kemp's Ridley	*Lepidochelys kempii*
Coastal Plain	Endangered	Sea Turtle, Leatherback	*Dermochelys coriacea*
Coastal Plain	Endangered	Stork, Wood	*Mycteria americana*
Coastal Plain	Endangered	Sturgeon, Shortnose	*Acipenser brevirostrum*

Region	Status	Common Name	Scientific Name
Coastal Plain	Endangered	Tern, Roseate	*Sterna dougallii*
Coastal Plain	Endangered	Whale, Finback	*Balaenoptera physalus*
Coastal Plain	Endangered	Whale, Humpback	*Megaptera novaeangliae*
Coastal Plain	Endangered	Whale, Right	*Balaena glacialis*
Coastal Plain	Endangered	Whale, Sea	*Balaenoptera borealis*
Coastal Plain	Endangered	Whale, Sperm	*Physeter catodon*
Coastal Plain	Endangered	Wolf, Red	*Canis rufus*
Coastal Plain	Endangered	Woodpecker, Red-cockaded	*Picoides borealis*
Coastal Plain	Threatened	Alligator, American	*Alligator mississippiensis*
Coastal Plain	Threatened	Eagle, Bald	*Haliaeetus leucocephalus*
Coastal Plain	Threatened	Plover, Piping	*Charadrius melodus*
Coastal Plain	Threatened	Sea Turtle, Green	*Chelonia mydas*
Coastal Plain	Threatened	Sea Turtle, Loggerhead	*Caretta caretta*
Coastal Plain	Threatened	Silverside, Waccamaw	*Menidia extensa*
Coastal Plain	Endangered	Sparrow, Bachman's	*Aimophila aestivalis*

Breeding bird surveys show continuing declines in species and species populations. The avian species most adversely affected by fragmentation and habitat degradation include those that are area-sensitive (dependent on large continuous blocks of hardwood forest); those that depend on forest interiors; those that depend on special habitat requirements, such as mature forests or a particular food source; and/or those that depend on good water quality. Increased nest parasitism from brown-headed cowbirds is also common in fragmented forests.

More that 300 species of breeding migratory songbirds are found in the region. Some of these species, including Swainson's warbler, prothonotary warbler, swallow-tailed kites, wood thrush, and cerulean warbler, have declined substantially and need the benefits of large forested blocks to recover and sustain their existence.

Fragmentation has also brought the forest edge and brown-headed cowbird (a seed-eating bird common in agricultural areas) closer to the natural nesting sites of many forest interior-nesting birds. The brown-headed cowbird is a parasitic nester that lays eggs in the nests of other birds, rather than building a nest of its own. Nestling cowbirds are typically bigger and more aggressive and out-compete the young of the species building the nest. This results in poor reproductive success and declining populations of forest interior-nesting species that are forced to nest near forest edges.

Fragmentation of bottomland hardwood forests has left many of the remaining forested tracts surrounded by a sea of agricultural lands. Intensive agriculture has removed most of the forested corridors along sloughs that formerly connected the forest patches. The loss of connectivity between the remaining forested tracts hinders the movement of wildlife between tracts and reduces the functional values of many remaining smaller forest tracts. The lost connections also result in a loss of gene flow. Restoring the connections to allow gene flow and reestablish travel corridors is particularly important for some wide-ranging species, such as the black bear and red wolf.

ALTERATIONS TO HYDROLOGY

In addition to the loss of vast acreages of bottomland forested wetlands, there have been substantial alterations in the region's hydrology. This is due to managed stream flows from flood control and hydroelectric power generation reservoirs, drainage ditches, river channel modification, flood control levees, deforestation, and degradation to aquatic systems from excessive sedimentation, contaminants, and urban development.

The natural hydrology of a region is directly responsible for the connectedness of forested wetlands and indirectly responsible for the complexity and diversity of habitats through its effects on topography and soils. Natural resource managers recognize the importance of dynamic hydrology to forested wetlands and waterfowl-habitat relationships (Fredrickson and Heitmeyer 1988).

Instead of natural hydrology, large-scale man-made hydrological alterations have changed the spatial and temporal patterns of flooding throughout the entire South Atlantic Coastal Plain. In addition, these alterations have modified both the extent and duration of annual seasonal flooding. The alteration of this annual flooding regime has had a tremendous effect on the forested wetlands and their associated wetland-dependent species. Specifically, the combination of managed stream flows and drainage ditches in bottomland forests exposes the forests to more frequent flooding than occurs naturally, drains back swamps through natural levees, and floods the back swamps at low flows through the ditches.

In view of the hydrologic changes, it is very difficult, if not impossible, to fully emulate and reconstruct the structure and functions of a natural wetland. According to Mitsch and Gosselink (1993), restoration of wetland functions is especially difficult since wetlands depend on a dynamic interface of hydrologic regimes to maintain water, vegetation, and animal complexes and processes.

SILTATION OF AQUATIC ECOSYSTEMS

Siltation from deforestation and hydrologic alteration has degraded aquatic systems, including lakes, rivers, sloughs and bayous. Clearing of bottomland hardwood forests has led to an accelerated accumulation of sediments and contaminants in all aquatic systems. Sediment now fills many water bodies, greatly reducing their surface area and depth. It also reduces light penetration in shallow water and the growth of submerged aquatic vegetation growing in the water. Concurrently, the non-point source runoff of excess nutrients and contaminants is threatening the area's remaining aquatic resources. Six species of federally threatened aquatic organisms and twelve species of federally endangered aquatic species occur in North Carolina and Virginia.

Hydrologic alterations have basically eliminated the geomorphologic processes that created oxbow lakes, sloughs, and river meander scars. Consequently, the protection, conservation, and restoration of these aquatic resources take on an added importance in light of the alterations associated with flood control and navigation.

PROLIFERATION OF INVASIVE AQUATIC PLANTS

Compounding the problems faced by aquatic systems is the growing threat from invasive aquatic vegetation. Static water levels caused by the lack of annual flooding and reduced water depths resulting from excessive sedimentation have created conditions favorable for the establishment and proliferation of several species of invasive aquatic plants. Additionally, the introduction of exotic (non-native) vegetation capable of aggressive growth is further threatening viability of aquatic systems. These invasive aquatic species threaten the natural aquatic vegetation important to aquatic systems, and choke waterways to a degree that limits biodiversity and often prevents recreational use.

CONSERVATION PRIORITIES

The declines in the South Atlantic Coastal Plain's bottomland hardwood forests and their associated fish and wildlife resources have prompted the Service to designate these forest systems as areas of special concern. A collaborative effort involving private, State, and Federal conservation partners is now underway to implement a variety of tools to restore the functions and values of wetlands in the South Atlantic Coastal Plain. The goal is to prioritize and manage wetlands to most effectively maintain and possibly restore the biological diversity in the South Atlantic Coastal Plain. Some areas are prioritized as focus areas for reforestation.

Conservation agencies and organizations have initiated several coordinated efforts to set priorities and establish focus areas to overcome the impacts of hydrologic changes and forest fragmentation. A cooperative private-State-Federal partnership, known as the North American Waterfowl Management Plan, Atlantic Coast Joint Venture, was established in 1986 to help provide sufficient wintering waterfowl habitat throughout the Atlantic Coastal Plain.

The initial Atlantic Coast Joint Venture effort for waterfowl has expanded to also establish breeding bird objectives for shorebirds, marsh birds, wading birds, and neotropical migratory songbirds. The Atlantic Coast Joint Venture is working with the U.S. Shorebird Conservation Working Group to establish step-down objectives for shorebird foraging habitat for the fall and spring migration period throughout the South Atlantic Coastal Plain.

Partners in Flight has developed bird conservation plans to focus a number of private, State, and Federal restoration programs into specific areas in an effort to provide maximum program benefits for neotropical migratory songbirds. The goal of this collaborative restoration effort is to provide islands or blocks of habitat in an otherwise highly fragmented landscape. The targeted block sizes of forest habitat range from 10,000 to 100,000 acres. Such areas are large enough to support viable populations of various suites of neotropical migratory interior forest-dwelling songbirds. Of course, these areas will also support other species that depend on large forested blocks. The plans are anchored by existing or proposed State wildlife management areas or national wildlife refuges. These public lands serve as centers of biodiversity that are enhanced and supported by the expansion of blocks of habitat, either through public or private management.

One of the biggest challenges to the management and restoration efforts underway in the South Atlantic Coastal Plain, and one that affects refuges in particular, is the need to meet long-term management objectives that address comprehensive ecosystem needs, including those of wintering migratory waterfowl, neotropical migratory birds, shorebirds, wading birds, threatened and endangered species, large mammals, and other wide-ranging species. Often a management strategy for one species or species' group conflicts with that of another species or species' group. The tendency is to pursue short-term priorities that frequently change as scientific knowledge expands and interests in special resources shift. Land managers must exercise caution to prevent the start-up of management and restoration actions that are difficult to reverse and fail to meet the long-term, comprehensive management needs of the ecosystem or a specific area within the ecosystem. An example might be a tendency to manage the forests on Pocosin Lakes NWR in an effort to provide habitat for many species of neotropical migratory songbirds that use dense understories of shrubs. Such an approach may overlook the critical habitat needs of other songbirds that prefer forests with sparse understories.

Partners in the Atlantic Coast Joint Venture can only meet their habitat goals through active management of croplands, moist-soil areas, and forested wetlands on both public and private land (Reinecke and Baxter 1996). Biologists must actively manage land (i.e., vegetation manipulation and hydrology restoration) to compensate for the spatial and temporal habitat changes that deforestation and hydrologic alterations have caused throughout the South Atlantic Coastal Plain. Properly managed, the Pocosin Lakes NWR will make a substantial contribution to meeting the objectives of the Atlantic Coast Joint Venture. Setting habitat and species objectives from the perspective of the South Atlantic Coastal Plain is advantageous, because it looks at the big picture and enables managers to plan and provide habitat for a diversity of species throughout their range.

Although forest stand management is probably the best solution for restoring the vast forests in the region, land managers must remember that hydrology (i.e., flooding) drives the ecological system in the South Atlantic Coastal Plain. The plant and animal community throughout the South Atlantic Coastal Plain is dependent upon the hydrologic cycle. It is incumbent upon land managers to manage hydrology in an effort to restore the ecological diversity that once characterized the South Atlantic Coastal Plain. Refuges can install impoundments and structures to control and manage water in an effort to mimic historic flood cycles and to meet wildlife habitat objectives.

PHYSICAL RESOURCES

CLIMATE

Since the flow of air over North Carolina is predominantly from west-to-east, the continental influence has a great influence on precipitation patterns while the maritime influence affects climatological factors, such as length of growing season. The Gulf Stream current flows only a short distance off the North Carolina coast. Its direct effects are limited by the fact that the prevailing winds in winter are from the southwest most of the year and from the northeast in the winter

Lows usually form along the coast as "Cape Hatteras lows" and then move north along the coast. Winter's low-pressure storms are usually more intense because of the large north-to-south contrasts.

Winter's storms bring prolonged periods of steady rain and are responsible for most of the winter precipitation. The forms of precipitation in spring begin to change from these steady rains to occasional thunderstorms. The Gulf of Mexico's warm, moist air produces warm, humid weather throughout the summer. Rainfall comes from occasional thunderstorms that occur on an average of 45 days. Autumn is slightly drier than the other three seasons and is to many people the most pleasant with its many clear, warm days and cool nights with relatively little rain. This weather usually lasts from October through December.

Occasional hurricanes do have major impacts on Tyrrell, Washington, and Hyde Counties. The storms usually pass off the coast east of the Pocosin Lakes NWR, but may bring large quantities of rain to the refuge. Most North Carolina tornadoes occur in the Piedmont and the interior of the coastal plain, which spares Tyrrell, Washington, and Hyde Counties.

The average annual precipitation is 51.51 inches, and the average snowfall is 4.2 inches. Snow accumulations of more than 1 inch for more than a day are rare. Rainfall is evenly distributed throughout the year without a pronounced wet or dry season: average monthly rainfall ranges from 3.10 inches in April and November to 6.39 inches in July. Eight months have average precipitation between 4 and 6 inches. Of the total annual precipitation, about 30 inches usually fall in April through September. The growing season for most crops falls within this period.

The average relative humidity in mid-afternoon is about 60 percent. Humidity is higher at night, and the average at dawn is about 85 percent. The sun shines 65 percent of the time in summer and 60 percent in winter. The prevailing wind is from the southwest. Average wind speed is highest, 11 miles per hour, in late winter and early spring. In January, the average temperature is 42 degrees, the average daily minimum temperature is 30 degrees and the average daily maximum is 53 degrees. In July, the average temperature is 78 degrees, the average daily maximum temperature is 89 degrees, and the average daily minimum is 67 degrees.

The average growing season is 192 days long. The average last date of frost in the spring is April 15 and the first frost in the fall is October 25.

GEOLOGY

The Coastal Plain Province lies east of the Piedmont Province. The Piedmont begins at the "Fall Line," which is a broad transition zone where the crystalline rocks of the Piedmont (i.e., the igneous and metamorphic rocks that cause the rapids in the Roanoke River at Roanoke Rapids) become buried by the marine sediments of the Coastal Plain.

Thin beds of Quaternary sediments were deposited on the surface of the Coastal Plain during the past three million years (Riggs and Belknap 1988). This Quaternary history and the resulting surface veneer of unconsolidated sediments directly dictates the general characteristics of the Coastal Plain, including the regional morphology and character of the drainage systems and flooded estuaries, soil types, and potential land use. Quaternary sediments were deposited by the coastal system, which rapidly migrated back and forth across the Coastal Plain-Continental Shelf as sea-level fluctuated in response to repeated episodes of glaciation and deglaciation. Within this rapidly changing coastal system, extremely varied sediments, including gravel, sands, clays, and peat in all possible combinations, were deposited in river, estuarine, barrier island, and continental shelf environments. Thousands of feet of sedimentary rock underlie the refuge with sand and shale closer to the surface and limestone at greater depths.

SUBSURFACE RESOURCES

Sand and peat are the only subsurface resources occurring in economic quantities on the refuge. There are no commercial sand pits adjacent to the refuge.

SOILS

Soil types identified on the refuge are Pungo muck,* Belhaven muck,* Scuppernong muck.* Ponzer muck,* Dorovan muck,* Wasda muck,* Pettigrew muck,* Gullrock muck,* Longshoal muck,* Arapahoe fine sandy loam,* Hyde loam,* Weeksville silt loam,* Cape Fear loam,* Portsmouth loam,* Newholland mucky loamy sand,* Udorthents (sands), Tomotley fine sandy loam,* Perquimens silt loam,* Augusta fine sandy loam, Altavista fine sandy loam, Argent silt loam*, Seabrook fine sand, Roanoke loam*, Fortescue silt loam,* Arapahoe fine sandy loam,* Conetoe loamy fine sand, Yonges loam,* Chowan silt loam,* Wysocking very fine sandy loam,* and State loamy fine sand (USDA, Soil Conservation service, 1988) (Table 4). Soils with an asterisk are listed as hydric in "Hydric Soils of the United States" (USDA, Soil Conservation Service 1985) (Table 4) and (Figure 3). Hydric soils are . . . "soils that in their undrained condition are saturated, flooded or ponded long enough during the growing season to develop anaerobic conditions that favor the growth and regeneration of hydrophytic (water loving) vegetation" (USDA, Soil Conservation Service 1985). These soils have seasonally high water tables within a foot of the surface of the soil.

Pocosin wetlands are characterized by deep organic soils known as mucks or peats. The depth of organic soil depth over mineral soil, though not evident at the surface, has a tremendous influence on the potential uses of the land. Typically, the deeper the muck surface layer, the shorter the vegetation in the native plant community growing on the soil. The dominant species in the plant communities are dense shrubs tolerant of the wet, acid soils. Tall trees are unable to establish their deep root systems on the deep organic soils. Wind easily topples trees that do grow on the deep organic soils. Over the years, natural selection has favored trees that are shorter. Formation of peat is an ongoing process in areas sufficiently wet to prevent oxidation of organic matter deposited by plants.

Soils with more than 51 inches of muck over mineral soil identified in the refuge are Pungo (66,675 acres; 65 percent of land), Dorovan (3,644 acres; 3.5 percent), and Longshoal (13 acres). The following soils have surface layers of 16 to 51 inches of muck: Belhaven (16,490 acres; 16 percent), Scuppernong (6,179 acres; 5.9 percent), and Ponzer (3,289 acres: 3.1 percent). These six soils make up 95 percent of the terrestrial area of the refuge. They are excessively wet, characterized by layers of peat over mineral soil, and are mostly unsuitable for agriculture (Skaggs et al., 1980, Lilly 1981). Forest productivity is lower on these soils, compared to mineral soils with less than 16 inches of organic soil. With appropriate drainage and bedding, productivity can be increased. However, the refuge would not likely engage extensively in such practices on these deep organic soils due to accelerated oxidation of peat and release of nitrogen and mercury – a negative impact on water quality.

Table 4. Characteristics of soils of Pocosin Lakes NWR

Series	Approximate Acreage	Surface Texture	Muck Depth	Water Table Depth	Flooding Frequency
Dorovan	3,644	Muck	90"	0-1'	Frequent
Longshoal	13	Mucky Peat	72"	0-0.5'	Frequent
Pungo	66,675	Muck	65"	0-1'	Rare
Belhaven	16,490	Muck	45"	0-1'	Rare
Scuppernong	6,179	Muck	33"	0-1'	Rare
Ponzer	3,289	Muck	30"	0-1'	Rare
Wasda	710	Muck	15"	0-1'	Rare
Conaby	418	Muck	13"	0-1'	Rare
Gullrock	44	Muck	13"	0-1'	Rare
Pettigrew	539	Muck	12"	0-1'	Rare
Roper	218	Muck	10"	0-1'	Rare
Hyde	1,306	Loam	None	0-1'	Rare
Cape Fear	648	Loam	None	0-1'	Rare
Portsmouth	635	Loam	None	0-1'	Rare
Perquimens	137	Loam	None	0-1'	Rare
Roanoke	35	Loam	None	0-1'	Never
Yonges	6	Loam	None	0-1'	Rare
Weeksville	779	Silt Loam	None	0-1'	Rare
Argent	41	Silt Loam	None	0-1'	Rare

Series	Approximate Acreage	Surface Texture	Muck Depth	Water Table Depth	Flooding Frequency
Fortescue	37	Silt Loam	None	0-0.5'	Rare
Chowan	2	Silt Loam	None	0-0.5'	Frequent
Tomotley	286	Fine Sandy Loam	None	0-1'	Rare
Arapahoe	33	Fine Sandy Loam	None	0-1'	Rare
Wysocking	1	Very Fine Sandy Loam	None	0-1	Rare
Newholland	401	Mucky Loamy Sand	None	0-1'	Rare
Augusta	65	Fine Sandy Loam	None	1-2-	Never
Altavista	59	Fine Loamy Sand	None	1-2-	Never
Seabrook	37	Fine Sand	None	2-3'	Rare
State	1	Loamy Fine Sand	None	4-6'	Never
Conetoe	7	Loamy Fine Sand	None	>6'	Never
Udorthents	334	Sand	None	>6'	Rare
Total Land	**103,069**				
Water	**7,000**				
Total	**110,069**				

Comprehensive Conservation Plan

Figure 3. Characteristics of soils of Pocosin Lakes NWR

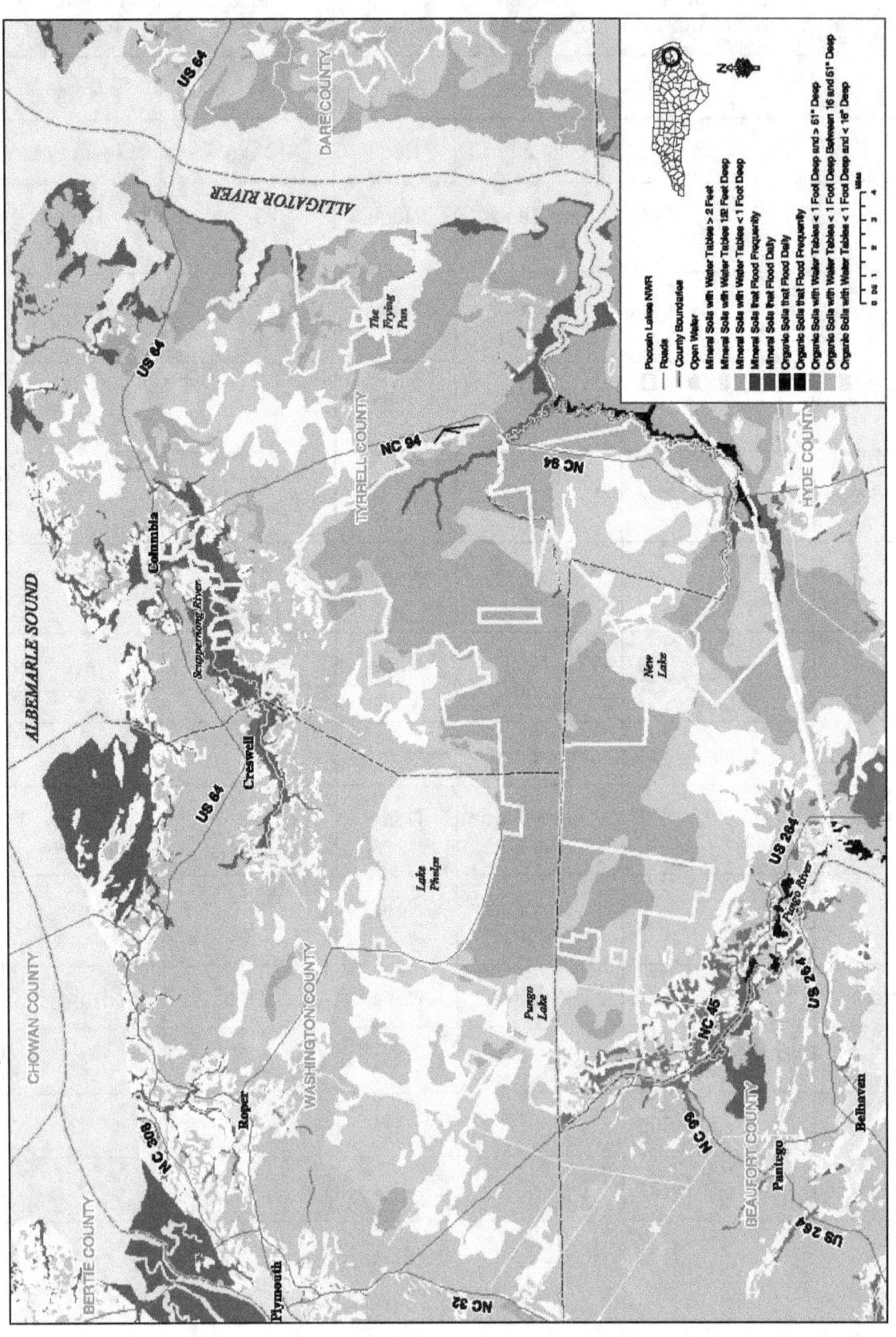

Four soils (1,929 acres, 1.9 percent) have less than 16 inches of muck over mineral soil: Wasda (710 acres, 0.6 percent), Pettigrew (539 acres), Conaby (418), Roper (218 acres), and Gullrock (44 acres). The native vegetation on these soils is typical of that on mineral soils and the productivity of the soils is similar to mineral soils. When drained, these soils are among the most productive agricultural soils in the area. The USDA, Natural Resources Conservation Service, classifies Wasda, Pettigrew, Conaby, Roper, and Gullrock as prime farmland soils. Part of the refuge farmland is in Conaby muck.

Mineral soils make up 4,850 acres (4.7 percent) of the land area of the refuge. The soil with the largest area is Hyde (1,306 acres mostly in the Frying Pan Unit, 1.2 percent of land area), followed by Weeksville (779 acres), Cape Fear (648), Portsmouth (635), Newholland (401), Udorthents (334), Tomotley (286), Perquimans (137), Augusta (65), Altavista (59), Argent (41), Seabrook (37), Roanoke (35), Fortescue (37), Arapahoe (33), Conetoe (7), Yonges (6), Chowan (2), Wysocking (1), and State (1). Most mineral soils are more productive than organic soils for crops and forest trees. Most on the refuge is poorly drained and would grow loblolly pine, bald cypress, Atlantic white cedar, or pond pine, and those underlain by clayey subsoil would be good for bottomland hardwoods, such as water oak, willow oak, and swamp white oak. The USDA, Natural Resources Conservation Service, classifies Altavista, Arapahoe, Augusta, Cape Fear, Conetoe, Fortescue, Hyde, Newholland, Perquimens, Portsmouth, Roanoke, State, Tomotley, Weeksville, Wysocking, and Yonges as prime farmland soils. Part of the refuge cropland is on Newholland, Portsmouth, and Seabrook soils.

The Udorthents, Augusta, Altavista, State, Conetoe, and Seabrook soils are well-drained to droughty and are more suitable for native tree species, such as loblolly pine, and for upland oak species, such as white oak and red oak. Udorthents are the dredge spoils from the Intracoastal Waterway and are extremely droughty.

The volume of peat on the Albemarle peninsula is probably less than half the original amount due to the effects of drainage, agriculture, and fire (Lilly 1995). There are descriptions of subsidence greater or equal to 3 feet as a consequence of drainage and agriculture (Ruffin 1861, Dolman and Buol 1967, Lilly 1981, Roberts and Cruikshank 1941, Whitehead and Oaks 1979). In general, drainage of organic soils results in the loss of at least one-third of the peat (Farnham and Finney 1965), and sometime much greater (Dolman and Buol 1967, Lilly 1981). Some of the initial loss in volume is due to mechanical shrinkage (Dolman and Buol 1967, Skaggs et al., 1980). In addition, drainage makes pocosins drier, increasing the frequency and severity of fires. Last, drainage causes peat to oxidize rather than accumulate. If subjected to drainage, fire, and tillage over a long enough period of time, all blackland soils will become mineral soils (Lilly 1981).

HYDROLOGY

Soil on the refuge is more than 99 percent hydric and is maintained as natural or managed wetlands. These wetlands are in the coastal plain province. Water is the driving force of the Pocosin Lakes NWR's pocosin, marsh, and hardwood/pine forest communities. Water forms and maintains the wetlands by transporting and redistributing sediments from watersheds upstream. It provides seasonal access for aquatic organisms to the marsh and forest and transports nutrients and detritus across the marsh. Sources of water to the Albemarle Sound system include precipitation and runoff and groundwater that originate from it.

Groundwater is the source of the area's water supply. The depth to freshwater is generally less than 100 feet in the vicinity of the Albemarle Sound and more than 400 feet in the center of the peninsula. The freshwater is contained in the upper sandy and shaly aquifer, which is capable of yielding up to 1,000 gallons per minute. The lower limestone aquifer is capable of yielding thousands of gallons per minute except near the Albemarle Sound where the water is salty. The maximum available groundwater is estimated at one million gallons per day per-square-mile. The water is characteristically very hard and may contain excessive iron. Water from shallow wells may be hard or soft and may also contain excessive iron (T. M. Robison 1977).

WATER QUALITY

The water quality on most of Pocosin Lakes NWR is related directly to the water quality in Albemarle Sound, Scuppernong River, Lake Phelps and Alligator River. Nutrient loading in the Albemarle Sound, Scuppernong River, and Alligator River and related non-point source pollution will affect the water quality on most of the refuge in the future.

There are sixteen facilities in the counties around the refuge in the National Pollution Discharge Elimination System (NPDES) (Table 5). The State of North Carolina has classified the water bodies around Pocosin Lakes NWR for minimum water quality standards (Table 6). All the water bodies and streams meet the standards established for the minimum uses.

The high water tables in the soils in the three counties represent a great potential for non-point pollution. The residences in the three counties have onsite treatment of domestic wastewater. Those systems are more likely to fail on soils with high water tables. Agricultural operations are also more likely to pollute on the soils in the area. Nutrients and pesticides applied to crops have a great potential to reach the water table before plants utilize the nutrients or the pesticides break down. The drainage of organic soil has the potential to release nitrogen and mercury in the muck into the water table.

AIR QUALITY

The laws of the State of North Carolina specify that no source of air pollution shall cause any listed ambient air quality standard (Section .0400) to be exceeded or contribute to a violation of any listed ambient air quality standard (Section .0400) except as allowed by Rules .0531 or .0532 [.0401(c), NCAC, Title 15A, Subchapter 2D - Air Pollution Control Requirements (North Carolina Department of Environment and Natural Resources)].

Subchapter 2D lists ambient air quality standards for sulfur oxides (measured as sulfur dioxide), total suspended particulates, carbon monoxide, ozone, hydrocarbons, nitrogen dioxide, lead, and particulate matter. Section 0.0520 (7) indicates that prescribed fires purposely set to forest lands for forest management practices acceptable to the North Carolina Division of Forestry and the Environmental Management Commission are permissible if not prohibited by ordinances and regulations of governmental entities having jurisdiction. The regulation also includes a disclaimer that addresses certain potential liabilities of prescribed burning even though permissible.

The area closest to the refuge that the Environmental Protection Agency monitors continuously is the Virginia Beach-Norfolk metropolitan area. Despite the large population with the industry, traffic, and power plants, the area did not violate any air quality standards in 2004, due to the breezes blowing through the area from the ocean. The North Carolina Department of Environment and Natural Resources monitors air sporadically at stations in Martin, Pitt, and Edgecombe Counties, west of the refuge. No reading at any of the three stations violated air quality standards in 2004.

Table 5. Active National Pollution Discharge Elimination System (NPDES) permits in Tyrrell, Washington, and Hyde Counties, North Carolina

Permit Number	Applicant	Type of Facility	Receiving Stream
Tyrrell County			
NC0086924	Tyrrell County	Water Treatment Plant	Bulls Bay
NC0087092	Tyrrell County	Water Treatment Plant	Riders Creek
NC0007510	Columbia	Water Treatment Plant	Scuppernong River
NC0020443	Columbia	Waste Treatment Plant	Scuppernong River
NC0085081	Dalton House	Domestic Waste Treatment	Scuppernong River
Hyde County			
NC0068233	Hyde County	Water Treatment Plant	Lake Mattamuskeet
NC0077992	Hyde County	Water Treatment Plant	Pungo Lake Canal
NC0000744	Captain Charlie	Industrial Waste Treatment	Far Creek
NC0076571	Gullrock Seafood	Industrial Waste Treatment	Gray Ditch
NC0070211	Rose Bay Oyster	Industrial Waste Treatment	Rose Bay
NC0085002	Eastern Fuels	Groundwater Remediation	Far Creek
NC0035751	Regional Housing authority	Domestic Waste Treatment	Swanquarter Bay
Washington County			
NC0002313	Plymouth	Water Treatment Plant	Conaby Creek
NC0020028	Plymouth	Waste Treatment Plant	Roanoke River
NC0027600	Creswell	Water Treatment Plant	Scuppernong River
NC0031925	Roper	Water Treatment Plant	Main Canal

Table 6. Classifications of water bodies and streams surrounding the Pocosin Lakes NWR

Water Body or Stream	Classification	Minimum Uses
Albemarle Sound Bulls Bay	SB – Saltwater	Primary Recreation, Fishing, Aquatic Life
Intracoastal Waterway Little Alligator River Goose Pond	SC – Saltwater Sw – Swamp Waters	Secondary Recreation, Fishing, Aquatic Life
Grapevine Bay Rattlesnake Bay The Straits The Frying Pan Coopers creek Babbitt Bay	SC – Saltwater Sw – Swamp Waters ORW-Outstanding Resource water	Secondary Recreation, Fishing, Aquatic Life
Phelps Lake Goose creek Second Creek	B – Freshwater Sw – Swamp Waters ORW-Outstanding Resource Water	Primary Recreation, Fishing, Aquatic Life
Pungo Lake	C – Freshwater Sw – Swamp Waters NSW- Nutrient Sensitive Water	Secondary Recreation, Fishing, Aquatic Life
Gum Neck Creek Southwest Fork, Alligator River Northwest Fork, Alligator River Juniper Creek Alligator River	C – Freshwater Sw – Swamp Waters ORW-Outstanding Resource Water	Secondary Recreation, Fishing, Aquatic Life
Dunbar Creek Basnight Creek Grays Canal Bush Harrell Canal Riders Creek Second Creek Bee Tee Canal Bunton Creek (source to Bulls Bay) Bonarva Creek Scuppernong River Transportation Canal New Lake	C – Freshwater Sw – Swamp Waters	Secondary Recreation, Fishing, Aquatic Life

Visual Resources/Aesthetics

Pocosin Lakes NWR is part of an extensive complex of pocosins (shrub wetlands), forested wetlands, and freshwater marshes interspersed with cropland. Farmers and logging companies have cleared and drained many of these wetlands in the past, but conservation agencies and organizations have acquired and protected them. They have restored the areas or allowed them to go through succession to native vegetation. In addition to the 110,106-acre Pocosin Lakes NWR, the counties have natural vegetative cover on 64,000 acres at the Mattamuskeet and Swanquarter NWRs, 47,000 acres at eight State game lands, 18,000 acres on the Buckridge National Estuarine Research Reserve, and 4,531 acres at the Pettigrew State Park.

Visitors to the refuge have the opportunity to experience solitude, wildness, uninterrupted quiet, spirit and adventure, and observe the signs and the sounds of activity in the pocosin, marsh, and forested wetlands. Most people will only experience the refuge from gravel roads due to the prevalence of deep, organic soil that will not support a person's weight. The casual observer will see large expanses of freshwater marsh and hardwood and pine forest. During the growing season, the marshes appear alive with neotropical songbirds, raptors, wading birds, marsh birds, mink, otter, and other wildlife species. The forests of loblolly pine, red maple, black gum, sweetgum, green ash, and wax myrtle echo the sounds of songbirds, wood ducks, red wolves, bear, and deer. The pocosins of evergreen shrubs attract songbirds and bears to their fruit-bearing branches.

BIOLOGICAL RESOURCES

HABITAT

The term "pocosin" includes several distinct plant communities (Table 7) (Figure 4) (Richardson 1991, Weakely and Schafale 1991) whose characteristics and dynamics are still poorly understood (Weakely and Schafale 1991). In the great peatlands, fire frequency and depth of peat are two master factors determining the distribution and structure of many plant communities. Much of the land within Pocosin Lakes NWR is not forest; yet forests clearly grew there in the past. Swamp forests are dynamic, not static (Drayton and Hook 1988, Hinsely 1999, Odum 1984). It is one thing to note the presence of tree residue, but it is more difficult to say exactly when these stands existed. Through the millennia, peat accumulated around these residues as they were deposited. Offsetting the process of accumulation were the effects of subsidence, mostly in response to drainage, as well as loss of peat in fires, both of which left material at the surface that might be very old. Some soil profiles contain strata composed of very different plant species, each group with different requirements for establishment and growth. Ruffin (1861) described a peat profile near Pungo Lake in which there were three major layers of embedded woody material: pond pine (upper), cypress (middle), and Atlantic white cedar (lower). Peat profiles near Pungo Lake also contain several distinct layers of tree residue (Dolman and Buol 1967).

Species composition of the swamp vegetation in eastern North Carolina has undergone several major changes through its history (Dolman and Buol 1968, Lewis and Cocke 1929, Whitehead and Oaks 1979). Otte (1981) said he had never observed a pocosin (underlain by deep peat soils) that had been dominated by a single vegetation type throughout the history of the wetland. No single vegetation type has always existed on these sites. Analysis reveals many localized changes and successional sequences during the last several thousand years, indicating a state of dynamic equilibrium and a modest capacity for self-repair over long periods without disturbance, say several centuries (Whitehead and Oaks 1979). This tenuous equilibrium is constantly threatened by activities of man. Preserving pocosin systems requires recognition of the many factors that permitted them to develop and of the variety of forces that have maintained them for thousands of years (Whitehead and Oaks 1979).

Table 7. Habitat types by approximate acreage for Pocosin Lakes NWR

Habitat Type	Acreage
Pocosin	63,896
Bay Forest	4,280
Peatland Atlantic White Cedar Forest	3,124
Mixed Pine Flatwoods	13,649
Hardwood Swamp Forest	14,045
Cypress/Gum Swamp	970
Marsh	987
Xeric Sandhill Scrub	276
Cropland	1,250
Moist Soil Areas (Managed Wetlands)	443
Natural Lake Shoreline	446
Open Water	6,740
TOTAL	**110,106**
Roads, Roadsides	970
Canals	909
Firebreaks	1,200
Administrative Areas	10

NOTE: Roads, roadsides, canals, firebreaks, and administrative areas occur within the various habitat types listed above. Firebreak maintenance (mowing, burning, chemical treatment) results in these acres being maintained in a pocosin (grass stage) habitat type.

Figure 4. Vegetative habitat types of Pocosin Lakes NWR

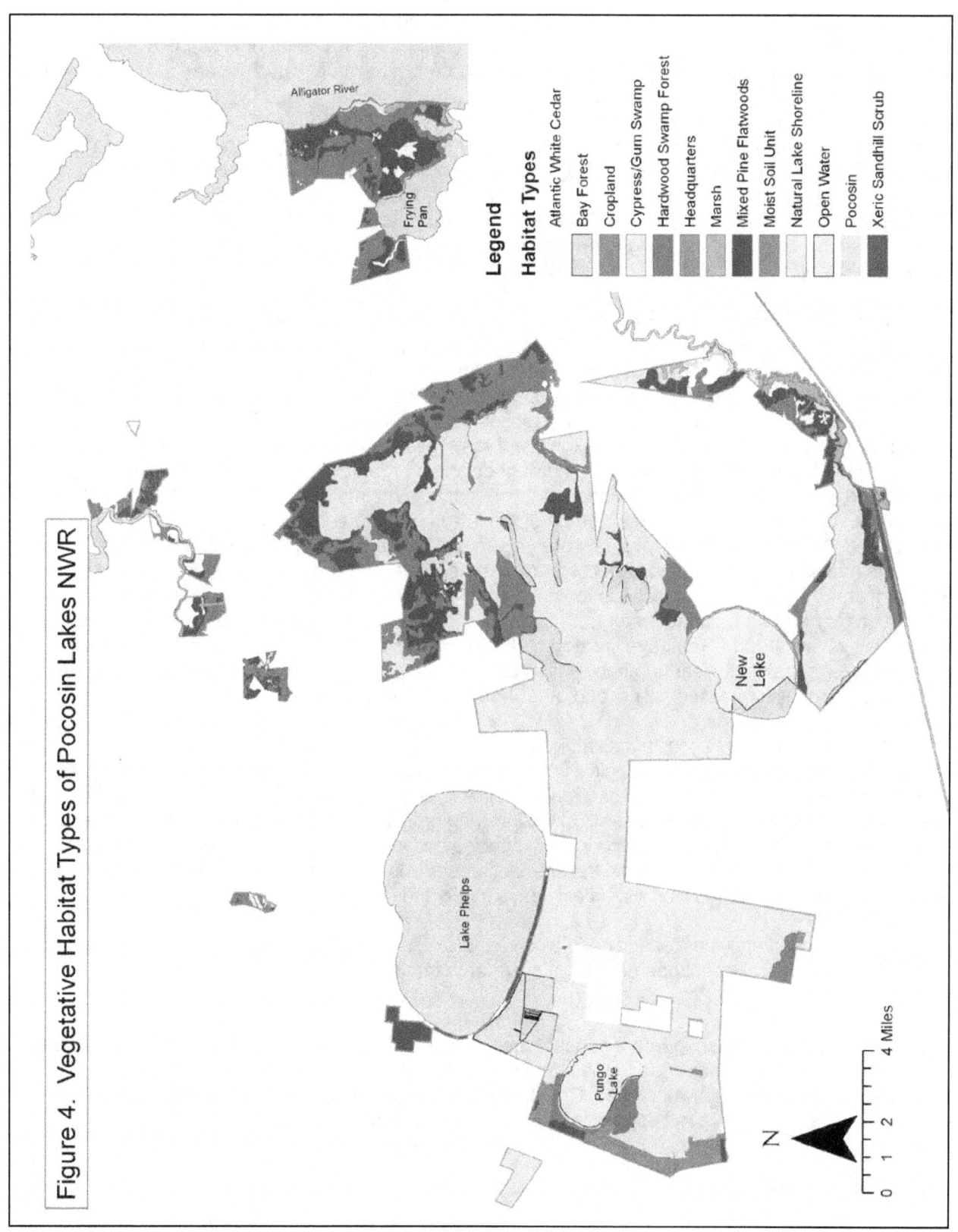

South of Phelps Lake, in the vicinity of Boerma Road and County Line Road, the peat is 7 to 9 feet thick (Pungo soil) and contains thousands of tons of logs and stumps. The age of the woody material is approximately 7,000 years just above the sand at the bottom of the peat and approximately 3,400 years at mid-depth (Courtney Hackney, University of North Carolina-Wilmington, personal communication). The woody material throughout the peat is Atlantic white cedar (Hackney, personal communication).

Other references from Hinsely's Forest Habitat Management Plan (1999) indicate that the vegetation south of Phelps Lake on present-day refuge land was mostly pond pine pocosin. There is no reference documenting the existence of Atlantic white cedar there in the last 150 years. However, the Superintendent of Pettigrew State Park, Mr. Sidney Shearin, remembers observing Atlantic white cedars south of Lake Phelps along Allen Road prior to the 1985 wild fires. The site is currently dominated by typical pocosin and bay forest habitats.

Pocosins: There are 63,896 acres of typical pocosin wetlands on the refuge. Pocosin wetlands, also called southeastern shrub bog, are characterized by high organic content peat soils and a dense layer of shrub vegetation. Shrub species include fetterbush (*Lyonia lurida*), inkberry (*Ilex glabra*), sweet gallberry (*Ilex coriacea*), and sweet pepperbush (*Clethra alnifolia*). An overstory of pond pine (*Pinus serotina*), from scattered to densely stocked, is also often present. Pocosins have been classified in many different ways. For example, Frost describes two types of low pocosin: true ombrotrophic low pocosin (influenced by nutrient deficient organic soils deeper than 4 feet) and fire-maintained low pocosin. The fire influenced low pocosin is maintained by frequent burn cycles from 1 to 7 years. Canebrakes and a large portion of the shrub-dominated pocosins on the refuge are fire-maintained pocosins on shallower peat soils (< 4 feet). These fire-maintained sites often have more nutrients available because of the shallower peat soils overlaying mineral soil. In the absence of frequent fire, the canebrake succeeds to shrub pocosin and eventually to climax community with a pine overstory and a shrub understory. Pitcher plant bogs occur throughout many of these pocosins, especially where ground fires have created potholes in the soil. Due to past land management practices (e.g., draining, clearing, timber harvest, agriculture, pasture, and wildfire), some of these areas contain mostly grasses, ferns, and other herbaceous vegetation.

In this CCP, we divide the pocosin habitat, including the 362 acres of true ombrotrophic low pocosin that occurs on the refuge, into three ecological successional stages based on the current vegetation. These three stages include forest (tree) pocosin, shrub pocosin, and herbaceous (grass) pocosin. In the grass stage, the recovering vegetation consists of low-growing grasses, forbs, ferns, and other herbaceous vegetation. In the shrub stage, mid-story shrub species dominate the site. Pond pine saplings may also be visible. In the forest (climax) stage, the site is characterized by a pond pine overstory, from widely scattered to fully stocked, with an extremely dense shrub understory.

The Nature Conservancy has ranked pond pine canebrake, a type of pocosin on shallow peat soils (< three feet), as a critically endangered ecosystem. Large tracts of this community type are found on the eastern side of the refuge.

Key wildlife species of management concern include the endangered red wolf, the endangered red-cockaded woodpecker, black bear, small mammals, brown-headed nuthatch, red-headed woodpecker, American bobwhite quail, Chuck-will's-widow, American woodcock, neotropical migratory birds, canebrake rattlesnake, carnivorous plants, and green treefrog.

Bay Forest: Bay forest is a special type of pocosin wetland. There are 4,280 acres of bay forest on the refuge. It has a dominant cover of loblolly bay (*Gordonia lasianthus*), sweetbay magnolia (*Magnolia virginiana*), and red bay (*Persea palustris*). Bay forests are late-successional communities, replacing peatland Atlantic white cedar or pond pine woodland after a long absence of fire (Buell and Cain 1943, Kologiski 1977). Other tree species, such as red maple (*Acer rubrum*), Atlantic white cedar (*Chamaecyparis thyoides*), pond pine (*Pinus serotina*), and bald cypress (*Taxodium distichum*), may be present in the understory or canopy. Bay forests typically have a dense shrub layer component. Shrub species include fetterbush (*Lyonia lurida*), inkberry (*Ilex glabra*), sweet gallberry (*Ilex coriacea*), and sweet pepperbush (*Clethra alnifolia*).

Key wildlife species of management concern in bay forests include: Swainson's warbler, American woodcock, and prothonotary warbler.

Peatland Atlantic White Cedar Forest: Atlantic white cedar forest is a special type of pocosin wetland. There are 3,124 acres of peatland Atlantic white cedar (*Chamaecyparis thyoides*) forest on the refuge. The Nature Conservancy has ranked Atlantic white cedar as an imperiled ecosystem. Historically, Atlantic white cedar was the most valuable tree on the Albemarle Peninsula. The acreage of Atlantic white cedar today is probably less than five percent of the original (Davis et al., 1997, Frost 1987). Less than 10,000 acres of Atlantic white cedar remain in North Carolina, with more than half in Dare County (Davis et al., 1997). The occurrence of Atlantic white cedar is affected by the frequency and intensity of fires and other disturbances. Results are often unpredictable, resulting in conversion to hardwood swamps rather than Atlantic white cedar. Where possible, land managers must carefully control disturbance in order to encourage, not deter, cedar regeneration (Roman et al., 1990).

Atlantic white cedar forests are the product of a low frequency, relatively high intensity fire regime that is probably related to their marginally moist-soil conditions. Too frequent fire either prescribed or as the result of lower water tables, will convert such areas to pocosin shrub bogs. Infrequent fires result in decreased importance of white cedar and pine (Christensen 1981). In other words, Atlantic white cedar stands will succeed to bay forests following a catastrophic wildfire and/or long-term fire suppression. The most extensive development of Atlantic white cedar forests occurred on medium-to-deep peat soils overlying sandy soil, or in sandy creek bottoms with soils high in organic matter. Fire intervals are 100 - 300 years (Frost 1995). One hundred years allow stands to mature and accumulate an extensive seed bank in the upper few inches of peat. Three hundred years is the approximate longevity of Atlantic white cedar, but at that age, too few trees still remain on the site to maintain a good seed bank or prevent succession to other species (Frost 1995). Atlantic white cedar stands can sustain themselves with fire intervals of 50 to 100 years; sometimes, small patches might appear with fire intervals of 13 to 25 years (Frost 1995). Atlantic white cedar, a pioneer species, often grows in dense, even-aged stands.

It appears that the limiting factors to Atlantic white cedar on the refuge are altered hydrology and the absence of a seed source, which prevents it from naturally regenerating after disturbances, including fire. For this reason, the Service should establish stands of Atlantic white cedar throughout the refuge to serve as a future source of regeneration (Hinsley 1999). Several plantings at Pocosin Lakes NWR have conclusively shown that seedlings grown to large transplants (3 feet in height) give better results in the field, especially when subjected to browsing and heavy weed competition (Hughes 1995, Hinsley et al., 1999). As of 2001, approximately 425 acres south of Phelps Lake have been planted with Atlantic white cedar.

Key wildlife species of management concern in Atlantic white cedar forests include the black-throated-green warbler, American woodcock, Swainson's warbler, and yellow-throated warbler.

Mixed Pine Flatwoods: Mixed pine flatwoods is another special type of pocosin wetland. There are 13,649 acres of mixed pine flatwoods forest on the refuge, mostly in the northeast corner in the Frying Pan area, and in the area south of Columbia and west of State Route 94 where the organic soils are deeper than 16 inches. This habitat type contains loblolly (*Pinus taeda*) and pond pine (*Pinus serotina*) and a wide variety of hardwood tree species. The hardwood species are soft mass species, such as red maple (*Acer rubrum*), swamp tupelo (*Nyssa biflora*), and slippery elm (*Ulmus rubra*).

Key wildlife species of management concern include the endangered red wolf, red-cockaded woodpecker, black bear, white-tailed deer and small mammals (red wolf prey base), brown-headed nuthatch, red-headed woodpecker, Chuck-wills's-widow, American woodcock, prothonotary warbler, Swainson's warbler, cerulean warbler, wood thrush, yellow-billed cuckoo, northern parula, yellow-throated warbler, rusty blackbird, hooded warbler, Kentucky warbler, yellow-throated vireo, summer tanager, yellow-crowned night-heron, acadian flycatcher, Louisiana waterthrush, and eastern wood-pewee.

In areas with surface water, additional species of concern are the bald eagle, nesting and wintering wood duck, wintering black duck, anhinga, and the following anadromous fish species: blue back herring, alewife, and hickory shad.

Hardwood Swamp Forest: There are 14,045 acres of hardwood swamp forest, including examples of nonriverine swamp forest and wet hardwood forest on the refuge. These habitat types contain a variety of hard and soft mast bearing species of trees and ideally should contain a midstory of younger trees along with understories of ferns, grasses, forbs, and leaf litter. The swamp forests occur on soils with organic topsoil and have soft mast species, such as red maple (*Acer rubrum*), swamp tupelo (*Nyssa biflora*), and slippery elm (*Ulmus rubra*). The wet hardwood forests occur on mineral soil and have hard mast species, such as water oak (*Quercus nigra*), willow oak (*Quercus phellos*), laurel oak (*Quercus laurelifolia*), cherrybark oak (*Quercus pagodafolia*), and swamp chestnut oak (*Quercus michauxii*).

Key wildlife species of management concern in the forests include: endangered red wolf, wood duck, Swainson's warbler, American woodcock, cerulean warbler, American black duck, white-tailed deer, black bear, and other mammals.

Cypress/Gum Swamps: There are 970 acres of cypress/gum swamps on the refuge. This habitat type varies greatly in response to past management practices, hydrology, and soils. In general, it is some mixture of bald cypress (*Taxodium distichum*) and swamp hardwood species, including swamp tupelo (*Nyssa biflora*) in wetter areas, and black gum (*Nyssa sylvatica*) in drier areas.

Bald cypress usually occurs in even-aged groups in all-aged stands (Matoon 1915), and rarely constitutes more than 25 percent of the stand (Pinchot and Ashe 1897). Although much of the swampland west of Lake Phelps and Pungo Lake had bald cypress and swamp tupelo in the early 1800s (Ruffin 1839), today approximately 2,800 acres exist around Pungo Lake, and in Tyrrell County.

Key wildlife species of management concern in bald cypress/gum swamps include: red wolf, bald eagle, American alligator, black bear, wood duck, Swainson's warbler, cerulean warbler, and American woodcock.

Marsh: This habitat type includes 987 acres of freshwater marshes along the Alligator River and Intracoastal Waterway. The marshes are dominated by sawgrass (*Cladium jamaicense*). Invasion of common reed (*Phragmites australis*) has been a major problem in many of the marshes.

Key wildlife species of management concern include the endangered red wolf, American alligator, peregrine falcon, American black duck and other waterfowl, black bear, yellow rail, king rail, Virginia rail, American bittern, least bittern, and northern harrier.

Xeric Sandhill Scrub: This habitat type includes 276 acres on the sandy spoil banks created by excavating the Intracoastal Waterway along the southern edge of the refuge. It features an open canopy of loblolly pine (*Pinus taeda*) with an open to dense understory of scrub oaks and sparse to moderately dense herb layer, including wiregrass (*Aristida stricta*). It is the least productive of the longleaf pine-dominated communities, occupying the most xeric end of the gradient, but still subject to frequent low intensity fires. There is low plant diversity and the absence of most scrub oaks, other than turkey oak (*Quercus laevis*), helps distinguish this type.

Key wildlife species of management concern include the endangered red wolf, red-cockaded woodpecker, black bear, white-tailed deer and small mammals (red wolf prey base), brown-headed nuthatch, red-headed woodpecker, northern bobwhite, chuck-wills's-widow, American woodcock, prothonotary warbler, and Swainson's warbler.

Cropland: There are 1,250 acres of cropland on the refuge, all of which is on the Pungo Unit. It is managed primarily to provide grain and green browse for wintering waterfowl. The cropland is managed through a Cooperative Farming Program. Local farmers are allowed to farm the ground in exchange for leaving 20 percent (about 250 acres annually) of the crop standing in the field for wildlife. The refuge normally takes its share in corn and specifies to the farmer which rows to leave. Normally, about 200 acres of winter wheat are also planted behind corn and provides winter green browse for swans and geese. Some corn and wheat is harvested, stored in grain bins, and used to support waterfowl banding operations at refuges throughout eastern North Carolina.

Moist-soil Units (Managed Wetlands): There are 443 acres of moist-soil habitat on the refuge in six moist-soil units (Smartweed, Jones Pond, Marsh A, Van's Pond, Hyde Park, and Evan's Pond). There are also about 550 acres of other wetlands managed for waterfowl (Marsh C, North Smartweed, and part of the Triangle Block). The acreages for these areas are included under their appropriate habitat types, such as Hardwood Swamp Forest, Cypress/Gum Swamp, and Mixed Pine Flatwoods. Water supply (which has historically been from rainfall only) for flooding the moist-soil units in the fall has been a limiting factor in providing excellent habitat conditions for wintering, migratory waterfowl.

The 84-acre Smartweed Impoundment is located between D-Canal Road and West Lake Drive. The impoundment has been flooded annually since 1977, when dikes were constructed on its west and south sides. Fifteen acres of the unit were in agricultural production from 1969 to 1978. In 1978, excellent stands of smartweed (*Polygonum spp.*), wild millet (*Echinochloa crusgalli*), and fall panicum (*Panicum dichotomiflorum*) were observed, resulting in a habitat management decision to convert the unit to a moist-soil impoundment. In 1988, a dike was constructed to completely impound the area to provide independent water management. The current habitat management strategy is to plow or burn the impoundment at 2- to 5-year intervals to maintain and restore desirable, early ecological successional plant species. If the unit is left undisturbed, these desirable species will be replaced with undesirable, later successional species, such as cattail (*Typha spp.*), black willow (*Salix nigra*), and wool grass (*Scirpus cyperinus*). The encroachment of invasive species, including sesbania (*Sesbania* sp.), common reed (*Phragmites austrailis*), and alligator weed (*Alternathera philoxeroides*), continues to be a management challenge in the Smartweed Impoundment. The refuge has used herbicide treatments, including a glyphosate product labeled for aquatic use, and the herbicide, Habitat, successfully to set back invasive species encroachments.

Water levels for the impoundment are controlled at a water control structure at the southern end and the Hyde Park water control structure located 4 miles downstream. The structures are closed in September to flood the impoundment from October to December. Water in the Smartweed Impoundment gradually spreads from the lower elevation located at the south end. Approximately 2 to 3 feet of water in the south end are required to provide flooding for the north end of the unit. This is the first moist-soil unit to flood each year.

The Service flooded the southern third of the 200-acre Jones Pond from 1973 to 1977, and has completely flooded the pond each winter since 1978. Historically, the staff flooded the impoundment from November through February to provide habitat for wintering, migratory waterfowl. To facilitate flooding capabilities, the staff places boards in the Hyde Park water control structure in September to provide gravity flow of water and to collect accumulated rainfall. In 2004, the Service installed an artesian well and pump. This greatly increased water management capabilities in the Jones Pond unit for waterfowl and shorebird management. The staff inundated the area by blocking water at the Hyde Park structure. Boards were placed in the structure in September but flooding occurred from November-February, depending on rainfall. In October 1992, the Service completed dike construction to impound the entire unit. In 2004, the refuge installed a well and pump.

Vegetation in the area includes black willow (*Salix nigra*), sweet gum (*Liquidambar styraciflua*), smartweed (*Polygonum spp.*), fall panicum (*Panicum dichotomiflorum*), sedges (*Carex spp.*), wool grass (*Scirpus cyperinus*), and river cane (*Arundinaria gigantea*). The Service plows or burns the area every 2 to 5 years depending on the extent of encroachment by the undesirable, later successional species. The early detection of and rapid response to the exotic common reed (*Phragmites australis*) have continued to successfully minimize encroachment of this highly invasive species in Jones Pond. Herbicides labeled for aquatic use have been successfully implemented on small patches of common reed as part of the management program for this unit.

Marsh A was created in 1971. Water management in this 84-acre unit is extremely limited because the land elevation is too high to permit flooding in any but extremely wet years. The marsh was periodically burned until burning was eliminated in 1981. No management or manipulation was accomplished until the fall of 1988 when the area was double plowed. Marsh A was successfully burned by prescription in 1999. Three potholes were dug in 1989 and the area flooded in November. A small patch of the invasive common reed (*Phragmites australis*) continues to be managed with a formulation of the herbicide glyphosate, labeled for aquatic use. Three potholes were dug in 1989 and the area flooded in November. Two thousand ducks used the area consistently during the years 1989-90 and 1990-91, and 500 ducks used the area in the 1996 and 1997 waterfowl seasons.

Van's Pond was created in late summer of 1987. Although much of this 10-acre unit was bare due to the lateness in the growing season, 250-500 tundra swans daily used the cleared area during most of the winter of 1987-88. During the 1997-98 waterfowl season, 80 tundra swans and 100 ducks were observed in the unit.

The Hyde Park structure controls the flooding of the area of Van's Pond. Normally, the staff closes the structure in September but the area normally does not flood until December – February, depending on rainfall.

The 25-acre Hyde Park Pond has been flooded annually since 1973. The Hyde Park water control structure, located at the southwest corner of the field, floods this pond, Jones Pond, and Smartweed Pond. The staff closes the structure in September, but this area normally does not flood until between December and February, depending on rainfall. This pond has the highest elevation on the drainage system and is the last to flood and the first to be drawn down.

Initially, cooperative farmers "clean" farmed this area for corn, milo, and soybeans with conventional tillage and application of pre-emergent herbicides before planting, cultivation in the early stages of the crop's development, and post-emergent herbicide use later in the crop's development. When a few excellent natural foods, such as giant foxtail (*Setaria magna*), were observed growing with the crops, the staff conducted some experiments to grow corn and natural foods together. The experimental treatments included the elimination of late tilling after crops are 12 inches high, the elimination of post-emergent herbicides, and the use of no-till techniques to grow crops. Conclusions from the experiments showed that the longest sustained high use by waterfowl occurred when this area was clean farmed and the staff flooded the standing corn. Biologists have observed Canada geese in this unit.

The Service began initial waterfowl work on the 40-acre Evan's Pond unit in 1993, when the Service plowed the unit twice in July and August to set back succession and began pumping in December. The old dike has several leaks that have been scheduled for repair since 1994.

Natural Lake Shoreline: The majority of the 446-acre natural lake shoreline community on the refuge occurs around Pungo Lake, Phelps Lake, and New Lake. High water levels driven by wind tides prevent the establishment of trees. Vegetative cover in these areas includes rare, naturally occurring non-estuarine marshes. This community features a marsh and shrub zone along the lake shoreline. Common herbaceous species include broad-leaf cattail (*Typha latifolia*), common three-square (*Scirpus americanus*), and soft rush (*Juncus effusus*). The dominant tree species beyond the shrub zone include bald cypress (*Taxodium distichum*) and swamp tupelo (*Nyssa biflora*). Common reed or Phragmites (*Phragmites australis*) has encroached on the majority of the natural lake shoreline around Pungo Lake. Phragmites is a noninvasive species native to the northeastern United States, but invasive ecotypes entered the country from Europe as packing material on ships at the turn of the century (Saltonstahl 2002). The invasive ecotypes have spread throughout the east and are threatening marsh ecosystems throughout the area. The presence of Phragmites has also been observed around Lake Phelps and New Lake. Efforts to control the spread and eradicate the presence of Phragmites are essential to optimize natural lake shoreline ecosystems.

Key wildlife species of management concern on the natural lake shoreline include wood ducks and other waterfowl, marsh and wading birds, neotropical migratory birds, and muskrat and other mammal species.

Open Water: The 6,740 acres of open water include Pungo Lake and New Lake. The 2,800-acre Pungo Lake is a natural lake, which may have formed by ground fires that burned deep into the peat soils. The resulting depression filled with rainwater and became a lake. Remnant logs and stumps show evidence of historic Atlantic white cedar and bald cypress forests. Frequent fires converted these forests to the more common pocosin species, including titi (*Cyrilla racemiflora*), inkberry (*Ilex glabra*), waxmyrtle (*Myrica cerifera*), red maples (*Acer rubrum*), and scattered pond pine (*Pinus serotina*). The northern and western shorelines consist of swamp forest with a dominant species of swamp tupelo (*Nyssa biflora*)).

Pungo Lake can be lowered much easier than it can be refilled. Water inflow into the lake is from the property line drainage ditch through a one-way flap gate structure located on the west side of the lake. The property line ditch is not a significant water source, as it must be completely full before water can flow into the lake. Rainfall is essentially the only source of water for the lake. On the southeast part of the lake, a 60-inch culvert, with stopboard riser, allows water to be released.

The lake water has a pH of 4.9 and is darkly stained by tannic acid and suspended organic matter that limits sunlight penetration. The lack of sunlight penetration and low pH prevents germination of aquatic plants in the lake. Potential waterfowl food production is along the natural lake shoreline. The lake level was lowered yearly from 1964 to 1971, and in 1976, 1981, and 1985. The exposed shoreline produced good stands of desirable natural foods, primarily American threesquare (*Scirpus americana*), and undesirable stands of black willow (*Salix nigra*) and Phragmites (*Phragmites australis*). There was seldom enough precipitation to refill the lake after the drawdowns.

Pungo Lake's primary benefit to waterfowl has been for roosting and resting. Maximum acreage should be maintained with water to accommodate the large number of birds that use it. Pungo Lake receives extensive use by tundra swans, snow geese, ducks, and Canada geese. Duck numbers peak when the lake is full and there is standing water in the lakeshore marshes and adjacent moist-soil units. Biologists have observed peaks of 38,000 tundra swans, 10,000 Canada geese, 80,000 snow geese (2006/07), and 60,000 ducks on the lake within the past 13 years.
Recommended water management is to maintain a year-round full lake level (10 feet above mean sea level) to ensure adequate water when migrating birds return in the fall; however, water levels in the lake fluctuate throughout the year due to climatic conditions.

The refuge includes 3,940 acres of the 4,800-acre New Lake (sometimes called Alligator Lake), and approximately half of its shoreline. The outflow of this lake is discharged through two water control structures. A landowner plugged the canal that was channeled into the lake in 1985 to fight a large wildfire in the summer of 1993. The lake was full for the first time since 1985 during the winter of 1995 and was full again at the end of 1997.

Natural Areas: In the early 1980s, the Coastal Energy Impact Program funded efforts to construct natural area inventories for Washington, Hyde, and Tyrrell Counties. This work was undertaken partly in anticipation of proposed peat mining activities in the region. Inventories excluded land already within Federal ownership. The mission was "... to identify natural areas containing highly unique, endangered, or rare natural features, or high-quality representations of relatively undisturbed natural habitats, and which may be vulnerable to threats and damage from land use changes. The resulting inventory and recommendations were designed to help State and Federal agencies, county officials, resource managers, landowners, and developers work out effective land management and preservation mechanisms to protect outstanding or exemplary natural areas...."(Lynch and Peacock 1982a, 1982b: McDonald and Ash 1981).

These inventories are useful in developing a picture of plant communities that previously existed in certain areas and/or on certain soil types. Legrand and his associates prepared updated inventories of natural areas in the Albemarle-Pamilico Peninsula (Legrand et al., 1992). Natural areas total 62,300 acres, representing 58 percent of the terrestrial area within Pocosin Lakes NWR. They suggested that management activities be directed toward maintaining and/or conserving the unique botanical and fauna of these areas. Under some situations, prescribed fire might be required. Due to the inaccessibility of some areas, active management is probably not feasible.

Hyde County: An area south and southeast of New Lake, extending to the Intracoastal Waterway, was called New Lake Fork Pocosin (9,300 acres total; 7,300 acres in Pocosin Lakes NWR) (Lynch and Peacock 1982a). Prior to a severe fire that burned the entire area in 1982, it was mostly high pocosin, with some pond pine woodland. Legrand and his associates also included this area and suggested that the Service consider prescribed fire to perpetuate the type, especially if it could restore the wetland hydrology (Legrand et al., 1992).

Tyrrell County: The inventory of McDonald and Ashe included several natural areas within present-day refuge property in Tyrrell County. The largest was Upper Alligator River Pocosin, the drainage basin for the Northwest and Southwest Forks of Alligator River. The vegetation was mostly pond pine pocosin. The area, described as "vast inaccessible," was given a State Natural Heritage rating of "high" (statewide significance) (McDonald and Ashe 1982).

McDonald and Ashe described a small area on the western side as "forest that was cut within the last 15-20 years, but the loggers left behind some huge bald cypress trees (cull remnants of earlier logging), most with their tops blown out, and some as large as 5 feet in diameter." The authors speculated that the area might contain a State-record tree. Other trees were mostly blackgum (*Nyssa sylvatica*).

Insect and Disease Pests of Habitats: In recent years, the forest tent caterpillar *(Malacosoma disstria)* has caused widespread defoliation in the State (Collins 2005). Prolonged flooding and saturation on coastal plain soils adversely impacts the parasitic wasp that preys on the forest tent caterpillar. The parasitic wasp spends part of its life cycle in the ground. Prolonged flooding kills the wasp so it can no longer serve as a check on the populations of the forest tent caterpillar. This may account for the large outbreaks resource managers have been observing the last decade on the coastal plain.

The gypsy moth (*Lymantria dispar Linnaeus*) is now well established as far south as northeastern North Carolina. The North Carolina Division of Plant Industry and the USDA Forest Service closely monitors gypsy moth populations. They utilize pheromone traps located throughout the State, including refuge lands. When they detect large-scale outbreaks, they use integrated pest management techniques to suppress the outbreak, but not necessarily eliminate the species from the area (McManus 1989).

The southern pine beetle (*Dendroctonus frontalis*) is becoming a more common pest of pines in northeastern North Carolina. The beetles feed on the inner bark of stress-weakened trees. The needles turn yellow or straw-colored within two or three weeks of the attack, before finally turning reddish-brown. Land managers treat infected stands by cutting down a swath of trees around the area where the beetles are actively feeding, thus removing their food and starving them. Managers must monitor their pine stands and investigate any trees that appear infected (Townsend and Rieske-Kinney 2000).

Fire ants (*Solenopsis* spp) were introduced into the United States from South America during the 1940s (Tvedten 2005). This species is associated with disturbed, open habitats, including roadsides, turf, farm fields, and firebreaks. The fire ant mounds are on average between 10 to 24 inches in diameter and approximately 18 inches in height. During prescribed burns, the drier soil, which makes up the ant mounds, often introduce ground fire in the peat soils on the refuge. This has resulted in a continual management challenge for the refuge's prescribed fire program.

WILDLIFE

Many wildlife species occur in a variety of habitats across the refuge. Surveys are needed to document presence and establish population estimates for many of the classes of wildlife.

Amphibians: Although surveys have not been conducted, Pocosin Lakes NWR may provide habitat for up to 36 species of amphibians. There are approximately 20 species of frogs and toads, including the more common spring peeper, gray and barking treefrogs, southern toad, and bullfrog. Over 15 species of salamanders, including the eastern newt and spotted salamander, may occur on the refuge.

Reptiles: Over 40 species of reptiles, including lizards, snakes, turtles, and American alligator, occur throughout the refuge. Eight species of turtles frequently observed on the refuge include the yellow-bellied slider, painted turtle, spotted turtle, eastern box turtle, eastern musk turtle, eastern mud turtle, common snapping turtle, and Florida cooter. There are at least 9 species of lizards frequently observed on the refuge. The more common species include the green anole, broadhead skink, six-lined racerunner and five-lined skink.

The refuge provides habitat for a diverse array of snakes, including four venomous snakes: copperhead, pigmy rattlesnake, timber rattlesnake (canebrake), and cottonmouth. Other common species of snakes observed on the refuge include black rat snake, redbelly water snake, and eastern hognose snake.

Mammals: Pocosin Lakes NWR provides habitats for over 40 mammal species, including the endangered red wolf. Other species frequently observed on the refuge include black bear, white-tailed deer, Virginia opossum, raccoon, and the exotic nutria. Other more secretive mammals found on the refuge include river otter, bobcat, mink, and long-tailed weasel.

Although very little is known about the flying mammals on the refuge, approximately nine species of bats may occur on the refuge. Some of these include southeastern myotis, eastern pipistrel, red bat, big brown bat, and eastern big-eared bat.

During 2003 and 2004, graduate student Catherine Tredick from the Virginia Polytechnic Institute and State University conducted a study to determine population abundance and genetic structure of black bears on Pocosin Lakes NWR, using noninvasive genetic techniques. Black bear density estimates were derived from DNA samples extracted from hair samples. The estimated densities on Pocosin Lakes NWR were some of the highest reported in the literature and ranged from 1.23 to 1.66 bears per square kilometer in the areas sampled. The number of bears on Pocosin Lakes NWR in suitable habitat (i.e., ~ 300 km2 of hardwood, pocosin, and cypress-gum forests) would range 369-498 bears. However, this range is likely an underestimate because bears also inhabit areas of low-quality habitat (i.e., low pocosin and marsh) at lower densities (C. Tredick 2005). Genetic variability and structure was substantially higher on the refuge compared to other bear populations in North America (C. Tredick 2005).

Migratory Birds: Throughout the year, over 200 species of migratory birds (e.g., shorebirds, marsh birds, wading birds, waterfowl, and neotropical migratory songbirds) occur in the abundant habitats found at Pocosin Lakes NWR. Additional surveys are needed to document the diversity of species that migrate through the refuge.

Shorebirds and Marsh and Wading Birds: More intensive surveys are required to document shorebird and marsh and wading bird use on the refuge. Climatic conditions, especially rainfall, determine habitat availability to support most shorebird species on the refuge. The most abundant and diverse shorebird species occur during drought years. The staff conducts shorebird surveys depending on habitat availability (exposed mudflats) around the lake, firebreaks, and moist-soil units.

Waterfowl: Intensive surveys, including bi-monthly ground surveys and bi-monthly aerial surveys, have documented waterfowl peak use and use days since the establishment of the Pungo Unit as Pungo National Wildlife Refuge in 1963. Over 1,000 acres of moist-soil units, other managed wetlands, and three lakes provide abundant wintering habitat for migratory waterfowl. The refuge provides breeding habitat for wood ducks, hooded mergansers, American black ducks, and mallards. See Tables 8 – 13 for waterfowl use of the refuge.

Neotropical Migratory Birds and other Land Birds: The refuge provides breeding, wintering, and stopover habitat for neotropical migratory birds and other land bird species. The staff must perform more intensive surveys to more accurately document population parameters for the various species that occur on the refuge throughout the year.

Threatened and Endangered Species: Two federally listed species occur on the refuge. These are the endangered red wolf and the endangered red-cockaded woodpecker. The bald eagle, previously listed as threatened, was recently removed from the list of threatened and endangered species. Biologists have documented the presence of American alligators on land adjacent to the refuge. This species is listed as "threatened" due to similarity of appearance to other endangered crocodilian species.

State listed species that do or could occur on the refuge include: star-nosed mole, Rafinesque's big-eared bat, Southern dismal swamp shrew, southern bald eagle, loggerhead shrike, Bachman's sparrow, black vulture, red-cockaded woodpecker, little blue heron, tri-colored heron, Cooper's hawk, American eastern peregrine falcon, glossy ibis, and American alligator.

Table 8. 1999-2000 Monthly peak waterfowl use on Pocosin Lakes NWR

Species	PEAK USE					
	October	November	December	January	February	March
Snow Geese	0	3,502	45,000	36,009	22,360	23
Mallard	239	501	2,939	3,125	1,843	765
Green-winged Teal	432	779	2,530	1,720	4,280	1,132
Ring-necked Duck	15	161	864	38	18	0
Northern Pintail	3	172	791	613	314	3
American Wigeon	25	401	583	1,375	1,046	119
Black Duck	179	169	583	499	385	441
Canada Geese	310	100	380	645	488	135
Wood Duck	7	116	321	528	710	56
Ruddy Duck	22	160	371	80	3	3
Northern Shoveler	0	94	190	383	274	134
Bufflehead	4	87	168	13	10	27
Gadwall	35	33	25	124	0	38
Hooded Merganser	0	4	16	10	19	0
Blue-winged Teal	30	3	0	0	0	2
Redhead	0	0	0	25	0	0

Table 9. 1999-2000 Monthly waterfowl use days on Pocosin Lakes NWR

Species	USE DAYS					
	October	November	December	January	February	March
Snow Geese	0	27,618	707,854	813,016	539,980	356
Mallard	7,332	8,598	58,249	63,106	50,682	12,508
American Wigeon	11,036	11,334	29,971	40,920	73,834	24,955
Ring-necked Duck	279	2,304	11,718	703	193	0
Northern Pintail	465	2,418	10,986	9,992	4,408	46
Black Duck	3,022	2,160	9,691	7,130	4,485	6,913
Canada Geese	6,913	942	6,690	7,543	5,017	2,092
Northern Shoveler	0	912	5,326	6,045	5,104	3,240
Wood Duck	108	1,224	4,290	6,851	11,349	868
Ruddy Duck	512	966	2,982	827	48	46
Bufflehead	62	522	1,290	134	126	418
Hooded Merganser	0	48	273	103	203	0
Gadwall	542	666	236	1,829	0	852
Blue-winged Teal	465	18	0	0	0	31
Redhead	0	0	0	258	0	0

Table 10. 1988-2005 annual peak waterfowl use on Pungo Unit

TOTAL	PEAK USE				
	Ducks	Canada Geese	Snow Geese	Tundra Swans	Coots
1988-1989	35,000	4,500	15,000	30,000	20
1989-1990	60,000	10,000	17,000	34,000	30
1990-1991	26,200	1,436	16,000	20,000	5
1991	25,100	1,000	16,000	20,000	0
1991-1992	11,250	1,400	26,000	28,000	50
1992-1993	31,400	3,000	20,000	20,000	150
1993-1994	26,000	1,939	25,000	26,473	40
1994-1995	35,000	1,200	20,000	38,715	100
1994-1995	11,100	1,205	30,000	31,377	50
1996-1997	10,000	705	30,000	32,000	540
1997-1998	18,210	450	38,520	16,355	129
1998-1999	14,260	380	43,000	25,000	402
1999-2000	7,599	425	45,000	23,930	167
2000-2001	11,325	720	46,000	28,062	41
2001-2002	6,055	700	44,000	19,985	5
2002-2003	13,217	1,110	65,000	11,105	10
2003-2004	21,915	477	70,000	11,105	0
2004-2005	28,283	380	57,000	15,577	5

Table 11. 1988-2005 annual waterfowl use days on Pungo Unit

YEAR	USE DAYS			
	Ducks	Canada Geese	Snow Geese	Tundra Swans
1988-1989	2,632,162	230,401	924,800	1,248,621
1989-1990	2,907,846	398,290	848,800	1,716,550
1990-1991	1,876,346	106,989	1,313,500	1,477,514
1991	2,090,760	103,495	1,277,150	1,496,439
1991-1992	834,680	103,915	1,406,365	1,904,175
1992-1993	1,959,909	130,529	1,245,300	1,734,334
1993-1994	1,235,086	89,694	1,685,375	1,623,989
1994-1995	2,513,940	78,716	1,043,666	1,562,838
1995-1996	837,529	56,157	1,419,140	1,984,691
1997-1998	888,740	35,516	1,548,799	2,087,401
1998-1999	570,563	34,727	2,017,493	818,669
1999-2000	540,946	20,085	1,992,877	1,451,992
2000-2001	527,363	12,504	1,579,964	592,300
2001-2002	374,310	60,620	1,341,091	359,950
2002-2003	281,232	14,926	1,321,375	696,666
2003-2004	1,261,648	38,071	2,407,533	1,317,500
2004-2005	434,712	22,496	2,512,536	787,443

Comprehensive Conservation Plan

Table 12. 2002-2005 (aerial survey only) annual peak waterfowl use on Pocosin Lakes NWR (including the Pungo Unit)

Year	Ducks	Canada Geese	Snow Geese	Tundra Swans	American Coots
2002-2003	16,111	1,177	47,500	13,324	10
2003-2004	22,552	774	40,000	22,805	5
2004-2005	30,161	795	23,000	23,000	5

Table 13. 2002-2005 (aerial survey only) annual waterfowl use days on Pocosin Lakes NWR (including the Pungo Unit)

Year	Ducks	Canada Geese	Snow Geese	Tundra Swans	American Coots
2002-2003	814,758	75,354	1,876,450	822,260	100
2003-2004	1,879,796	69,718	2,272,300	2,850,600	202
2004-2005	1,059,211	34,696	1,318,854	1,104,580	183

Animal Damage Control: The majority of animal damage control is focused around feral hogs, beavers, white-tailed deer, rabbits, black bears, and nutria. Feral hogs grub in the ground for food and can cause significant soil disturbance and damage to native vegetation. Feral hog sightings in the Frying Pan area began increasing around 2002, and they were seen in the central parts of the refuge (harvester road area) in 2006. Beavers can be a high-maintenance challenge on the refuge by damming culverts and water control structures. White-tailed deer and rabbits have been a continual challenge to the refuge's Atlantic white cedar restoration. Seedlings below approximately 36 inches in height are severely browsed, resulting in either stunting or killing the seedlings. Dr. Eric Hinesley, a professor from North Carolina State University, has been researching various exclosure treatments to protect the seedlings. Nutria can potentially cause problems with erosion from their foraging behaviors. Although several litters of nutria are observed throughout the year, the nutria population appears to be heavily preyed upon by the red wolf and other predator species on the refuge. It is difficult to determine any adverse effects of the presence of nutria on the native muskrats due to unknown historic muskrat population estimates. However, more nutria are being observed than muskrats.

Visual observations of black bears on the refuge suggest an increase in the population. Bears are attracted to and will damage salt-treated lumber used to post staff gauges and signs and anything made of plastic or vinyl. There are legitimate concerns of bears becoming bold on the Pungo Unit. Bears seem to have learned to associate the sound of gunfire with food -- deer carcass. There have been increasing hunter complaints concerning bears tearing up deer stands and scratching truck beds that had residual deer scent from carcasses or blood remains present. Refuge bird banding programs are also experiencing bold bears taking over banding sites and damaging rocket net equipment. Valid, scientific data on population estimates is essential to develop black bear management strategies.

Insects and Diseases: Very little is known about the insect populations on the refuge. Several diseases potentially transmittable to humans associated with insects that do or potentially could occur on the refuge include: Lyme and other tick-borne diseases and West Nile's virus encephalitis and other mosquito-borne diseases.

Other diseases transmitted to humans documented on land adjacent to the refuge include rabies and distemper.

INVASIVE AND/OR EXOTIC SPECIES

There are several invasive and/or exotic species found on the refuge. These include common reed or Phragmites (*Phragmites australis*), alligator weed (*Alternanthera philoxeroides*), Japanese stiltgrass (*Microstegium* sp.), parrot feather (*Myriophyllum aquaticum*), Sesbania (*Sesbania exaltata*), Japanese honeysuckle (*Lonicera japonica*), Canada thistle (*Cirsium arvense*), Chinese privet (*Ligustrum sinense*), fire ants (*Solenopsis invicta*), gypsy moth (*Lymantria dispar)*, nutria (*Myocastor coypus*), European starling (*Sturnis vulgaris*), house sparrow (*Passer domesticus*), coyote (Canis latrans), and feral hog (*Sus scrofa*).

Alligator weed and parrot feather are exotic aquatic plants which out-compete native vegetation. Alligator weed has significantly spread and can be found in the majority of the refuge canals located on the east side of the refuge and, for the first time in 2005, on the Pungo Unit. Large mats of this weed are found floating in the Alligator River, Scuppernong River, and their tributaries, sometimes limiting or preventing accessibility to remote locations of the rivers. Parrot feather, originally an ornamental aquarium plant, is spreading at a slower rate but is becoming more frequently prevalent in refuge canals and small ponds.

The staff deploys up to five phermone-gypsy moth traps at high public use areas across the refuge to monitor the spread of gypsy moths. During the last 10 years of monitoring, two male moths were captured, one in 1997 and one in 1998.

Nutria, an exotic and invasive mammal species, was introduced in the United States in 1899. Nutria are polyestrus and can produce between 2 to 3 litters per year. This generalist species out-competes the native muskrat and can cause erosion problems around dikes from their foraging behavior. Biologists observe sites that nutria use frequently in the Pungo Unit.

Fire ants have continued to spread throughout the refuge. Scientists know little about the adverse effects to ground nesting birds, herpetofauna, and small mammals on the refuge. The presence of large fire ant mounds has caused concerns for introducing ground fires during prescribed burn operations because the mounds are higher and drier than the surrounding terrain, burn more readily, and may carry the fire down into organic soil.

Small patches of Sesbania were first observed while conducting the 1999 vegetation surveys in the Smartweed impoundment. Within the last two growing seasons, the size of the patches has considerably increased. Treatments with glyphosate herbicide to eradicate this invasive species began during the fall of 2000 and continued through 2005. The presence of common reed will require continued early detection and rapid response to its detection through active management.

Control of common reed on the refuge is a top priority. This species has invaded approximately 300 acres of refuge habitat, including the natural shoreline community around Pungo Lake. Once established, this invasive species out-competes the preferred vegetation and eventually becomes a monoculture of reeds. Between 2000 and 2006, the refuge treated between 100 and 200 acres of Phragmites annually with glyphosate or imazapyr herbicides.

CULTURAL RESOURCES

There have been limited archaeological investigations within the refuge. No significant artifacts have been found. The wetland environment makes it unlikely that there are many cultural resources on the refuge. The small area of uplands (170 acres of the 110,106 acres on the refuge) is the most likely site of settlements or encampments. The staff must conduct management activities so as to avoid compromising sensitive sites.

SOCIOECONOMIC ENVIRONMENT

The current area of Pocosin Lakes NWR lies in Tyrrell, Washington, and Hyde Counties, North Carolina. Tyrrell, Washington, and Hyde Counties are in northeastern North Carolina with Dare County and the Atlantic Ocean to the east, Pamlico Sound to the south, Martin and Beaufort Counties, North Carolina, to the west, and the Albemarle Sound to the north. The areas have had little growth since 1900 despite rapid growth in Dare County on the coast to the east and the major highway to the coast passing through Tyrrell and Washington Counties. The lack of growth is due in large part to the poorly drained, deep organic soil that makes development expensive and environmentally hazardous. Unemployment and poverty rates are much higher than the State average; high school and college graduation rates are below the State average.

The area is still predominantly rural, and the largest towns and county seats are Columbia (2000 population: 819), Plymouth (2000 population 4,107), and Swan Quarter (2000 population 300). Like other rural areas throughout the country, outdoor activities are both popular and necessary. Hunting and recreational fishing are popular pastimes and farming, commercial fishing, and forestry are important elements of the economy.

HISTORY OF THE AREA

Tyrrell County: The inhabitants of Tyrrell County at the time of European settlement were Coastal Algonquians called the Secotan. These Algonquians were the southernmost extent of a tribe that inhabited the Atlantic Coast north to Canada. They settled in relatively dispersed patterns with capital villages, villages, seasonal villages, and camps for specialized activities. The settlements were along the sounds, estuaries, major rivers, and tributaries. Some of the villages had regular internal organization with palisades and some were less organized with an open structure. They settled where they could conduct agriculture, fishing, shell fishing, hunting, and gathering close to the village. The farmsteads were occupied by extended families. The Coastal Algonquians grew corn, squash, sunflowers, beans, and native plants on sandy ridges. They traded extensively with the Tuscarora that inhabited the area west of the Tidewater region (Mathis, M.A. and J.J. Crow 2000).

The governor of colonial North Carolina established the Tyrrell Precinct in 1729 from parts of present-day Chowan, Bertie, Currituck, and Pasquotank Counties. The precinct was large and stretched from Roanoke Island to Tarboro. From 1774 to 1870, governors formed Martin, Washington, and Dare Counties from parts of the Tyrrell Precinct. The North Carolina General Assembly chartered the town of Elizabeth in 1793, chartered it as the county seat in 1799, and changed its name to Columbia in

1810. The town had a population of 100 in 1810 and a diverse economy of mercantile trade, milling, county administration, and maritime occupations.

Agriculture and forest products have been important to the county from the time of early settlement. The rich soil with an organic topsoil layer has been the resource responsible for the county's high productivity. The first settlers farmed for survival and absentee landowners in Edenton. Landowners established large, nearly self-sufficient plantations. After the Civil War and the end of slavery, these large plantations failed and agricultural production declined, but the timber industry thrived. In the twentieth century, the use of mechanization and adoption of modern production techniques led the county's return to prominence as an agricultural area.

In the later part of the twentieth century, conservation agencies and organizations began to purchase areas less suited for agriculture and production forestry due to the deep organic soils. They managed those areas for wildlife habitat, the protection of unique ecological communities, and outdoor recreation. Recreation based on natural and cultural resources is a growing part of the local lifestyle.

Hyde County: The inhabitants of Hyde County at the time of European settlement were also Coastal Algonquians called the Machapungo and Mattamuskeets. By the early 1700s, most of the Indians lived on a reservation in the eastern part of the county. In 1711, the number of Indians was about 30, and by 1761, only 6 remained.

English explorers first arrived in the county in 1585. The early history of the county was dominated by maritime trade and featured the exploits of Edward Teach, also known as Blackbeard the Pirate. The first settlers were castaways from ships.

The North Carolina General Assembly formed Hyde County from Bath County in 1705, and originally named it Wickam County. It was given the name Hyde County in 1712, in honor of Edward Hyde, the first governor of North Carolina.

In the 1800s, residents built many plantation homes in the county. The best known is the Octagon House in the eastern part of the county. With its rich soil with an organic topsoil layer, Hyde County has always had a good reputation for agricultural production, especially in corn. People traveled to the county from across the State for corn.

In 1837, the State Literary Board owned Lake Mattamuskeet and ordered the lake drained with a canal to the Pamlico Sound that decreased the size from 120,000 to 50,000 acres and its depth from a range of six to nine feet to two to three feet. The State established Mattamuskeet Drainage District to drain Lake Mattamuskeet completely with more drainage canals and a pumping plant in 1910 for crop production. The cost of maintaining the water levels necessary for production exceeded the profits from the crops. In 1932, the developers abandoned the operation. The large pumping plant built for the project was first converted into a hunting lodge and is now Mattamuskeet Lodge.

In 1934, the lake and the surrounding area became the Mattamuskeet National Wildlife Refuge. The lake attracts large populations of wintering waterfowl and the area is a haven for hunters and bird-watchers.

Agriculture has remained the most important part of the county's economy and lifestyle. The acreage in cropland increased dramatically in the 1970s, when soybean prices increased substantially. Much of that land was difficult to drain and maintain water levels necessary for production, and has been abandoned.

In the later part of the twentieth century, conservation agencies and organizations began to purchase areas less suited for agriculture and production forestry due to the deep organic soils. They manage those areas for wildlife habitat, the protection of unique ecological communities, and outdoor recreation. Recreation based on natural and cultural resources is a growing part of the local lifestyle. Some of the recreation has presented business opportunities to local residents in the form of guide services for hunting and fishing and the sale of hunting leases.

Washington County: The inhabitants of Washington County at the time of European settlement were also Coastal Algonquians called the Moratucs and the Secotans, who lived in the area as early as 10,000 years ago. By 1755, less than 100 years after settlement, the total Indian population in the northeastern part of North Carolina was less than 365 (Lee 1963).

Trapping, logging, and farming were the main sources of livelihood in the early years of the colony. Trade was begun with the West Indies and the northern colonies. The main exports were tar, pitch, turpentine, lumber, corn, and tobacco.

In 1702, entrepreneurs built a gristmill and sawmill in an area known as Lee's Mill. By 1799, the North Carolina General Assembly established Washington County and the town of Lee's Mill became the first county seat. Lee's Mill became Roper in 1890.

Several landowners built large estates in the county, chiefly Buncombe Hall, built in Roper, and Josiah Collins' Somerset Place on Lake Phelps. Traders shipped corn produced on Collins' plantation worldwide. Collins attempted to drain Lake Phelps into the Scuppernong River by way of a 6-mile-long canal, 20 feet wide, dug by 80 slaves imported directly from Africa. The canal helped with drainage, irrigation, and shipping. The plantation eventually grew to 100 buildings and 300 slaves (Tetterton 1998).

Plymouth, which was an important seaport until the Civil War, was laid out in 1785. It became the first incorporated town in the county in 1807, and is the present county seat. Its founders named it after Plymouth, Massachusetts, from which the early settlers came (USDA Soil Conservation Service 1981).

During the Civil War, Union forces occupied the town from May 1862 to April 1864. Between April 17-20, 1864, 15,000 Confederate soldiers under the command of General Robert Hoke retook the town with the assistance of the ironclad ship C.S.S. Ram Albemarle. The Albemarle held the Union Navy on the Roanoke River. Three days later, the Union Army and Navy retook Plymouth (Tetterton 1998).

In the twentieth century, life in Washington County evolved around agriculture, forest management, and the forest products industry.

LAND USE IN THE AREA

The historic land use in the area depended for the most part by the nature of the land. Hydric soils cover 97 percent of Tyrrell County, 99 percent of Hyde County, and 86 percent of Washington County. The hydric soils remained in forest, pocosin (shrubby plant communities), or marsh until the twentieth century. The major historic land uses have revolved around hunting upland game and waterfowl. Native Americans and farmers descended from European settlers cultivated crops on the uplands on the shoreline of the Albemarle Sound and Lake Mattamuskeet and terraces of streams for centuries. In the twentieth century, farmers drained much of the hydric mineral soil and shallow organic soil.

Tyrrell County: Today, Tyrrell County is 61 percent forested (153,400 acres) and 28 percent cropland (69,749 acres).

From 1997 to 2002, the land in farms increased 35 percent from 54,638 acres to 73,608 acres; the average size of farms increased 22 percent from to 661 acres to 809 acres; full-time farm operators increased 30 percent from 56 farms to 73 farms; total market value of agricultural products sold decreased 18 percent from $35,687,000 to $29,403,000; and average market value of agricultural products sold per farm decreased 24 percent from $429,966 to $323,110 (Table 14).

In 2002, soybeans accounted for 35,753 acres of cropland, the largest of any single crop in the county. Corn and wheat have also been important crops in Tyrrell County (Table 15) (USDA 2002).

Hyde County: Today, Hyde County is 60 percent forested (235,800 acres), 24 percent cropland (95,327 acres), and 11 percent marsh (44,729 acres).

From 1997 to 2002, the land in farms increased 8 percent from 95,327 acres to 103,089 acres; the average size of farms decreased 25 percent from 953 acres to 716 acres; full-time farm operators increased 22 percent from 74 farms to 90 farms; total market value of agricultural products sold decreased slightly from $32,996,000 to $32,868,000; and average market value of agricultural products sold per farm decreased 31 percent from $329,965 to $228,251 (Table 16).

In 2002, corn and soybeans accounted for 31,059 and 30,013 acres of cropland, the largest crops in the county. Cotton and wheat have also been important crops in Hyde County (Table 17) (USDA 2002).

Washington County: Today, Washington County is 38 percent forested (84,200 acres) and 45 percent cropland (100,388 acres).

From 1997 to 2002, the land in farms decreased 6 percent from 107,280 acres to 100,388 acres; the average size of farms increased 11 percent from 528 acres to 593 acres; full-time farm operators increased 13 percent from 126 farms to 143 farms; total market value of agricultural products sold decreased 32 percent from $67,555,000 to $46,149,000; and average market value of agricultural products sold per farm decreased 28 percent from $332,784 to $239,113 (Table 18).

In 2002, soybeans accounted for 33,365 acres of cropland, the largest of any single crop in the county. Corn, wheat, and cotton have also been important crops in Washington County (Table 19). The county produces more than 6 million broiler chickens (USDA 2002).

On the land surrounding the refuge, the major land use is farming and hunting. There is little residential construction in the wetlands surrounding the refuge. The well-drained areas of the county have had extensive residential and commercial development.

DEMOGRAPHICS IN THE AREA

Tyrrell County: Tyrrell County is primarily rural with a total estimated population of 4,149 in 2000 (U.S. Census Bureau 2000). The county gained 7.6 percent of its population between 1990 and 2000 (U.S Census Bureau 2000). Columbia, the county seat, is the largest town but the population is widely dispersed throughout the unincorporated areas of the county.

The population is 56.5 percent white, 39.4 percent black, 3.6 percent hispanic, 0.2 percent Native American, and 0.7 percent Asian (U.S. Census Bureau 2000). In 2000, the mean family income was $21,616, substantially below the State average of $35,320. The poverty rate was 25.7 percent of the population, well above the State average of 12.6 percent (U.S. Census Bureau 2000). The average unemployment rate in 2004 was 7.8 percent, well above the State of North Carolina unemployment rate of 5.5 percent (North Carolina Employment Security Commission 2004).

Table 14. Tyrrell County agricultural statistics from the 2002 USDA Census

Number of Farms	91
Acres in Farms	73,608
Average Size of Farms (Acres)	809
Market Value of Land Per Farm	$1,380,993
Market Value of Land Per Acre	$1,809
Market Value of Equipment Per Farm	$257,269
Total Cropland (Acres)	68,406
Market Value of All Products Sold	$29,403,000
Market Value of Products Sold Per Farm	$323,110
Market Value of Crops Sold	$21,334,000
Market Value of Livestock Sold	$8,069,000
Operators with Farm as Principal Occupation	73
Operators with Another Occupation as Principal Occupation	18
Hogs in Inventory	0
Hogs Sold	0
Beef Cows in Inventory	214
Beef Cows Sold	51
Land in Soybeans (Acres)	35,753
Land in Corn (Acres)	27,654
Land in Wheat (Acres)	18,118
Land in Cotton (Acres)	1,540

Table 15. Commodity production in Tyrrell County in 2002 and 1997 from the 2002 and 1997 USDA Census

Commodity	2002 Production	1997 Production	1997-2002 Change
Soybeans (acres)	35,753	27,490	Increased 30%
Corn (acres)	27,654	18,999	Increased 45%
Wheat (acres)	18,118	13,065	Increased 39%
Cotton (acres)	1,540	1,311	Increased 17%
Hog Inventory	0	39,087	N/A
Hogs Sold	0	156,539	N/A
Cattle Sold	51	250	Decreased 80%

Table 16. Hyde County agricultural statistics from the 2002 USDA Census

Number of Farms	144
Acres in Farms	103,089
Average Size of Farms (Acres)	716
Market Value of Land Per Farm	$1,264,802
Market Value of Land Per Acre	$1,819
Market Value of Equipment Per Farm	$208,106
Total Cropland (Acres)	91,524
Market Value of All Products Sold	$32,868,000
Market Value of Products Sold Per Farm	$228,251
Market Value of Crops Sold	$32,151,000
Market Value of Livestock Sold	$717,000
Operators with Farm as Principal Occupation	90
Operators with Another Occupation as Principal Occupation	54
Hogs in Inventory	3,300
Hogs Sold	7,160
Beef Cows in Inventory	180
Beef Cows Sold	99
Land in Corn (Acres)	31,059
Land in Soybeans (Acres)	30,013
Land in Cotton (Acres)	22,906
Land in Wheat (Acres)	10,614

Table 17. Commodity production in Hyde County in 2002 and 1997 from the 2002 and 1997 USDA Census

Commodity	2002 Production	1997 Production	1992-1997 Change
Corn (acres)	31,059	31,990	Decreased 3%
Soybeans (acres)	30,013	36,381	Decreased 17%
Cotton (acres)	22,906	4,212	Increased 444%
Wheat (acres)	10,614	18,989	Decreased 44%
Hog Inventory	3,300	9,890	Decreased 67%
Hogs Sold	7,160	25,059	Decreased 71%
Cattle Inventory	180	427	Decreased 58%
Cattle Sold	99	142	Decreased 30%

Table 18. Washington County agricultural statistics from the 2002 USDA Census

Number of Farms	193
Acres in Farms	114,423
Average Size of Farms (Acres)	593
Market Value of Land Per Farm	$1,124,786
Market Value of Land Per Acre	$1,924
Market Value of Equipment Per Farm	$157,276
Total Cropland (Acres)	100,388
Market Value of All Products Sold	$46,149,000
Market Value of Products Sold Per Farm	$239,113
Market Value of Crops Sold	$34,027,000
Market Value of Livestock Sold	$12,122,000
Operators with Farm as Principal Occupation	143
Operators with Another Occupation as Principal Occupation	50
Broilers	6,051,300
Hogs in Inventory	0
Hogs Sold	9,090
Beef Cows in Inventory	637
Beef Cows Sold	643
Land in Soybeans (Acres)	33,365
Land in Corn (Acres)	28,346
Land in Cotton (Acres)	26,901
Land in Wheat (Acres)	15,727
Land in Peanuts (Acres)	3,016
Land in Tobacco (Acres)	311

Table 19. Commodity production in Washington County in 2002 and 1997 from the 2002 and 1997 USDA Census

Commodity	2002 Production	1997 Production	1997-2002 Change
Soybeans (acres)	33,365	40,792	Decreased 18%
Corn (acres)	28,346	30,734	Decreased 8%
Cotton (acres)	26,901	7,692	Increased 250%
Wheat (acres)	15,727	25,381	Decreased 38%
Peanuts (acres)	3,016	2,785	Increased 8%
Tobacco (acres)	311	449	Decreased 31%
Broilers	6,051,300	4,868,100	Increased 24%
Hog Inventory	0	72,730	N/A
Hogs Sold	9,090	201,676	Decreased 95%
Cattle Sold	643	607	Increased 6%

The percentage of high school graduates in the population older than 25 is 51 percent; the percentage of college graduates is 7 percent. The state averages are 78.1 percent for high school graduation and 22.5 percent for college graduation (U.S. Census Bureau 2000). Home ownership rate is 74.9 percent, above the State average rate of 69.4 percent. There are 2.42 persons per household in Tyrrell County, slightly below the State average of 2.49.

Hyde County: Hyde County is primarily rural with a total estimated population of 5,826 in 2000 (U.S. Census Bureau 2000). The county gained 7.7 percent of its population between 1990 and 2000 (U.S Census Bureau 2000). Swan Quarter, the county seat, is the largest town but the population is widely dispersed throughout the unincorporated areas of the county.

The population is 62.7 percent white, 35.1 percent black, 2.2 percent hispanic, 0.3 percent Native American, and 0.4 percent Asian (U.S. Census Bureau 2000). In 2000, the mean family income was $23,568, substantially below the State average of $35,320. The poverty rate was 24.8 percent of the population, well above the State average of 12.6 percent (U.S. Census Bureau 2000). The average unemployment rate in 2004 was 7.2 percent, well above the State of North Carolina unemployment rate of 5.5 percent (North Carolina Employment Security Commission 2004).

The percentage of high school graduates in the population older than 25 is 52 percent; the percentage of college graduates is 7 percent. The state averages are 78.1 percent for high school graduation and 22.5 percent for college graduation (U.S. Census Bureau 2000). Home ownership rate is 78.4 percent, above the State average rate of 69.4 percent. There are 2.36 persons per household in Hyde County, slightly below the State average of 2.49.

Washington County: Washington County is primarily rural with a total estimated population of 13,723 in 2000 (U.S. Census Bureau 2000). The county lost 2.0 percent of its population between 1990 and 2000 (U.S Census Bureau 2000). Plymouth, the county seat, is the largest town but the population is widely dispersed throughout the unincorporated areas of the county.

The population is 48.3 percent white, 48.91 percent black, 2.3 percent hispanic, 0.1 percent Native American, and 0.3 percent Asian (U.S. Census Bureau 2000). In 2000, the mean family income was $27,726, substantially below the State average of $35,320. The poverty rate was 20.5 percent of the population, well above the State average of 12.6 percent (U.S. Census Bureau 2000). The average unemployment rate in 2004 was 7.3 percent, well above the State of North Carolina unemployment rate of 5.5 percent (North Carolina Employment Security Commission 2004).

The percentage of high school graduates in the population older than 25 is 56 percent; the percentage of college graduates is 9 percent. The state averages are 78.1 percent for high school graduation and 22.5 percent for college graduation (U.S. Census Bureau 2000). Home ownership rate is 73.6 percent, above the State average rate of 69.4 percent. There are 2.52 persons per household in Hyde County, slightly above the State average of 2.49.

EMPLOYMENT IN THE AREA

Tyrrell County: Agriculture is the largest employer in Tyrrell County, employing 186 of the county's 530 employees with an annual payroll of $8.3 million in 2000 (U.S. Department of Commerce, County Business Patterns 2000). There is no single large employer in the county (North Carolina Economic Security Commission 2002). Refer to Table 20.

Table 20. Economic and population data for northeastern North Carolina Counties

County	Average Income[1]	Poverty Rate (%)[1]	Average 2004 Unemployment Rate (%)[2]	2000 Population[1]	Population Trend[1]
N. Carolina	$35,320	12.6	5.5		+21% since 1990
Counties in the Vicinity of the Pocosin Lakes NWR					
Hyde	$23,568	24.8	7.2	5,826	-37% since 1900
Tyrrell	$21,616	25.7	7.8	4,149	-17% since 1900
Washington	$27,726	20.5	7.3	13,723	Same as 1960
Other Northeastern North Carolina Counties					
Beaufort	$28,614	17.4	6.9	44,958	+6% since 1990
Bertie	$22,816	12.6	8.2	19,773	Same as 1990
Camden	$35,423	12.2	3.8	6,885	+16% since 1990
Carteret	$34,348	11.8	4.7	59,383	+13% since 1990
Chowan	$27,900	18.7	4.9	14,526	+7% since 1990
Craven	$33,214	13.8	4.9	91,436	+12% since 1990
Currituck	$36,287	10.8	2.8	18,190	+166% since 1970
Dare	$35,258	8.1	5.1	29,967	+328% since 1970
Gates	$30,087	15.4	4.2	10,516	Same as 1900
Halifax	$24,471	23.6	8.1	57,370	Same as 1950
Hertford	$23,724	23.1	6.0	22,601	Same as 1960
Martin	$26,058	20.1	7.1	25,593	Same as 1940
Northampton	$24,218	23.1	7.3	22,086	Same as 1980
Pamlico	$28,629	16.8	4.7	12,934	+14% since 1990
Pasquotank	$29,305	19.0	4.7	34,897	+11% since 1990
Perquimens	$26,489	19.5	4.8	11,368	Same as 1920

[1] U.S. Census Bureau, 2000 Census of the United States
[2] North Carolina Economic Security Commission, December 2004

In 2000, the sectors employing the largest numbers of persons were in decreasing order as follows: agriculture, retail trade, manufacturing, construction, finance, lodging, and food service (U.S. Census Bureau 2000).

Hyde County: Lodging and food service and retail trade are the largest employers in Hyde County, employing 277 and 223 of the county's 1,044 employees with an annual payroll of $22.4 million in 2000 (U.S. Department of Commerce, County Business Patterns 2000). This is due in large part to the tourists attracted to the Outer Banks of Hyde County (North Carolina Economic Security Commission, 2002).

In 2000, the sectors employing the largest numbers of persons were in decreasing order as follows: lodging and food service, retail trade, agriculture, manufacturing, construction, wholesale trade, health care, finance, forestry and fishing, real estate, administrative support services, and recreation (U.S. Census Bureau, Economic Census 2000).

Washington County: Manufacturing is the largest employer in Washington County, employing more than 1,000 of the county's 3,998 employees with an annual payroll of $129.8 million in 2000 (U.S. Department of Commerce, County Business Patterns 2000). This is due in large part to the wood products industry (North Carolina Economic Security Commission 2002).

In 2000, the sectors employing the largest numbers of persons were in decreasing order as follows: manufacturing, retail trade, health care, agriculture, lodging and food service, transportation, wholesale trade, transportation, administrative support, forestry and fishing, and finance (U.S. Census Bureau, Economic Census 2000).

FORESTRY IN THE AREA

Tyrrell County: Timber had always been a source of wealth for Tyrrell County. However, much of the timber was cleared in order to cultivate the land for corn, soybeans, and other crops.

Today, Tyrrell County is approximately 61 percent forested, with 153,400 acres of forestland. In contrast, 60 percent of North Carolina is forested. Fifty-four percent of the county's forest is in oak-gum-cypress, 25 percent is in pine, 19 percent is in oak-pine, and 2 percent is in oak-hickory (USDA Forest Service 2002).

In 2000, private landowners and the Federal Government were the largest forest landowners and each owned 34 percent of the county's forested land. The State owned 19 percent and forest industry owned 13 percent (USDA Forest Service 2002).

Hyde County: Timber had always been a source of wealth for Hyde County. However, much of the timber was cleared in order to cultivate the land for corn, soybeans, and other crops.

Today, Hyde County is approximately 60 percent forested, with 235,800 acres of forestland. In contrast, 60 percent of North Carolina is forested. Fifty-two percent of the county's forest is in pine, 32 percent is in oak-gum-cypress, 11 percent is in oak-hickory, and 5 percent is in oak-pine (USDA Forest Service 2002).

In 2000, private landowners were the largest forest landowners with 55 percent of the county's forestland. The Federal Government owned 28 percent, forest industry owned 15 percent, and the State owned 2 percent (USDA Forest Service 2002).

Washington County: Timber had always been a source of wealth for Washington County. However, much of the timber was cleared in order to cultivate the land for corn, soybeans, and other crops.

Today, Washington County is approximately 38 percent forested, with 84,200 acres of forestland. In contrast, 60 percent of North Carolina is forested. Forty-one percent of the county's forest is in pine, 19 percent is in oak-gum-cypress, 18 percent is in oak-hickory, and 11 percent is in oak-pine, and 5 percent in elm-ash-cottonwood (USDA Forest Service 2002).

In 2000, private landowners were the largest forest landowners with 54 percent of the county's forestland. Forest industry owned 27 percent, the Federal Government owned 15 percent, and the State owned 4 percent (USDA Forest Service 2002).

OUTDOOR RECREATION IN THE AREA

Fish and wildlife resources have had a profound effect on recreation in the area. Tyrrell, Hyde, and Washington Counties have always had an abundance of fish and game, due to its diversity of lands and waters. Early in history, sportsmen-established clubs were created in the area for the purpose of protecting game and wildlife. Later, as part of a comprehensive wildlife management program, Mattamuskeet, Swanquarter, and Pocosin Lakes NWRs were created to conserve and restore habitat for native wildlife and migratory birds. In addition to the refuges, there are eight North Carolina state game lands, a state park, an area managed by the Conservation Fund, and several parcels protected by the Nature Conservancy in the area.

Recreation in the area is also based on the water in the Albemarle and Pamlico Sounds, Scuppernong and Alligator Rivers, and Lake Phelps and Lake Mattamuskeet. Boat ramps provide access to the rivers and sounds. Numerous outfitters provide boats and guided tours. The North Carolina Coastal Plain Paddle Trails Guide lists eighty-nine miles on nine trails in Tyrrell, Hyde, and Washington Counties (North Carolina Division of Parks and Recreation 2001). Pettigrew State Park has 16,600 acres of water on Lake Phelps, 1,293 acres of land around Lake Phelps, and 3,238 acres on the Scuppernong River (including the Nature Conservancy Property which plans to deed the Scuppernong River property to Pettigrew State Park.

The State of North Carolina manages the 1,825-acre Lantern Acres Game Land; 614-acre Pungo River Game Land; 5,426-acre Bachelor Bay Game Land; 5,482-acre Van Swamp Game Land; 600-acre J. Morgan Futch Game Land; 1,394-acre New Lake Game Land; and 31,057-acre Gull Rock Game Land in Tyrrell, Hyde, and Washington Counties for wildlife management and hunting opportunities.

The Partnership for the Sounds is a non-governmental organization that promotes and supports ecotourism in the region and has been proactive in publicizing recreation opportunities on the refuge. The Partnership's headquarters is in Columbia at the North Carolina Department of Transportation's visitor center adjacent to the refuge office and visitor center.

OUTDOOR RECREATION ECONOMICS

Fish and wildlife are the focuses of the refuge, but they are also important to the local economy. First, a commercial fishery is present in both the Albemarle and Pamlico Sounds and the Alligator River. Blue crab and flounder are the major species harvested. Second, hunting and fishing are economically important to local businesses, both directly as the local population spends money and indirectly as an attraction that draws sportsmen from outside the county.

Unfortunately, a general lack of regard for the conservation of fish and wildlife resources combined with wetland clearing and draining, has led to the loss of valuable fishery spawning grounds and the loss of habitat for many wildlife species. In the attempt to restore and protect some of these resources, Pocosin Lakes NWR serves an important role, not only by providing habitat for a diversity of plant and wildlife species, but also as a place where people can go to enjoy these resources, either through observation or through hunting or fishing.

The Fish and Wildlife Service surveyed participants in wildlife-dependent recreation in North Carolina in 2001. The survey documented an average expenditure of $69 per day by anglers, $74 per day for hunters, and $199 per day for wildlife observers and photographers (U.S. Fish and Wildlife Service 2001).

The Partnership for the Sounds had a study done of the economic impact of its facilities. The study demonstrated that the average visitor spent $108 per visit, with a range of $63.70 to $332.55 per day (Vogelsang 2001). A similar study of visitors at the Chincoteague National Wildlife Refuge in Virginia also showed a range of expenditures from $62 to $101 per day (U.S. Environmental Protection Agency 1997).

A study commissioned by the State of New Jersey demonstrated that the average visitor to the shorebird migration spent $130 per day (New Jersey Department of Environmental Protection 2000). Birdwatchers on eight national wildlife refuges in New Jersey reported a range of expenditures from $25 to $41 per day (Kerlinger 1994).

Ecotourists on Dauphin Island, Alabama, spent an average of $60 per visitor per day (Kerlinger 1999).

Bird watchers on High Island, Texas, reported an average expenditure of $46 per day; and non-residents reported $693 per trip (Eubanks, Kerlinger, and Payne 1993). The average visitor to the Great Texas Coastal Birding Trail spent $78 per day (Eubanks and Stoll 1999).

Studies at the Santa Ana National Wildlife Refuge in south Texas demonstrated a range of expenditures from $88 to $145 per day on nature-based tourist activities. The Laguna Atascosa National Wildlife Refuge in south Texas reported a range of $83 to $117 per day (U.S. Environmental Protection Agency 1997).

Bird watchers to the Salton Sea National Wildlife Refuge in California spent an average of $57 per day (National Audubon Society 1998).

When improved access, facilities, and staffing are added, Pocosin Lakes NWR can serve as an important role in the economic life of the community. Local officials consider eco-tourism, hunting, fishing, wildlife observation and photography, and environmental interpretation elements of a desirable industry. As the population increases and the number of places left to enjoy wildlife decreases, the refuge may become even more important to the local community. It can benefit the community directly by providing recreational opportunities for the local population, and indirectly by attracting tourists from outside the county to generate additional dollars to the local economy.

TOURISM IN THE AREA

Tourism in the area is based on the natural resources and cultural attractions in the area. Boat ramps provide access to the rivers, bays, and sounds for fishing, hunting, and boating. Numerous outfitters provide boats and guided tours. The Atlantic Ocean attracts swimmers, surfers, sunbathers, and anglers to the Outer Banks of Dare County. The Outer Banks attract 7 million tourists per year.

More developed tourist attractions based on natural resources include the Mattamuskeet and Swanquarter NWRs, Alligator River NWR, Pettigrew State Park, Buckridge National Estuarine Research Reserve, and Palmetto Peartree Preserve.

Pocosin Lakes NWR could serve as an additional attraction to tourists visiting the area. If the Service provided better roads and more facilities within the refuge, tourists might stay longer in the area to enjoy the opportunities provided for wildlife-dependent recreation and environmental education. This could generate more income for the local economy.

TRANSPORTATION

In its early days, residents of the area relied on water transportation. The rivers and streams that crisscross the counties served as a means for transportation, trade, and communication between almost every community in the area. The Scuppernong River, Alligator River, and Albemarle Sound were once the major transportation avenues in the area. As the area grew and the railroad arrived, river and boat traffic declined. The waterways are still important as sources of income and for recreation.

In the twentieth century with the popularity of automobiles, the State developed a network of highways connecting the county to all areas of the eastern United States. North Carolina Highway 32 and U.S. Highway 17 connect the refuge with the Virginia Beach, Norfolk, and Chesapeake areas. U.S. Highway 64 connects the refuge with Raleigh, North Carolina, and the northeastern United States by way of Interstate 95. A number of smaller roads connect the various communities in the area. There is an international airport in Norfolk/Virginia Beach 100 miles north of the refuge and a regional airport in Greenville 90 miles west of the refuge.

CULTURAL ENVIRONMENT

The local area features cultural activities in small local art galleries, antique shops, and at fairs and festivals.

Virginia Beach is in a major metropolitan area 100 miles north of the refuge that supports a wide range of cultural facilities and events. The Virginia Beach Pavilion is a 63,000-square-foot convention center that hosts dozens of events annually from craft shows to musical and theatrical performances. The Little Theater of Virginia Beach hosts plays throughout the year. The 20,000-seat Virginia Beach Amphitheater is the site of live musical performances. The Contemporary Art Center of Virginia features changing exhibitions by national and international artists, as well as performing arts performances. It attracts 400,000 visitors annually. The Atlantic Wildfowl Museum celebrates the art of decoy making that was instrumental in attracting the first settlers to the area.

The Scope in Norfolk is a 12,600-seat arena that hosts live music performances, as well as sports events. The 2,400-seat Chrysler Hall is the site of theatrical performances. The historic Wells Theater is the 600-seat home to the Virginia Stage Company. The 675-seat Attucks Theater is the site of African-American stage performances. The 1,632-seat Harrison Opera House is home to the Virginia Opera. The Chrysler Museum of Art is a venue for 30,000 paintings, sculptures, and decorative arts from the world over. The 12,067-seat Harbor Park is home to the Norfolk Tides baseball team.

REFUGE ADMINISTRATION AND MANAGEMENT

LAND PROTECTION AND CONSERVATION

Congress established the 12,000-acre Pungo National Wildlife Refuge in 1963 by the authority of the Migratory Bird Conservation Act of 1929. The Service established the Pocosin Lakes NWR in 1990 and made the Pungo Refuge a unit of the refuge. The refuge now includes 110,106 acres. The Service did not establish an acquisition boundary before establishment or since, so there is no approved acquisition boundary beyond the refuge ownership (Figure 5).

There are other lands in the area protected by State agencies and non-governmental organizations in Tyrrell, Washington, and Hyde Counties (Table 21).

Table 21. Protected lands in Tyrrell, Washington, and Hyde Counties

Agency or Organization	Name of Property	Acreage
North Carolina Division of Parks and Recreation	Pettigrew State Park	Land-4,531 Water-16,600
North Carolina Division of Coastal Management	Buckridge Coastal Reserve	18,000
North Carolina Wildlife Resources Commission	Alligator River Game Land	5,401
North Carolina Wildlife Resources Commission	Lantern Acres Game Land	1,825
North Carolina Wildlife Resources Commission	Pungo River Game Land	614
North Carolina Wildlife Resources Commission	Bachelor Bay Game Land	5,426
North Carolina Wildlife Resources Commission	Van Swamp Game Land	5,482
North Carolina Wildlife Resources Commission	J. Morgan Futch	600
North Carolina Wildlife Resources Commission	New Lake Game Land	1,394
North Carolina Wildlife Resources Commission	Gull Rock Game Land	31,057
Conservation Fund	Palmetto Peartree Preserve	9,700
The Nature Conservancy	Scuppernong River Preserve	653
Total		**92,551**

Figure 5. Existing boundary of the Pocosin Lakes NWR

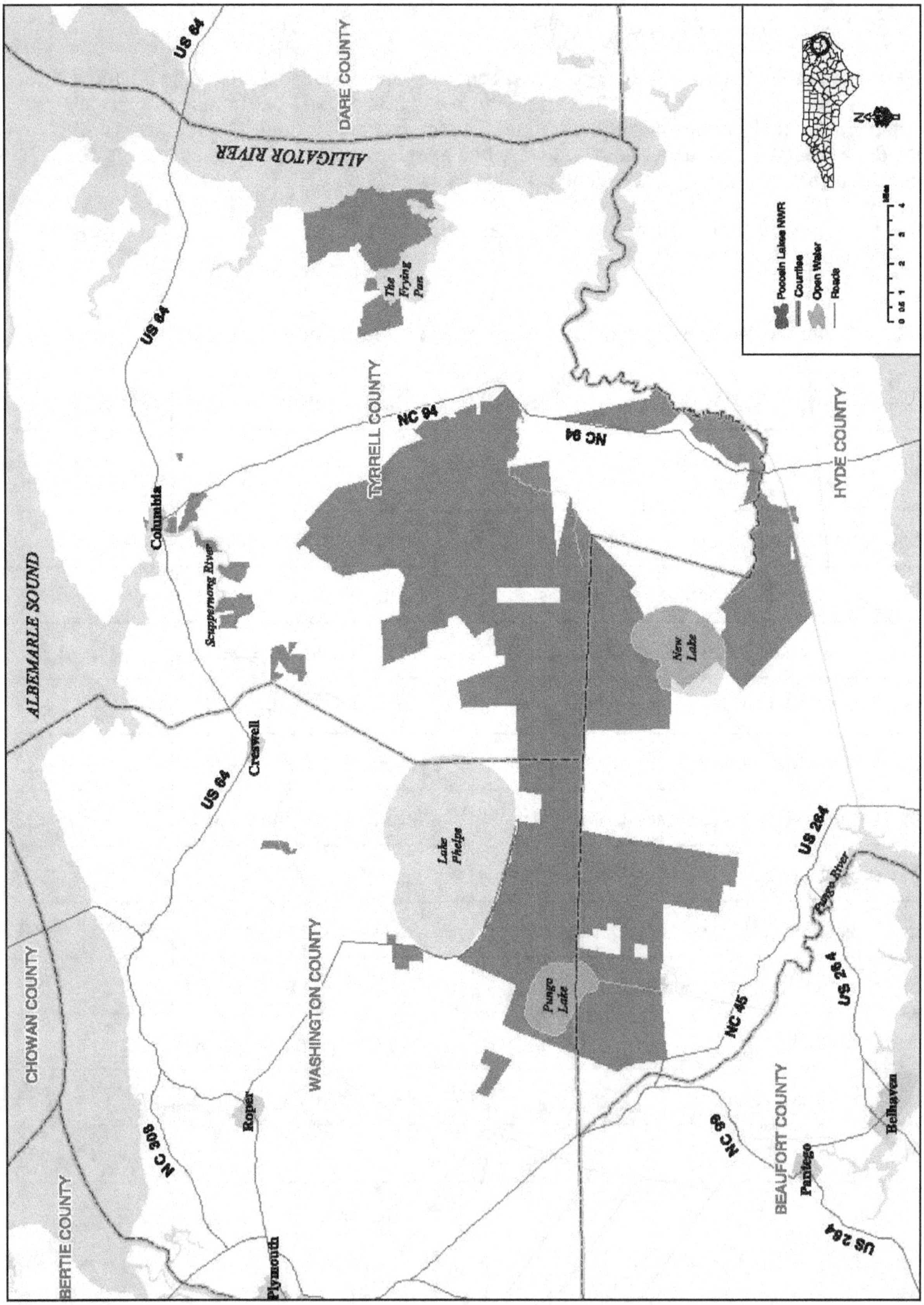

Pocosin Lakes National Wildlife Refuge

Visitor Services

The National Wildlife Refuge System Improvement Act of 1997 recognized six wildlife-dependent priority public uses as recreation activities the refuge should support if it had the staff and funding to conduct them safely. Those priority public uses are: hunting, fishing, wildlife observation, wildlife photography, and environmental education and interpretation.

In the FY 2007 Refuge Annual Performance Plan, the staff estimated approximately 65,850 people visited the refuge in FY 2006. This estimate was based on observations during daily refuge activities and the number of visitors signing the guest registration book at the refuge's visitor center in Columbia (which was open only 24 to 32 hours per week). A good method for measuring the total number of actual visitors a year is currently unavailable. Therefore, these estimates are probably not accurate. Many visitors to the refuge participate in wildlife observation (up to 20,000) and hunting (up to 10,000). Education and outreach efforts away from the refuge at local festivals, events, and field days are the leading tools in generating interest in the refuge. Visitation estimates were much higher in previous years but have declined since the loss of a visitor services' specialist position in 2005.

The refuge's visitor center/office complex, which opened in 2001, attracts many visitors to the refuge. The visitor center, dedicated as the Walter B. Jones, Sr., Center for the Sounds (named after a long-time North Carolina Congressional Representative), is adjacent to the North Carolina Department of Transportation's Tyrrell County Visitor Center in Columbia. The staff of the Partnership for the Sounds, Inc., which operates the visitor center, estimates that over 460,000 people stop for information. Therefore, actual refuge visitor numbers may be significantly higher than the estimates above. The refuge visitor center offers a range of displays and a gift shop. A video about the refuge and the Roanoke-Tar-Neuse-Cape Fear Ecosystem is available for the public to view in the 68-seat auditorium.

Access

The location of the refuge headquarters is 205 South Ludington Drive, just south of North Carolina Highway 64 in Columbia, North Carolina, at the Walter B. Jones, Sr., Center for the Sounds. The new headquarters is located on the eastern bank of the Scuppernong River. There the refuge maintains a three-quarter-mile interpretive boardwalk and an outdoor classroom. The visitor center contains a gift shop and 68-seat auditorium. There is an environmental education classroom located in the office complex portion of the center and an outdoor classroom along the Scuppernong River Interpretive Boardwalk.

The refuge maintains a field station for interns and education programs at the former office headquarters in Creswell, North Carolina, on the west side of Lake Phelps at 3157 Shore Drive. The Pocosin Lakes NWR maintenance facility is located on the southwest corner of the Pungo Unit at 601 Refuge Road in Pantego, North Carolina.

The Pungo Unit is accessible from North Carolina Highway 45 in Pantego. The Frying Pan Unit can be accessed from North Carolina Highway 94, south of Columbia. Other access points to the refuge are North Carolina Highway 94 and Northern Road south of Columbia, Shore Drive in Creswell, and New Lake Road.

The Pungo Unit comprises approximately 12,500 acres of the refuge. This unit includes Pungo Lake, which is roughly 2,800 acres, and several impoundments that provide food and a resting place for migratory waterfowl in winter. There is an observation tower and Kuralt Trail kiosk located on the south side of Pungo Lake (Figure 6). The Kuralt Trail of the refuge is composed of 12 miles of designated roads on the Pungo Unit.

Comprehensive Conservation Plan

Figure 6. Current visitor facilities at Pocosin Lakes NWR

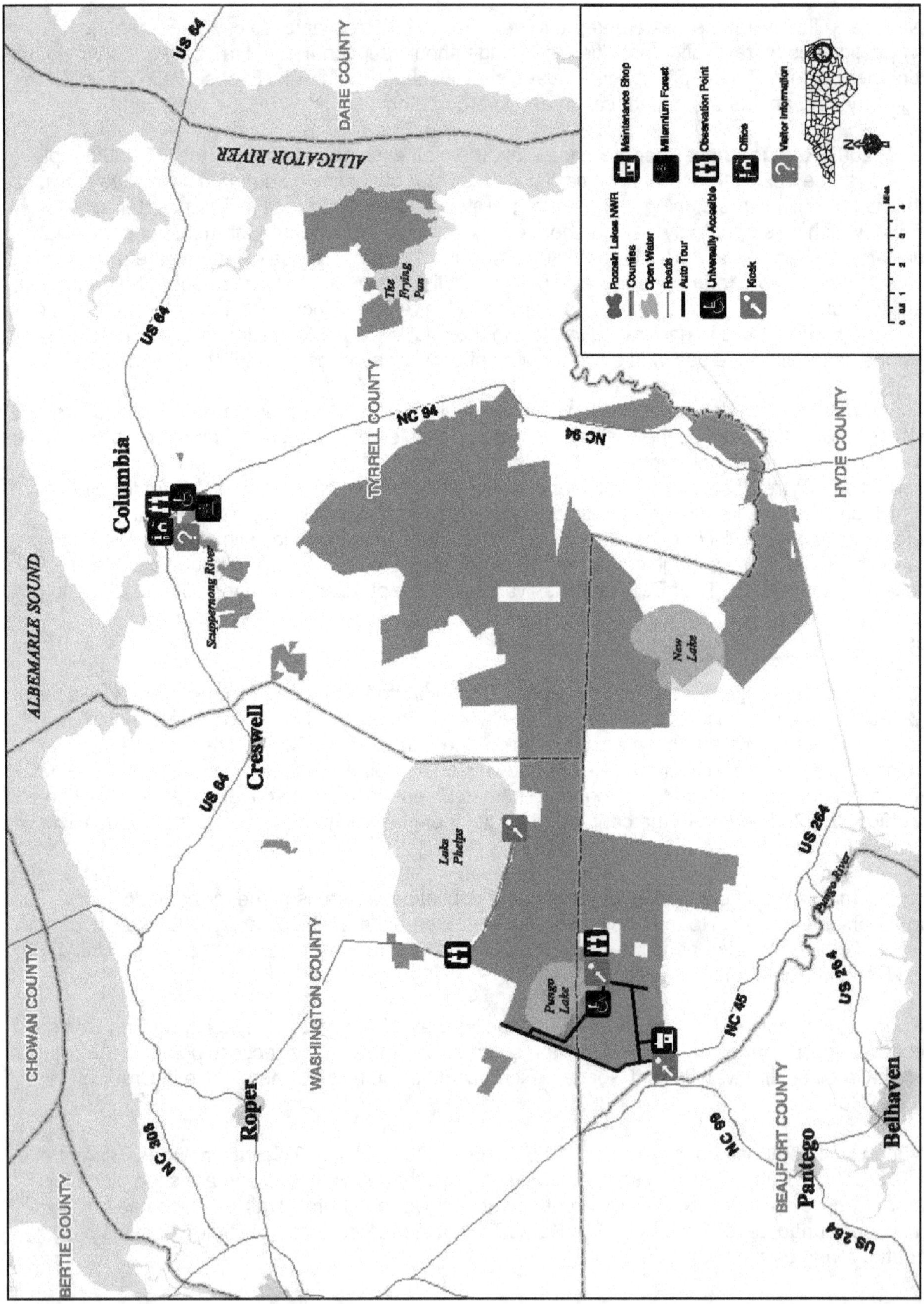

60 Pocosin Lakes National Wildlife Refuge

The Frying Pan Unit is approximately 5,700 acres. Trux Road, on this unit, is open to all-terrain vehicles during the hunting season. This part of the refuge also offers good fishing opportunities. There is a State-maintained boat ramp located on refuge property that provides access to Frying Pan Lake and the Alligator River.

New Lake lacks adequate public access. Most access roads leading to the lake are private. Boundary Road, located south of New Lake Road away from the lake, is open to all-terrain vehicles (ATVs) during the hunting season. Much of the road runs parallel to the Intracoastal Waterway.

Most of the interior of refuge is open to public use during daylight hours only. An area that is closed will either have a locked gate at the entrance with an "Area Closed" sign or will have the boundary posted with "Area Closed" signs. Gates and "No Vehicle" signs indicate when the public cannot drive on a road.

There are many opportunities to observe wildlife and participate in photographic opportunities throughout the refuge.

The refuge has approximately 250 miles of dirt roads which are accessible to the public. Approximately 80 miles of roads are open to public licensed vehicular travel. Horseback riding is also allowed on these roads with a special use permit. Another approximately 27 miles of roads are designated ATV trails that hunters may use to access remote hunting areas during the hunting season. The remaining roads are closed to all motorized vehicles. A person can walk or take a bicycle on all of the dirt roads, even those closed to motorized vehicles, unless the area is posted as a closed area due to refuge activities. No off-road vehicle travel of any kind is allowed.

Some refuge lands can be accessed by boat from the northwest and southwest forks of the Alligator River, the Intracosatal Waterway, the Scuppernong River, and the Alligator River (Frying Pan Unit).

Hunting

State seasons and bag limits apply with the exception of the Pungo Unit. On the Pungo Unit, hunting with bow for deer begins on the date the State designates and lasts through the end of November. The refuge allows gun hunting for deer on the Pungo Unit by special permit only and accepts applications for the 1,125 permits issued. The refuge permit hunts usually consist of four to five 2-day hunts on weekends beginning in late September and continuing into October. For the 2007/2008 hunting season, the refuge is partnering with the NCWRC in administering the hunt. The NCWRC is now taking applications, conducting the lottery and issuing the special permits under their *Special Hunt Opportunities* program. The Service does not allow general archery hunting during the 2-day permit hunts although archery equipment, as well as muzzleloaders or shotguns, can be used by permitted hunters.

The service has closed Pungo and New Lakes to all hunting activities. Other areas closed to hunting are specified in regulations and on brochures.

Over 8,000 hunting visits occur on Pocosin Lakes NWR each year.

Fishing

The Service allows fishing on the waters of Pungo from March 1 to October 31. All other waters on the Pungo Unit are open year-round except during the special 2-day (Friday/Saturday) permit hunts in late September and October. Fishing in canals is popular during spring and summer months. Primary species caught include black fish, black crappie, several species of sunfish, and catfish. Approximately 1,500 anglers use the refuge every year.

The refuge permits fishing on New Lake except during the wintering waterfowl period (November – February), but access is difficult.

Interpretive and Environmental Education Programs

The refuge staff gives twelve talks and slide presentations to various groups annually. The refuge has also participated in various local festivals and field days, setting up displays and presenting educational demonstrations. The new visitor center/office complex provides a number of displays, both static and interactive. The gift shop offers a variety of merchandise, including field guides, nature books, and other materials. Guided group tours or field trips are sometimes available upon request. The staff reached an estimated 200,000 people with education, interpretive, or outreach programs in 2004, but that number has dropped significantly since the abolishment of the park ranger position.

Wildlife Observation and Photography

The majority of the refuge's 20,000 to 30,000 wildlife observers and photographers generally visit the Pungo Unit. This area of the refuge is known for its large concentration of wintering waterfowl and a dense population of black bear. The Pungo Unit has an elevated observation platform overlooking Pungo Lake, which the Service built in 1977, and replaced in 2004. The unit also contains several moist-soil units and impoundments that provide food and a resting place for wintering waterfowl.

The interpretive trail located on the Scuppernong River in Columbia is another area that may be used for observation and photography. Neotropical migratory songbirds and wildflowers are plentiful here during the spring and summer.

Walking/Hiking/Bicycling

The Service permits walking and hiking anywhere on the refuge unless the area is posted as closed. Bicycling is allowed on all established roads and trails (off-road bicycling is not permitted). The Service considers these modes of transportation that facilitate the priority public uses.

Canoeing/Kayaking/Boating

The Service does not allow boating on Pungo Lake and does not allow boating on New Lake from November through February. The parts of the refuge that have access by boat are the north and southwest forks of the Alligator River. Other local areas that allow boating include New Lake Fork Canal, Alligator and Scuppernong Rivers, and Frying Pan Lake. The Service considers these modes of transportation that facilitate the priority public uses.

PERSONNEL, OPERATIONS, AND MAINTENANCE

The refuge's current staff is listed in Table 22 below.

Table 22. Staff of the Pocosin Lakes NWR

Position	Program	Employment Status
Project Leader (GS-0485-13)	Refuge	PFT
Deputy Project Leader (GS-0485-12)	Refuge	PFT
Wildlife Biologist (GS-0486-11)	Refuge	PFT
*Park Ranger (GS-0025-09)	Refuge	PFT
Office Assistant (GS-0303-06)	50% Refuge 50% Fire	PFT
*Office Assistant (GS-0303-04)	Refuge	TFT
Crane Operator (WG-5725-09)	Refuge	PFT
*Maintenance Mechanic (WG-5716-09)	Refuge	PFT
Equipment Operator (WG-5716-08)	Refuge	PFT
Fire Management Officer (GS-0401-11)	Fire	PFT
Equipment Operator (Fire) (WG-5716-08)	Fire	PFT
Equipment Operator (Fire) (WG-5716-08)	Fire	PFT
Equipment Operator (Fire) (WG-5716-08)	Fire	PFT
Forestry Technician (Fire) (GS-0462-06)	Fire	PFT
Forestry Technician (Fire) (GS-0462-05)	Fire	PFT
Forestry Technician (Fire) (GS-0462-04)	Fire	PFT

PFT = permanent full time, TFT = temporary full time, PS = permanent seasonal

*Since this planning effort began, the Park Ranger, Maintenance Mechanic, and TFT Office Assistant positions have been abolished.

The Fish and Wildlife Service administers Pocosin Lakes NWR from an office located in Columbia along the Scuppernong River near the northeastern-most portion of the refuge. The Service houses the maintenance and fire crews at a shop facility on the Pungo Unit in the southwestern corner of the refuge.

The refuge staff administers 110,106 acres of fee title land in Tyrrell, Washington, and Hyde Counties, North Carolina. Most of the land is wetlands, with much having peat soils that cannot support equipment, roads, or buildings. The refuge has an extensive road and drainage ditch system installed by previous owners. The principal habitat management activity is water management to provide optimum conditions for waterfowl, wading birds, and shorebirds in managed wetlands on the Pungo Unit and water table management throughout the natural habitat on the refuge. The staff conducts prescribed burns according to the fire management plan and maintains roads and roadsides as firebreaks to manage wild fires. Cooperative farmers manage the refuge cropland.

Refuge Infrastructure

Roads and Trails

There are 250 miles of roads on the refuge that are open to the public. The Service allows use of these roads for travel by foot or bicycle for hunting, fishing, wildlife observation, wildlife photography, and environmental education and interpretation. Approximately 80 miles of these roads are open to public licensed vehicular travel and another approximately 27 miles of roads are open to all-terrain vehicle travel for hunting. The refuge also maintains roads for administrative access for wildlife and habitat management and law enforcement. The refuge has a three-quarter-mile interpretive trail on the east bank of the Scuppernong River outside the visitor center.

Communication Systems

The refuge communications system is currently limited to mobile radios with base stations at the headquarters and shop. Cellular phones are also used for communication between the field and office.

Solid Waste Collection and Disposal

Presently, there is no solid waste collection and disposal on refuge lands.

III. Plan Development

PUBLIC INVOLVEMENT AND THE PLANNING PROCESS

In accordance with Service guidelines and National Environmental Policy Act recommendations, public involvement has been a crucial factor throughout the development of this comprehensive conservation plan for Pocosin Lakes NWR. This plan has been written with input and assistance from interested citizens, conservation organizations, and employees of local and state agencies. The participation of these stakeholders and their ideas has been of great value in setting the management direction for the refuge. The Service, as a whole, and the reuge staff, in particular, are very grateful to each one who has contributed time, expertise, and ideas to the planning process. The staff remains impressed by the passion and commitment of so many individuals for the lands and waters administered by the refuge.

Representatives from the Fish and Wildlife Service and State wildlife agency personnel attended initial planning meetings that included a review of the biological program. At these initial meetings, they discussed strategies for completing the comprehensive conservation plan, identified the staff's issues and concerns, and compiled a mailing list of likely interested government agencies, non-governmental organizations, businesses, and individual citizens. The Service invited these agencies, organizations, businesses, and citizens to participate in six public scoping meetings on February 15, 16, 20, 22, and 23, 2001, in Washington, Plymouth, Columbia, Swanquarter, and Manns Harbor, North Carolina. They introduced the audience to the refuge and its planning process and asked them to identify their issues and concerns. The Service published announcements giving the location, date, and time for the public meeting in the *Federal Register* and legal notices in local newspapers. They also sent press releases to local newspapers and public service announcements to television and radio stations. Fish and Wildlife Service personnel placed fifty posters announcing the meeting in local post offices, local government buildings, and stores.

The planning teams (Appendix X) expanded the issues and concerns to include those generated by the agencies, organizations, businesses, and citizens from the local community. The objectives were subjects of discussion at a second round of public meetings on April 25 and 28, 2001, in Plymouth and Columbia, North Carolina. The Service published announcements giving the location, date, and time for the public meeting as legal notices in local newspapers. Service personnel also sent press releases to local newspapers and public service announcements to television and radio stations. Service personnel placed seventy-five posters announcing the meetings in local post offices, local government buildings, and stores.

A number of issues and concerns was generated from the input of local citizens and public agencies, the team members' knowledge of the area, and the resource needs identified by the refuge staff and biological review team. A Fish and Wildlife Service planning team was assembled to evaluate the resource needs. The team then developed a list of goals, objectives, and strategies to shape the management of the refuge for the next fifteen years.

The Draft Comprehensive Conservation Plan and Environmental Assessment for Pocosin Lakes NWR was released for public review and comment in July 2007. A news release and flyers were prepared announcing the deadline for accepting public comments as August 15, 2007. Also, a *Federal Register* notice was published announcing the comment period. In addition, two open house meetings were held on Wednesday, July 25, at the Vernon James Center in Washington County and on Thursday, July 26, at the Walter B. Jones, Sr., Center for the Sounds in Tyrrell County.

Comments were compiled and responses were developed. Some changes were incorporated into the plan. Appendix IV includes both scoping and Draft CCP public comments.

SUMMARY OF ISSUES, CONCERNS, AND OPPORTUNITIES

The input of local citizens and public agencies, the team members' knowledge of the area, and the resource needs identified by the refuge staff and biological review team all contributed to the issues and concerns addressed in the plan. These issues provided the basis for developing the refuge's alternative management objectives and strategies, played a role in determining the desired future conditions for the refuge, and were considered in the preparation of the long-term comprehensive conservation plan. The issues and concerns are described below. They are of local, regional, and national significance and reflect similar issues that were, in part, identified by the public at the planning meetings.

HYDROLOGY

Drainage

Prior to refuge ownership, the previous landowners dug drainage ditches to facilitate crop production and logging. The ditches effectively lower the water table, draining subsurface water in the vicinity of the ditch. The drainage affects the plant communities on the refuge by providing habitat for species adapted to better drainage close to the ditches and on the tops of spoil piles. When the peat soils dry out, they oxidize/degrade. This can lead to heavy metals, such as naturally occuring mercury, leaching out of the soil as well as nitrogen and carbon being released. Artificially dry peat soils are also more susceptible to wildfire and the soil can burn for long periods of time.

FISH AND WILDLIFE POPULATIONS

Threatened and Endangered Species

Recovery and protection of threatened and endangered plants and animals is an important responsibility delegated to the Service and its national wildlife refuges. Three threatened or endangered animals are thought to use (or could use) Pocosin Lakes NWR: red-cockaded woodpecker, red wolf, and American alligator.

Bald eagles, recently de-listed, travel the river corridor and shoreline of the Sound. The refuge's habitat protection and management activities provide suitable habitat for nesting or wintering eagles.

The endangered red-cockaded woodpecker currently inhabits Tyrrell County just north of the refuge. A December 2003 aerial survey observed six active colonies of red-cockaded woodpeckers in the Frying Pan Unit in the northeastern part of the refuge. As the forest ages and pine trees develop suitable nesting cavities, the refuge could support additional woodpecker colonies. Sustaining viable populations will require proper understory management.

American alligators reside in Tyrrell and Hyde Counties. They nest in grassy marshes on and around the refuge. The American alligator is listed as threatened due to similarity in appearance to other threatened crocodilian species.

The endangered red wolf currently inhabits large areas of habitat on the refuge. Northeastern North Carolina has the only wild surviving population of red wolves in the world.

Waterfowl

The scoping process identified the management of all refuge marshes, managed wetlands (moist-soil units), and forests for waterfowl and expanding waterfowl hunting opportunities as issues. In order to meet the refuge's waterfowl purpose, the refuge must manage the marshes, forests, and managed wetlands (moist-soil units) to meet waterfowl habitat needs, including sufficient rest areas to provide undisturbed resting and feeding areas for waterfowl. The Service can provide waterfowl hunting opportunities as the refuge acquires additional land outside the proclamation boundary within which the Service prohibits waterfowl hunting. The core waterfowl rest areas need to remain intact to meet the needs of waterfowl.

The refuge's waterfowl purpose guides all operation and management actions on the refuge. The refuge protects forested wetlands to meet the feeding, resting, and breeding needs of migratory and resident waterfowl. Staff of the Fish and Wildlife Service and cooperating agencies and organizations conducted a Biological Review of Pocosin Lakes NWR in 1999 and 2000, as part of the comprehensive conservation planning process. They identified objectives to meet the minimum water, food, and resting/loafing habitat requirements of waterfowl.

Neotropical Migratory Birds

Neotropical migratory birds are a species group of special management concern. Providing habitat (e.g., forests and marshes) for these birds is one of the refuge's major objectives. Strategic forest management compatible with the refuge's waterfowl habitat objectives would contribute to the forest needs of neotropical migratory birds. Neotropical migratory birds are also a major focus of the refuge wildlife observation program as many birders visit the refuge to observe nesting, feeding, and loafing birds.

HABITATS

Freshwater Marsh and Managed Wetlands

Participants at the public scoping meetings expressed the expectation that the refuge was established to protect and manage the marshes in various locations on the refuge and managed wetlands (moist-soil units) on the Pungo Unit. Local interest still exists in managing the refuge. The area's cultural tradition has a strong history of fishing and hunting, and marsh and moist-soil unit management is the first step toward maintaining the opportunities for hunting on adjacent lands (primarily for waterfowl).

Pocosin Lakes NWR is near several large marshes in the South Atlantic Coastal Plain Physiographic Zone. Cooperative private-State-Federal partnerships under the North American Waterfowl Management Plan, Partners in Flight, and the Atlantic Coast Joint Venture recommend maintenance and stabilization of the marsh. With strategic management, the staff can provide quality marsh habitat with the proper water management, prescribed burning, and aquatic weed control.

Woody Plant Communities

There is public recognition of the role of the refuge's pocosins and forests in white-tailed deer, black bear, red wolf, and neotropical migratory bird populations and the public use associated with deer hunting and wildlife observation. At the public scoping meetings, the public also expressed an appreciation for the function of the forest in support of the other aspects of the refuge's public use program. The refuge has not developed a management plan for its forestlands, but does treat insect and disease infestations as they occur and conducts prescribed burning as opportunities present themselves. The public and the members of the biological review team encouraged the refuge staff to make forest management a higher priority than it has been.

WILDERNESS REVIEW

Refuge planning policy requires a wilderness review as part of the comprehensive conservation planning process. The Wilderness Act of 1964 defines a wilderness area as an area of Federal land that retains its primeval character and influence, without permanent improvements or human inhabitation, and is managed so as to preserve its natural conditions and which:

1. generally appears to have been influenced primarily by the forces of nature, with the imprint of man's work substantially unnoticeable;

2. has outstanding opportunities for solitude or primitive and unconfined type of recreation;

3. has at least 5,000 contiguous roadless acres or is of sufficient size to make practicable its preservation and use in an unimpeded condition, or is a roadless island regardless of size;

4. does not substantially exhibit the effects of logging, farming, grazing, or other extensive development or alteration of the landscape, or its wilderness character could be restored through appropriate management at the time of review; and

5. may contain ecological, geological, or other features of scientific, educational, scenic, or historic value.

As a part of the planning process, the lands within the Pocosin Lakes NWR boundary were reviewed for their suitability in meeting the criteria for wilderness, as defined by the Wilderness Act of 1964. The Wilderness Review identified 17, 342 acres that meet the criteria for a wilderness study area.

In examining the nature of the 17,342 acres selected as a wilderness study area more closely, it was determined that there would be mostly passive management whether the lands were designated as wilderness areas or not. There is little opportunity for recreation because the deep organic soils and dense understory vegetation allow for very little pedestrian traffic. The nature of the habitat does not invite pedestrian traffic and frequent pedestrian traffic would result in habitat destruction.

Any future land acquisition outside the currently approved acquisition boundary would be evaluated independently for possible proposed wilderness designation. The Wilderness Review is attached as Appendix IX.

PUBLIC USE

Visitor Services and Education

The refuge is in Tyrrell County, North Carolina (2000 population 4,149), Washington County, North Carolina (2000 population 13,723), and Hyde County, North Carolina (2000 population 5,826). There is a need to promote nature-based tourism in northeastern North Carolina in the rural counties that have an abundance of natural resources to attract tourists, but they are dominated by wetlands that limit traditional economic development. The Outer Banks attract 7 million tourists per year who pass by the refuge on U.S. Highway 64. A few commercial interests guide canoeing and angling adventures. The refuge is an important link to other natural areas that together make these experiences possible. Carefully selected and managed staff, programs, and facilities will provide the wildlife-dependent environmental education and interpretation programs, as well as recreation opportunities visistors have come to expect.

Hunting

Hunting is an integral part of rural North Carolina culture. It is not surprising that there is a considerable interest from State agencies and local citizens in expanding hunting opportunities. The initial refuge strategy must be maintenance of the quality of hunting at existing levels. Any additional hunting opportunities will be dependent on providing safe, quality experiences that are compatible with refuge purposes. The refuge requires additional law enforcement personnel to administer additional hunts. In the future, there may be an opportunity to add additional hunting opportunities on the refuge.

Fishing

Anglers utilize the refuge canals, ditches, impoundments, a pier on the Scuppernong River, and State-maintained boat ramps for fishing opportunities. The public expressed an interest in improving access to the refuge for fishing. The refuge has the potential to add a boat ramp and expand safe access to bank fishing areas.

Roads and Trails, Interior and Exterior

The Service limits access to refuge roads when wet conditions limit their use. The public expressed an interest in more and better access to the refuge. As resources are available for roads, the staff may consider increasing access to the refuge, based on compatibility with refuge objectives. The refuge must limit access to areas where wintering waterfowl rest and feed on the Pungo Unit and other areas where human disturbance would be detrimental to wildlife and habitat objectives.

RESOURCE PROTECTION

Cultural Resources

Local residents, the refuge staff, and the Fish and Wildlife Service in the regional and national office are all aware of the potential of the Pocosin Lakes NWR for Native American sites.

Land Acquisition and Habitat Fragmentation

When the Service established the Pungo National Wildlife Refuge, it established the refuge as an inviolate waterfowl sanctuary for wintering migratory waterfowl and other migratory birds. The refuge's role in providing managed wetlands (moist-soil units) was to provide additional habitat types for migratory waterfowl. Establishment of the Pocosin Lakes NWR has added extensive areas of habitat that are more important for neotropical migratory songbirds (in support of Partners in Flight) and red wolves than they are for wintering migratory waterfowl habitat. These areas also provide important breeding habitat for wood ducks. In the biological review, the Service identified private properties for acquisition that have value as pine habitat for red-cockaded woodpecker, nonriverine swamp forest habitat for songbirds, and cropland for high-energy foods for wintering migratory waterfowl and other wildlife species. Those properties are important links in protecting areas along the Alligator and Scuppernong Rivers and the Albemarle Sound. To maintain the potential to protect these lands, the Service must have the ability and authority to manage and protect (through acquisition of fee title interest or conservation easements) the important habitat beyond the refuge's

Comprehensive Conservation Plan

current acquisition boundary. Also, acquisition of fee title interest in new lands will provide expanded public use opportunities when compatible; conservation easements would not.

Law Enforcement and Refuge Regulation

The refuge has enforced the applicable laws and regulations through the use of a dual function officer, currently the refuge manager, and the assistance of a law enforcement officer from Mattamuskeet NWR who covers four refuges. The use of the dual function officer to perform enforcement functions utilizes a great deal of the time he could devote to refuge administration and support of the biological, public use, and maintenance programs. This is particularly evident during hunting season when the law enforcement workload is at its highest. He is also limited in the amount of time he can devote to permit monitoring and enforcement of the conditions on the permits.

Other Resource Protection

There are other threats to refuge resources that require closer monitoring and management. Pest plants and animals, as well as wildlife disease, are all issues which the refuge needs to diligently monitor and respond to rapidly in order to prevent degradation of ecological integrity.

As resources become available, natural hydrology is being restored on large tracts of pocosin habitat that were drained prior to refuge ownership.

IV. Management Direction

INTRODUCTION

The Service manages fish and wildlife habitats considering the needs of all resources in decision-making. But first and foremeost, fish and wildlife conservation assumes priority in refuge management. A requirement of the National Wildlfie Refuge System Improvement Act of 1997 is for the Service to maintain the ecological health, diversity, and integrity of refuges. Public uses are allowed if they are appropriate and compatible with wildlife and habitat conservation. The above-mentioned Act identified hunting, fishing, wildlife observation, wildlife photography, and environmental education and interpretation as priority wildife-dependent public uses of the refuge system. Each of these uses is therefore emphasized in this CCP.

This chapter describes the CCP for managing the refuge over the next 15 years. This management direction contains the goals, objectives, and strategies that will be used to achieve the refuge vistion.

Four alternatives for managing the refuge were considered in the Draft CCP/EA. These were: 1) current management/no action, 2) address highest priority goals/objectives, 3) address all goals/objectives, and 4) place in caretaker status. Each of the alternatives was described in the Alternatives section of the Draft CCP/EA. The Service chose Alternative 2 as the preferred management direction.

Implementing the preferred alternative will result in moderate program increases to address the refuge's highest priorities. The refuge will manage its impoundments very intensively by controlling water levels and vegetation to create optimum habitat for migrating waterfowl. It will also manage pine forests and marshes with prescribed fire and will manage the vegetative composition of habitats in selected areas. Waterfowl will be surveyed on a routine basis. The staff will develop inventory plans for all species and implement them in selected habitats. The staff will develop and implement a black bear management plan. The staff will maintain the visitor center with volunteers and cooperating agency personnel supplementing refuge personnel. There will be eighteen staff members (17.5 full-time equivalents) dedicated to refuge management and eight staff members (7.5 full-time equivalents) dedicated to fire management. The volunteer program will be expanded to recruit volunteers to contribute 4,000 hours of service. Two workamper pads will be built to attract volunteers with recreational vehicles. The six priority public uses will be allowed and the staff will conduct environmental education and interpretation programs to meet local needs.

VISION

The Pocosin Lakes National Wildlife Refuge will restore and maintain natural processes and biodiversity of a functional pocosin wetland and provide habitat for threatened, endangered, and other Federal trust species. On the Pungo Unit, the refuge will provide optimum wintering habitat for migratory waterfowl and breeding habitat for wood ducks throughout the refuge on suitable habitats in conjunction with other refuges in the National Wildlife Refuge System.

The refuge will reduce habitat fragmentation by establishing corridors to other protected areas in the central Albemarle - Pamlico Peninsula. The visitor center will be a gateway for visitors to refuges in eastern North Carolina. The refuge will serve as a destination for nature-based tourism that will contribute to the economic health of rural communities. It will provide opportunities for priority public uses. The refuge staff will continue to use partnerships to accomplish goals.

GOALS

Wildlife Populations: Conserve, protect, and maintain healthy and viable populations of migratory birds, wildlife, fish, and plants, including Federal and State endangered and trust species.

Habitat: Restore, protect, and enhance pocosin wetlands and other natural habitats for optimum biodiversity. Intensively manage habitats specific to waterfowl on the Pungo Unit.

Public Use: Develop programs and facilities to increase public use opportunities, including hunting, fishing, wildlife observation, wildlife photography, and environmental education and interpretation.

Resource Protection: Protect and perpetuate refuge resources by limiting the adverse effects of human activities and development on refuge resources.

Administration: Acquire resources and infrastructure to accomplish the other refuge goals. Support local efforts to sustain economic health through nature-based tourism.

OBJECTIVES AND STRATEGIES

The goals, objectives, and strategies addressed below are the Service's response to the issues, concerns, and needs expressed by the planning team, the refuge staff, and the public. These goals, objectives, and strategies reflect the Services' commitment to achieve the mandates of the National Wildlife Refuge System Improvement Act of 1997, the mission of the National Wildlife Refuge System, the North American Waterfowl Management Plan, and the purpose and vision for Pocosin Lakes NWR. The Service intends to accomplish these goals, objectives, and strategies during the next 15 years.

FISH AND WILDLIFE POPULATIONS

Fish

Objective: Manage refuge resources to protect species of fish and other aquatic organisms in refuge and adjacent waters.

Discussion: There is little data about the fish and other aquatic resources on the refuge or the effect of refuge management on those resources. The North Carolina Wildlife Resources Commission has conducted species surveys of Lake Phelps, Pungo Lake, and New Lake in the past, but there have been no recent quantitative surveys. The plan provides for the Service to perform those surveys and cooperate with other agencies, organizations, and universities conducting studies.

Strategies:

- Cooperate with other agencies, universities, and organizations performing studies and investigations on the refuge.
- Inventory fishery resources utilizing the technical assistance office fisheries biologist or a consultant.
- Explore management options in consultation with the technical assistance office fisheries biologist.

Invertebrate Species

Objective: Document presence of invertebrate species.

Discussion: There is little data about the invertebrate species on the refuge or the effect of refuge management on those invertebrates. The plan provides for the Service to perform surveys systematically in moist-soil units and as opportunities occur on other places on the refuge.

Strategies:

- Document presence of invertebrate species as they are encountered.
- Cooperate with other agencies, universities, and organizations performing studies and investigations on the refuge.

Land Birds

Objective: Provide resting, nesting, and foraging habitat for about 100 speices of land birds.

Discussion: There is little data about the land birds on the refuge or the effect of refuge management on those species. The plan provides for the Service to inventory land birds. The refuge will also coordinate management of turkey, quail, and mourning doves with the NCWRC.

Strategies:

- Cooperate with other agencies, universities, and organizations performing studies and investigations on the refuge.
- Assist with banding activities as directed.
- Develop an inventory plan for neotropical migratory songbirds, including migration surveys with mist nets, within five years of the date of this CCP and implement the plan on selected habitats within ten years of the date of this CCP.
- Develop an inventory plan for raptors within five years of the date of this CCP and implement the plan on selected habitats within ten years of the date of this CCP.
- Identify priority species for management based on inventory results and status of the species found.
- Correlate land bird inventory results to habitat studies to give direction to habitat management.
- Inventory turkeys, quail, and mourning doves using the protocols used by the North Carolina Wildlife Resources Commission.
- Coordinate turkey management with the NCWRC to maintain sustainable populations.

Mammals

Objective: Provide suitable habitat for and manage selected mammal populations associated with pocosin wetlands.

Discussion: Data about the mammals on the refuge are limited to white-tailed deer, red wolves, and black bears. There is little data on the effect of refuge management on those mammals. The plan provides for the Service to monitor selected mammals.

Strategies:

- Cooperate with other agencies, universities, and organizations performing studies and investigations on the refuge.
- Maintain communication with the Red Wolf Recovery Team and its population monitoring efforts.
- Monitor populations of black bear, white-tailed deer, and up to two other species (based on emerging management issues).
- Adapt management based on an evaluation of the data.
- Develop and implement a plan for managing black bears based on the results from USGS cooperative bear study within ten years of the completion of the study.

Red Wolves

Objective: Assist the Red Wolf Recovery Team with red wolf reintroduction.

Discussion: The Service has established a population of red wolves to reintroduce this endangered species to the landscape. There is a Red Wolf Recovery Team headquartered in Manteo, North Carolina, that closely monitors the population. The staff assists the team by giving them access to the refuge through gates and on roads that are often in poor condition, assisting with outreach and hosting workshops for teachers and the general public. The staff is also assisting in the development of a small wolf eduation and veterinary care facility on refuge land south of Columbia.

Strategies:

- Provide refuge access to Red Wolf Recovery Team.
- Maintain communication with the Red Wolf Recovery Team and its population monitoring efforts.
- Host workshops for teachers and the general public.
- Develop, operate, and maintain a wolf education and veternairy care facility in partnership with the Recovery Team and others.

Red-cockaded Woodpecker

Objective: Monitor red-cockaded woodpecker nests and populations to document their presence in accordance with the red-cockaded woodpecker recovery plan.

Discussion: There is little data about the red-cockaded woodpeckers on the refuge or the effect of refuge management on those birds. The refuge staff has located cavity trees from the air and is attempting to cut trails to allow the staff to monitor the cavities from the ground. There are woodpecker populations on land surrounding the refuge. The Fish and Wildlife Service's Ecological Services' office and the Conservation Fund are both involved in monitoring those populations. The plan provides for the Service to monitor red-cockaded woodpeckers on the refuge.

Strategies:

- Develop and implement a refuge-specific red-cockaded woodpecker management plan based on the national recovery plan within five years of the date of this CCP.
- Survey the refuge aerially for the occurrence of red-cockaded woodpecker cavity trees according to the protocol in the plan.

- Document the location of cavity trees in a geographic information system (GIS) within three years of the date of this CCP.
- Clear and maintain roads and trails to active cavity trees on the ground by contract within five years of the date of this CCP.
- Monitor existing clusters according to the recovery plan.
- Band woodpeckers and manage existing cavities.
- Cooperate with other agencies, universities, and organizations performing studies and investigations on the refuge.

Reptiles and Amphibians

Objective: Inventory use of selected sites on selected habitats by reptiles and amphibians.

Discussion: There is little data about the reptiles and amphibians on the refuge or the effect of refuge management on those species. This CCP provides for the Service to inventory reptiles and amphibians.

Strategies:

- Develop and implement an inventory plan in selected habitats.
- Conduct two annual alligator surveys during May on selected sites.
- Cooperate with other agencies, universities, and organizations performing studies and investigations on the refuge.

Shorebirds and Marsh Birds

Objective: Monitor shorebirds and marsh birds annually to document their populations and evaluate habitat management.

Discussion: The refuge staff has been conducting regular surveys of shorebirds in conjunction with waterfowl surveys. This CCP continues that effort and also provides for intensive callback surveys of marsh birds.

Strategies:

- Conduct weekly surveys during peak migration months (April, May, July, and August).
- Conduct intensive callback surveys of marsh birds annually in selected habitats.
- Assist and cooperate with other agencies, universities, and organizations performing studies and investigations on the refuge.

Wading Birds

Objective: Survey wading birds annually to document their populations and evaluate habitat management.

Discussion: The refuge staff has been conducting regular surveys of wading birds in conjunction with waterfowl and shorebird surveys. This CCP continues that effort and also provides for surveys of rookeries.

Strategies:

- Conduct surveys annually in conjunction with shorebird and waterfowl surveys.
- Conduct two surveys annually on all potential rookery sites for rookeries.
- Assist and cooperate with other agencies, universities, and organizations performing studies and investigations on the refuge.

Waterfowl

Objective: Monitor waterfowl annually to document their populations and evaluate habitat management.

Strategies:

- Monitor wintering waterfowl populations annually by conducting 12 aerial surveys performed every other week and 12 ground surveys performed every other week throughout the wintering waterfowl season.
- Conduct banding as directed.
- Assist with banding when requested.
- Continue supporting banding operations on refuges in eastern North Carolina with grain harvested from refuge croplands.
- Conduct productivity surveys of tundra swans and snow geese when requested.
- Check up to 100 wood duck boxes for productivity every 35-40 days during peak nesting season annually.
- Band summer wood ducks and other waterfowl as requested.
- Assist and cooperate with other agencies, universities, and organizations performing studies and investigations on the refuge.

HABITAT MANAGEMENT

Pocosin

Objective: Manage 61,288 acres of pocosin, including forest, shrub, and herbaceous stages, to maintain it as a natural community. Depending on locations and timing of oppoturnities, convert 2,900 acres of herbaceous or shrub stage pocosin to Atlantic white cedar, hardwood swamp forests, moist-soil units, and firebreaks.

Discussion: Altered hydrology has a great impact on the refuge staff's ability to manage the pocosin habitat for wildlife. Previous owners installed ditches and canals to farm and harvest timber in the area. When it is drained, the deep, organic soil oxidizes, decomposing and evaporating into the atmosphere. The drained soil also burns when wildfires occur. Finally, drained soil will not support the healthy hydrophytic plant communities typical of saturated organic soils or the wildlife populations that have evolved in those communities.

Successful maintenance or management of the pocosin will require restoration of hydrology to hold the water table at the surface of the soil. The saturated soil profile will sustain the vegetative community and allow prescribed burning and management of wildfires to achieve habitat manipulation.

The plan provides for hydrology restoration, fire management, habitat surveys, development and implementation of management plans, and conversion of some pocosin to Atlantic white cedar and hardwood swamp forest.

Strategies:

- Restore hydrology on areas specified in the hydrology restoration plan by installing infrastructure to facilitate water management within the 15-year life of this CCP.
- Manage hydrology to mimic the natural condition as closely as possible and in accordance with the hydrology restoration plan and the forest habitat management plan.
- Revise the fire management plan.
- Manage wildfires and prescribed burning as specified in the fire management plan.
- Initiate studies and surveys to provide baseline information on habitat conditions and use of habitat by wildlife within five years of the date of this CCP.
- Develop management plans based on the results of the studies and surveys within two years of the completion of studies and surveys.
- Implement management plans in selected areas.
- Monitor the effects of implementing the plans and change the plans as needed.
- Develop a refuge-specific red-cockaded woodpecker habitat management plan after receipt of the national plan. Initiate implementation of the plan on habitat around active clusters within one year of its development.
- Restore 700 acres of shrub or grass stage pocosin to Atlantic white cedar forest.
- Restore 1,500 acres of shrub or grass stage pocosin to bottomland hardwood forest.
- Assist and cooperate with other agencies, universities, and organizations performing studies and investigations on the refuge.

Peatland Atlantic White Cedar Forest

Objective: Manage 3,824 acres (3,124 existing acres and 700 newly restored acres) of functional peatland Atlantic white cedar forest habitat to maintain it as a natural community.

Discussion: The refuge staff currently protects the peatland Atlantic white cedar forest from wildfires and conducts no surveys and little management. Researchers from the North Carolina State University and Christopher Newport University have conducted research on revegetation and community volunteers have planted a small area, known as the Millennium Forest. The plan provides for fire management, habitat surveys, development and implementation of management plans, and restoration of 700 acres from pocosin.

Strategies:

- Revise the fire management plan.
- Manage wildfires and prescribed burning as specified in the fire management plan.
- Develop a forest management plan and implement it on selected areas within ten years of the date of this CCP.
- Convert 700 acres of pocosin habitat in the shrub or grass stage to peatland Atlantic white cedar forest.
- Assist and cooperate with other agencies, universities, and organizations performing studies and investigations on the refuge.

Hardwood Swamp Forest

Objective: Manage 15,545 acres (14,045 existing acres and 1,500 newly restored acres) of healthy, functional hardwood swamp forest habitat to maintain it as a natural community.

Discussion: The refuge staff currently protects the hardwood swamp forest from wildfires and conducts no surveys or management. The plan provides for fire management, habitat surveys, and development and implementation of management plans.

Strategies:

- Revise the fire management plan.
- Manage wildfires and prescribed burning as specified in the fire management plan.
- Plant 1,500 acres of pocosin with shallow peat soil in the shrub or grass stage to hardwoods to maintain a healthy, functional hardwood swamp forest habitat community.
- Inventory vegetation and correlate to wildlife occurrence within ten years of the date of this CCP.
- Develop a forest management plan and implement it on selected areas within ten years of the date of this CCP.
- Assist and cooperate with other agencies, universities, and organizations performing studies and investigations on the refuge.

Cypress Gum Swamp

Objective: Manage 970 acres of healthy, functional cypress/gum swamp habitat to maintain it as a natural community.

Discussion: The refuge staff currently protects the cypress-gum swamp from wildfires and conducts no surveys or management. The plan provides for fire management, habitat surveys, and development and implementation of management plans.

Strategies:

- Revise the fire management plan.
- Manage wildfires and prescribed burning as specified in the fire management plan.
- Develop management plans based on the results of the studies and surveys within ten years of the completion of the studies and surveys.
- Inventory vegetation and correlate to wildlife occurrence within ten years of the date of this CCP.
- Implement management plans in selected areas.
- Assist and cooperate with other agencies, universities, and organizations performing studies and investigations on the refuge.

Marsh

Objective: Manage 987 acres of healthy, functional marsh habitat to maintain it as a natural community.

Discussion: The refuge staff currently conducts no surveys or management in the marsh. This CCP provides for fire management, habitat surveys, and development and implementation of management plans.

Strategies:

- Revise the fire management plan.
- Manage wildfires and prescribed burning as specified in the fire management plan.
- Develop management plans based on the results of the studies and surveys within ten years of the completion of the studies and surveys.
- Inventory vegetation and correlate to wildlife occurrence within ten years of the date of this CCP.
- Implement management plans in selected areas.
- Assist and cooperate with other agencies, universities, and organizations performing studies and investigations on the refuge.

Cropland

Objective: Manage 1,410 acres (1,250 existing and 160 newly acquired acres) of cropland in accordance with the cropland management plan. Annually provide 400 acres of grain and 300 acres of green browse for wintering waterfowl.

Discussion: The refuge currently manages 1,250 acres of cropland habitat through the use of the cooperative farming program and provides up to 250 acres of standing corn and 200 acres of winter wheat for wintering waterfowl annually. The ultimate goal of the program is to provide 400 acres of unharvested corn for wintering waterfowl.

Strategies:

- Use cooperative farming program, contract farming, force account farming, or acquisition of land (fee simple purchase, easement purchase, or cooperative agreements) to provide 400 acres of unharvested corn and 300 acres of winter wheat annually.
- Revise the cooperative farming agreements annually.
- Assist and cooperate with other agencies, universities, and organizations performing studies and investigations on the refuge.

Moist-soil Units (Managed Wetlands)

Objective: Manage 593 acres (443 existing and 150 newly acquired or converted acres) of moist-soil habitat and manage water on 550 acres of other wetlands (hardwood swamp forests, mixed pine flatwoods, etc.), to provide wintering habitat for migratory waterfowl, shorebirds, wading birds, and land birds and breeding habitat for marsh birds and land birds.

Discussion: The refuge's moist-soil units are one of the most intensively managed habitats on the refuge. They include the Smartweed, Jones Pond, Marsh A, Hyde Park, Van's Pond, and Evan's Pond units; however, the Evan's Pond unit is currently not managed due to a deteriorated dike system. The moist-soil units provide plants that produce high-quality seeds and other foods for waterfowl in the fall and winter and mudflats that produce invertebrates for shorebird food in the spring and late summer. Other managed wetlands include diked and partially diked areas where water levels can be managed.

Strategies:

- Manage all areas according to the water management plan using a combination of natural water sources and pump/well systems.

- Manage the moist-soil habitat to achieve a 70 percent cover of moist-soil plants rated as good every year.
- Manage the moist-soil habitat to provide 50 percent of the acreage in mudflats during the peak of the spring migration (May).
- Construct two additional moist-soil habitat units of 150 acres total within ten years of the date of this CCP. This will require acquisition of additional prior converted farm land (fee simple purchase or cooperative agreements).
- Install five pump/well systems to provide dependable water supply to existing and proposed moist-soil habitat units within five years of the date of this CCP.
- Maintain dikes and renovate failed dikes.
- Construct new dikes for existing moist-soil areas without dikes (Hyde Park) and new moist-soil areas.
- Raise existing dikes/roads and manage water to increase the amount of wetlands available for wintering waterfowl.
- Assist and cooperate with other agencies, universities, and organizations performing studies and investigations on the refuge.

Natural Lake Shoreline

Objective: Manage 446 acres of healthy, functional natural lake shoreline habitat to maintain it as a natural community.

Discussion: The lake shoreline of Pungo Lake has great potential for producing high-quality waterfowl food plants, but common reed (*Phragmites australis*) currently occupies some of these areas. The refuge staff is taking actions to manage this invasive species.

This CCP provides for management of shoreline vegetation with fire and herbicide to reduce the encroachment of undesirable vegetation.

Strategies:

- Revise the fire management plan.
- Manage wildfires and prescribed burning as specified in the fire management plan.
- Manage undesirable vegetation as necessary.
- Assist and cooperate with other agencies, universities, and organizations performing studies and investigations on the refuge.

Open Water

Objective: Manage water levels to maximize the amount of open water and provide waterfowl food plants in the lake margins for wintering waterfowl.

Discussion: Pungo and New Lakes provide important roosting and loafing habitat for wintering waterfowl. Water levels in Pungo Lake fluctuate widely and are often not at optimum levels for the wintering waterfowl season. The lake margins of Pungo Lake have great potential for producing high-quality waterfowl food plants, but common reed (*Phragmites australis*) currently occupies some of these areas. The refuge is taking actions to manage this invasive species. Fifteen percent of New Lake is privately owned.

Strategies:

- Manage the water levels to maximize the amount of open water for wintering waterfowl in the 6,740 acres of lakes.
- Install a pump/well system and manage the margins of Pungo Lake for foraging habitat for waterfowl.
- Seek partnerships to conserve and manage refuge and private sections of New Lake for wintering waterfowl habitat.
- Assist and cooperate with other agencies, universities, and organizations performing studies and investigations on the refuge.

Roads, Roadsides, and Canals

Objective: Maintain 80 miles of road surface for public vehicular access, 27 miles for hunting season all-terrain vehicle access, and up to 143 miles on a 1- to 3-year cycle for administrative, fire, and non-vehicular public access. Maintain 250 miles of canals to maintain water management capability. Manage roads, roadsides, and canals to optimize wildlife habitat.

Discussion: Roads on the refuge and throughout the Albemarle-Pamlico Peninsula were created by digging canals and using the spoil to create roadbeds. Maintenance of roads built on top of piles of organic soil is extremely difficult; driving on these roads is also extremely difficult, especially in wet weather. The staff currently tries to maintain 80 miles of road surface for public vehicular access. Construction (upgrading) of one all-weather road passing north and south through the refuge and one road passing east and west through the refuge is critical to dependable access to the refuge by the staff and the public. As the Service restores hydrology on the refuge, the refuge must raise the elevation of certain sections of roads to facilitate maintenance in areas that will be saturated to the current road surface. The staff will implement early detection and rapid response to invasive species during the road raising process. Presence of the exotic Japanese stiltgrass (*Microstegium vimineum*) has increased along roadsides throughout parts of the refuge. Roadsides have the potential to be early successional habitat dominated by native grasses and wildflowers when they are managed properly with rotational mowing and prescribed fire.

Strategies:

- Provide constant and continuous maintenance of road surface to assure passable condition.
- Provide all weather access on at least one north-south and one east-west road and one auto tour route within ten years of the date of this CCP.
- Raise the elevation of certain sections of roads as described in the hydrology restoration plan to facilitate hydrology restoration and provide continued access within the 15-year life of this CCP.
- Maintain all roads open to the public to Federal Highway Administration standards.
- Manage vegetation on 364 acres of roadside to provide early successional habitat for wildlife.
- Maintain 909 acres of canals according to the hydrology restoration plan.
- Implement early detection and rapid response to invasive species during the road raising process.

Wood Duck Nest Boxes

Objective: Maintain up to 150 wood duck nest boxes in appropriate wood duck habitat annually.

Discussion: Wood ducks require large trees in flooded areas with cavities in which to nest. Due to the harvest of large trees in flooded habitat, the wood ducks need artificial cavities to replace the large trees. These artificial cavities are called wood duck nest boxes. They must be checked annually to document their use and evaluate the need to install more as the existing boxes are utilized. They also must have old nest material replaced and unhatched eggs removed. The boxes must be repaired as weather and black bears damage them.

Strategies:

- Check up to 150 wood duck boxes and clean and repair them annually.
- Erect 50 new boxes within five years of the date of this CCP.

Firebreaks

Objective: Manage 1,750 acres of firebreaks on a 3-year rotation according to the fire management plan to facilitate wild fire suppression and also provide early successional habitat for wildlife.

Strategies:

- Manage vegetation in firebreaks by mechanical means, with herbicides, and with prescribed burning.
- Maintain roads and canals as part of the firebreak system.

PUBLIC USE

Access

Objective: Maintain a level of access to the refuge during daylight hours that is compatible with refuge purposes (Figure 7).

Discussion: The entire refuge is currently open to the public during daylight hours throughout the year unless restricted by refuge operations or wildlife activity. The public has access to the Pungo impoundment areas during the period when waterfowl are resting and this access results in disturbance to the birds. The plan proposes to maintain the current access except for selected areas of impoundments when waterfowl are resting to minimize disturbance.

Strategies:

- Continue to open the refuge to the public during daylight hours throughout the year unless restricted by refuge operations or wildlife activity.
- Restrict access to Pungo and New Lakes, selected Pungo impoundment areas, and other refuge areas as necessary to minimize waterfowl disturbance during the period November through February.
- Restrict access to Pungo Lake during the wood duck breeding season.
- Restrict access to the firearms range and maintenance and storage areas year-round.

Hunting

Objective: Provide 10,000 annual quality daylight hunting opportunities for selected species of game animals during the State hunting season on the entire refuge except the Pungo Unit.

Figure 7. Proposed visitor facilities of the Pocosin Lakes NWR

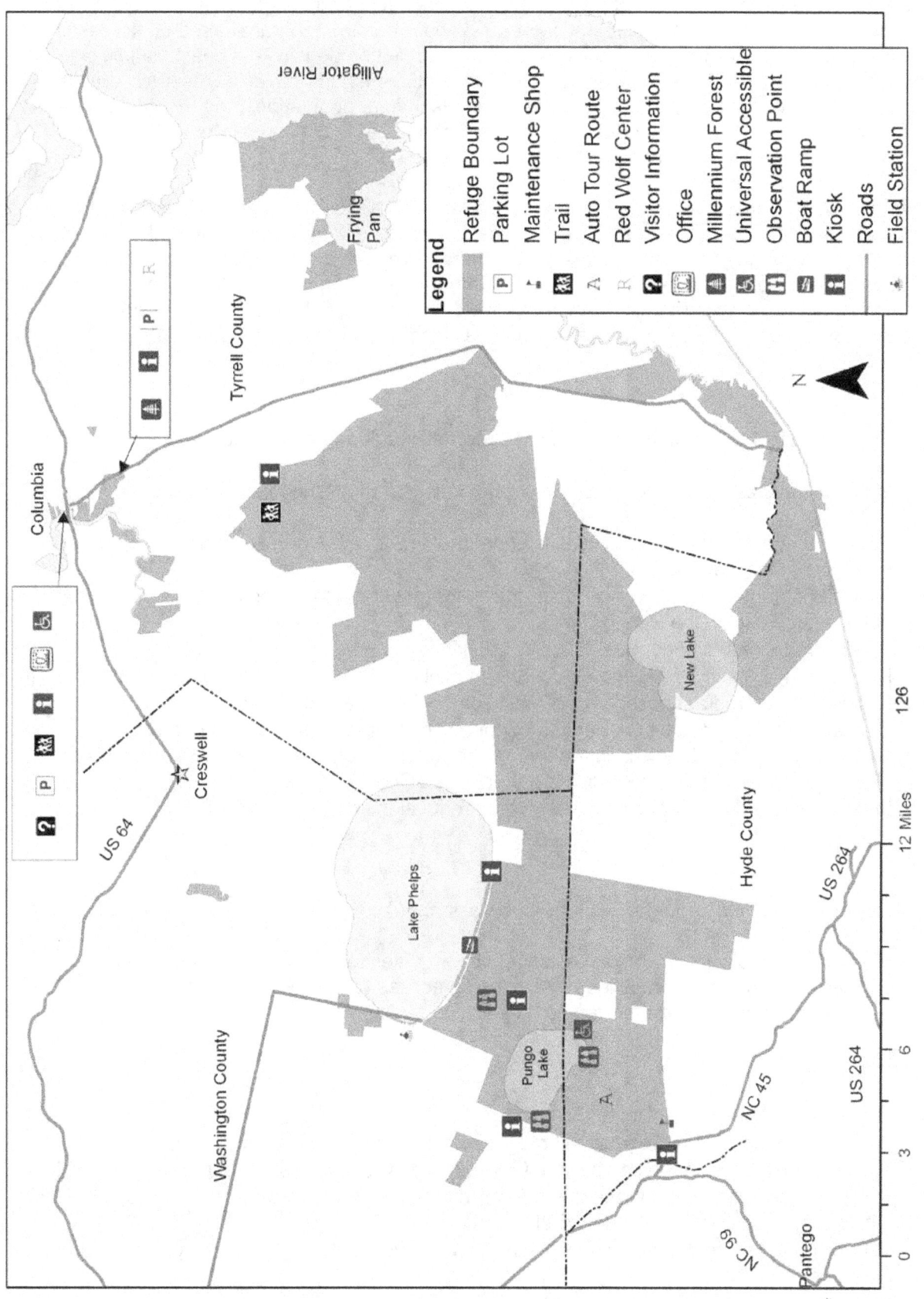

Comprehensive Conservation Plan

Discussion: The refuge currently provides up to 8,000 hunting opportunities annually. The plan provides for 10,000 annual hunting opportunities. It increases opportunities for hunting on the Pungo Unit by permit. It also provides consideration of a new bear hunting program based on the results of the 2005 black bear study, which demonstrated a bear population density that could sustain a conservative hunt. The U.S. Geological Survey (Cooperative Fish and Wildlife Research Unit at Virginia Tech) has conducted a thorough study of the black bear populations on the refuge. The results of the study also recommended continued monitoring of the black bear population to determine population increases and declines.

The State of North Carolina allows hunting on all the land in the Coastal Plain. Bears currently interfere with banding operations on the refuge, destroy wood duck nest boxes, and take deer shot by hunters before the hunters can retrieve the deer. There have also been numerous dangerous bear/human interactions reported by deer hunters, refuge interns, and other refuge staff. The black bears also attract many visitors to the refuge to observe the bears in their habitat. The number of incidental observations of bears on the refuge has declined since Hurricane Isabel in 2003.

Strategies:

- Provide up to 1,200 annual deer hunting opportunities during a permitted hunt with shotguns and muzzleloaders on the Pungo Unit.
- Provide 3,000 annual archery hunting opportunities on the Pungo Unit according to the hunt plan.
- Provide turkey hunting opportunities in coordination with the North Carolina Wildlife Resources Commission.
- Provide 50 annual night hunting opportunities for raccoon and opossum by permit on the entire refuge except the Pungo Unit.
- Sponsor one youth hunt annually.
- Revise refuge hunting regulation brochure annually.
- Adapt hunting program based on the biological and cultural carrying capacity.
- Consider providing black bear hunting opportunities based on the results of the study conducted by the U.S. Geological Survey (Cooperative Fish and Wildlife Research Unit at Virginia Tech) within five years of the date of this CCP.
- Increase law enforcement staffing to enforce regulations during hunts.

Fishing

Objective: Provide fishing opportunities for 2,000 visits annually.

Discussion: The refuge currently provides fishing opportunities for 1,500 visits annually. This CCP provides for an increase in opportunities by developing access to Lake Phelps and hosting one fishing event annually to publicize the refuge as a fishing destination.

Strategies:

- Maintain boardwalk as a fishing pier.
- Develop a refuge fishing regulation brochure within five years of the date of this CCP.
- Develop boat ramp on the south side of Lake Phelps within five years of the date of this CCP.
- Develop a cooperative agreement with Pettigrew State Park on boat ramp access to the lake within ten years of the date of this CCP.
- Conduct one fishing event (such as fishing derby or fishing tourmament for youth) annually.

Environmental Education

Objective: Provide education opportunities for 3,600 users annually.

Strategies:

- Maintain four environmental education facilities (auditorium, indoor classroom, outdoor classroom, and field station).
- Develop and provide eighteen planned environmental education programs annually.
- Participate in three environmental field days annually.
- Serve as an outdoor classroom for ten college course single day field trips annually.
- Utilize partners and volunteers to conduct education programs.
- Equip and develop the classroom/laboratory facility at the Center for the Sounds for use by refuge staff and local teachers within five years of the date of this CCP.
- Develop a plan for use of the outdoor classroom facility along the interpretive boardwalk and equip the facility within ten years of the date of this CCP.
- Continue existing and develop new programs in cooperation with the Partnership for the Sounds, Eastern North Carolina 4H Environmental Education Center, Tyrrell County Board of Education, Pocosin Arts Center, Pettigrew State Park, North Carolina Wildlife Resources Commission, and North Carolina Museum of Natural Science.

Interpretation

Objective: Provide interpretation opportunities for 400,000 visitors annually.

Strategies:

- Conduct ten tours of the refuge by request annually.
- Relocate the Kuralt trail kiosk to the new northwest Pungo Lake observation platform.
- Develop and maintain a trail and universally accessible observation platform and boardwalk on the northwest side of Pungo Lake within ten years of the date of this CCP.
- Develop two kiosks at the Millennium Forest and Northern Road within the 15-year life of this CCP.
- Maintain seven information kiosks.
- Maintain the refuge web site.
- Maintain Scuppernong River interpretive boardwalk and trail.
- Develop additional and replacement exhibits for the Walter B. Jones Center for the Sounds as needed.
- Increase the amount of exhibit space in the Walter B. Jones Center for the Sounds within five years of the date of this CCP.
- Develop three videos over the 15-year life of this CCP and utilize the refuge videos as interpretive tools.
- Develop brochures on the refuge, wildlife, interpretive boardwalk, refuge trails, refuge native plants, Pungo auto tour route, and the Millennium Forest Trail within ten years of the date of this CCP or within two years of facility development.
- Revise one of the eight refuge brochures (refuge, refuge trails, refuge native plants, Pungo auto tour route, Millennium Forest Trail, wildlife brochure, interpretive boardwalk) annually.
- In cooperation with the Red Wolf Coalition, develop a captive red wolf viewing facility within ten years of the date of this CCP.

Comprehensive Conservation Plan

- Develop Millennium Forest Access Trail with signs within ten years of the date of this CCP.
- Maintain Millennium Forest Trail and parking lot.
- Develop a new trail and interpretive boardwalk through the pocosin off of Northern Road within ten years of the date of this CCP.
- Develop interpretive material for a new trail and interpretive boardwalk through the pocosin off of Northern Road within ten years of the date of this CCP.
- Explore the possibility of developing a Vistor Contact Station for the Pungo Unit to be staffed by volunteers.

Wildlife Observation

Objective: Provide wildlife observation opportunities for 50,000 users annually.

Strategies:

- Maintain the southeast Pungo Lake observation platform to facilitate observation.
- Develop and maintain a trail and universally accessible observation platform and boardwalk on the northwest side of Pungo Lake within ten years of the date of this CCP.
- Convert and maintain the fire tower on Allen Road to an observation tower within five years of the date of this CCP.
- Provide Kuralt Trail information to encourage use of auto tour route for observation.
- Develop and maintain a universally accessible boardwalk trail along Northern Road within five years of the date of this CCP.
- Promote the wildlife observation opportunities from the water on the Scuppernong River and Northwest Fork of the Alligator River within five years of the date of this CCP. Partner with Pettigrew State Park, which is actively purchasing property along the river.

Wildlife Photography

Objective: Provide wildlife photography opportunities for 1,500 users annually.

Strategies:

- Develop and maintain one photo-blind on north Pungo Lake within ten years of the date of this CCP.
- Maintain interpretive boardwalk and biking trail to facilitate photography continuously.
- Develop and maintain a trail and observation platform and boardwalk on the northwest side of Pungo Lake within five years of the date of this CCP.
- Convert and maintain the fire tower on Allen Road to an observation tower within five years of the date of this CCP.
- Develop and maintain a universally accessible boardwalk trail along Northern Road within five years of the date of this CCP.
- Provide Kuralt Trail information to encourage use of auto tour route for photography.
- Develop a brochure for the Pungo auto tour route within three years of the date of this CCP.
- Develop and maintain one canoe trail and associated signage and wildlife checklists within five years of the date of this CCP.

Outreach

Objective: Target outreach efforts for an audience of 16 million people in the Atlantic Coast states from New York to Georgia.

Strategies:

- Participate in Swan Days, Wings over Water, Scuppernong River Festival, Farm City Days, International Migratory Bird Day, and the North Carolina State Fair annually.
- Develop a refuge-based wildlife festival and conduct it annually.
- Make six presentations to local organizations annually.
- Develop twelve news releases annually.
- Develop one traveling refuge exhibit within ten years of the date of this CCP.
- Conduct an open house every year in conjunction with the Scuppernong River Festival.
- Develop three videos over fifteen years and utilize the refuge videos as outreach tools.

Reptile and Amphibian Collection and Harvest

Objective: Allow collection and harvest of reptiles and amphibians if populations will allow collection and harvest.

Discussion: The refuge does not currently permit collection or harvest of reptiles or amphibians. There is traditional use of reptiles and amphibians in the local diet. The actual population size of frogs on the refuge is unknown but appears to be plentiful based on staff observations. They tend to be concentrated in ephemeral ponds and wet areas.

Strategies:

- Permit harvest of bullfrogs or southern leopard frogs by gigging at specified locations under special use permits.
- Permit no collection of turtles, snakes, lizards, toads, salamanders, and other frog species.

Refuge Support

Objective: Develop and maintain local support for refuge programs.

Strategies:

- Develop a Friends Group to support refuge programs.
- Work with the Partnership for the Sounds to promote nature-based tourism and public use in the region as an economic development strategy with refuges and other conservation lands providing the natural resource base.
- Work with the Red Wolf Coalition to support the red wolf program, the Pocosin Arts Center to support restoration efforts on the refuge, and the Conservation Fund to support land acquisition and restoration.

RESOURCE PROTECTION

Cultural Resources

Objective: Avoid all impacts to cultural resources by coordinating with the Regional Office.

Discussion: The refuge staff currently protects known cultural resource sites and coordinates with the Regional Archaeologist when construction is planned.

Strategies:

- Evaluate all proposed projects and coordinate with the Regional Office before beginning a project.
- Protect identified cultural resource sites.

Interagency Coordination and Cooperative Agreements

Objective: Facilitate and enhance refuge programs and protect refuge resources by coordinating with State, Federal, local, and public and private agencies.

Discussion: This CCP provides for a continuation of the current level of coordination with other agencies and organizations. As the Service adds staff in specialized areas, such as law enforcement and environmental education, that coordination will be more effective since the staff will have adequate time to follow up after meetings and comply with the terms of agreements.

Strategies:

- Review and revise formal cooperative agreements annually.
- Coordinate with North Carolina Forest Service and other refuges on wildfire suppression activities annually.

Land Protection

Objective: Develop land protection plans and acquire land from willing sellers.

Discussion: The refuge currently owns all the land within its approved acquisition boundary. Due to the opportunistic nature of former land acquisition, the refuge boundary is extremely irregular and does not extend to highways or other means of access. The nature of the boundary makes habitat management and law enforcement very difficult. The Service approved the acquisition boundary after the land was acquired and did not include valuable habitat such as red-cockaded woodpecker cavity trees and riparian corridors along streams, rivers, lakes, and sounds. An expansion of the approved acquisition boundary will give the refuge opportunities to conduct more effective wildlife and habitat management and law enforcement, and protect important habitat.

Strategy:

- Develop minor expansion proposals and land protection plans to protect important habitat and facilitate habitat management and law enforcement.

Law Enforcement

Objective: Ensure public safety and protect refuge resources by enforcing refuge regulations.

Discussion: The refuge currently enforces regulations with a dual function law enforcement officer, the refuge manager, and assistance from the full-time officer at Mattamuskeet National Wildlife Refuge. The plan provides for the hiring of two full-time officers for the refuge who will substantially increase law enforcement visibility, protect visitors, and assist in conducting a safe hunting program.

Strategies:

- Post boundaries according to Service policy.
- Double the amount of regular law enforcement patrols.
- Implement a law enforcement outreach program.
- Provide assistance to and coordinate with appropriate State, Federal, and local law enforcement agencies to facilitate compliance with their laws.
- Develop written agreements with and improve cooperation with law enforcement agencies.

Permits

Objective: Protect refuge resources by evaluating use proposals on a case-by-case basis, developing conditions for the permits, and monitoring compliance with the conditions.

Discussion: The refuge staff currently has the capacity to review 40 proposals for use of the refuge annually. With an increased visibility of the refuge, the staff anticipates an increased number of proposals. Part of the duties of the increased staff proposed in this CCP will be the evaluation of proposals, development of conditions of the permits, and monitoring compliance with the conditions.

Strategies:

- Limit impacts to refuge resources by evaluating up to 80 use proposals per year on a case-by-case basis.
- Protect refuge resources by developing special conditions for those permitted uses that are compatible.
- Develop standardized special conditions where possible.
- Monitor permitted activities to ensure compliance and assess the effect of the use on the environment.

Pest Animals

Objective: Limit impacts to refuge resources by monitoring, controlling, or eradicating pest animals as necessary.

Discussion: This CCP proposes to continue the current management. Red wolves currently seem to be controling the exotic nutria that damage herbaceous plant communities on the refuge. Feral hogs are numerous in the Frying Pan unit, are expanding to other areas on the refuge, and are causing significant damage. The refuge staff will maintain vigilance of nutria, feral hogs, coyotes, and other selected species that have an impact on refuge resources. As resources become available, staff will control the pests as necessary and evaluate the effectiveness of control measures.

Strategies:

- Develop a Pest Animal Control Plan within five years of the date of this CCP.
- Train the staff to be aware of pest animals and report their occurrence.
- Monitor selected pest animals on a systematic basis.
- Implement pest animal control measures with refuge staff, contractors, volunteers, and permit holders.
- Evaluate the effectiveness of control measures.

Pest Plants

Objective: Improve plant communities and limit impacts to refuge resources by monitoring, controlling, or eradicating pest plants as necessary.

Discussion: The plan proposes to continue the current management. Phragmites and alligatorweed are the most dominant pest plants on the refuge, but others, such as sesbania, Japanese stiltgrass, Chinese privet, and Japanese honeysuckle, are highly visible. The refuge staff will maintain vigilance of the dominant species that have an impact on refuge resources. Pests will be controlled as necessary and the staff will evaluate the effectiveness of control measures.

Strategies:

- Develop and implement a Pest Plant Control Plan within five years of the date of this CCP. Include specific strategies for controlling phragmites and alligatorweed.
- Develop a cooperative agreement with the State of North Carolina and other agencies and organizations to control alligatorweed in waterways through and adjacent to the refuge.
- Train the staff to be aware of pest plants and report their occurrence.
- Monitor selected pest plants on a systematic basis.
- Implement early detection and rapid response pest plant control measures with refuge staff, contractors, and cooperating agencies and organizations.
- Evaluate the effectiveness of control measures.

Significant Natural Heritage Areas

Objective: Limit impacts to the area to retain its natural character.

Discussion: The North Carolina Natural Heritage Program has recognized the nature of the vegetative communities on the refuge by designating most of the refuge as a Significant Natural Heritage Area. The Service has signed a non-binding agreement with the State of North Carolina to manage the areas to retain its natural character. The plan continues the current management. The primary management tool on the refuge is prescribed fire. The refuge staff establishes the fire frequency to mimic the natural fire cycle. The restoration of hydrology will not only maintain the existing vegetative communities, but also will ensure their long-term sustainability and facilitate fire management.

Strategies:

- Limit impacts to the area to retain the natural character of the area.
- Revise the fire management plan with fire frequencies on Significant Natural Heritage Areas established to mimic natural fire cycles.
- Manage wildfires and prescribed burning as specified in the fire management plan.

- Implement a prescribed burning program as data becomes available to guide the program and as hydrology is restored.
- Review the fire management plan and update it to adapt the plan based on the results of prescribed fires on the refuge and research being conducted in pocosin habitats.
- Restore hydrology on the refuge.

Water Quality

Objective: Manage the refuge to maintain and monitor water quality.

Discussion: The Service manages the refuge with little disturbance that would cause erosion and sedimentation and few pesticides and nutrients that would pollute water. Cooperative farmers and refuge staff use pesticides and fertilizers according to pesticide labels and crop management plans. This CCP continues the current management and implements monthly monitoring.

Strategies:

- Monitor water quality in selected lakes, canals, and at pump stations quarterly.
- Cooperate with other agencies and organizations performing water quality sampling on the refuge.

Wildlife Disease Control and Prevention

Objective: Limit impacts to refuge resources by coordinating with Federal, State, and local agencies as necessary to monitor and control wildlife disease.

Discussion: The refuge has not experienced any large-scale wildlife disease outbreaks in the past. With high concentrations of wintering waterfowl, the possibility exists that any disease organism that enters the wintering population could become a problem. Other wildlife species, such as raccoons and foxes, could contract rabies or other canine diseases. The plan continues the current management of training staff, maintaining vigilance, and cooperating with agencies and organizations.

Strategies:

- Train refuge staff to recognize clinical signs of wildlife diseases and exercise vigilance of wildlife disease.
- Coordinate with Federal, State, and local agencies as necessary to monitor and control wildlife disease.

REFUGE ADMINISTRATION

General Administration

Objective: Obtain resources to meet requirements of budgets, such as making purchases, reporting progress, administering travel, maintaining filing system, maintaining computer systems, responding to information requests, developing and revising plans, performing compatibility determinations, and maintaining relationships with the public, local government officials, and congressional delegations.

Strategies:

- Manage budgets, request funding from various sources, make purchases, report progress, and administer travel.
- Manage filing, computer systems, and databases.
- Respond to information requests.
- Develop and revise plans and perform compatibility determinations.
- Maintain relationships with the public, local government officials, and congressional delegations.

Capital Property Management

Objective: Obtain resources to operate, effectively maintain, and dispose of capital property.

Discussion: The plan improves on the current management by providing for acquisition of all the equipment necessary to support refuge programs and replace equipment frequently enough to maximize the efficiency of refuge operations.

Strategies:

- Acquire minimum equipment necessary to support refuge programs.
- Conduct a capital property inventory annually.
- Maintain adequate administrative records on capital and non-capitalized property.
- Evaluate the operating condition of capital property.
- Maintain and upgrade capital and non-capital property to ensure safety of staff and the general public.

Columbia Office and Visitor Center

Objective: Operate and maintain the office space to ensure efficiency of operation, the safety of the staff and the public, and an aesthetically pleasing appearance.

Discussion: The plan improves on the current management by staffing the receptionist and maintenance worker functions at the office and visitor center with permanent full-time positions and staffing the visitor center full time.

Strategies:

- Handle office reception duties with a permanent full-time receptionist.
- Maintain the visitor center and operate it a minimum of 40 hours per week in cooperation with the Partnership for the Sounds and volunteers.
- Utilize permanent full-time staff for maintenance of the office and visitor center.

Pungo, Lake Phelps, and Columbia Shop Facilities

Objective: Operate and maintain the existing field station, house, and workspace in an adequate condition to ensure efficiency of operation and the comfort and safety of the staff and the public.

Discussion: The refuge was originally the 12,500-acre Pungo National Wildlife Refuge that is now known as the Pungo Unit in the southwest corner of the existing 110,106-acre refuge. The shop facility established to manage the Pungo National Wildlife Refuge is not centrally located to serve the entire refuge. Due to the wetland nature of the refuge, construction of a new shop facility in the current center of the refuge is not possible. The plan provides for the construction of a new additional shop facility near Columbia from which staff could serve the northern and eastern part of the refuge. There is a former refuge residence on the shore of Lake Phelps now called the Field Station. Interns, volunteers, and emergency firefighters use it as a residence. The building must be maintained to provide safe housing for these important personnel. The old office and a small residence (occupied by a resident with deeded life-time use of the house and yard) are located next to the Field Station.

Strategies:

- Construct a new maintenance facility near Columbia.
- Replace the old office building on Lake Phelps with a residential building for use by interns, volunteers, and emergency firefighters.
- Take over maintenance and make necessary repairs to small residence on Shore Drive between Field Station and old office when the life-time occupant vacates and use it to provide employee housing.
- Operate and maintain all maintenance and other facilities in an adequate condition to ensure efficiency of operation, as well as the comfort and safety of the staff.

Financial Management

Objective: Develop budget and develop and administer contracts in accordance with Fish and Wildlife Service policy.

Strategy:

- Manage budgets, request funding from various sources, make purchases, report progress, administer travel, and maintain databases in accordance with Fish and Wildlife Service policy.

Personnel Management

Objective: Recruit, hire, and manage staff at adequate full-time equivalent levels (FTE) to accomplish the highest priority refuge goals and objectives (25 FTEs).

Discussion: This CCP provides for a moderate increase in staff to implement the proposed goals, objectives, and strategies. It also proposes to contract intermittent staff functions. Both the increased staff and contract employees will require additional personnel management. Service policy prescribes the level of management for evaluation, training, recruiting, and hiring.

Strategies:

- Provide staff with professional technical and leadership development training in accordance with Service policy.
- Evaluate and manage performance in accordance with Service policy.
- Recruit and hire additional staff positions in accordance with Service policy.

Comprehensive Conservation Plan

Real Property Management

Objective: Manage resources to adequately maintain buildings, grounds, firebreaks, roads, bridges, structures, and public use facilities in a clean and acceptable condition that protects the health and safety of the refuge staff and the public.

Discussion: The plan improves on the current management by providing for not only the maintenance of existing facilities, but also the rehabilitation of refuge roads that severely limit access for staff and visitors.

Strategies:

- Acquire adequate buildings and structures to support refuge programs, as resources are available.
- Conduct one real property inventory annually.
- Manage all real property according to the Fish and Wildlife Service Manual.

Volunteer Management

Objective: Recruit, train, support, and manage volunteers in accordance with Service policy.

Discussion: The refuge currently utilizes up to 2,500 hours of labor donated by volunteers to maintain the refuge, conduct biological surveys, and implement environmental education programs. College interns contribute the majority of the labor. The interns live in a refuge residence (the Field Station) on Lake Phelps and receive a stipend for food. The refuge has attempted to recruit volunteers from the community with limited success. The counties in which the refuge is located are some of the poorest in the State and residents with time to contribute are scarce. Area refuges have had a great deal of success recruiting workampers who contribute their labor in exchange for a pad for their recreational vehicle. This CCP proposes to hire a part-time coordinator to recruit, train, and manage volunteers and develop recreational vehicle pads to attract workampers.

Strategies:

- Employ a part-time coordinator to support designated refuge programs by recruiting, training, and coordinating volunteers to donate 4,000 hours of service annually.
- Develop two pads at the Field Station for recreational vehicles to attract workamper volunteers.

V. Plan Implementation

INTRODUCTION

The Service will implement this CCP utilizing existing staff, facilities, and equipment and by acquiring additional staff, facilities, and equipment. The tables below outline the strategies from Chapter IV and list the existing and new staff, facilities, and equipment required to implement this CCP. Appendix VIII contains details of the new staff, facilities, and equipment as Refuge Operation Needs System (RONS) Projects or Maintenance Management System (MMS) Projects. The appendix also includes the priorities of those projects. MMS projects were recently converted to the Service Asset Maintenance Management System (SAMMS). RONS and MMS project lists represent a snapshot in time of a dynamic set of projects and priorities. The refuge staff will implement the strategies associated with specific projects as the Service funds those projects.

PROPOSED PROJECTS

Table 23. Projects supporting fish and wildlife population strategies

Personnel Projects	
Strategy	**Projects**
Conduct surveys, monitoring, studies, and investigations.	Use existing wildlife biologist. Recruit, hire, and train two biological technicians (RONS 00011, 97001, 00005).
Protect wildlife.	Use existing dual function officer and law enforcement officer from Mattamuskeet NWR. Recruit, hire, and train one law enforcement officers (RONS 97009, 03001).
Manage budget, contracts, personnel, and property.	Use existing refuge manager, assistant manager, wildlife biologist, fire management officer, and office assistant. Recruit, hire, and train an assistant manager (RONS 00006) and an office assistant (RONS 99012).
Apply for flexible funding and other grants.	Use existing wildlife biologist. Recruit, hire, and train two biological technicians (RONS 00011, 97001, 00005).
Equipment Projects	
Maintain, repair, and replace equipment to survey and protect wildlife.	Replace equipment (various MMS projects). Replace vehicles (various MMS projects).

Table 24. Projects supporting habitat strategies

Personnel Projects	
Strategy	Projects
Conduct surveys, monitoring, studies, and investigations.	Use existing wildlife biologist. Recruit, hire, and train two biological technicians (RONS 00011, 97001, 00005).
Conduct prescribed burning.	Use existing fire management officer, wildlife biologist, forestry technicians, and engineering equipment operators.
Protect habitat.	Use existing dual function officer and law enforcement officer from Mattamuskeet Refuge. Recruit, hire, and train one law enforcement officers (RONS 97009, 03001).
Manage budget, contracts, personnel, and property.	Use existing refuge manager, assistant manager, wildlife biologist, fire management officer, and office assistant. Recruit, hire, and train an assistant manager (RONS 00006) and an office assistant (RONS 99012).
Apply for flexible funding and other grants.	Use existing wildlife biologist. Recruit, hire, and train two biological technicians (RONS 00011, 97001, 00005)
Equipment Projects	
Maintain, repair, and replace equipment to manage habitat.	Replace equipment (various MMS projects). Replace vehicles (various MMS projects).
Facility Projects	
Maintain, repair, and replace facilities to manage habitat.	Replace bulkheads and water control structures (various MMS projects).

Table 25. Projects supporting public use strategies

Personnel Projects	
Strategy	**Projects**
Plan, design, and conduct programs and outreach.	Use existing park ranger (public use) position that was recently lost and recruit, hire, and train a park ranger (environmental education) (RONS 99012), park ranger (volunteer coordinator) (RONS 01001), and recreation aid (visitor center).
Maintain education, interpretation, wildlife observation, and photography facilities.	Use existing maintenance staff and volunteers. Recruit, hire, and train two equipment operators and one maintenance worker.
Protect visitors.	Use existing dual function officer and law enforcement officer from Mattamuskeet Refuge. Recruit, hire, and train one law enforcement officer (RONS 97009, 03001).
Manage budget, contracts, personnel, and property.	Use existing refuge manager, assistant manager, park ranger, and office assistant. Recruit, hire, and train a new assistant manager (RONS 00006) and office assistant (RONS 99012).
Apply for flexible funding and other grants.	Use existing refuge manager, assistant manager, wildlife biologist, and park ranger (public use). Recruit, hire, and train new park ranger (environmental education) (RONS 99012), and recreation aid (visitor center).
Equipment Projects	
Maintain, repair, and replace equipment to maintain facilities as necessary.	Replace equipment (various MMS projects). Replace vehicles (various MMS projects).
Facility Projects	
Maintain, repair, and replace facilities as necessary.	Replace parking lots, kiosks, boat ramp, and boat dock (various MMS projects).

Table 26. Projects supporting resource protection strategies

Personnel Projects	
Strategy	Projects
Maintain cooperation with agencies, organizations, and permit holders. Review permits and develop conditions for uses allowed by permits. Monitor pest animals and plants and permitted uses.	Use existing refuge manager, assistant manager, and wildlife biologist. Recruit, hire, and train an assistant manager (RONS 00006) and two biological technicians (RONS 00011, 97001, 00005).
Maintain equipment and facilities.	Use existing maintenance staff and volunteers. Recruit, hire, and train two equipment operators, and one maintenance worker.
Enforce regulations.	Use existing dual function officer and law enforcement officer from Mattamuskeet Refuge. Recruit, hire, and train one law enforcement officer (RONS 97009, 03001).
Manage budget, contracts, personnel, and property.	Use existing refuge manager, assistant manager, fire management officer, and office assistant. Recruit, hire, and train an assistant manager (RONS 00006) and an office assistant/receptionist (RONS 99012).
Apply for flexible funding and other grants.	Use existing refuge manager, assistant manager, and wildlife biologist. Recruit, hire, and train an assistant manager (RONS 00006) and two biological technicians (RONS 00011, 97001, 00005).
Equipment Projects	
Maintain, repair, and replace equipment as necessary.	Replace equipment (various MMS projects). Replace vehicles (various MMS projects).
Facility Projects	
Maintain, repair, and replace facilities as necessary.	Replace parking lots and kiosks (various MMS projects).

Table 27. Projects supporting refuge administration strategies

Personnel Projects	
Strategy	Projects
Manage budget, contracts, personnel, and property.	Use existing refuge manager, assistant manager, fire management officer, and office assistant. Recruit, hire, and train an assistant manager (RONS 00006) and an office assistant/receptionist (RONS 99012).
Maintain equipment and facilities.	Use existing maintenance staff. Recruit, hire, and train two equipment operators one maintenance worker.
Equipment Projects	
Maintain, repair, and replace equipment as necessary.	Replace equipment (various MMS projects). Replace vehicles (various MMS projects).
Facility Projects	
Maintain, repair, and replace facilities as necessary.	Replace bulkheads, water control structures, parking lots, wildlife observation platforms, and kiosks (various MMS projects).

REFUGE ADMINISTRATION

Periodic upgrading of facilities is necessary for safety and accessibility and to support staff and management needs. The staff has identified funding and staffing needs for several projects, including additional facilities and equipment to support refuge operation and maintenance.

FUNDING AND PERSONNEL

Until recently, the Service had approved a staff of 7.5 full-time equivalent permanent positions for the refuge (the park ranger and maintenance mechanic positions were abolished after becoming vacant). There are 7.5 full-time equivalent positions funded for fire management.

To complete the extensive wildlife habitat management and restoration projects and conduct the necessary inventorying, monitoring, and mapping activities, the refuge requires more staff. The proposed staffing plan (Table 28) would enable the refuge to achieve the plan objectives and strategies of this CCP within a reasonable time. The annual cost (including salaries and benefits) would be $2,151,000.

Table 28. Proposed staff for the Pocosin Lakes NWR

Position	Program	Employment Status
Management Staff		
Project Leader (GS-0485-13)*	Refuge	PFT
Deputy Project Leader (GS-0485-12)*	Refuge	PFT
Assistant Manager (Restoration) (GS-0485-9)**	Refuge	PFT
Office Assistant (GS-0303-07)*	50% Refuge 50% Fire	PFT
Office Assistant/Receptionist (GS-0303-04)**	Refuge	PFT
Biological Staff		
Wildlife Biologist (GS-0486-11)*	Refuge	PFT
Biological Technician (GS-0404-9)**	Refuge	PFT
Biological Technician (GS-0404-7)**	Refuge	PFT
Visitor Service Staff		
Park Ranger (GS-0025-09)*	Refuge	PFT
Park Ranger (Environmental Education)(GS-0025-07)**	Refuge	PFT
Refuge Aid (Visitor Center)(GS-0189-03)**	Refuge	PFT
Maintenance Staff		
Crane Operator (WG-5725-09)*	Refuge	PFT
Maintenance Mechanic (WG-5716-08)*	Refuge	PFT
Equipment Operator (WG-5716-08)*	Refuge	PFT
Equipment Operator (WG-5716-09)**	Refuge	PFT
Equipment Operator (WG-5716-09)**	Refuge	PFT
Maintenance Worker (WG-5716-08)**	Refuge	PFT
Law Enforcement Staff		
Law Enforcement Officer (GS-0025-9)**	Refuge	PFT
Fire Management Staff		
Fire Management Specialist (GS-0401-11)*	Fire	PFT
Equipment Operator (Fire) (WG-5716-08)*	Fire	PFT
Equipment Operator (Fire) (WG-5716-08)*	Fire	PFT
Equipment Operator (Fire) (WG-5716-08)*	Fire	PFT
Forestry Technician (Fire) (GS-0462-06)*	Fire	PFT
Forestry Technician (Fire) (GS-0462-05)*	Fire	PFT
Forestry Technician (Fire) (GS-0462-04)*	Fire	PFT

*Existing Positions, ** Proposed Additional Positions*
PFT = permanent full time, TFT = temporary full time, PS = permanent seasonal

VOLUNTEERS

The refuge currently uses 2,000 hours of volunteer service annually. College interns contribute the majority of the volunteer service. The interns reside at the field station on Lake Phelps and receive a stipend for their meals. The plan projects an increase of volunteer service to 4,000 hours. The refuge will increase recruiting of college interns and volunteers from the community. The refuge will also construct pads for recreational vehicles to facilitate the recruitment of workampers, who volunteer on the refuge in exchange for the recreational vehicle pad.

PARTNERSHIP OPPORTUNITIES

A major objective of this CCP is to establish partnerships with local volunteers, landowners, private organizations, and State and Federal natural resource agencies. In the immediate vicinity of the refuge, opportunities exist to establish partnerships with sporting clubs, elementary and secondary schools, and community organizations. At regional and State levels, the Service might establish partnerships with organizations such as the North Carolina Wildlife Resources Commission, North Carolina Division of Marine Fisheries, The Nature Conservancy, Ducks Unlimited, Partnership for the Sounds, North Carolina Coastal Reserve Program, Pettigrew State Park, National Audubon Society, and the National Wildlife Federation.

STEP-DOWN MANAGEMENT PLANS

A comprehensive conservation plan is a strategic plan that guides the future direction of the refuge. Before the refuge staff can implement some of the strategies and projects, it must prepare or update detailed step-down management plans. To assist in preparing and implementing the step-down plans, the refuge staff will develop partnerships with local agencies and organizations. The plans will be developed in accordance with the National Environmental Policy Act, which requires the identification and evaluation of alternatives and public review and involvement prior to their implementation.

Habitat Management Plan (Develop). This plan will describe the overall desired future habitat conditions needed to fulfill refuge purpose and objectives. The plan will include sections on management for moist-soil and water-management units, forest habitat, croplands, and other habitat types. The staff will develop the procedures, techniques, and timetables for achieving desired future conditions into an overall plan.

Moist Soil/Water Management Section of Habitat Management Plan (Update). This plan will describe the strategies and procedures (timing and duration of flooding and disturbance) for manipulating the refuge's water management units to meet habitat management objectives.

Forest Habitat Section of Habitat Management Plan (Develop). This plan will describe strategies for meeting refuge forest management objectives. It will include direction on reforestation, stand improvement, and harvest. Also, the plan will address scrub/shrub habitat management.

Fire Management Plan (Update). This plan will describe wild and prescribed fire management techniques that the refuge will employ. Wildfire control descriptions will include initial attack strategies and cooperative agreements with other agencies.

Biological Inventory/Monitoring Plan (Develop). This plan will describe inventory and monitoring techniques and time frames. The refuge staff will inventory all plant communities and associations in the refuge; all trust species (migratory birds, including songbirds, neotropical passerines, and waterfowl); listed species (Federal and State threatened, endangered, and species of concern); and key resident species. It will monitor population trends. These data are essential to guide wildlife habitat management.

Integrated Pest Management Plan (Develop and Update). This plan will address the complex issue of bringing exotic and nuisance plants and animals to a maintenance control level on the refuge. It will cover chemical pesticide use (aerial and ground application), mechanical eradication, and biological controls. The Nuisance/Exotic Animal and Plant Control plans will be sections of this plan.

Nuisance/Exotic Animal Control Plan (Update). This plan (as part of the Integrated Pest Management Plan) will describe survey, removal or control, and monitoring techniques for both terrestrial and aquatic nuisance and exotic animals (vertebrate and invertebrate). This plan will include nutria and feral hog control.

Nuisance/Exotic Plant Control Plan (Develop). This plan (as part of the Integrated Pest Management Plan) will describe survey, removal or control, and monitoring techniques for both terrestrial and aquatic nuisance and exotic plants.

Visitor Services Plan (Develop). This plan will describe the refuge's wildlife-dependent recreation programs. It will address specific issues or items, such as facility requirements, site plans, and handicapped accessibility. The environmental education and interpretation, fishing, hunting, and sign plans will be sections of this plan.

Environmental Education Section of Visitor Services Plan (Develop). This plan will reflect the objectives and strategies of the CCP and address environmental education guidelines following Service standards.

Fishing Section of Visitor Services Plan (Update). This plan will address specific aspects of the refuge's fishing program. It will define fishing areas, methods, handicapped accessibility, facilities needed, and refuge-specific regulations.

Hunting Section of Visitor Services Plan (Update). This plan will address specific aspects of the refuge's hunting program. It will define species to be hunted, season structures, hunt areas, methods, all-terrain vehicle use, handicapped accessibility, facilities needed, and refuge-specific hunting regulations.

Sign Section of Visitor Services Plan (Update). This plan will describe the refuge's strategy for informing visitors via signage. It will incorporate Service guidelines.

Law Enforcement Plan (Develop). This plan will provide a reference to station policies, procedures, priorities, and programs concerning law enforcement.

Land Protection Plan (Develop). This plan will propose to expand the boundaries of the approved acquisition boundaries to include land between irregular boundaries and roads, and important habitats (red-cockaded woodpecker habitat and riparian areas). The plan will facilitate habitat management (prescribed fire and water), law enforcement, and the protection of important habitats. As stated earlier in the plan, no acquisition boundary was identified when the refuge was established.

MONITORING AND ADAPTIVE MANAGEMENT

Adaptive management is a flexible approach to long-term management of biotic resources under which the staff utilizes the results of ongoing monitoring activities and other information to evaluate and change practices. More specifically, adaptive management is a process by which projects are implemented within a framework of scientifically driven experiments to test the predictions and assumptions outlined within a CCP.

To apply adaptive management, the staff would adopt specific survey, inventory, and monitoring protocols for the refuge. It would evaluate habitat management strategies systematically to determine management effects on wildlife populations, and utilize the information to refine approaches and determine how effectively the objectives are being accomplished. Evaluations would include ecosystem team and other appropriate partner participation. If monitoring and evaluation indicate undesirable effects for target and non-target species and/or communities, then the refuge would alter management projects. Subsequently, the staff would revise this CCP.

The Service would describe specific monitoring and evaluation activities in the step-down management plans.

Appendix I. Glossary

Adaptive Management	A process in which projects are implemented within a framework of scientifically driven experiments to test predictions and assumptions outlined within the comprehensive conservation plan. The analysis of the outcome of project implementation helps managers determine whether current management should continue as is or whether it should be modified to achieve desired conditions.
Alternative	Alternatives are different means of accomplishing refuge purposes, goals, and objectives and contributing to the mission of the National Wildlife Refuge System.
Approved Acquisition Boundary	A project boundary that the Director of the Fish and Wildlife Service approves upon completion of the detailed planning and environmental compliance process.
Biological Diversity	The variety of life and its processes, including the variety of living organisms, the genetic differences among them, and the communities and ecosystems in which they occur. The National Wildlife Refuge System focus is on indigenous species, biotic communities, and ecological processes.
Biological Integrity	The biotic composition, structure, and functioning at genetic, organism, and community levels comparable with historic conditions including the natural biological processes that shape genomes, organisms, and communities.
Canopy	A layer of foliage; generally the upper-most layer in a forest stand. It can be used to refer to mid- or under-story vegetation in multi-layered stands. Canopy closure is an estimate of the amount of overhead tree cover (also canopy cover).
Categorical Exclusion	A category of actions that do not individually or cumulatively have a significant effect on the human environment and have been found to have no such effect in procedures adopted by a federal agency pursuant to the National Environmental Policy Act of 1969.
CFR	Code of Federal Regulations.

Compatible Use	A wildlife-dependent recreational use or any other use of a refuge that, in the sound professional judgment of the refuge manager, will not materially interfere with, or detract from, the fulfillment of the mission or the purposes of the refuge. A compatibility determination supports the selection of compatible uses and identifies stipulations or limits necessary to ensure compatibility.
Comprehensive Conservation Plan	A document that describes the desired future conditions of the refuge; provides long-range guidance and management direction for the refuge manager to accomplish the purposes, goals, and objectives of the refuge; and contributes to the mission of the National Wildlife Refuge System and meets relevant mandates.
Conservation Easement	A legal document that provides specific land-use rights to a secondary party. A perpetual conservation easement usually grants conservation and management rights to a party in perpetuity.
Cooperative Agreement	A simple habitat protection action in which no property right is acquired. An agreement is usually long-term and can be modified by either party. Lands under a cooperative agreement do not necessarily become part of the National Wildlife Refuge System.
Corridor	A route that allows movement of individuals from one region or place to another.
Cover Type	The present vegetation of an area.
Cultural Resources	The remains of sites, structures, or objects used by people of the past.
Cypress and Tupelo Swamp	Found in low-lying areas, swales, and open ponds that hold water several months, if not all of the year. Large hollow trees are used as bear den sites.
Deciduous	Pertaining to perennial plants that are leafless for sometime during the year.
Ecological Succession	The orderly progression of an area through time in the absence of disturbance from one vegetative community to another.
Ecosystem	A dynamic and interrelating complex of plant and animal communities and their associated non-living environment.
Ecosystem Management	Management of natural resources using systemwide concepts to ensure that all plants and animals in ecosystems are maintained at viable levels in native habitats and basic ecosystem processes are perpetuated indefinitely.

Environmental Health	It is the composition, structure, and functioning of soil, water, air, and other abiotic features comparable with historic conditions, including the natural abiotic processes that shape the environment.
Even-Aged Forests	Forests that are composed of trees with a time span of less than 20 years between oldest and youngest individuals.
Endangered Species	A plant or animal species listed under the Endangered Species Act that is in danger of extinction throughout all or a significant portion of its range.
Endemic Species	Plants or animals that occur naturally in a certain region and whose distribution is relatively limited to a particular locality.
Environmental Assessment	A concise document, prepared in compliance with the National Environmental Policy Act, that briefly discusses the purpose and need for an action, alternatives to such action, and provides sufficient evidence and analysis of impacts to determine whether to prepare an environmental impact statement or finding of no significant impact.
Fauna	All the vertebrate or invertebrate animals of an area.
Federal Trust Species	All species where the Federal Government has primary jurisdiction including federally threatened or endangered species, migratory birds, anadromous fish, and certain marine mammals.
Fee-title	The acquisition of most or all of the rights to a tract of land. There is a total transfer of property rights with the formal conveyance of a title. While a fee title acquisition involves most rights to a property, certain rights may be reserved or not purchased, including water rights, mineral rights, or use reservation (the ability to continue using the land for a specified time period, or the reminder of the owner's life).
Finding of No Significant Impact	A document prepared in compliance with the National Environmental Policy Act and supported by an environmental assessment that briefly presents why a federal action will have no significant effect on the human environment and for which an environmental impact statement, therefore, will not be prepared.
Floodplain Woods	Bottomland Hardwood Forests. Consists of hardwoods (old growth and mid-succession age timber) and cypress tupelo stands found on low ridges that drain slowly and are subject to flooding. Species include overcup, willow, water oaks, sweetgum, and green ash, and old growth - typically exceeding 120 years of age. Red oaks were removed in the 1940s. Mid-succession - logged timber that may need restoration to improve wildlife habitat; missing several key oak species.

Fragmentation	The process of reducing the size and connectivity of habitat patches; the disruption of extensive habitats into isolated and small patches.
Goal	Descriptive, open-ended, and often broad statements of desired future conditions that convey a purpose but does not define measurable units.
Geographic Information System	A computer system capable of storing and manipulating spatial data.
Ground Story (flora)	Vascular plants less than one meter in height, excluding tree seedlings.
Herbaceous Wetland	Annually or seasonally inundated with vegetation consisting primarily of grasses, sedges, rushes, and cattail.
Historic Conditions	These are the composition, structure, and functioning of ecosystems resulting from natural processes that we believe, based on sound professional judgment, were present prior to substantial human-related changes to the landscape.
Habitat	The place where an organism lives. The existing environmental conditions required by an organism for survival and reproduction.
Indicator Species	A species of plants or animals that is assumed to be sensitive to habitat changes and represents the needs of a larger group of species.
In-holding	Privately owned land inside the boundary of a national wildlife refuge.
Issue	Any unsettled matter that requires a management decision.
Migratory	The seasonal movement from one area to another and back.
Monitoring	The process of collecting information to track changes of selected parameters over time.
National Environmental Policy	Requires all agencies, including the Service, to examine the environmental impacts of their actions, incorporate environmental information, and use public participation in the planning and implementation of all actions. Federal agencies must integrate this Act with other planning requirements, and prepare appropriate policy documents to facilitate better environmental decision-making.
National Wildlife Refuge	A designated area of land, water, or an interest in land or water within the National Wildlife Refuge System.

National Wildlife Refuge System	Various categories of areas administered by the Secretary of the Interior for the conservation of fish and wildlife, including species threatened with extinction, all lands, waters, and interests therein administered by the Secretary as wildlife refuges, wildlife ranges, game ranges, wildlife management areas, or waterfowl production areas.
Native Species	Species that normally live and thrive in a particular ecosystem.
Neotropical Migratory Bird	A bird species that breeds north of the United States/Mexican border and winters primarily south of that border.
Objective	An objective is a concise quantitative (where possible) target statement of what will be achieved. Objectives are derived from goals and provide the basis for determining management strategies. Objectives should be attainable and time-specific.
Planning Area	A planning area may include lands outside existing planning unit boundaries that are being studied for inclusion in the unit and/or partnership planning efforts. It may also include watersheds or ecosystems that affect the planning area.
Planning Team	A planning team prepares the comprehensive conservation plan. Planning teams are interdisciplinary in membership and function. A team generally consists of the a planning team leader; refuge manager, and staff biologists; staff specialists or other representatives of Service programs, ecosystems, or regional offices; and State partnering wildlife agencies, as appropriate.
Preferred Alternative	This is the alternative determined by the decision maker to best achieve the refuge purpose, vision, and goals; contributes to the Refuge System mission, addresses the significant issues; and is consistent with principles of sound fish and wildlife management.
Purpose of the Refuge	The purpose of the refuge is specified in or derived from the law, proclamation, executive order, agreement, public land order, donation document, or administrative memorandum establishing, authorizing, or expanding a refuge and refuge unit.
Refuge Operating Needs System	This is a national database that contains the unfunded operational needs of each refuge. Projects included are those required to implement approved plans and meet goals, objectives, and legal mandates.
Refuge Purposes	The purposes specified in or derived from the law, proclamation, executive order, agreement, public land order, donation document, or administrative memorandum establishing, authorizing, or expanding a refuge, refuge unit, or refuge subunit.

Seral Forest	A forest in the mature stage of development, usually dominated by large, old trees.
Sink	A habitat in which local mortality exceeds local reproductive success for a given species.
Sink Population	A population in a low-quality habitat in which birth rate is generally less than the death rate and population density is maintained by immigrants from source populations.
Source	A habitat in which local reproductive success exceeds local mortality for a given species.
Source Population	A population in a high-quality habitat in which birth rate greatly exceeds death rate and the excess individuals leave as migrants.
Step-down Management Plans	Step-down management plans provide the details necessary to implement management strategies and projects identified in the comprehensive conservation plan.
Strategy	A specific action, tool, or technique or combination of actions, tools, and techniques used to meet unit objectives.
Threatened Species	Species listed under the Endangered Species Act that are likely to become endangered within the foreseeable future throughout all or a significant portion of their range.
Trust Species	Species for which the Fish and Wildlife Service has primary responsibility, including most federally listed threatened and endangered species, anadromous fish once they enter the inland coastal waterways, and migratory birds.
Understory	Any vegetation with canopy below or closer to the ground than canopies of other plants.
Wildlife Corridor	A landscape feature that facilitates the biologically effective transport of animals between larger patches of habitat dedicated to conservation functions. Such corridors may facilitate several kinds of traffic, including frequent foraging movement, seasonal migration, or the once in a lifetime dispersal of juvenile animals. These are transition habitats and need not contain all the habitat elements required by migrants for long-term survival or reproduction.
Wildlife-Dependent Recreation	A use of a refuge involving hunting, fishing, wildlife observation, wildlife photography, and environmental education and interpretation. The National Wildlife Refuge System Improvement Act of 1997 specifies that these are the six priority general public uses of the system.

Appendix II. References and Literature Cited

Barick, F.B. and T.S. Critcher. 1975. Wildlife and land use planning with particular reference to coastal counties. North Carolina Wildlife Resources Commission. Raleigh, NC. 168 pp.

Bellrose, F.C. 1976. Ducks, geese, and swans of North America. Stackhole Books, Harrisburg, PA. 544 pp.

Buell, M.F., and R.L. Cain. 1943. The successional role of white cedar (Chamaecyparis thyoides) in southeastern North Carolina. Ecology 24:85-93

Chapman, J. A., G. A Feldhamer. 1987. Wild Mammals of North America. p. 1059 – 1076. The Johns Hopkins University Press. Baltimore, MD.

Christensen, N. L. 1981. Fire regimes in southeastern ecosystems. p. 112-136. In: H. A. Mooney et al. (eds). Fire regimes and ecosystem properties. USDA Forest Service General Technical Report. WO-26, Washington, DC.

Christensen, N. L., R. B. Burchell, A. Liggett, and E. L. Simms. 1981. The structure and development of pocosin vegetation. p. 43-61. In: C. J. Richardson (ed.). Pocosin wetlands: an integrated analysis of Coastal Plain freshwater bogs in North Carolina. Hutchinson Ross. Stroudsburg, PA.

Christopher Newport University. 1997. Proceedings of Symposium: Atlantic white cedar: ecology and management. Aug. 6-7, 1997, Newport News, VA.

Collins, J. 2005. Tent Caterpillars. University of Kentucky, College of Agriculture, Department of Entomology. Accessed website on October 5, 2005. www.uky.edu/agriculture/entomology/entfacts/trees/ef424.htm.

Cowardin, L. et. al. 1979. Classification of Wetlands and Deepwater Habitats of the United States. United States Fish and Wildlife Service Office of Biological Services FWS/OBS-79/31. 131 pgs.

Cowardin, L. M., V. Carter, F. C. Golet, and E. T. Laroe. 1995. Classification of wetlands and deepwater habitats of the United States. U. S. Fish and Wildlife Service, Office of Biological Service, U.S. Department of the Interior, Washington, DC. FWS/OBS-79/31. 131 pp.

Davis, K. N., B. Henderson and S. Daniels. 1997. Inventory of Atlantic white-cedar remnant stands in North Carolina. U. S. Air Force, BPA No. F31610-95-AV026

Dolman, J. D. and S. W. Buol. 1968. Organic soils on the Lower Coastal Plain of North Carolina. Soil Science Society of America Proceedings 32: 414-418.

Drayton, E. R. III and D. D. Hook. 1988. Water management of a baldcypress-tupelo wetland for timber and wildlife. p. 54-58. In: D. D. Hook and R. Lea (eds). Proceedings of Symposium - The Forested Wetlands of the Southeastern United States, 12-14 July 1988. Orlando, FL Southeastern Forest Experiment Station, Clemson University, North Carolina State University, The Man and the Biosphere Program.

Eubanks, Ted, Paul Kerlinger, and R.H. Payne 1993. High Island, Texas, A Case Study in Avitourism, Birding 25(6):415-420).

Eubanks, Ted, and John Stoll. 1999. Avitourism in Texas: Two Studies of Birders in Texas and Their Potential Support for the Proposed World Birding Center. Texas Parks and Wildlife Contract No. 44467.

Frayer, W.E., T.J. Monahan, D.C. Bowen and F.A. Graybill. 1983. Status and trends of wetlands and deepwater habitats in the conterminous United States: 1950's to 1970's. U.S. Fish and Wildlife Service, Washington, DC. 32pp.

Fredrickson, L.H. and M.E. Heitmeyer. 1988. Waterfowl Use of Forested Wetlands of the Southern United States: An Overview. Pages 307-323 in M.W. Weller, editor. Waterfowl in Winter. University of Minnesota Press, Minneapolis, Minnesota.

Frost, C.C. 1987. Historical overview of Atlantic white cedar in the Carolinas. p. 257-264. *In*: A. D. Laderman (ed). Atlantic white cedar wetlands. Westview Press, Boulder, CO.

Frost, C. C. 1995. Presettlement fire regimes in southeastern marshes, peatlands, and swamps. p. 39-60. *In:* S. I. Cerulean and R. T. Engstrom (eds). Fire in wetlands: a management perspective. Proceedings 19th Tall Timbers Research Conference, Tall Timbers Research Station, Tallahassee, FL.

Frost, C. C., H. E. LeGrand, Jr., and R. E. Schneider. 1992. Regional inventory for critical natural areas, wetland ecosystems and endangered species habitats of the Albemarle-Pamlico estuarine region : phase 1. North Carolina Natural Heritage Program, Division of Parks and Recreation; Department of Environment, Health, and Natural Resources, Raleigh, NC. Albemarle-Pamlico Estuarine Study No. 90-01. 441 pp.

Hamel, P.B. 1992. The Land Manager's Guide to the Birds of the South. The Nature Conservancy and the United States Department of Agriculture Forest Service. Atlanta, Georgia.

Hefner, J.H. and J.D. Brown. 1984. Wetland trends in the southeastern United States. Wetlands 4:1-11.

Hinesley, L.E. 1999. Pocosin Lakes National Wildlife Refuge Forest Habitat Management Plan. North Carolina State University. 80 pp.

Hinesley, L. E. and A. M. Wicker. 1996. Atlantic white cedar wetland restoration project, Pocosin Lakes National Wildlife Refuge: report for 1st year of 319 Demonstration Project. North Carolina State University., Raleigh, NC, and U. S. Fish & Wildlife Service, Raleigh, NC. 30 pp.

Hinesley, L. E. and A. M. Wicker. 1997. Atlantic white cedar wetland restoration project, Pocosin Lakes National Wildlife Refuge: report for 2nd year of 319 Demonstration Project. North Carolina State Univ., Raleigh, NC, and U. S. Fish & Wildlife Service, Raleigh, NC. 38 pp.

Hinesley, L. E. and A. M. Wicker. 1998. Atlantic white cedar wetland restoration project, Pocosin Lakes National Wildlife Refuge: report for 3rd year of 319 Demonstration Project. North Carolina State University, Raleigh, NC, and U. S. Fish & Wildlife Service, Raleigh. NC, 16 pp.

Hinesley, L. E. and A. M. Wicker. 1999. Atlantic white cedar wetland restoration project, Pocosin Lakes National Wildlife Refuge: report for 4th year of 319 Demonstration Project. North Carolina State University, Raleigh, NC, and U. S. Fish & Wildlife Service, Raleigh, NC. 17 pp.

Hinesley, L. E., L. K. Snelling, G. A. Pierce, and A. M. Wicker. 1998. Effect of peat amendments, shade and seedling size on growth of Atlantic white cedar transplants. Southern Journal of Applied Forestry 23: 5-10.

Hinesley, L. E., L. K. Snelling, G. A. Pierce, and A. M. Wicker. In press. Effect of peat amendments, shade and seedling size on growth of Atlantic white cedar transplants. Southern Journal of Appled Forestry.

Hughes, J. 1995. Weyerhaeuser Company is helping with the effort to restore Atlantic white cedar in coastal North Carolina. Paper presented at workshop titled Current Developments with White-cedar Management. Sponsored by North Carolina Forest Service, Aug. 1-3, 1995. Washington, NC No published proceedings.

Hunter, W.C., D.N. Pashley and R.E.F. Escano.1992. Neotropical migratory land bird species and their habitats of special concern within the Southeast region. Pages 159-169 in D.M.

Hunter, W.C., L.H. Peoples, and J.A. Collazo. 2001. South Atlantic Coastal Plain Partners in Flight Bird Conservation Plan.

Kerlinger, P. 1994. The Economic Impact of Birding Ecotourism on Communities Surrounding Eight National Wildlife Refuges.

Kerlinger, P. 1999. Birding Tourism and Dauphin Island.

Kologiski, R. 1977. The phytosociology of the Green Swamp, North Carolina. North Carolina Agricultural Experiment Station technical Bulletin No. 250.

LeGrand, Jr., H. E., C. C. Frost, J. O. Fussell, III. 1992. Regional inventory for critical natural areas, wetland ecosystems and endangered species habitats of the Albemarle-Pamlico estuarine region: phase 2. North Carolina Natural Heritage Program, Division of Parks and Recreation, Department of Environment, Health, and Natural Resources, Raleigh, NC. Albemarle-Pamlico Estuarine Study No. 92-07, 506 pp.

Lynch, J. M. and S. L. Peacock. 1982a. Natural areas inventory of Hyde County, North Carolina. North Carolina Coastal Energy Impact Program Rpt. No. 28. Department of Natural Resources and Community Development, Raleigh, NC.

Lynch, J. M. and S. L. Peacock. 1982b. Natural areas inventory of Washington County, North Carolina. North Carolina Coastal Energy Impact Program Report No. 30. Department of Natural Resources and Community Development, Raleigh, NC.

Mathis, M.A. and J.J. Crow. 2000. The Prehistory of North Carolina: An Archaeological Symposium.

Matoon, W. R. 1915. Southern cypress. USDA Bulletin 272. 74 pp.

McDonald, C. B. and A. M. Ash. 1981. Natural areas inventory of Tyrrell County, North Carolina. North Carolina Coastal Energy Impact Program Report No. 8. Department of Natural Resources and Community Development, Raleigh, NC.

McManus, M., N. Schneeberger, R. Reardon, G. Mason,. 1989, revised 1992. Forest Insect and Disease Leaflet. USDA, United States Forest Service. Accessed website on 10/5/2005. www.na.fs.fed.us/spfo/pubs/fidls/gypsymoth/gypsy.htm.

Mitsch, W.J. and J.G. Gosselink. 1993. Wetlands. Second Edition. Van Nostrand Reinhold, New York, New York. 722 pp.

National Audubon Society. 1998. Campaign on HR 3267.

New Jersey Department of Environmental Protection, 2000. Wildlife-Associated Recreation on the New Jersey Delaware Bayshore.

North Carolina Economic Security Commission. 2002. Largest Employers by County.

North Carolina Economic Security Commission. 2004. Unemployment Rates by County.

North Carolina Division of Parks and Recreation. 2001. North Carolina Coastal Plain Paddle Trails Guide.

Odum, H. T. 1984. Summary: cypress swamps and their regional role. p. 416-443. *In*: C. E. Katherine and H. T. Odum (eds). 1984. Cypress swamps. University Presses of Florida, Gainsville, FL.

Pinchot, G. and W. W. Ashe. 1897. Timber trees and forests of North Carolina. M. I. & J. C. Stewart, North Carolina Geological Survey Bulletin No. 6, 227 pp.

Radford, A. E., H. E. Ahles, C. R. Bell. 1968. Manual of the Vascular Flora of the Carolinas. The University of North Carolina Press, Chapell Hill, NC, 1183 pp.

Richardson, C. J. 1991. Pocosins: An ecological perspective. Wetlands 11: 335-354.

Richardson, C. J., R. Evans, and D. Carr. 1981. Pocosins: an ecosystem in transition. p. 3-19. *In*: C. J. Richardson (ed). Pocosin wetlands: an integrated analysis of coastal plain freshwater bogs in North Carolina. Hutchinson Ross Publishing Company, Stroudsburg, PA.

Riggs, S.R. and D.K. Belknap. 1988. Upper Cenozoic processes and environments of continental margin sedimentation: eastern United States, p. 131-176 *in* Sheridan, R.E., and J.A. Graw, eds. The Geology of North America, Vol. 1-2, the Atlantic Continental Margin, U.S. Geological Society of America.

Robison, T.M. 1977. Public water supplies of North Carolina, Northern Coastal Plain. U.S. Department of the Interior, pp. 49-50.

Roman, C. T., R. E. Good, and S. Little. 1990. Ecology of Atlantic white cedar swamps in the New Jersey pinelands. p. 163-173. *In*: D. F. Whigham, R. E. Good, J. Kvet, and N. F. Good (eds). Wetland ecology and management: case studies. (Tasks for vegetation science 25). Kluwer Academic Publishers, London.

Ruffin, E. 1839. "Jottings Down in the swamps". Farmers Register III: 698-733. Edmund Ruffin, Publisher, Petersburg, VA.

Ruffin, E. 1861. The origin and manner of geological formation of the great swamps of the Atlantic Coast. p. 155-249. *In*: Agricultural, geological and descriptive sketches of lower North Carolina and the similar adjacent lands. North Carolina Agricultural and Geological Survey, Raleigh, NC. Printed at the Institution for the Deaf & Dumb & the Blind, Raleigh, NC.

Schafale, M.P. and Weakely, A.S. 1990. Classification of the Natural Communities of North Carolina. Third Approximation. North Carolina Natural Heritage Program. Raleigh, NC. 325 pp.

Saltonstall, K. 2002. Cryptic invasion by a non-native genotype of *Phragmites australis* into North America. Proceedings of the National Academy of Sciences, USA. 99(4): 2445-2449.

Tetterton B. and G. Tetterton. (1998) North Carolina County Fact Book. Vols. I and II. Broadfoot's of Wendell, Wendell, NC.

Townsend, L., Rieske-kinney, L. 2000. Southern Pine Beetle Biology. University of Kentucky, College of Agriculture, Department of Entomology. Accessed website on October 5, 2005. www.uky.edu/agriculture/entomology/entfacts/trees/ef423.htm.

Tuedten, S. accessed website on 10/5/2005. The Best Control (second ed). Fire Ant-Factoids. Biology and Identification of Fire Ants. www.safe2use.com/pests/fireants/factoids.htm.

U.S. Department of Agriculture. 1997. Census of Agriculture, North Carolina, 1997. Washington, D.C.: U.S. Department of Agriculture.

U.S. Department of Agriculture, Forest Service. 1991. Forest Statistics for North Carolina Counties - 1991. Resource Bulletin SE-120, Washington, D.C.: U.S. Government Printing Office.

U.S. Department of Agriculture, Natural Resources Conservation Service. 1999. Soil Survey of Hyde County, North Carolina.

U.S. Department of Agriculture, Soil Conservation Service. 1988. Soil Survey of Tyrrell County, North Carolina.

U.S. Department of Agriculture, Soil Conservation Service. 1981. Soil Survey of Washington County, North Carolina.

U.S. Department of Agriculture. Soil Conservation Service. 1985. Hydric soils of the State of North Carolina 1985. U.S. Department of Agriculture, Soil Conservation Service in cooperation with the National Technical Committee for Hydric Soils. Washington, DC. unpaginated.

U.S. Department of Commerce, Bureau of the Census. 2000. U.S.A. Counties 2000, General Profile, Hyde County, North Carolina. Washington, D.C.:U.S. Government Printing Office.

U.S. Department of Commerce, Bureau of the Census. 1997. Economic Census, Hyde County, North Carolina. Washington, D.C.: U.S. Government Printing Office.

U.S. Department of Commerce, Bureau of the Census, Small Area Income and Poverty Estimates Program. 2000. Model-Based Income and Poverty Estimates for Hyde County, North Carolina. Washington, D.C.: U.S. Government Printing Office.

U.S. Department of Commerce, Bureau of the Census. 2000. U.S.A. Counties 2000, General Profile, Tyrrell County, North Carolina. Washington, D.C.:U.S. Government Printing Office.

U.S. Department of Commerce, Bureau of the Census. 1997. Economic Census, Tyrrell County, North Carolina. Washington, D.C.: U.S. Government Printing Office.

U.S. Department of Commerce, Bureau of the Census, Small Area Income and Poverty Estimates Program. 2000. Model-Based Income and Poverty Estimates for Tyrrell County, North Carolina. Washington, D.C.: U.S. Government Printing Office.

U.S. Department of Commerce, Bureau of the Census. 2000. U.S.A. Counties 2000, General Profile, Washington County, North Carolina. Washington, D.C.:U.S. Government Printing Office.

U.S. Department of Commerce, Bureau of the Census. 1997. Economic Census, Washington County, North Carolina. Washington, D.C.: U.S. Government Printing Office.

U.S. Department of Commerce, Bureau of the Census, Small Area Income and Poverty Estimates Program. 2000. Model-Based Income and Poverty Estimates for Washington County, North Carolina. Washington, D.C.: U.S. Government Printing Office.

U.S. Environmental Protection Agency. 1997. Nature-Based Tourism.

U.S. Fish and Wildlife Service. 1981. Significant wildlife resource areas of North Carolina. U.S. Fish and Wildlife Service. Asheville Area Office. Asheville, NC. 139 pp.

U.S. Fish and Wildlife Service. 2001. National Survey of Fishing, Hunting and Wildlife Associated Recreation.

U.S. Fish and Wildlife Service. 2001. National Survey of Fishing, Hunting, and Wildlife Associated Recreation - North Carolina.

U.S. Fish and Wildlife Service. 2005. Banking on Nature 2004: The Economic Benefits to Local Communities of National Wildlife Refuge Visitation. 444 pp.

Vogelsang, Hans, 2001. Assessing the Economic Impact of Ecotourism Developments on the Albemarle/Pamlico Region.

Weakely, A. S. and M. P. Schafale. 1991. Classification of pocosins of the Carolina coastal plain. Wetlands 11: 355-374. North Carolina Natural Heritage Program, Raleigh, NC.

Whitehead, D. R. 1972. Development and environmental history of the Dismal Swamp. Ecological Monograph 42: 301-305.

Whitehead, D. R. and R. Q. Oaks, Jr. 1979. Developmental history of the Dismal Swamp. p. 25-43. *In*: P. W. Kirk (ed). The Great Dismal Swamp. University Press of Virginia, Charlottesville, VA.

Appendix III. Relevant Legal Mandates

National Wildlife Refuge System Authorities
The mission of the Fish and Wildlife Service is to conserve, protect, and enhance the Nation's fish and wildlife and their habitats for the continuing benefit of the American people. The Service is the primary Federal agency responsible for migratory birds, endangered plants and animals, certain marine mammals, and anadromous fish. This responsibility to conserve our Nation's fish and wildlife resources is shared with other Federal agencies and State and Tribal governments.

As part of this responsibility, the Service manages the National Wildlife Refuge System. This system is the only nationwide system of Federal land managed and protected for wildlife and their habitats. The mission of the National Wildlife Refuge System is to administer a national network of lands and waters for the conservation, management, and where appropriate, restoration of the fish, wildlife, and plant resources and their habitats within the United States for the benefit of present and future generations of Americans.

Pocosin Lakes NWR is managed as part of this system in accordance with the National Wildlife Refuge System Administration Act of 1966, as amended by the National Wildlife Refuge System Improvement Act of 1997, the Refuge Recreation Act of 1962, Executive Order 12996 (Management and General Public Use of the National Wildlife Refuge System), and other relevant legislation, executive orders, regulations, and policies.

Key Legislation/Policies for Plan Implementation
The Pocosin Lakes NWR Comprehensive Conservation Plan describes and illustrates management area projects with standards and guidelines for future decision-making and the staff may adjust them through monitoring and evaluation, as well as amendment and revision. The plan approval establishes conservation and land protection goals, objectives, and specific strategies for the refuge and its expansion. The refuge manager has identified and approved compatible recreation uses specific to the refuge. This plan provides for systematic stepping down from the overall direction as outlined when making project or activity level decisions. This level involves site-specific analysis (e.g., Forest Habitat Management Plan) to meet National Environmental Policy Act requirements for decision-making.

Antiquities Act (1906): Authorizes the scientific investigation of antiquities on federal land and provides penalties for unauthorized removal of objects taken or collected without a permit.

Migratory Bird Treaty Act (1918): Designates the protection of migratory birds as a federal responsibility. This Act enables the setting of seasons, and other regulations including the closing of areas, federal or non-federal, to the hunting of migratory birds.

Migratory Bird Conservation Act (1929): Establishes procedures for acquisition by purchase, rental, or gift of areas approved by the Migratory Bird Conservation Commission.

Migratory Bird Hunting and Conservation Stamp Act (1934): Authorized the opening of part of a refuge to waterfowl hunting.

Fish and Wildlife Act (1956): Established a comprehensive national fish and wildlife policy and broadened the authority for acquisition and development of refuges.

Fish and Wildlife Coordination Act (1958): Allows the Fish and Wildlife Service to enter into agreements with private landowners for wildlife management purposes.

Refuge Recreation Act (1962): Allows the use of refuges for recreation when such uses are compatible with the refuge's primary purposes and when sufficient funds are available to manage the uses.

Land and Water Conservation Fund Act (1965): Uses the receipts from the sale of surplus Federal land, outer continental shelf oil and gas sales, and other sources for land acquisition under several authorities.

National Wildlife Refuge System Administration Act of 1966 as amended by the National Wildlife Refuge System Improvement Act of 1997, 16 U.S.C. 668dd-668ee. (Refuge Administration Act): Defines the national wildlife refuge system and authorizes the Secretary of the Interior to permit any use of a refuge provided such use is compatible with the major purposes for which the refuge was established. The Refuge Improvement Act clearly defines a unifying mission for the Refuge System; establishes the legitimacy and appropriateness of the six priority public uses (hunting, fishing, wildlife observation, wildlife photography, and environmental education and interpretation); establishes a formal process for determining compatibility; established the responsibilities of the Secretary of the Interior for managing and protecting the Refuge System; and requires a comprehensive conservation plan for each refuge by the year 2012. This Act amended portions of the Refuge Recreation Act and National Wildlife Refuge System Administration Act of 1966.

Architectural Barriers Act (1968): Requires federally owned, leased, or funded buildings and facilities to be accessible to persons with disabilities.

National Environmental Policy Act (1969): Requires the disclosure of the environmental impacts of any major Federal action significantly affecting the quality of the human environment.

Endangered Species Act (1973): Requires all Federal agencies to carry out programs for the conservation of threatened and endangered species.

Rehabilitation Act (1973): Requires that programmatic and physical accessibility be made available in any facility funded by the Federal Government, ensuring that anyone can participate in any program.

Clean Water Act (1977): Requires consultation with the U.S. Army Corps of Engineers for major wetland modifications.

Executive Order 11988 (1977): Each Federal agency shall provide leadership and take action to reduce the risk of flood loss and minimize the impact of floods on human safety, and conserve the natural and beneficial values served by the flood plain.

Emergency Wetlands Resources Act (1986): The purpose of the Act is to promote the conservation of migratory waterfowl and to offset or prevent the serious loss of wetlands by the acquisition of wetlands and other essential habitat.

Federal Noxious Weed Act (1990): Requires the use of integrated management systems to control or contain undesirable plant species; and an interdisciplinary approach with the cooperation of other Federal and State agencies.

Americans with Disabilities Act (1992): Prohibits discrimination in public accommodations and services.

Executive Order 12996 Management and General Public Use of the National Wildlife Refuge System (1996): Defines the mission, purpose, and priority public uses of the National Wildlife Refuge System. It also presents four principles to guide management of the system.

Executive Order 13007 Indian Sacred Sites (1996): Directs Federal land management agencies to accommodate access to and ceremonial use of Indian sacred sites by Indian religious practitioners, avoid adversely affecting the physical integrity of such sacred sites, and where appropriate, maintain the confidentiality of sacred sites.

Emergency Wetland Resources Act of 1986: This Act authorized the purchase of wetlands with Land and Water Conservation Fund moneys, removing a prior prohibition on such acquisitions. The Act also requires the Secretary of the Interior to establish a National Wetlands Priority Conservation Plan, requires the states to include wetlands in their Comprehensive Outdoor Recreation Plans, and transfers to the Migratory Bird Conservation Fund an amount equal to import duties on arms and ammunition.

Endangered Species Act of 1973 (16 U.S.C. 1531-1544, 87 Stat. 884), as amended: Public Law 93-205, approved December 28, 1973, repealed the Endangered Species Conservation Act of December 5, 1969 (P.L. 91-135, 83 Stat. 275). The 1969 Act amended the Endangered Species Preservation Act of October 15, 1966 (P.L. 89-669, 80 Stat. 926). The 1973 Endangered Species Act provided for the conservation of ecosystems upon which threatened and endangered species of fish, wildlife, and plants depend, both through Federal action and by encouraging the establishment of State programs. The Act authorizes the determination and listing of species as threatened and endangered; prohibits unauthorized taking, possession, sale, and transport of endangered species; provides authority to acquire land for the conservation of listed species, using land and water conservation funds; authorizes establishment of cooperative agreements and grants-in-aid to states that establish and maintain active and adequate programs for threatened and endangered wildlife and plants; authorizes the assessment of civil and criminal penalties for violating the Act or regulations; and authorizes the payment of rewards to anyone furnishing information leading to arrest and conviction of anyone violating the Act and any regulation issued thereunder.

Environmental Education Act of 1990(20 USC 5501-5510; 104 Stat. 3325): Public Law 101-619, signed November 16, 1990, established the Office of Environmental Education within the Environmental Protection Agency to develop and administer a federal environmental education program. Responsibilities of the Office include developing and supporting programs to improve understanding of the natural and developed environment, and the relationships between humans and their environment; supporting the dissemination of educational materials; developing and supporting training programs and environmental education seminars; managing a federal grant program; and administering an environmental internship and fellowship program. The Office is required to develop and support environmental programs in consultation with other federal natural resource management agencies, including the Fish and Wildlife Service.

Executive Order 11988, Flood Plain Management: The purpose of this Executive Order, signed May 24, 1977, is to prevent Federal agencies from contributing to the adverse impacts associated with occupancy and modification of floodplains and the direct or indirect support of flood plain development. In the course of fulfilling their respective authorities, Federal agencies shall take action to reduce the risk of flood loss, to minimize the impact of floods on human safety, health and welfare, and to restore and conserve the natural and beneficial values served by flood plains.

Fish and Wildlife Improvement Act of 1978: This Act was passed to improve the administration of fish and wildlife programs and amends several earlier laws, including the Refuge Recreation Act, the National Wildlife Refuge System Administration Act, and the Fish and Wildlife Act of 1956. It authorizes the Secretary of the Interior to accept gifts and bequests of real and personal property on behalf of the United States. It also authorizes the use of volunteers on Service projects and appropriations to carry out volunteer programs.

Historic Preservation Acts include:

Antiquities Act (16 USC 431 - 433)--The Act of June 8, 1906, (34 Stat. 225): This Act authorizes the President of the United States to designate as National Monuments objects or areas of historic or scientific interests on lands owned or controlled by the United States. The Act required that a permit be obtained for examination of ruins, excavation of archaeological sites and the gathering of objects of antiquity on lands under the jurisdiction of the Secretaries of Interior, Agriculture, and Army, and provided penalties for violations.

Archaeological Resources Protection Act (16 U.S.C. 470aa - 47011) -- Public Law 96-95, approved October 31, 1979, (93 Stat. 721): This Act largely supplanted the resource protection provisions of the Antiquities Act for archaeological items. It established detailed requirements for issuance of permits for any excavation for or removal of archaeological resources from Federal and Indian lands. It also established civil and criminal penalties for the unauthorized excavation, removal, or damage of any such resources; for any trafficking in such resources removed from Federal and Indian lands in violation of any provision of Federal law; and for interstate and foreign commerce in such resources acquired, transported or received in violation of any State or local law.

Public Law 100-588, approved November 3, 1988, (102 Stat. 2983) lowered the threshold value of artifacts triggering the felony provisions of the Act from $5,000 to $500, made attempting to commit an action prohibited by the Act a violation, and required the land managing agencies to establish public awareness programs regarding the value of archaeological resources to the nation.

Archaeological and Historic Preservation Act (16 U.S.C. 469-469c) -- Public Law 86-523, approved June 27, 1960, (74 Stat. 220), and amended by Public Law 93-291, approved May 24, 1974, (88 Stat. 174): This Act directed Federal agencies to notify the Secretary of the Interior whenever a Federal, federally assisted, or licensed or permitted project may cause loss or destruction of significant scientific, prehistoric or archaeological data. The Act authorized use of appropriated, donated and/or transferred funds for the recovery, protection, and preservation of such data.

Historic Sites, Buildings and Antiquities Act (16 U.S.C. 461-462, 464-467) -- The Act of August 21, 1935, (49 Stat. 666) popularly known as the Historic Sites Act, as amended by Public Law 89-249, approved October 9, 1965, (79 Stat. 971): This Act declared it a national policy to preserve historic sites and objects of national significance, including those located on refuges. It provided procedures for designation, acquisition, administration and protection of such sites. Among other things, National Historic and Natural Landmarks are designated under authority of this Act. As of January 1989, thirty-one national wildlife refuges contained such sites.

National Historic Preservation Act of 1966 (16 U.S.C. 470-470b, 470c-470n) -- Public Law 89-665, approved October 15, 1966, (80 Stat. 915) and repeatedly amended: This Act provided for preservation of significant historical features (buildings, objects, and sites) through a grant-in-aid program to the states. It established a National Register of Historic Places and a program of matching grants under the existing National Trust for Historic Preservation (16 U.S.C. 468-468d).

The Act established an Advisory Council on Historic Preservation, which was made a permanent independent agency in Public Law 94-422, approved September 28, 1976 (90 Stat. 1319). That Act also created the Historic Preservation Fund. Federal agencies are directed to take into account the effects of their actions on items or sites listed in, or eligible for listing in, the National Register of Historic Places. As of January 1989, ninety-one such sites on national wildlife refuges are listed in this Register.

Land and Water Conservation Fund Act of 1948: This Act provides funding through receipts from the sale of surplus Federal land, appropriations from oil and gas receipts from the outer continental shelf, and other sources of land acquisition under several authorities. Appropriations from the fund may be used for matching grants to states for outdoor recreation projects and for land acquisition by various Federal agencies, including the Fish and Wildlife Service.

Migratory Bird Hunting and Conservation Stamp Act (16 U.S.C. 718-718j, 48 Stat. 452), as amended: The Duck Stamp Act, of March 16, 1934, requires each waterfowl hunter, 16 years of age or older, to possess a valid Federal hunting stamp. Receipts from the sale of the stamp are deposited in a special Treasury account known as the Migratory Bird Conservation Fund and are not subject to appropriations.

National and Community Service Act of 1960 (42 U.S.C. 12401:104 Stat. 3127), Public Law 101-610, signed November 16,1990: This Act authorizes several programs to engage citizens of the United States in full- and/or part-time projects designed to combat illiteracy and poverty, provide job skills, enhance educational skills, and fulfill environmental needs. Several provisions are of particular interest to the Fish and Wildlife Service.

American Conservation and Youth Service Corps: A Federal grant program established under Subtitle C of the law, the Corps offers an opportunity for young adults between the ages of 16-25, or in the case of summer programs, 15-21, to engage in approved human and natural resources projects which benefit the public or are carried out on Federal or Indian lands. To be eligible for assistance, natural resource programs must focus on improvement of wildlife habitat and recreational areas, fish culture, fishery assistance, erosion, wetlands protection, pollution control and similar projects. A stipend of not more than 100 percent of the poverty level will be paid to participants. A Commission established to administer the Youth Service Corps will make grants to States, the Secretaries of Agriculture and Interior, and the Director of ACTION to carry out these responsibilities.

National Environmental Policy Act of 1959 (P.L. 91-190, 42 U.S.C. 4321-4347, January 1, 1970, 83 Stat. 852) as amended by Public Law 94-52, July 3, 1975, 89 Stat. 258, and Public Law 94-83, August 9, 1975, 89 Stat. 424): Title I of the 1969 National Environmental Policy Act requires that all Federal agencies prepare detailed environmental impact statements for every recommendation or report on proposals for legislation and other major Federal actions significantly affecting the quality of the human environment. The 1969 statute stipulated the factors to be considered in environmental impact statements, and required that Federal agencies employ an interdisciplinary approach in related decision-making and develop means to ensure that unquantified environmental values are given appropriate consideration, along with economic and technical considerations. Title II of this statute requires annual reports on environmental quality from the President to the Congress, and established a Council on Environmental Quality in the Executive Office of the President with specific duties and functions.

National Wildlife Refuge System Improvement Act of 1997: Public Law 105-57, amended the National Wildlife Refuge System Act of 1966 (16 U.S.C. 668dd-ee), and provided guidance for management and public use of the Refuge System. The Act mandates that the Refuge System be consistently directed and managed as a national system of lands and waters devoted to wildlife conservation and management. The Act establishes priorities for recreational uses of the Refuge

System. Six wildlife-dependent uses are specifically named in the Act: hunting, fishing, wildlife observation, wildlife photography, and environmental education and interpretation. These activities are to be promoted in the Refuge System, while all non-wildlife-dependent uses are subject to compatibility determinations. A compatible use is one that, in the sound professional judgment of the refuge manger, will not materially interfere with, or detract from, fulfillment of the National Wildlife Refuge System mission or refuge purpose(s). As stated in the Act, the mission of the system is to administer a national network of lands and waters for the conservation, management, and where appropriate, restoration of the fish, wildlife, and plant resources and their habitats within the United States for the benefit of present and future generations of Americans. The Act also requires development of a comprehensive conservation plan for each refuge and that management is consistent with the plan. When writing a plan for expanded or new refuges, and when making management decisions, the Act requires effective coordination with other Federal agencies, State fish and wildlife or conservation agencies, and refuge neighbors. A refuge must also provide opportunities for public involvement when making a compatibility determination.

North American Wetlands Conservation Act (103 Stat. 1968; 16 U.S.C. 4401~4412) Public Law 101-233, enacted December 13, 1989: This Act provides funding and administrative direction for implementation of the North American Waterfowl Management Plan and the Tripartite Agreement on Wetlands between Canada, the United States, and Mexico. The Act converts the Pittman-Robertson account into a trust fund, with the interest available without appropriation through the year 2006, to carry out the programs authorized by the Act, along with an authorization for annual appropriation of $15 million plus an amount equal to the fines and forfeitures collected under the Migratory Bird Treaty Act. Available funds may be expended, upon approval of the Migratory Bird Conservation Commission, for payment of not to exceed 50 percent of the United States' share of the cost of wetlands conservation projects in Canada, Mexico, or the United States (or 100 percent of the cost of projects on Federal lands). At least 50 percent and no more than 70 percent of the funds received are to go to Canada and Mexico each year.

Refuge Recreation Act of 1952: This Act authorizes the Secretary of the Interior to administer refuges, hatcheries, and other conservation areas for recreational use, when such uses do not interfere with the area's primary purposes. It authorizes construction and maintenance of recreational facilities and the acquisition of land for incidental fish and wildlife-oriented recreational development or protection of natural resources. It also authorizes the charging of fees for public uses.

Refuge Revenue Sharing Act (16 U.S.C. 715s): Section 401 of the Act of June 15,1935, (49 Stat. 383) provided for payments to counties in lieu of taxes, using revenues derived from the sale of products from refuges. Public Law 88-523, approved August 30, 1964, (78 Stat. 701) made major revisions by requiring that all revenues received from refuge products, such as animals, timber and minerals, or from leases or other privileges, be deposited in a special Treasury account and net receipts distributed to counties for public schools and roads. Public Law 93-509, approved December 3, 1974, (88 Stat. 1603) required that moneys remaining in the fund after payments be transferred to the Migratory Bird Conservation Fund for land acquisition under provisions of the Migratory Bird Conservation Act. Public Law 95-469, approved October 17, 1978, (92 Stat. 1319) expanded the revenue sharing system to include national fish hatcheries and Service research stations. It also included in the Refuge Revenue Sharing Fund receipts from the sale of salmonid carcasses. Payments to counties were established as follows: on acquired land, the greatest amount calculated on the basis of 75 cents per acre, three-fourths of one percent of the appraised value, or 25 percent of the net receipts produced from the land; and on land withdrawn from the public domain, 25 percent of net receipts and basic payments under Public Law 94-565 (31 U.S.C. 1601-1607, 90 Stat. 2662). This amendment also authorized appropriations to make up any difference between the amount in the fund and the amount scheduled for payment in any year. The stipulation that payments be used for schools and roads was removed, but counties were required to pass payments along to other units of local government within the county that suffer losses in revenues due to the establishment of Service areas.

Wilderness Act of 1954: Public Law 88-577, approved September 3, 1964, directed the Secretary of the Interior, within 10 years, to review every roadless area of 5,000 or more acres and every roadless island (regardless of size) within National Wildlife Refuge and National Park Systems for inclusion in the National Wilderness Preservation System.

Appendix IV. Public Involvement

SUMMARY OF PUBLIC SCOPING

The Service invited these agencies, organizations, businesses, and citizens to participate in six public scoping meetings on February 15, 16, 20, 22, and 23, 2001, in Washington, Swan Quarter, Plymouth, Columbia, and Manns Harbor, North Carolina. The staff introduced the audience of 176 citizens to the refuge and its planning process and asked them the attendees to identify their issues and concerns. The Service published announcements giving the location, date, and time for the public meetings in the Federal Register and legal notices in local newspapers. Press releases were also sent to local newspapers and public service announcements to television and radio stations. Service personnel placed fifty posters announcing the meeting in local post offices, local government buildings, and stores.

The planning teams expanded the issues and concerns to include those generated by the agencies, organizations, businesses, and citizens from the local community. These issues and concerns formed the basis for the development and comparison of the objectives in the different alternatives described in the environmental assessment, which was Section B of the Draft Comprehensive Conservation Plan for Pocosin Lakes NWR.

The objectives were subjects of discussion at a second round of public meetings on April 25 and 28, 2005, in Plymouth and Columbia, North Carolina. The Service published announcements giving the location, date, and time for the public meetings as legal notices in local newspapers. Press releases were also sent to local newspapers and public service announcements to television and radio stations. Service personnel placed seventy-five posters announcing the meetings in local post offices, local government buildings, and stores.

The issues raised at the meetings are on the next pages, followed by worksheets the workshop participants completed at each workshop.

DRAFT PLAN COMMENTS AND SERVICE RESPONSES

The following summarizes all comments that were received on the Draft Comprehensive Conservation Plan and Environmental Assessment (Draft CCP/EA) for Pocosin Lakes NWR. Public comments on the Draft CCP/EA were accepted from July 11 to August 15, 2007.

Approximately 70 copies of the Draft CCP/EA were sent out to individuals who placed their name on the mailing list during the scoping phase. Copies of the Draft CCP/EA were also distributed to the Hyde, Tyrrell and Washington County libraries, as well as several individuals who requested a copy. Notice of the availability of the Draft CCP/EA and the comment period was sent to five area newspapers (Coastland Times, Washington Daily News, Scuppernong Reminder, Roanoke Beacon, Virginia Pilot) and posted in the Hyde, Tyrrell, and Washington County libraries and at the Walter B. Jones, Sr., Center for the Sounds in Columbia, North Carolina. In addition, notification was sent via email to all the refuge manager's contacts, many of whom, in turn, distributed the notification further.

A total of 12 people submitted comments on the Draft CCP/EA, either in writing or at public forums held on July 25 and July 26, 2007.

POCOSIN LAKES NWR
COMPREHENSIVE CONSERVATION PLAN SCOPING MEETINGS
FEBRUARY 15, 16, 20, 22, 23, 2001

Area of Concern	Issue	Disposition
Wildlife-General	Continue surveys.	In plan.
	Conduct surveys.	In plan.
	Consider non-game species in management.	In plan.
	Share data with other agencies.	In plan.
Wildlife-Invertebrates	Investigate the occurrence of butterflies.	In Alternatives 2 and 3.
Wildlife-Mammals	Bear populations too high.	Completed black bear study with Virginia Tech. Results may justify hunting for bear.
	Prevent deer and bear from damaging neighbors' crops.	Currently conducting population survey. Results may justify hunting for bear. Deer hunting in plan.
	Evaluate deer predation by red wolves.	Being evaluated by red wolf recovery team.
	Keep red wolves on the refuge.	Not practical.
	Increase cooperation between red wolf biologists and private landowners.	Recommendation forwarded to Red Wolf Recovery Team.
	Investigate the occurrence of bats.	In Alternative 3.
Wildlife-Reptiles and Amphibians	Evaluate pygmy rattlesnake populations.	Inventory plan fully implemented in Alternative 3.
Wildlife-Waterfowl	Control tundra swan and snow goose populations that are too high.	Control by hunting is a State responsibility in cooperation with migratory bird program.
	Increase Tundra swan bag limits to control populations.	Control by hunting is a State responsibility in cooperation with migratory bird program.
	Increase waterfowl bag limits.	Control by hunting is a State responsibility in cooperation with migratory bird program.

Area of Concern	Issue	Disposition
Habitat-General	Allow natural species to dominate.	Basis of plan.
	Utilize species natural requirements to manage habitats.	Basis of plan.
	Consider natural processes in management.	Basis of plan.
	Cooperate with State to ensure that natural processes take place.	Refuge has no control over State activities (fire control, pest control, etc.) beyond refuge boundaries.
	Develop restoration objectives that enable self-maintenance.	Basis of plan.
	Cooperate with the State to develop cooperative management plans.	State has been involved in plan development and will be involved in step-down plan development.
	Cooperate with Pettigrew State Park to improve water quality in Phelps Lake.	Can manage refuge land to improve water quality from refuge lands. The refuge cannot affect pollution from private land.
	Cooperate with Pettigrew State Park to reduce the threat of flooding to Tyrrell County.	Can manage refuge land to improve the conveyance of water from refuge land to natural streams and water
	Create corridors between refuges to connect habitat.	Will be addressed in land protection plan.
	Develop and evaluate landscape level inter-relationships.	Will be addressed in land protection plan.
	Manage habitats for non-game species.	Refuge managed for all species.
	Create more habitat types across the refuge.	Service policy is to manage natural habitats, not create artificial habitats.
	Restore hydrology.	Basis of plan.
	Restore hydrology for anadromous fish.	Water control structures for hydrology restoration will be adapted as best as they can for fish passage.

Area of Concern	Issue	Disposition
	Manage existing water control structures.	Basis of plan.
	Improve water management.	Hydrology restoration planned for wetlands, pumps and wells planned for waterfowl management areas.
	Design and install additional water control structures.	Water control structures for hydrology restoration are planned.
	Remove roads and ditches that are no longer used.	Current roads and ditches serve as firebreaks as much as access or drainage conduits.
	Establish quail habitat.	Potential is minimal in wetland habitat.
	Evaluate the use of controlled burns to create quail habitat.	Emphasis in plan is on managing natural habitats.
	Plant species that attract wildlife.	Potential is minimal in wetland habitat.
Habitat-Cropland	Protect cropland adjacent to refuge.	Cropland cannot realistically be protected from predation from waterfowl.
	Develop cropland in the refuge interior to attract wildlife away from private land.	Service policy does not allow for converting wetlands to cropland.
Habitat-Nonriverine Wet Hardwood Forest	Increase hardwood planting.	In Alternatives 2 and 3.
Habitat-Open Water	Improve fish habitat in Lake Phelps.	Can manage refuge land to improve water quality from refuge lands. The refuge cannot affect pollution from private land. Refuge does partner with Pettigrew State Park on fish projects.

Area of Concern	Issue	Disposition
Public Use-General	Cooperate more with partners in providing public use opportunities.	Refuge does cooperate with several partners. Cooperation will increase if park ranger is rehired.
	Cooperate more with communities in providing public use opportunities.	Refuge does cooperate with schools and partners from the communities. Cooperation will increase if park ranger is rehired.
	Make public aware of priority public uses.	New refuge brochure available since 2001.
	Consider public comments in decision-making.	Required by the National Environmental Policy Act for major decisions.
	Revise proposed appropriate use policy to eliminate the need for an activity not to be possible in the area to be appropriate on the refuge.	Appropriate use policy dictated by the U.S. Fish and Wildlife Service national headquarters.
Public Use-Hunting	Coordinate with state to change hunting regulations.	Coordination on the refuge in plan.
	Increase waterfowl bag limits.	State responsibility in cooperation with migratory bird program.
	Provide access for disabled hunters.	Disabled hunter access is provided and covered in step-down plan.
	Increase law enforcement presence during hunting season.	Full time law enforcement officer planned in Alternatives 2 and 3.
	Establish safety buffers or no-hunting zones adjacent to neighbors.	Several such buffers have been established.
Public Use-Environmental Education	Educate the public more on the effects of management practices.	Will be incorporated into environmental education step-down plan.
	Educate the public more on ecosystem functions across all habitats.	Will be incorporated into environmental education step-down plan.
	Educate the public more on the relationship between habitat and public use.	Will be incorporated into environmental education step-down plan.

Area of Concern	Issue	Disposition
Public Use-Interpretation	Improve access to view the full array of habitats on the refuge.	Access will improve as funds become available to improve roads.
	Develop list of plant species utilized by migratory birds.	Will be incorporated into interpretation step-down plan; lists available in fact sheets and books..
Public Use-Wildlife Observation	Allow more access for wildlife observation.	Access will improve as funds become available to improve roads.
	Provide access for disabled wildlife observers.	Not all facilities will be accessible, but Scuppernong Trail and Pungo Lake platform are accessible.
Public Use-Access	Establish one good north-south road and one good east-west road.	Access will improve as funds become available to improve roads.
	Restrict public access to the refuge during hunting season.	Access not restricted due to use for wildlife observation, but users urged to be cautious.
	Restrict access to large trucks during hunting season.	Access dependent on road condition.
Public Use-Non-Wildlife Dependent Public Use	Allow horseback riding on existing public access roads.	Horseback riders may apply for special use permits.
	Allow uses that are compatible with local community objectives.	Priority is given to the six priority public uses. Manager does have authority to approve special use permits.
	Allow manager to make decisions on public use.	Manager does have authority to approve special use permits.
Public Use-Visitor Protection	Increase visibility of law enforcement officers.	Full time law enforcement officer in Alternatives 2 and 3.
	Patrol the refuge on weekends.	Full time law enforcement officer in Alternatives 2 and 3.
	Establish a hotline to report violations.	The North Carolina Wildlife Resources Commission has a hotline.

Area of Concern	Issue	Disposition
Resource Protection-Land Protection	Acquire land from willing sellers.	In land protection step-down plan.
	Consider corridor development in land protection planning.	In land protection step-down plan.
	Consider uses of and public uses on adjacent land in land protection plans.	In land protection step-down plan.
Resource Protection-Law Enforcement	Increase law enforcement activity.	Full time law enforcement officer in Alternatives 2 and 3.
	Eliminate bear poaching.	In plan.
	Establish, monitor, and enforce a hunter sign-in area.	Not practical due to the number of hunters, multiple access points, and shortage of staff.
	Develop a permit system to regulate hunter activity.	Would not be more effective than the current system.
	Require hunter safety card.	State hunter safety certification adequate.
	Develop a refuge hunter safety certification.	State hunter safety certification adequate.
	Make hunters accountable for their actions.	Increased law enforcement should enable the refuge to hold more hunters accountable.
	Create buffer zone between refuge and private property to minimize trespass onto private property.	Will be considered in the law enforcement step down plan.
	Educate public on their rights concerning defense from red wolf damage.	Will be considered in the law enforcement step down plan.
	Enforce poaching regulations on private lands from refuge rights-of-way.	Trespassing is the responsibility of county law enforcement officials; poaching is the responsibility of state wildlife officials.
Resource Protection-Pest Animals	Allow trapping to control pest animals.	Trapping will be considered in pest animal control step-down plan.

Appendices

Area of Concern	Issue	Disposition
Resource Protection-Wilderness	Designate wilderness areas.	No wilderness study areas are proposed, but certain areas will not be managed intensively due to site restrictions and the nature and condition of the habitat.
Resource Protection-Wilderness	Do not designate wilderness areas.	No wilderness study areas are proposed, but certain areas will not be managed intensively due to site restrictions and the nature and condition of the habitat.
	Evaluate the limits on use of adjacent land by designating wilderness.	No wilderness study areas are proposed, but certain areas will not be managed intensively due to site restrictions and the nature and condition of the habitat.
	Clarify approved uses in wilderness to the public before the designation.	No wilderness study areas are proposed, but certain areas will not be managed intensively due to site restrictions and the nature and condition of the habitat.
	Consider the impacts of wilderness designation on prescribed fire.	Prescribed fire can be designated as a minimum management tool.

POCOSIN LAKES NATIONAL WILDLIFE REFUGE PLANNING ISSUES WORKSHEET				
ACTIVITY	**WHAT WOULD YOU LIKE US TO DO?**			
	Keep the Same	Eliminate	Increase	Decrease
WILDLIFE SURVEYS AND MANAGEMENT				
Waterfowl Survey and Management	58%	8%	34%	0%
Shorebird Survey and Management	46%	15%	31%	8%
Land Bird Survey and Management	46%	8%	31%	14%
Reptile/Amphibian Survey and Management	43%	7%	35%	15%
Fish Survey and Management	20%	13%	67%	0%
Endangered Species Survey and Management	35%	14%	43%	8%
Black Bear Management	34%	8%	50%	8%
White-tailed Deer Management	55%	9%	36%	0%
WILDLIFE HABITAT ACTIVITIES				
Water Management (Farming, Moist Soil Management)	30%	20%	40%	10%
Prescribed Burning	50%	10%	10%	30%
Forest Thinning	34%	8%	50%	8%
Mechanical Vegetation Management (Mowing, Disking)	60%	0%	30%	10%
Chemical Vegetation Management	70%	20%	0%	10%
Shoreline Maintenance	50%	17%	25%	8%
Planting, Seeding, Clearing for Habitat Improvement	45%	0%	55%	0%
Habitat Restoration (Hydrology, Reforestation)	29%	7%	64%	0%

Appendices

POCOSIN LAKES NATIONAL WILDLIFE REFUGE PLANNING ISSUES WORKSHEET					
ACTIVITY	WHEN WOULD YOU LIKE US TO DO?			
	Keep the Same	Eliminate	Increase	Decrease
Wildlife Management	36%	0%	64%	0%
Insect and Disease Management	33%	22%	45%	0%
Exotic and Invasive Species Eradication	15%	7%	78%	0%
Special Protection Status (Wilderness)	13%	37%	50%	0%
PUBLIC USE ACTIVITIES AND FACILITIES				
Fishing	50%	0%	50%	0%
Hunting	50%	13%	37%	0%
PUBLIC USE ACTIVITIES AND FACILITIES (Cont'd)				
Environmental Education (School Students)	33%	0%	67%	0%
Environmental Education (School Teachers)	35%	0%	65%	0%
Wildlife Interpretation (Formal Programs)	55%	0%	45%	0%
Wildlife Interpretation (Printed Material)	40%	0%	60%	0%
Wildlife Interpretation (Walking Trails)	36%	0%	64%	0%
Wildlife Interpretation (Canoeing Trails)	45%	0%	55%	0%
Wildlife Interpretation (Buildings, Kiosks)	45%	10%	45%	0%
PUBLIC USE ACTIVITIES				
Wildlife Interpretation (Interpretative Signs)	40%	10%	50%	0%
Wildlife Photography Opportunities	41%	0%	59%	0%
Wildlife Observation Opportunities	45%	0%	55%	0%
Vehicle Parking Lots	63%	0%	37%	0%

POCOSIN LAKES NATIONAL WILDLIFE REFUGE PLANNING ISSUES WORKSHEET				
ACTIVITY	WHAT WOULD YOU LIKE US TO DO?			
	Keep the Same	Eliminate	Increase	Decrease
Access for Fishing, Boating, Canoeing	22%	0%	78%	0%
LAW ENFORCEMENT ACTIVITIES				
Visitor Protection	40%	0%	60%	0%
Wildlife Protection	14%	0%	86%	0%
Trespass Violations	17%	0%	83%	0%
Littering/Dumping Violations	0%	0%	100%	0%
Hunting and Fishing Compliance Checks	20%	0%	80%	0%
OPERATION AND MAINTENANCE				
Canal Maintenance	33%	0%	67%	0%
Road and Firebreak Maintenance	50%	0%	50%	0%
Facilities Maintenance (Signs, Buildings)	60%	0%	40%	0%
Dike and Trail Maintenance	40%	0%	60%	0%
Water Control Structures, Pump Stations	40%	0%	60%	0%
Boundary Posting	50%	0%	50%	0%

PUBLIC FORUMS

During the July 11 – August 15, 2007 public review period, the refuge and planning staffs hosted two public forums, one on July 25 at the Vernon James Center (Tidewater Research Station) in Washington County and one on July 26 at the Walter B. Jones Center for the Sound (the refuge's visitor center) in Tyrrell County. Each forum began at 5 p.m. and concluded at 7 p.m. The forums were an open house style with the refuge staff available to discuss the Draft CCP/EA and refuge operations with the attendees. Several posters and an unmanned power point presentation were displayed to assist the public in understanding the document. A clipboard with a comment sheet was offered to each person to solicit written comments. Refuge staff also collected oral comments and transcribed them after the forums. A total of 12 people attended and five offered comments during these two public forums.

AFFILIATIONS OF RESPONDENTS

The table below identifies the names and affiliations of respondents who commented on the Draft CCP/EA, either in writing or at the two public forums. The State of North Carolina has many agencies with interests in the Albermarle/Pamlico Peninsula. The refuge has close relationships with those agencies, as well as non-governmental organizations that have been instrumental in protecting the lands of the peninsula and promoting ecotourism in the area.

Name of Respondent	Affiliation
Stephen Rynas	North Carolina Department of Environment and Natural Resources, Division of Coastal Management
Bill Pickens	North Carolina Department of Environment and Natural Resources, Forest Service
Sid Shearin	North Carolina State Parks, Pettigrew State Park
Isaac Harrold	North Carolina Wildlife Resources Commission, Raleigh, NC
Andrew Page	The Humane Society of the United States, Washington, DC
B. Sachau	Concerned Citizen, Florham Park, NJ
Emily and Blake Scott	Star Trak Recording, Washington, NC
Brian Roth	Mayor, Plymouth, NC
Gus Shad	Adjacent landowner and Concerned Citizen, Hyde County, NC
Doris Morris	Concerned Citizen, Plymouth, NC
Marco Gibbs	Concerned Citizen, Engelhard, NC
Frances Armstrong	Concerned Citizen, Bath, NC

The number of affiliations represented in the above table can be summarized as follows: state agencies: 4; local government: 1; public citizens (general public): 5; non-governmental organizations: 1, and businesses: 1.

Other organizations that were represented at the public forums, but did not provide comments, included the Town of Columbia, NC; the Town of Plymouth, NC; Tyrrell County, NC; and the Washington County No-OLF group.

COMMENT MEDIA

The types of media used to deliver the comments received by the refuge and planning staffs are categorized as follows: oral (given at the two public forums): 4; written: 8.

GEOGRAPHIC ORIGIN OF RESPONDENTS

The geographic origins of the individual respondents who submitted comments are North Carolina: 12; Washington DC: 1; New Jersey: 1.

SUMMARY OF CONCERNS AND THE SERVICE'S RESPONSES

The public comments received and the Fish and Wildlife Service's responses to each are included below.

North Carolina Division of Coastal Management (Comments submitted by Stephen Rhynas)

Comment 1:

The proposed action will be occurring within portions of the following North Carolina counties, Tyrrell, Washington, and Hyde. Each of these counties is a coastal county within the meaning to the Coastal Zone Management Act of 1972, as amended (CZMA). The CZMA requires that Federal agencies proposing activities[1] within a State's coastal zone to provide the State, in this case, the NC Division of Coastal Management with a consistency determination prior to implementing the activity to document that the proposed activity would comply with the enforceable policies of North Carolina's approved coastal management program and would be conducted consistent with the State's coastal management program. Conformance of the proposed Federal activity with the enforceable policies of the State's certified coastal management program was not evaluated in the Draft.

Response:
Comment noted.

Comment 2:

Though inclusion of the consistency analysis into the draft document **not** a requirement, 15 CFR 930.37 allows a Federal agency to use its NEPA documents *"as a vehicle"* for its consistency determination. Inclusion of the consistency analysis into the environmental documents simplifies the environmental review process and focuses the decision-making process by condensing the required analysis into one document. At this point in time, USFWS may either incorporate the consistency analysis into the final document or it may prepare a stand-alone consistency determination. DCM recommends that, Appendix II (Relevant Legal Mandates), the Socioeconomic Environment Section, and the Regulatory Effects Section of the final document be revised to incorporate a review of the proposed action with the Coastal Zone Management Act and North Carolina's coastal management program.

Response:
The Federal Consistency Determination for the Pocosin Lakes NWR Draft CCP/EA was submitted to the Division of Coastal Management for review on August 23, 2007. The refuge's review concluded with the determination that the proposed Federal activity is consistent, to the maximum extent practical, with the enforceable policies of the North Carolina Coastal Management Program. We further understand that development projects (as determined by statutory definition) will require additional consistency review as they are funded and plans become finalized.

Comment 3:
Based on our review of the Draft, the broad goals, objectives, and strategies outlined appear to be consistent with the State's coastal program. DCM also recognizes that the proposed management program would be environmentally beneficial. Nevertheless the Draft raises substantial questions with how the US Fish and Wildlife Service is preparing these plans. Over the past two years DCM has reviewed a total of six[2] prior draft comprehensive conservation plans plus this recently submitted plan for a total of seven plans. Of the six prior submissions, only two have been subsequently submitted to DCM for consistency review. Moreover, DCM has not observed any adaptation of the plans in response to the previous comments made by DCM. For example, in our first letter of July 12, 2005 on the Draft Comprehensive Conservation Plan and Environmental Assessment for the Roanoke River National Wildlife Refuge we wrote the following concerning the necessity for the USFWS to provide a CZMA analysis:

> *"The proposed action will be occurring within Bertie County; a coastal county within the meaning to the Coastal Zone Management Act of 1972, as amended (CZMA). The CZMA requires that Federal agencies proposing activities[3] within a State's coastal zone provide the State, in this case, the NC Division of Coastal Management with a consistency determination prior to implementing the activity to document that the proposed activity complies with the enforceable policies of North Carolina's approved coastal management program and will be conducted consistent with the State's coastal program. Conformance of the proposed Federal activity with the enforceable policies of the State's certified coastal management program was not evaluated in the Draft."*

Response:
It's unclear to us from this comment how the Pocosin Lakes Draft CCP/EA raises "substantial questions" about how the Service is preparing CCPs. It is also unclear to us what questions are raised.

The staff at Pocosin Lakes NWR is committed to working cooperatively with all State and Federal agencies to ensure full compliance with laws, regulations, and policies. The Federal Consistency Determination for the Pocosin Lakes NWR Draft CCP/EA was submitted to the Division of Coastal Management for review on August 23, 2007. The refuge's review concluded with the determination that the proposed Federal activity is consistent, to the maximum extent practical, with the enforceable policies of the North Carolina Coastal Management Program. We further understand that development projects (as determined by statutory definition) will require additional consistency review as they are funded and plans become finalized.

The manager at Roanoke River NWR informs us that a Consistency Determination on its Draft CCP/EA was sent in August 2005 and CD05-042 was issued on September 6, 2005. The Roanoke River NWR refuge manager can be reached at 252/794-3808 for more information on that CCP.

Comment 4:
As noted above, the current submission still lakes a CZMA analysis. In addition, we have not yet received copies of the final documents[4] with an analysis of how our comments, as well as the comments of others, may have been handled by the USWFS.

Response:
The Federal Consistency Determination for the Pocosin Lakes NWR Draft CCP/EA was submitted to the Division of Coastal Management for review on August 23, 2007. The refuge's review concluded with the determination that the proposed Federal activity is consistent, to the maximum extent practical, with the enforceable policies of the North Carolina Coastal Management Program. We further understand that development projects (as determined by statutory definition) will require additional consistency review as they are funded and plans become finalized.

We have confirmed that Division of Coastal Management Federal Consistency Division is included with the mailing addresses to receive, upon completion, a copy of the Comprehensive Conservation Plan for Pocosin Lakes NWR, to include this appendix addressing all comments received.

Comment 5:
The Pocosin Lakes National Wildlife Refuge is adjacent to the location of the Navy's proposed Outlying Landing Field (OLF). The Navy's draft supplemental environmental impact statement for the proposed OLF notes that the Navy will be implementing a variety of measures to discourage birds from using the OLF as habitat. Additionally aircraft operations passing through the wildlife refuge could have an effect on how birds use of the wildlife refuge. Based on the proximity of the OLF to the Pocosin Lakes National Wildlife Refuge and the fact that this is a known proposed action, DCM staff would have expected the Draft to: 1) develop a fifth management alternative for consideration that could be implemented if the Navy implements the OLF and 2) have included the OLF potential in the cumulative impact assessment section. DCM recommends that the final version of the Pocosin Lakes Comprehensive Conservation Plan and Environmental Assessment address how the Refuge would potentially adjust to the OLF.

Response:
At this point, the Navy has not completed the Draft Supplemental Environmental Impact Statement (Draft SEIS) for the Outlying Landing Field (OLF) site and therefore has not made a final decision on the location of the proposed OLF. Recent congressional actions seem to be moving towards rescinding authorization and appropriations for an OLF at Site C (the one near the refuge). In addition, the Navy is reportedly looking at alternative sites suggested by officials in Virginia and North Carolina. Therefore, it is far from certain that an OLF will be established near the refuge and thus detailed planning for an OLF seems to be premature.

At the request of the Navy, the Service assisted with the development of the Draft SEIS as a Cooperating Agency. The Navy concluded in its Draft SEIS that the impact of an OLF at Site C on waterfowl at Pocosin Lakes NWR would be relatively minor. The Service disagrees with this conclusion and believes the potential for substantial negative impacts to be higher than does the Navy. Since we do not know exactly how the OLF will affect how the birds use the refuge, we will have to take an adaptive approach to managing the situation if it occurs. The CCP is a general planning document that establishes broad goals and objectives and general direction for management of the refuge. As a result of the CCP, there will be a number of step-down plans written for the purpose of achieving those broad goals and objectives. These step-down plans will be prepared at the level of detail necessary to address complex management needs, such as would be created by the construction and operation of an OLF at Site C.

Comment 6:
The proposed project will be environmentally beneficial since it proposes to improve habitat values. Nevertheless, the Mitigation Measures Section is vague and generic as it lacks specific commitments. For example, Table 34 lists proposed projects. Implementing some of these projects could have adverse effects to wildlife habitat. The Mitigation Measures Section itself notes" *Temporary initial disturbances to wildlife and habitat would occur during the construction of new facilities, such as trails, wildlife observation platforms, photo blinds, and interpretive sites.* Some of these adverse effects could be avoid by undertaking work during periods of low biological productivity. DCM recommends that the Mitigation Measures Section be strengthened through specific commitments.

Appendices

Response:
Comment noted.

It is stated in Section B, Chapter IV: Environmental Consequences, page 151, that these initial disturbances to wildlife and habitat due to construction would be *temporary*. It is also stated that the refuge would monitor the impacts of activities and adjust as needed to limit disturbances to acceptable thresholds. All projects or groups of projects on the refuge are planned and designed to minimize disturbance to wildlife and habitat.

Comment 7:

The statement "*Land ownership by the Service also precludes any future economic development by the private sector.*"[5] while true in a limited sense must be balanced by the fact that the Pocosin Lakes National Wildlife Reserve itself generates economic activity through tourism and recreational activities such as hunting and fishing. DCM recommends that the economic benefits of the Reserve be highlighted in the final document.

Response:
Comment noted.
Text in the CCP was revised to include that the presence of the refuge provides many outdoor recreational opportunities, such as hunting, fishing, wildlife photography, wildlife observation, and interpretation and outreach. This would benefit local economies by providing opportunities for ecotourism and business infrastructures to support these activities.

Comment 8:

Furthermore, DCM recommends that North Carolina's Coastal Reserve Program be considered for inclusion as a State Partner. This request has been previously made as a comment as a result of our prior review of the other draft comprehensive conservation plans that were circulated for review and comment.

Response:
The Fish and Wildlife Service in general and the refuge staff in particular welcome the opportunity to partner with the North Carolina Coastal Reserve Program. It is only through mutual cooperation that a better understanding of each agency's mission and purpose will occur, and more importantly, our natural resources will realize greater benefits through a collaborate effort. The text was revised in the CCP to include the North Carolina Coastal Reserve Program as a state partner.

Comment 9:

North Carolina's coastal zone management program consists of, but is not limited to, the Coastal Area Management Act, the State's Dredge and Fill Law, and the land use plan of the County and/or local municipality in which the proposed project is located. In preparing the consistency determination the USFWS will need to review these documents and to evaluate the conformance of proposed comprehensive conservation plan with the State's coastal program. The website for the Division of Coastal Management can be found at: http://dcm2.enr.state.nc.us/index.htm. The State's consistency webpage is located at: http://dcm2.enr.state.nc.us/Permits/consist.htm. Additionally, NOAA's Office of Ocean and Coastal Resources Management (OCRM) has a webpage on the consistency process at: http://coastalmanagement.noaa.gov/czm/federal_consistency.html.

Response:
The Federal Consistency Review submitted on August 23, 2007, includes a review of the Coastal Area Management Act, the State's Dredge and Fill Law, and the Tyrrell, Washington and Hyde Counties Land Use Plans.

Comment 10:
DCM encourages the USFWS review the applicability of 15 CFR 930.33(a)(4) and 15 CFR 930.36(c). Pursuant to 15 CFR 930.33(a)(4), the USFWS may request that future environmentally beneficial activities conducted in compliance with the Pocosin Lakes National Wildlife Refuge's Comprehensive Conservation Plan[6] be excluded from further consistency review. Furthermore, pursuant to 15 CFR 930.36(c), the USFWS may propose a general consistency determination when a Federal agency proposes repeated activities other than development projects where the incremental actions do not affect any coastal use or coastal resource when performed separately. Prior to implementing the proposed comprehensive conservation plan the USFWS will need to submit to DCM a consistency determination and obtain the concurrence of DCM.

Response:
The Federal Consistency Determination for the Pocosin Lakes NWR Draft CCP/EA was submitted to the Division of Coastal Management for review on August 17, 2007. The refuge's review concluded with the determination that the proposed Federal activity is consistent, to the maximum extent practical, with the enforceable policies of the North Carolina Coastal Management Program. We further understand that development projects (as determined by statutory definition) will require additional consistency review as they are funded and plans become finalized.

<u>North Carolina Division of Forest Resources, Bill Pickens, Staff Forest-Conifer Silviculture</u>

Comment 1:
"The NC Division of Forest Resources (NCDFR) has reviewed the Draft Comprehensive Conservation Plan proposed for the Pocosin Lakes NWR (PLNWR). Our comments concerning that document and the long-term objectives and strategies for the refuge follow.

NCDFR supports the overall vision and goals listed in the CCP for PLNWR. The habitat and resource protection goals complement the Divisions mission to protect, manage, and develop the forest resources in North Carolina.

Response:
Comments noted.

Comment 2:
We concur with the selection of Alternative 2 as the preferred management alternative. It is well suited to meet the strategies and objectives of the CCP.

We specifically support the following Habitat Management objectives and strategies, and, when possible, offer our continued cooperation and technical assistance to implement them.
- Restoration of hydrology in specific areas to mimic natural conditions and to coordinate the forest habitat plan with the hydrology.
- Restore 700 acres of Atlantic white cedar.
- Restore 1,500 acres to a bottomland hardwood forest.
- Cooperate with other agencies, universities, and organizations performing studies on the refuge.
- Develop a forest management plan and implement it on selected areas.
- Revise the fire management plan.
- Manage firebreaks to facilitate wild fire suppression.

Response:
Comments noted.

Comment 3:
The Division is pleased that the biological review team encouraged the refuge staff to place a higher priority on forest management. We hope that adequate funding will be allocated for the personnel, equipment, and supplies to meet that priority and allow implementation of forest management and forest restoration projects.

We appreciate the opportunity to comment on the proposed CCP and look forward to continued cooperation between our agencies.

Response:
Pocosin Lakes NWR also looks forward to continued cooperation and partnership between our agencies. This cooperation is essential in providing the foundation for the protection and management of fish, wildlife, forest habitats, and other natural resources throughout North Carolina and the United States.

Pettigrew State Park, Park Superintendent Sidney Shearin

Comment 1:
After reviewing the draft of Pocosin Lakes' Comprehensive Plan, I have many comments particularly because Pettigrew State Park shares many similarities in resources and objectives.

On Table 6, I noticed some water bodies that may be misnamed: The Bee Tree Trail and Bonana Creek. Their names could be Bee Tree Canal and Bonarva Canal. Old Canal is more commonly known as Transportation Canal.

Response:
Text in Table 6 was revised to correct the names.

Comment 2:
Most of the draft's data was written several years ago and Pettigrew State Park has since increased its boundaries. The Park is acquiring any available property on the Scuppernong River and linking up to refuge property. The objective would be to preserve one of North Carolina's last undeveloped rivers and have a wildlife corridor. The Nature Conservancy has given the park most of its river property and eventually will deed Pettigrew all river property.

The current estimates for the park property are:
16,600 acres Lake Phelps
 1,293 acres around Lake Phelps
 3,238 acres on Scuppernong River (including Nature Conservancy Property)
21,131 total acres

By the time this comprehensive plan is completed, Pettigrew should have added over 1,000 acres. The park is also actively seeking any lake shore property on Lake Phelps. Corrections should be made on pages 21, 50, 54 and maybe other paces.

On page 50, in listing "Outdoor Recreation in the Area" it leaves out outdoor recreation which our Park provides such as hiking, picnicking, and camping. Opportunities for outdoor recreation are increasing as we construct facilities on the Scuppernong River.

On page 53, the state park system is completely left off "More developed tourist attractions based on natural resources...." The North Carolina State Park System has always had the philosophy that state parks are natural areas that are unique and need preserving for future generations.

Response:
The text was revised on pages 20, 22, 23, 50, 54, and 99 of the Draft CCP/EA to indicate correct acreages, and partnership and ecotourism opportunities for Pettigrew State Park.

Comment 3:
I was delighted to see on page 81 that the refuge developed a cooperative agreement for a ramp on the south side of Lake Phelps. The Division of Parks and Recreation would need to lease the property from the U.S. Fish and Wildlife and the Pettigrew would be in charge of construction, patrolling, and maintaining the facility. This project has been discussed for years and the only problem has been that the U.S. Fish and Wildlife does not want to lease the property. Pettigrew has to lease the land in order for its staff to legally enforce any laws or regulations. Even though refuge personnel have stated that they could patrol it, Pocosin Lakes NWR shares two law enforcement officers with other refuges. They do not have the staff to check the ramp every Saturday, Sunday, holiday, and evening, especially during peak seasons. The refuge staff would not able to empty trash on weekends and holidays or do weekly mowing. I strongly suggest that the U.S. Fish and Wildlife Service lease a small area on the refuge next to Lake Phelps for a boating access.

Response:
The details of individual construction projects are beyond the scope of this CCP. Following the completion of the CCP, the refuge staff will develop more detailed step-down plans. The details for the construction and operation of the boat launch would be addressed in the Visitor Services Step-down Plan.

Comment 4:
Pettigrew State Park has some cooperative projects that need to be mentioned. The U.S. Fish and Wildlife Service installed a fish ladder in the Bee Tree Canal to let the anadromous herring reach Lake Phelps. Repairs are still being made. Pettigrew sponsors the annual Audubon Christmas Bird Count where the search circle includes Lake Phelps and Pungo Lake. Pettigrew also hosts the annual butterfly count in the summer. Both agencies have been doing environmental programs together like the Scuppernong River Festival.

Response:
Although not specifically named, some of these projects have already been referred to in general terms in the CCP. In addition, the text of the CCP has also been changed to mention some of these projects. Pettigrew State Park does an excellent job of managing habitat on the park and coordinating various wildlife surveys. The refuge looks forward to continuing the partnership and coordination efforts to mutually benefit fish, wildlife, habitat, and other natural resources for North Carolina and the United States of America.

Comment 5:
On page 24, it states that there is no documented existence of Atlantic white cedars south of Lake Phelps. I saw a few Atlantic white cedars before the Allen Road fire. The Roper Lumber Company timbered the cedars in the early 1900s, and with the changing hydrology and massive fires, none of the original trees has survived. There should be a way to confirm the cedars existence.

Response:
The text on page 24 states that *Dr. Hinsely's Forest Habitat Management Plan (1999)* indicates that the vegetation south of Phelps Lake on present-day refuge land was mostly pond pine pocosin and continues that there was no other reference *in Hinsely's Plan* documenting the existence of Atlantic white cedar in the last 150 years. Above this statement, the CCP provides a reference from Dr. Courtney Hackney (personal communication) stating that the woody material throughout the peat is Atlantic white cedar. Text was added to the CCP to include Park Superintendent Sid Shearin's observation of Atlantic white cedars located south of Lake Phelps along Allen Road, prior to the 1985 wild fires.

Comment 6:
Page 35 lists the Waccamaw killifish existing in the area. D.N.A. analysis indicates that the killifish in Lakes Waccamaw and Phelps evolved separately and are now considered separate species. There is a Lake Phelps killifish here and not the Waccamaw killifish.

Response:
The Waccamaw killifish was removed from text on page 35.

Comment 7:
I question the identification of some of the trees and shrubs listed. I have not seen any black willows in the area but the coastal plain willow is quite common. I have not seen any red bays (*Persea borbonia*) but swamp bay (*Persea palustris*) is very common. The silky dogwood (*Cornus amomum*) is listed but it probably should be the swamp dogwood (*Cornus stricta*). I have not seen the Toothache Tree (*Zanthoxylum clava-herculis*) west of Dare County but the devil's walking stick (*Aralia spinosa*) is very common.

Response:
Comment noted. Text in the plant section in Appendix VI was reviewed and revised based on information from field guides, expert opinions including observations made by refuge staff, and the above comments.

Comment 8:
A species of note is the rough leaf dogwood (*Cornus aspirifolia*) discovered by the park staff on the banks of the Scuppernong River. This is a disjuct population that previously was known only to exist in North Carolina near Wilmington.

Response:
Text in the plant section in Appendix VI was revised to include the rough leaf dogwood (*Cornus aspirifolia*)

Comment 9:
The park also keeps species lists of plants and animals that have been observed on Petigrew. More than likely these plants and animals exist on the refuge. I will be glad to meet with the biologist and discuss the list because I question whether several more exist on the refuge.

Response:
Comment noted.

Comment 10:
We are thankful we have Pocosin Lakes NWR as a neighbor and we look forward to the future of working together to protect North Carolina's natural resources.

Response:
Pocosin Lakes NWR also looks forward to a continued cooperation and partnership between our agencies. This cooperation is essential in providing the foundation for the protection and management of fish, wildlife, forest habitats, and other natural resources throughout North Carolina and the United States.

North Carolina Wildlife Resources Commission, Isaac Harrold, Section Manager WRC State and Private Lands Programs

Comment 1:
Appropriate staff with the North Carolina Wildlife Resources Commission (WRC) has reviewed the Draft Pocosin Lakes NWR Comprehensive Conservation Plan and Environmental Assessment. We offer the following comments and recommendations:

The Plan is well written, very thorough, and addresses alternatives to reach refuge management goals.

Response:
Comment noted.

Comment 2:
WRC supports the modest increase in active habitat management and baseline biological monitoring identified in the preferred alternative (Alternative 2).

Response:
Comment noted.

Comment 3:
Page 54: Add Alligator River Game Land: 5,401 acres.

Response:
Text on page 54, Table 21 was revised to include Alligator River Game Land: 5,401 acres.

Comment 4:
Page 57: Update the text that refers to deer hunts on the refuge to state that these hunts are administered by the WRC through the Special Hunts Opportunity Program.

Response:
Text on page 57 under Hunting was revised to include the above comment.

Comment 5:
Page 67: WRC supports the Service's interest in acquiring lands for endangered species and to prevent habitat fragmentation.

Response:
Comment noted.

Appendices

Comment 6:
Page 70: Land Birds – We suggest the Service provide wild turkey hunting opportunities where available and we offer the WRC Special Hunts Opportunity Program as a possible means of implementation.

Response:
Comment noted. The last sentence of the discussion section under Land Birds (dealing with staffing constraints limiting management by permit hunting) was apparently misplaced as hunting is not considered a management tool for turkey, quail, and mourning doves on the refuge; instead, it's considered a public use activity. This statement has been deleted under Land Birds. Under Public Use: Hunting (page 80), the CCP includes providing turkey hunting opportunities (in coordination with the Commission) as a strategy for meeting the refuge hunting objective. As with all other strategies in the plan, a turkey hunting program will be considered in detail when resources allow for such a program.

The Humane Society of the United States, Andrew Page, Campaign Manager, Hunting

Comment 1:
On behalf of the nearly 10 million members and supporters of the Humane Society of the United States and The Fund for Animals (hereinafter collectively "HSUS"), over 214,000 of whom reside in North Carolina, The HSUS submits the following comments to be considered on the Draft Comprehensive Conservation Plan (CCP) for Pocosin Lakes National Wildlife Refuge (Refuge).

Response:
Comments noted.

Comment 2:
The HSUS is opposed to the draft plan and believes that the action proposed represents a continuing violation of federal law, namely the National Environmental Policy Act (NEPA), given the U.S. Fish and Wildlife Service's (FWS) ongoing failure to prepare an Environmental Impact Statement (EIS) on its national wildlife refuge sport-hunting program or, more broadly, its overall refuge recreation program.

Response:
Opposition to the plan noted. Obviously, we disagree with the contention that the Draft CCP/EA represents "a continuing violation of federal law."

Comment 3:
While the FWS apparently believes the National Wildlife Refuge System Improvement Act (NWRSIA) provides it carte blanche approval to allow sport hunting on Refuges, the Act retains and reemphasizes the compatibility requirements and imposes other standards that require more, not less, biological and ecological evidence to support decisions to open refuges to sport hunting activities. See 16 U.S.C. § 668dd(a)(2); see also Complaint filed in The Fund et al. v. Williams et al., Civ. No. 03-677. Nor does the NWRSIA relieve the FWS of its obligations to consider the environmental impacts of, and alternatives to, the agency's decisions with regard to hunting in the Refuge system when preparing CCPs.

Response:
Comments noted. The Improvement Act lists six priority public uses the Service should consider and allow if compatible with the purposes of the refuge. One of these six uses is hunting.

Comment 4:
The HSUS does not believe that sport hunting is compatible with the purposes for which many Refuges were created. See 16 U.S.C. § 460k. Moreover, there is no indication that the FWS ensured the availability of sufficient funds before it approved sport hunting initially at the Refuge and must, therefore, do so now if the FWS intends to continue to authorize and/or expand hunting under the CCP. Id. § 460k(b).

Response:
The Hunt Plan for Pocosin Lakes NWR was developed in the early 1990s, soon after establishment of the refuge. A compatibility and funding statement was signed by the refuge manger at that time. A draft Compatibility Determination for Hunting on Pocosin Lakes NWR at current levels, which includes a determination that adequate funding exists to administer the use, is included in the Draft CCP/EA, Appendix V. Prior to expanding the hunting program to include any additional species, the refuge will use sound professional judgment and best available science to make the decision with regard to species and the type of hunting pressure that would be allowed. In addition, the refuge will consult with professional wildlife biologists with the NCWRC before adding species to the hunting program. The first and foremost goal is to provide healthy wildlife populations with recreational opportunities being subordinate to that goal.

Comment 5:
The proposed CCP must take into account not only the effects of hunting on other wildlife species in the Refuge, but also the cumulative impacts of hunting on wildlife, migratory birds, and non-hunting visitors to Refuges throughout the Refuge System before permitting hunting to continue via CCP. The FWS has effectively admitted that its NEPA compliance on Refuge hunting and, indeed, all Refuge recreational and use activities, is lacking given its failure to ever complete its Refuges 2003 Plan and EIS (herein incorporated by reference). That Draft EIS, which was published on January 15, 1993, conceded that the National Wildlife Refuge System was experiencing a crisis in terms of increased use, increased damage to biotic and abiotic resources, increased user conflicts and, specifically, identified a number of potential adverse impacts associated with refuge hunting programs (i.e., disturbance to feeding or resting waterfowl; trampling of low ground vegetation; soil compaction and/or erosion; abandonment of nest sites and reduced productivity and survival; increased visitation resulting in a negative effect on refuge biodiversity; adverse impacts on the distribution, relative abundance, and sex and age composition of wildlife; changes in wildlife behavior due to increased disturbance by hunters).

To date, no final EIS has been published nor has the FWS explained the status of Refuges 2003 or why it has apparently elected to halt the process midstream. The FWS cannot, on the one hand, initiate an EIS process conceding that the environmental impacts of hunting and other Refuge uses have not been adequately evaluated only to, on the other hand, halt the process and then continue to open Refuge after Refuge to hunting with no substantive analysis of the Refuge-specific or program-wide impact of the activity on wildlife or the refuge system itself.

Response:
Comments noted. Considering the cumulative impacts of hunting to refuges "throughout the Refuge System" is beyond the scope of the Pocosin Lakes NWR CCP. Likewise, the Refuges 2003 Plan is beyond the scope of the Pocosin Lakes NWR CCP.

Comment 6:
Considering the various reports published over the past several decades emphasizing the adverse impacts of Refuge uses, including hunting activities, and the abject failure of the compatibility determination process in preventing incompatible uses (see, e.g., Leopold Committee report, the FWS report entitled Field Station Threats and Conflicts, the FWS report entitled Fish and Wildlife Service Resource Problems, and the 1989 GAO National Wildlife Refuges: Continuing Problems With Incompatible Uses Call for Bold Action), the need for an EIS cannot be disputed. The biological, ecological, social, economic, aesthetic, and other impacts inherent to the FWS's decision necessitate the preparation of an EIS to properly, objectively, and comprehensively evaluate the full range of environmental impacts associated with this action. Until and unless an EIS is prepared, the FWS cannot finalize the proposed CCP.

Response:
Comment noted, but we disagree that an EIS on hunting at refuges across the nation needs to be completed before the Pocosin Lakes NWR CCP can be finalized.

Comment 7:
In addition, in preparing the CCP and NEPA document, the FWS must analyze a full range of alternatives to the proposed action, including the hunting component of the Plan. This includes considering alternatives to sport hunting for achieving the FWS's management objectives for the Refuge and the wildlife that use the Refuge. NEPA requires federal agencies to "study, develop, and describe appropriate alternatives to recommended courses of action . . . ." 42 U.S.C. § 4332(E); 40 C.F.R. § 1508.9(b) (requiring analysis of alternatives in EAs). NEPA's alternatives analysis is "designed to insure that an agency's single-minded approach to a proposed action is tempered by the consideration of other feasible options that may have different (and fewer) environmental effects." Sierra Club v. Watkins, 808 F.Supp. 852, 875 (D.D.C. 1991).

Response:
Comments noted.

Comment 8:
Finally, Section 7 of the ESA requires that each federal agency shall "insure that any action authorized, funded or carried out by such agency . . . is not likely to jeopardize the continued existence of any endangered species . . . ." 16 U.S.C. § 1536(a)(2). To comply with this mandate, before taking an action which may affect listed species, the FWS must first engage in formal consultation with any agency taking such action and produce a Biological Opinion which details the steps necessary to avoid jeopardy. Id. § 1536(b). In this process, the FWS reviews "the best scientific and commercial data available or which can be obtained," evaluates the status of impacted species, determines the cumulative effects of the action, and formulates its Biological Opinion as to "whether the action, taken together with cumulative effects, is likely to jeopardize the continued existence of listed species . . . ." Id. § 402.14. If so, the FWS identifies alternatives which, if implemented, will avoid jeopardy. Id. If the action will result in a "take" of listed species, the Service must provide a take statement identifying what level, if any, of take will be permitted. Id. In addition, the Service identifies discretionary recommendations which will further reduce the impacts of the project on listed species. Id.

Prior to engaging in the consultation which results in such a Biological Opinion, an agency must prepare a Biological Assessment which contains the information that is provided to the Fish and Wildlife Service at the inception of formal consultation. The BA must present an analysis of the effects of the action on species, "including consideration of cumulative effects," and consideration of "alternate actions considered by the Federal agency for the proposed action." Id. § 402.12(f). Only if the BA concludes that a project will not adversely affect any listed species, and the Fish and Wildlife Service concurs in writing, may the agency avoid formal consultation. 50 C.F.R. § 402.13. The ESA prohibits an agency from proceeding with a project which may impact listed species before the analysis required by Section 7 is complete. 16 U.S.C. § 1536(c)(1) (BA must be completed before project begins); id. § 1536(d) (agency may not make irreversible commitment of resources while consultation is underway). Indeed, all federal agencies have an on-going obligation to ensure that ESA listed species are not jeopardized by their actions.

The FWS has engaged in a pattern of compromising the biological and ecological integrity of our National Wildlife Refuges by providing hunters the opportunity to kill for fun and sport the variety of wildlife species that inhabit these Refuges. The fact that the public overwhelmingly rejects hunting of wildlife on National Wildlife Refuges – lands that most believe should be sanctuaries for wildlife -- is evidently immaterial to the FWS.

The impact of hunters and hunting on non-consumptive Refuge users has also not been of significant concern to the FWS despite a fundamental purpose of the Refuge system to provide recreational opportunities (including non-consumptive opportunities). Considering that far more people use the Refuge to observe, enjoy, and photograph wildlife compared to the number of people who use this Refuge for hunting, the impacts of expanded hunting on the experience and potential socioeconomic contribution of these non-consumptive users must be taken into account.

The number of hunters has steadily declined over the last few decades. This trend is so startling, that the *Wildlife Society Bulletin* produced an issue dedicated to the topic of the changing trends in attitudes towards and participation in the "consumptive" use of wildlife. Data from the U.S. Department of Fish and Wildlife reveals that the number of hunters declined 18% from 1975 until 2000 with a 7% decline occurring between 1991 and 2001. [i][ii]

A study in Alabama found that the precipitous decline in hunting license sales in that state could be attributed to a lack of time and interest on the part of former hunters. The study also revealed that 2/3 of all non-hunters did not want to see animals killed for recreation.[iii]

Surveys and studies reveal that social, economic, and cultural changes over the last 30 years have resulted not only in a drop in the number of hunters but also a shift in the focus of wildlife manager education from consumption to conservation.[iv][v] In fact, one study indicated that those who had been in the wildlife profession for less than 5 years as of 1998 were much less likely to support the consumptive use of wildlife than those who had been in the profession for over 20 years.[iii]

A study that examined participation in wildlife-related activities in Canada revealed a similar trend. That analysis showed that the probability of participating in waterfowl hunting decreases with birth year and age. Not only is the number of young hunters decreasing every year, but the overall number of hunters is also decreasing. Additionally, the study revealed that the probability of participation in wildlife viewing has greatly increased over the last three generations.[vi]

From an economic standpoint, non-consumptive wildlife uses continue to increase revenue for local governments while the money spent on hunting has not kept pace with inflation. In 1991, non-consumptive wildlife enthusiasts spent $18.1 billion on all aspects of their hobbies while hunters spent $12.3 billion.[vii] In 1996, non-consumptive expenditures were up to $29.2 billion while hunters spent $20.6 billion.[viii] In 2001, the most recent date for which data is available, non-consumptive expenditures had increased to $38.3 billion while hunting expenditures remained the same at $20.6 billion, despite inflation.[ix] Even in this small subset for which data is readily available, it is clear that hunting expenditures and participation are down while non-consumptive wildlife activities are on the rise.

Such a small segment of the population currently participates in hunting and this number is dwindling with each passing year. The minority status of hunters also extends to patrons of National Wildlife Refuges. The 2004 economic benefit analysis of National Wildlife Refuge Visitation clearly states that 68% of the revenue from National Wildlife Refuges is from non-consumptive users, 27% from fishing activities and only 5% from hunting.[x] This report also states that "[s]urveys show refuge visitors would have been willing to pay more for their visit than it actually cost them." This is known as a consumer surplus. This same survey revealed that 63% of the potential consumer surplus is derived solely from non - consumptive visitors.

FWS must begin to realize the revenue potential of non-consumptive wildlife patrons and begin to reform their revenue base around this rapidly increasing segment of the population. The Refuge should conduct a survey of consumptive versus non-consumptive visitors to the Refuge in order to assess the economic input of each group. These data may be used to assess whether hunting is an economically viable option for the refuge or if it is simply retained as a means to appease a vocal minority.

The FWS has ignored these data and failed to capitalize on the potential economic gain that would come from these non-consumptive users. This seems especially foolhardy in light of the fact that budget and cost woes are often highlighted in the *Refuge Update* newsletter.[xi] Additionally, the wildlife experience of non-consumptive patrons can only be enhanced by the elimination of hunting in these refuges. The current system of setting aside small parcels of land for non-consumptive visitors while opening up large portions of the refuge to hunters is nonsensical and only serves to marginalize a lucrative majority for the sake of a dwindling minority. Removing the dangers and disturbances inherent in hunting areas and allowing for a more complete exploration of these areas for non-hunters can only lead to increased visitation and a subsequent increase in revenue from this segment of the wildlife recreation community.

Response:
Comments noted.

Comment 9:
Conclusion

For all these reasons, we respectfully request that the FWS not open/expand hunting on this Refuge. Thank you in advance for considering these comments.

Response:
Pocosin Lakes NWR was opened for hunting in the early 1990s. Prior to expanding the hunting program to include any additional species, the refuge will use sound professional judgment and best available science to make the decision with regard to species and the type of hunting pressure that would be allowed. In addition, the refuge will consult with professional wildlife biologists with NCWRC before adding species to the hunting program. The first and foremost goal is to provide healthy wildlife populations, with recreational opportunities being subordinate to that goal.

B. Sachau, concerned citizen

Please send me a paper copy so I can comment more fully. I oppose hunting in a refuge. This is not a compatible use. Wildlife watchers over spend gun wackos 20-1 so encouraging their use of this area would benefit tax payers nationally who support this area thru tax dollars.

Response:
Comments noted. As per this request, a copy of the Draft CCP/EA was mailed to B. Sachau.

Emily and Blake Scott, concerned citizens

Comment 1:
We are concerned about continued protection of the waterfowl when the boardwalk and observation tower are built on the west end of Pungo Lake.

Response:
Temporary initial disturbances to wildlife and habitat would occur during the construction of the boardwalk and observation platform on the west end of Pungo Lake. The construction would not be conducted during critical times that would cause substantial wildlife disturbances, such as during the wintering migratory waterfowl season. During and following construction, the staff would monitor the impacts of activities and adjust as needed to limit disturbances to acceptable thresholds. All projects

or groups of projects on the refuge are planned and designed to minimize disturbance to wildlife and habitat to the maximum extent possible.

Comment 2:
We are concerned about refuge violations occurring on the Pungo Unit "when no one is around."

Response:
Upon completion of the CCP, the staff will develop and update, as needed, a Law Enforcement Step-down Plan. This plan will provide a reference to station policies, procedures, priorities, and programs concerning law enforcement. The plan's preferred Alternative 2 provides for a full-time law enforcement officer for Pocosin Lakes NWR. This will provide additional law enforcement to patrol the refuge and enforce refuge policies and laws.

Brian Roth, Mayor of Plymouth, North Carolina

Comment 1:
The CCP looks good!

Response:
Comment noted.

Comment 2:
There is interest in starting a Friends Group for Pocosin Lakes NWR, utilizing the momentum from the NO OLF issue.

Response:
Comment noted. Pocosin Lakes NWR would welcome the presence of a Friends Group for the refuge.

Gus Shad, adjacent landowner and concerned citizen

Comment 1:
Mr. Gus Shad, owner of the former All Star Farms land located adjacent to the refuge, would like the refuge to include part of his land its Watershed 2 hydrology restoration work.

Response:
Comment noted. Pocosin Lakes NWR would be glad to discuss restoring the natural hydrology of the adjacent pocosin wetlands with any landowner.

Doris Morris, concerned citizen

Comment 1:
Would like to have a Welcome/Educational Center at Pat's Road.

Response:
The Service's preferred alternative (2) provides for additional staffing, building expansion, and exhibit replacements for the Walter B. Jones Center for the Sounds (refuge visitor center) located in Columbia, N.C. The CCP also provides for development and maintenance of a captive red wolf facility located in Tyrrell County. Because of their location (along a primary route to the Outer Banks), these strategies have the potential for reaching many people and are therefore high priorities. However, with the increasing popularity of the Pungo Unit following the proposed Navy OLF

controversy, a visitor contact station for the unit may become necessary in the future to deal with higher levels of visitation. A strategy was added under interpretation to address this issue.

Comment 2:
Schedule tours on a regular calendar FY.

Response:
The details of individual programs are beyond the scope of the CCP, which is a general planning document. Following the completion of the CCP and when resources become available, the staff will develop more detailed step-down plans to address program management at this level of detail. The Service's preferred alternative (2) calls for a park ranger, environmental educator, and refuge aid to support the visitor services' program.

Comment 3:
Provide walking trails and horse trails.

Response:
The Service's preferred alternative (2) provides for an increase in the refuge's visitor services' program. This increase includes the construction of a boardwalk and observation platform to be located on the west side of Pungo Lake. It also includes the development of a trail through the pocosin habitat from Northern Road, as well as other projects. At this time, the Scuppernong River Interpretive Boardwalk, located behind the Walter B. Jones, Sr., Center for the Sounds (Refuge Visitor Center) in Columbia, N.C., is open for wildlife observation and photography. Existing administrative roads are also available as hiking trails to support wildlife-dependent recreation to the extent that these opportunities do not materially interfere with, or detract from,the achievement of wildlife conservation or refuge operations. The refuge has determined that the use of horses to access the refuge for certain wildlife-dependent recreational activities is appropriate and compatible with certain limitations. These limitations are administered through issuance of special use permits and include how many horses are in a group, how many horses are on the refuge at one time, the locations where the horses can be used, and the time of year when the use of horses must be restricted to avoid conflicts with other user groups and wildlife needs. As the refuge's visitor services' program develops, the staff would continue to assess and adjust the program to avoid negative impacts on refuge resources.

Comment 4:
Install safety railing on side walk at Welcome Center.

Response:
The Scuppernong River Interpretive Boardwalk (SRIB) was designed to provide refuge visitors with an opportunity to observe wildlife and habitat in a natural setting. While the SRIB meets all Occupational Safety and Health Administration (OSHA), and the Fish and Wildlife Service safety guidelines, railings and other visual obstructions were intentionally minimized to maximize the visitor's experience.

Marco Gibbs, concerned citizen

Comment 1:
I looked through the Draft CCP/EA for Pocosin Lakes NWR, but I did not see anything on trapping of furbearers. Trapping has always been a necessary wildlife management tool and I would like to see a trapping program on Pocosin Lakes NWR to manage furbearers. It would also allow another recreational activity to many sportsmen, biologists, and young people wanting to learn something different, and providing a benefit to wildlife at the same time.

Trapping on Pocosin Lakes NWR would furnish some great photography, beautiful scenery, and peace and quiet for someone wanting to trap.

Response:
The Service's preferred alternative (2) has determined that trapping as a management tool is an appropriate use for certain furbearers, including beaver, raccoon, nutria, and feral hog. These species are at sufficiently high levels on the refuge to adversely affect ecosystem functions (see the draft Compatibility Determination at Appendix V). The Service will issue special use permits to administer a trapping program for the management of these species consistent with sound biology, refuge purposes, and conservation of ecosystem functions.

Frances Armstrong, concerned citizen

Comment 1:
The Draft CCP/EA is very thorough and comprehensive. Also I was able to get the answers that I needed at the Public Meeting on July 26, 2007, at the Walter B. Jones Center for the Sounds (Pocosin Lakes NWR Office) in Columbia, NC. It was nice to have an informative meeting on the proposed plan.

I want to put in writing some of the suggestions that I gave at the public meeting.

1. Since Alternative 2 is the proposed alternative, I think a prioritized list of other activities from Alternative 3 – (Substantial Increase) would be a good idea in case funds are available to do more than the activity list of Alternative 2. I think this is especially important since this is a long-term 15-year plan.

Response:
Comment noted. Alternative 2 represents the most feasible and prudent approach for achieving national, ecosystem, and refuge-specific purposes, goals, and objectives.

1. In Alternative 3 the Wildlife Drive along Northern Road is an activity which is not in Alternative
2. I think the Wildlife Drive would give visitors the opportunity to see more of the refuge habitat and wildlife, and would especially be good for summer visitors when it is hot and buggy and not desirable for hiking.

Response:
Comment noted. Alternative 2 represents the most feasible and prudent approach for achieving national, ecosystem, and refuge-specific purposes, goals, and objectives.

3. The endangered red wolves need added protection on the Albemarle/Pamlico Peninsula. The Red Wolf Recovery Team manages coyotes on the peninsula in the area inhabited by red wolves. A law must be passed to outlaw the hunting of coyotes in the area inhabited by red wolves because of the likelihood of shooting an endangered red wolf by mistake. At this time this area on the peninsula is east of State Highway 32, which includes the following five counties: Dare, Hyde, Tyrrell, Washington and Beaufort.

Response:
Comment noted. Red wolves are protected under the Endangered Species Act and other laws on the refuge. Providing protection for wolves outside the refuge is beyond the scope of the CCP.

1. The veterinary care facility for the red wolf is a very good idea. I would like to see it expanded to give care to other endangered species on the refuge.

Response:
Comment noted.

1. I think abundant grain crops and winter wheat in the area near and surrounding Pungo Lake are very important for the migratory birds and the red wolves. The migratory birds feed off the grain and the winter wheat and the red wolves find prey in these fields. For the red wolves to thrive, the red wolf territory needs expansion. I would like to have the farmers in the area have a strong incentive to cultivate grain crops and winter wheat and desire migratory birds and red wolves in these fields as well.

Response:
Comment noted.

1. I think a plan to tap into the Castle Haynes Aquifer for extra water is very important. With the changing weather patterns that are leading to periods of drought, Pungo Lake and the impoundments will benefit if there is a water supply to replenish the lake and impoundments when necessary.

Response:
Comments noted.

1. A new wildlife observation platform on the North Side of Pungo Lake is very important. It should be screened off from the lake so as not to disturb the waterfowl resting on Pungo Lake. The existing wildlife observation platform at Pungo Lake should also be screened off.

Response:
We agree that the proposed boardwalk and observation platform on the west side of Pungo Lake should be screened in some manner to limit disturbance to resting waterfowl. The platform would be carefully designed and constructed to minimize disturbance to wildlife and habitat. During and following construction, the refuge staff would monitor the use of the facility and make adjustments as needed to limit wildlife disturbance to acceptable levels.

1. With the increased interest in the Pungo Unit of the refuge because of the preferred Site C location for a Navy Outlying Landing Field next to Pungo Lake, extra special actions will need to be taken to protect the waterfowl from intentional and unintentional harassment. I have witnessed intentional harassment by very low-flying military aircraft numerous times at the Pungo Unit.

Response:
Comment noted. Alternative 2 proposes additional law enforcement protection.

1. Also because of the increased interest in the Pungo Unit for winter viewing of migratory birds, an additional Visitor Information Center near Pungo Lake is necessary.

Response:
The Service's preferred alternative (2) provides for additional staffing, building expansion, and exhibit replacements for the Walter B. Jones Center for the Sounds (refuge visitor center) located in Columbia, N.C. The CCP also provides for development and maintenance of a captive red wolf facility located in Tyrrell County. Because of their location (along a primary route to the Outer Banks)

these strategies have the potential for reaching many people and are therefore high priorities. However, with the increasing popularity of the Pungo Unit following the proposed Navy OLF controversy, a visitor contact station for the Pungo Unit may become necessary in the future to deal with higher levels of visitation. A strategy was added under interpretation to address this issue.

1. I like the red wolf on the cover but would also like some other photos to show the diversity of Pocosin Lakes NWR. For example: waterfowl, birds, black bears, red-cockaded woodpeckers, bald eagles, refuge habitats. The red wolf or red wolves could be the feature but include some other photos. The background of the cover could be eliminated with a collection of photos.

Response:
Comment noted.

1. I know you are short of staff. I wish that Pocosin Lakes NWR could find a way to hire local people that have grown up in the area and have knowledge and experience with the wildlife in the area, the refuge habitats, and the surrounding land. If this is possible, I know someone that I would highly recommend.

Response:
Comment noted.

Appendix V. Decisions and Approvals

INTRA-SERVICE SECTION 7 BIOLOGICAL EVALUATION

Originating Person: Howard Phillips
Telephone Number: 252-796-3004
E-Mail: howard_phillips@fws.gov
Date: December 5, 2005

Project Name: Pocosin Lakes National Wildlife Refuge Comprehensive Conservation Plan

I. Service Program:
  ___ Ecological Services
  ___ Federal Aid
  ___ Clean Vessel Act
  ___ Coastal Wetlands
  ___ Endangered Species Section 6
  ___ Partners for Fish and Wildlife
  ___ Sport Fish Restoration
  ___ Wildlife Restoration
  ___ Fisheries
  _x_ Refuges/Wildlife

II. State/Agency: North Carolina/ U.S. Fish and Wildlife Service

III. Station Name: Pocosin Lakes National Wildlife Refuge

IV. Description of Proposed Action (attach additional pages as needed): Implementation of the Comprehensive Conservation Plan for Pocosin Lakes National Wildlife Refuge by adopting the preferred alternative that provides guidance, management direction and operation plans for the next 15 years.

V. Pertinent Species and Habitat:

  A. Include species/habitat occurrence map:

  B. Complete the following table:

SPECIES/CRITICAL HABITAT	STATUS
Bald Eagle	Threatened
Red-cockaded Woodpecker	Endangered
Red Wolf	Endangered
American Alligator	Threatened

VI. **Location (attach map):**

   A. **Ecoregion Number and Name:** Roanoke - Tar - Neuse - Cape Fear No. 34

   B. **County and State:** Tyrrell, Washington, and Hyde, North Carolina

   C. **Section, township, and range (or latitude and longitude):**

   D. **Distance (miles) and direction to nearest town:** Adjacent to and immediately south of Columbia, North Carolina

   E. **Species/habitat occurrence:**

   Bald Eagle – Record of in Washington and Hyde Counties within 20 years, in Tyrrell County more than 20 years ago. Occasionally observed on refuge during the winter.

   Red-cockaded Woodpecker - Record of occurrence in Counties within 20 years. Observed on property adjacent to the refuge.

   Red Wolf – Record of occurrence in Counties within 20 years. Experimental population established and monitored on the refuge.

   American Alligator – Record of occurrence in Counties within 20 years. Observed on property adjacent to the refuge

VII. **Determination of Effects:**

   A. Explanation of effects of the action on species and critical habitats in item V. B (attach additional pages as needed).

SPECIES/CRITICAL HABITAT	IMPACTS TO SPECIES/CRITICAL HABITAT
Bald Eagle	Disturbance by staff and visitors during nesting season.
Red-cockaded Woodpecker	Disturbance by staff and visitors during nesting season. Lack of understory management.
Red Wolf	Disturbance by staff and visitors. Saturation of habitat by hydrology restoration.
American Alligator	Disturbance by boaters and anglers. Water quality degradation and lack of marsh habitat.

   B. Explanation of actions to be implemented to reduce adverse effects.

SPECIES/CRITICAL HABITAT	ACTIONS TO MITIGATE/MINIMIZE IMPACTS
Bald Eagle	Restrict access to nesting area.
Red-cockaded Woodpecker	Restrict access to nesting area. Allow pines to grow old enough to develop cavities. Manage understory to maintain height below cavities.
Red Wolf	Restrict access to den sites when wolves are in the area. Monitor the effect of hydrology restoration.
American Alligator	Restrict access when alligators are in the area. Cooperate with state agencies to monitor and improve water quality. Monitor the status of marsh habitat.

VIII. **Effect Determination and Response Requested:**

SPECIES/CRITICAL HABITAT	DETERMINATION			RESPONSE REQUESTED[1]
	NE	NA	AA	
Bald Eagle		X		
Red-cockaded Woodpecker		X		
Red Wolf		X		
American Alligator		X		

[1]DETERMINATION/RESPONSE REQUESTED:

NE = no effect. This determination is appropriate when the proposed action will not directly, indirectly, or cumulatively impact, either positively or negatively, any listed, proposed, candidate species or designated/proposed critical habitat. Response Requested is optional but a Concurrence is recommended for a complete Administrative Record.

NA = not likely to adversely affect. This determination is appropriate when the proposed action is not likely to adversely impact any listed, proposed, candidate species or designated/proposed critical habitat or there may be beneficial effects to these resources. Response Requested is a Concurrence.

AA = likely to adversely affect. This determination is appropriate when the proposed action is likely to adversely impact any listed, proposed, candidate species or designated/proposed critical habitat. Response Requested for listed species is Formal Consultation. Response Requested for proposed or candidate species is Conference.

[signature] 12/5/05
Signature (originating station)   Date

Refuge Manager
Title

IX. **Reviewing Ecological Services Office Evaluation:**

A. Concurrence ✓   Nonconcurrence _____

B. Formal consultation required _____

C. Conference required _____

D. Informal conference required _____

E. Remarks (attach additional pages as needed):

John S. Hammond   8-14-07
Signature   Date

Acting Field Supervisor   _Raleigh Ecological Services_
Title   Office

APPROPRIATE USE DETERMINATIONS

An appropriate use determination is the initial decision process a refuge manager follows when first considering whether or not to allow a proposed use on a refuge. The refuge manager must find that a use is appropriate before undertaking a compatibility review of the use. This process clarifies and expands on the compatibility determination process by describing when refuge managers should deny a proposed use without determining compatibility. If we find a proposed use is not appropriate, we will not allow the use and will not prepare a compatibility determination.

Except for the uses noted below, the refuge manager must decide if a new or existing use is an appropriate refuge use. If an existing use is not appropriate, the refuge manager will eliminate or modify the use as expeditiously as practicable. If a new use is not appropriate, the refuge manager will deny the use without determining compatibility. Uses that have been administratively determined to be appropriate are:

- Six wildlife-dependent recreational uses - As defined by the National Wildlife Refuge System Improvement Act of 1997 (Improvement Act), the six wildlife-dependent recreational uses (hunting, fishing, wildlife observation, wildlife photography, and environmental education and interpretation) are determined to be appropriate. However, the refuge manager must still determine if these uses are compatible.

- Take of fish and wildlife under State regulations - States have regulations concerning take of wildlife that includes hunting, fishing, and trapping. We consider take of wildlife under such regulations appropriate. However, the refuge manager must determine if the activity is compatible before allowing it on a refuge.

The appropriateness of following uses are considered below: The following uses were considered for compatibility determination reviews: 1) access for public uses; 2) trapping of selected furbearers and feral hogs for nuisance animal management; 3) refuge resource research studies; 4) cooperative farming program; 5) commercial photography; 6) commercial tours and guiding; 7) wood and reed gathering and cutting; 8) berry picking; 9) pine straw gathering; 10) bee keeping; and 11) meetings of non-service agencies and organizations.

Statutory Authorities for this policy:

National Wildlife Refuge System Administration Act of 1966, as amended by the National Wildlife Refuge System Improvement Act of 1997, 16 U.S.C. 668dd-668ee (Administration Act). This law provides the authority for establishing policies and regulations governing refuge uses, including the authority to prohibit certain harmful activities. The Administration Act does not authorize any particular use, but rather authorizes the Secretary of the Interior to allow uses only when they are compatible and "under such regulations as he may prescribe." This law specifically identifies certain public uses that, when compatible, are legitimate and appropriate uses within the Refuge System. The law states ". . . it is the policy of the United States that . . .compatible wildlife-dependent recreation is a legitimate and appropriate general public use of the System . . .compatible wildlife-dependent recreational uses are the priority general public uses of the System and shall receive priority consideration in refuge planning and management; and . . . when the Secretary determines that a proposed wildlife-dependent recreational use is a compatible use within a refuge, that activity should be facilitated . . . the Secretary shall . . . ensure that priority general public uses of the System receive enhanced consideration over other general public uses in planning and management within the System . . . ." The law also states "in administering the System, the Secretary is authorized to take the following actions: . . . issue regulations to carry out this Act." This policy implements the standards set in the Administration Act by providing enhanced consideration of priority general public uses and ensuring other public uses do not interfere with our ability to provide quality, wildlife-dependent recreational uses.

Refuge Recreation Act of 1962, 16 U.S.C. 460k (Recreation Act). This law authorizes the Secretary of the Interior to ". . . administer such areas [of the System] or parts thereof for public recreation when in his judgment public recreation can be an appropriate incidental or secondary use." While the Recreation Act authorizes us to allow public recreation in areas of the Refuge System when the use is an "appropriate incidental or secondary use," the Improvement Act provides the Refuge System mission and includes specific directives and a clear hierarchy of public uses on the Refuge System.

Other statutes that establish refuges, including the Alaska National Interest Lands Conservation Act of 1980 (ANILCA) (16 U.S.C. 410hh - 410hh-5, 460 mm - 460mm-4, 539-539e, and 3101 - 3233; 43 U.S.C. 1631 et seq.).

Executive Orders. We must comply with Executive Order (E.O.) 11644 when allowing use of off-highway vehicles on refuges. This order requires that we designate areas as open or closed to off-highway vehicles in order to protect refuge resources, promote safety, and minimize conflict among the various refuge users; monitor the effects of these uses once they are allowed; and amend or rescind any area designation as necessary based on the information gathered. Furthermore, E.O. 11989 requires us to close areas to off highway vehicles when we determine that the use causes or will cause considerable adverse effects on the soil, vegetation, wildlife, habitat, or cultural or historic resources. Statutes, such as ANILCA, take precedence over executive orders.

Definitions:

Appropriate Use
A proposed or existing use on a refuge that meets at least one of the following four conditions:

1) The use is a wildlife-dependent recreational use as identified in the Improvement Act.
2) The use contributes to fulfilling the refuge purpose(s), the Refuge System mission, or goals or objectives described in a refuge management plan approved after October 9, 1997, the date the Improvement Act was signed into law.
3) The use involves the take of fish and wildlife under State regulations.
4) The use has been found to be appropriate as specified in Section 1.11.

Native American
American Indians in the conterminous United States and Alaska Natives (including Aleuts, Eskimos, and Indians) who are members of federally recognized tribes.

Priority General Public Use
A compatible wildlife-dependent recreational use of a refuge involving hunting, fishing, wildlife observation, wildlife photography, and environmental education and interpretation.

Quality
The criteria used to determine a quality recreational experience include:

- Promotes safety of participants, other visitors, and facilities.
- Promotes compliance with applicable laws and regulations and responsible behavior.
- Minimizes or eliminates conflicts with fish and wildlife population or habitat goals or objectives in a plan approved after 1997.
- Minimizes or eliminates conflicts with other compatible wildlife-dependent recreation.
- Minimizes conflicts with neighboring landowners.
- Promotes accessibility and availability to a broad spectrum of the American people.
- Promotes resource stewardship and conservation.
- Promotes public understanding and increases public appreciation of America's natural resources and our role in managing and protecting these resources.
- Provides reliable/reasonable opportunities to experience wildlife.
- Uses facilities that are accessible and blend into the natural setting.
- Uses visitor satisfaction to help define and evaluate programs.

Wildlife-Dependent Recreational Use
As defined by the Improvement Act, a use of a refuge involving hunting, fishing, wildlife observation, wildlife photography, and environmental education and interpretation.

FINDING OF APPROPRIATENESS OF REFUGE USES
Use: **Access for Public Uses**

This form is not required for wildlife-dependent recreational uses, take regulated by the State, or uses already described in a refuge CCP or step-down management plan approved after October 9, 1997.

Decision Criteria:	YES	NO
(a) Do we have jurisdiction over the use?	X	
(b) Does the use comply with applicable laws and regulations (Federal, State, Tribal, and local)?	X	
(c) Is the use consistent with applicable executive orders and Department and Service policies?	X	
(d) Is the use consistent with public safety?	X	
(e) Is the use consistent with goals and objectives in an approved management plan or other document?	X	
(f) Has an earlier documented analysis not denied the use or is this the first time the use has been proposed?	X	
(g) Is the use manageable within available budget and staff?	X	
(h) Will this be manageable in the future within existing resources?	X	
(i) Does the use contribute to the public's understanding and appreciation of the refuge's natural or cultural resources, or is the use beneficial to the refuge's natural or cultural resources?	X	
(j) Can the use be accommodated without impairing existing wildlife-dependent recreational uses or reducing the potential to provide quality (see Section 1.6D, 603 FW 1, for description), compatible, wildlife-dependent recreation into the future?	X	

Where we do not have jurisdiction over the use [no to (a)], there is no need to evaluate it further as we cannot control the use. Uses that are illegal, inconsistent with existing policy, or unsafe [no to (b), (c), or (d)] may not be found appropriate. If the answer is "no" to any of the other questions above, we will generally not allow the use.

If indicated, the refuge manager has consulted with State fish and wildlife agencies. Yes __X__ No ___

When the refuge manager finds the use appropriate based on sound professional judgment, the refuge manager must justify the use in writing on an attached sheet and obtain the refuge supervisor's concurrence.

Based on an overall assessment of these factors, my summary conclusion is that the proposed use is:

        Not Appropriate____   Appropriate__X__

FINDING OF APPROPRIATENESS OF A REFUGE USE
Use: **Trapping of Selected Furbearers and Feral Hogs for Nuisance Animal Management**

This form is not required for wildlife-dependent recreational uses, take regulated by the State, or uses already described in a refuge CCP or step-down management plan approved after October 9, 1997.

Decision Criteria:	YES	NO
(a) Do we have jurisdiction over the use?	X	
(b) Does the use comply with applicable laws and regulations (Federal, State, Tribal, and local)?	X	
(c) Is the use consistent with applicable executive orders and Department and Service policies?	X	
(d) Is the use consistent with public safety?	X	
(e) Is the use consistent with goals and objectives in an approved management plan or other document?	X	
(f) Has an earlier documented analysis not denied the use or is this the first time the use has been proposed?	X	
(g) Is the use manageable within available budget and staff?	X	
(h) Will this be manageable in the future within existing resources?	X	
(i) Does the use contribute to the public's understanding and appreciation of the refuge's natural or cultural resources, or is the use beneficial to the refuge's natural or cultural resources?	X	
(j) Can the use be accommodated without impairing existing wildlife-dependent recreational uses or reducing the potential to provide quality (see Section 1.6D, 603 FW 1, for description), compatible, wildlife-dependent recreation into the future?	X	

Where we do not have jurisdiction over the use [no to (a)], there is no need to evaluate it further as we cannot control the use. Uses that are illegal, inconsistent with existing policy, or unsafe [no to (b), (c), or (d)] may not be found appropriate. If the answer is "no" to any of the other questions above, we will generally not allow the use.

If indicated, the refuge manager has consulted with State fish and wildlife agencies. Yes _X_ No ___

When the refuge manager finds the use appropriate based on sound professional judgment, the refuge manager must justify the use in writing on an attached sheet and obtain the refuge supervisor's concurrence.

Based on an overall assessment of these factors, my summary conclusion is that the proposed use is:

    Not Appropriate _____   Appropriate__X__

FINDING OF APPROPRIATENESS OF A REFUGE USE
Use: **Refuge Resource Research Studies**

This form is not required for wildlife-dependent recreational uses, take regulated by the State, or uses already described in a refuge CCP or step-down management plan approved after October 9, 1997.

Decision Criteria:	YES	NO
(a) Do we have jurisdiction over the use?	X	
(b) Does the use comply with applicable laws and regulations (Federal, State, Tribal, and local)?	X	
(c) Is the use consistent with applicable executive orders and Department and Service policies?	X	
(d) Is the use consistent with public safety?	X	
(e) Is the use consistent with goals and objectives in an approved management plan or other document?	X	
(f) Has an earlier documented analysis not denied the use or is this the first time the use has been proposed?	X	
(g) Is the use manageable within available budget and staff?	X	
(h) Will this be manageable in the future within existing resources?	X	
(i) Does the use contribute to the public's understanding and appreciation of the refuge's natural or cultural resources, or is the use beneficial to the refuge's natural or cultural resources?	X	
(j) Can the use be accommodated without impairing existing wildlife-dependent recreational uses or reducing the potential to provide quality (see Section 1.6D, 603 FW 1, for description), compatible, wildlife-dependent recreation into the future?	X	

Where we do not have jurisdiction over the use [no to (a)], there is no need to evaluate it further as we cannot control the use. Uses that are illegal, inconsistent with existing policy, or unsafe [no to (b), (c), or (d)] may not be found appropriate. If the answer is "no" to any of the other questions above, we will generally not allow the use.

If indicated, the refuge manager has consulted with State fish and wildlife agencies. Yes __X__ No ____

When the refuge manager finds the use appropriate based on sound professional judgment, the refuge manager must justify the use in writing on an attached sheet and obtain the refuge supervisor's concurrence.

Based on an overall assessment of these factors, my summary conclusion is that the proposed use is:

        Not Appropriate _____   Appropriate__X__

Appendices

FINDING OF APPROPRIATENESS OF A REFUGE USE
Use: **Cooperative Farming Program**

This form is not required for wildlife-dependent recreational uses, take regulated by the State, or uses already described in a refuge CCP or step-down management plan approved after October 9, 1997.

Decision Criteria:	YES	NO
(a) Do we have jurisdiction over the use?	X	
(b) Does the use comply with applicable laws and regulations (Federal, State, Tribal, and local)?	X	
(c) Is the use consistent with applicable executive orders and Department and Service policies?	X	
(d) Is the use consistent with public safety?	X	
(e) Is the use consistent with goals and objectives in an approved management plan or other document?	X	
(f) Has an earlier documented analysis not denied the use or is this the first time the use has been proposed?	X	
(g) Is the use manageable within available budget and staff?	X	
(h) Will this be manageable in the future within existing resources?	X	
(i) Does the use contribute to the public's understanding and appreciation of the refuge's natural or cultural resources, or is the use beneficial to the refuge's natural or cultural resources?	X	
(j) Can the use be accommodated without impairing existing wildlife-dependent recreational uses or reducing the potential to provide quality (see Section 1.6D, 603 FW 1, for description), compatible, wildlife-dependent recreation into the future?	X	

Where we do not have jurisdiction over the use [no to (a)], there is no need to evaluate it further as we cannot control the use. Uses that are illegal, inconsistent with existing policy, or unsafe [no to (b), (c), or (d)] may not be found appropriate. If the answer is "no" to any of the other questions above, we will generally not allow the use.

If indicated, the refuge manager has consulted with State fish and wildlife agencies. Yes _X_ No ___

When the refuge manager finds the use appropriate based on sound professional judgment, the refuge manager must justify the use in writing on an attached sheet and obtain the refuge supervisor's concurrence.

Based on an overall assessment of these factors, my summary conclusion is that the proposed use is:

       Not Appropriate _____   Appropriate _X_

FINDING OF APPROPRIATENESS OF A REFUGE USE
Use: **Commercial Photography**

This form is not required for wildlife-dependent recreational uses, take regulated by the State, or uses already described in a refuge CCP or step-down management plan approved after October 9, 1997.

Decision Criteria:	YES	NO
(a) Do we have jurisdiction over the use?	X	
(b) Does the use comply with applicable laws and regulations (Federal, State, Tribal, and local)?	X	
(c) Is the use consistent with applicable executive orders and Department and Service policies?	X	
(d) Is the use consistent with public safety?	X	
(e) Is the use consistent with goals and objectives in an approved management plan or other document?	X	
(f) Has an earlier documented analysis not denied the use or is this the first time the use has been proposed?	X	
(g) Is the use manageable within available budget and staff?	X	
(h) Will this be manageable in the future within existing resources?	X	
(i) Does the use contribute to the public's understanding and appreciation of the refuge's natural or cultural resources, or is the use beneficial to the refuge's natural or cultural resources?	X	
(j) Can the use be accommodated without impairing existing wildlife-dependent recreational uses or reducing the potential to provide quality (see Section 1.6D, 603 FW 1, for description), compatible, wildlife-dependent recreation into the future?	X	

Where we do not have jurisdiction over the use [no to (a)], there is no need to evaluate it further as we cannot control the use. Uses that are illegal, inconsistent with existing policy, or unsafe [no to (b), (c), or (d)] may not be found appropriate. If the answer is "no" to any of the other questions above, we will generally not allow the use.

If indicated, the refuge manager has consulted with State fish and wildlife agencies. Yes _X_ No ___

When the refuge manager finds the use appropriate based on sound professional judgment, the refuge manager must justify the use in writing on an attached sheet and obtain the refuge supervisor's concurrence.

Based on an overall assessment of these factors, my summary conclusion is that the proposed use is:

       Not Appropriate _____   Appropriate_X_

Appendices

FINDING OF APPROPRIATENESS OF A REFUGE USE
Use: **Commercial Tours and Guiding**

This form is not required for wildlife-dependent recreational uses, take regulated by the State, or uses already described in a refuge CCP or step-down management plan approved after October 9, 1997.

Decision Criteria:	YES	NO
(a) Do we have jurisdiction over the use?	X	
(b) Does the use comply with applicable laws and regulations (Federal, State, Tribal, and local)?	X	
(c) Is the use consistent with applicable executive orders and Department and Service policies?	X	
(d) Is the use consistent with public safety?	X	
(e) Is the use consistent with goals and objectives in an approved management plan or other document?	X	
(f) Has an earlier documented analysis not denied the use or is this the first time the use has been proposed?	X	
(g) Is the use manageable within available budget and staff?	X	
(h) Will this be manageable in the future within existing resources?	X	
(i) Does the use contribute to the public's understanding and appreciation of the refuge's natural or cultural resources, or is the use beneficial to the refuge's natural or cultural resources?	X	
(j) Can the use be accommodated without impairing existing wildlife-dependent recreational uses or reducing the potential to provide quality (see Section 1.6D, 603 FW 1, for description), compatible, wildlife-dependent recreation into the future?	X	

Where we do not have jurisdiction over the use [no to (a)], there is no need to evaluate it further as we cannot control the use. Uses that are illegal, inconsistent with existing policy, or unsafe [no to (b), (c), or (d)] may not be found appropriate. If the answer is "no" to any of the other questions above, we will generally not allow the use.

If indicated, the refuge manager has consulted with State fish and wildlife agencies. Yes __X__ No ___

When the refuge manager finds the use appropriate based on sound professional judgment, the refuge manager must justify the use in writing on an attached sheet and obtain the refuge supervisor's concurrence.

Based on an overall assessment of these factors, my summary conclusion is that the proposed use is:

        Not Appropriate _____   Appropriate __X__

FINDING OF APPROPRIATENESS OF A REFUGE USE
Use: **Wood and Reed Gathering and Cutting**

This form is not required for wildlife-dependent recreational uses, take regulated by the State, or uses already described in a refuge CCP or step-down management plan approved after October 9, 1997.

Decision Criteria:	YES	NO
(a) Do we have jurisdiction over the use?	X	
(b) Does the use comply with applicable laws and regulations (Federal, State, Tribal, and local)?	X	
(c) Is the use consistent with applicable executive orders and Department and Service policies?	X	
(d) Is the use consistent with public safety?	X	
(e) Is the use consistent with goals and objectives in an approved management plan or other document?	X	
(f) Has an earlier documented analysis not denied the use or is this the first time the use has been proposed?	X	
(g) Is the use manageable within available budget and staff?	X	
(h) Will this be manageable in the future within existing resources?	X	
(i) Does the use contribute to the public's understanding and appreciation of the refuge's natural or cultural resources, or is the use beneficial to the refuge's natural or cultural resources?	X	
(j) Can the use be accommodated without impairing existing wildlife-dependent recreational uses or reducing the potential to provide quality (see Section 1.6D, 603 FW 1, for description), compatible, wildlife-dependent recreation into the future?	X	

Where we do not have jurisdiction over the use [no to (a)], there is no need to evaluate it further as we cannot control the use. Uses that are illegal, inconsistent with existing policy, or unsafe [no to (b), (c), or (d)] may not be found appropriate. If the answer is "no" to any of the other questions above, we will generally not allow the use.

If indicated, the refuge manager has consulted with State fish and wildlife agencies. Yes __X__ No ____

When the refuge manager finds the use appropriate based on sound professional judgment, the refuge manager must justify the use in writing on an attached sheet and obtain the refuge supervisor's concurrence.

Based on an overall assessment of these factors, my summary conclusion is that the proposed use is:

        Not Appropriate _____   Appropriate __X__

FINDING OF APPROPRIATENESS OF A REFUGE USE
Use: **Berry Picking**

This form is not required for wildlife-dependent recreational uses, take regulated by the State, or uses already described in a refuge CCP or step-down management plan approved after October 9, 1997.

Decision Criteria:	YES	NO
(a) Do we have jurisdiction over the use?	X	
(b) Does the use comply with applicable laws and regulations (Federal, State, Tribal, and local)?	X	
(c) Is the use consistent with applicable executive orders and Department and Service policies?	X	
(d) Is the use consistent with public safety?	X	
(e) Is the use consistent with goals and objectives in an approved management plan or other document?		X
(f) Has an earlier documented analysis not denied the use or is this the first time the use has been proposed?	X	
(g) Is the use manageable within available budget and staff?	X	
(h) Will this be manageable in the future within existing resources?	X	
(i) Does the use contribute to the public's understanding and appreciation of the refuge's natural or cultural resources, or is the use beneficial to the refuge's natural or cultural resources?		X
(j) Can the use be accommodated without impairing existing wildlife-dependent recreational uses or reducing the potential to provide quality (see Section 1.6D, 603 FW 1, for description), compatible, wildlife-dependent recreation into the future?	X	

Where we do not have jurisdiction over the use [no to (a)], there is no need to evaluate it further as we cannot control the use. Uses that are illegal, inconsistent with existing policy, or unsafe [no to (b), (c), or (d)] may not be found appropriate. If the answer is "no" to any of the other questions above, we will generally not allow the use.

If indicated, the refuge manager has consulted with State fish and wildlife agencies. Yes __X__ No ____

When the refuge manager finds the use appropriate based on sound professional judgment, the refuge manager must justify the use in writing on an attached sheet and obtain the refuge supervisor's concurrence.

Based on an overall assessment of these factors, my summary conclusion is that the proposed use is:

       Not Appropriate __X__   Appropriate ____

FINDING OF APPROPRIATENESS OF A REFUGE USE
Use: **Pine Straw Gathering**

This form is not required for wildlife-dependent recreational uses, take regulated by the State, or uses already described in a refuge CCP or step-down management plan approved after October 9, 1997.

Decision Criteria:	YES	NO
(a) Do we have jurisdiction over the use?	X	
(b) Does the use comply with applicable laws and regulations (Federal, State, Tribal, and local)?	X	
(c) Is the use consistent with applicable executive orders and Department and Service policies?	X	
(d) Is the use consistent with public safety?	X	
(e) Is the use consistent with goals and objectives in an approved management plan or other document?		X
(f) Has an earlier documented analysis not denied the use or is this the first time the use has been proposed?	X	
(g) Is the use manageable within available budget and staff?	X	
(h) Will this be manageable in the future within existing resources?	X	
(i) Does the use contribute to the public's understanding and appreciation of the refuge's natural or cultural resources, or is the use beneficial to the refuge's natural or cultural resources?		X
(j) Can the use be accommodated without impairing existing wildlife-dependent recreational uses or reducing the potential to provide quality (see Section 1.6D, 603 FW 1, for description), compatible, wildlife-dependent recreation into the future?	X	

Where we do not have jurisdiction over the use [no to (a)], there is no need to evaluate it further as we cannot control the use. Uses that are illegal, inconsistent with existing policy, or unsafe [no to (b), (c), or (d)] may not be found appropriate. If the answer is "no" to any of the other questions above, we will generally not allow the use.

If indicated, the refuge manager has consulted with State fish and wildlife agencies. Yes _X_ No ___

When the refuge manager finds the use appropriate based on sound professional judgment, the refuge manager must justify the use in writing on an attached sheet and obtain the refuge supervisor's concurrence.

Based on an overall assessment of these factors, my summary conclusion is that the proposed use is:

       Not Appropriate _X_   Appropriate ___

Appendices

FINDING OF APPROPRIATENESS OF A REFUGE USE
Use: **Bee Keeping**

This form is not required for wildlife-dependent recreational uses, take regulated by the State, or uses already described in a refuge CCP or step-down management plan approved after October 9, 1997.

Decision Criteria:	YES	NO
(a) Do we have jurisdiction over the use?	X	
(b) Does the use comply with applicable laws and regulations (Federal, State, Tribal, and local)?	X	
(c) Is the use consistent with applicable executive orders and Department and Service policies?	X	
(d) Is the use consistent with public safety?	X	
(e) Is the use consistent with goals and objectives in an approved management plan or other document?		X
(f) Has an earlier documented analysis not denied the use or is this the first time the use has been proposed?	X	
(g) Is the use manageable within available budget and staff?	X	
(h) Will this be manageable in the future within existing resources?	X	
(i) Does the use contribute to the public's understanding and appreciation of the refuge's natural or cultural resources, or is the use beneficial to the refuge's natural or cultural resources?		X
(j) Can the use be accommodated without impairing existing wildlife-dependent recreational uses or reducing the potential to provide quality (see Section 1.6D, 603 FW 1, for description), compatible, wildlife-dependent recreation into the future?	X	

Where we do not have jurisdiction over the use [no to (a)], there is no need to evaluate it further as we cannot control the use. Uses that are illegal, inconsistent with existing policy, or unsafe [no to (b), (c), or (d)] may not be found appropriate. If the answer is "no" to any of the other questions above, we will generally not allow the use.

If indicated, the refuge manager has consulted with State fish and wildlife agencies. Yes __X__ No ___

When the refuge manager finds the use appropriate based on sound professional judgment, the refuge manager must justify the use in writing on an attached sheet and obtain the refuge supervisor's concurrence.

Based on an overall assessment of these factors, my summary conclusion is that the proposed use is:

        Not Appropriate __X__   Appropriate ____

FINDING OF APPROPRIATENESS OF A REFUGE USE
Use: **Meetings of Non-Service Agencies and Organizations**

This form is not required for wildlife-dependent recreational uses, take regulated by the State, or uses already described in a refuge CCP or step-down management plan approved after October 9, 1997.

Decision Criteria:	YES	NO
(a) Do we have jurisdiction over the use?	X	
(b) Does the use comply with applicable laws and regulations (Federal, State, Tribal, and local)?	X	
(c) Is the use consistent with applicable executive orders and Department and Service policies?	X	
(d) Is the use consistent with public safety?	X	
(e) Is the use consistent with goals and objectives in an approved management plan or other document?	X	
(f) Has an earlier documented analysis not denied the use or is this the first time the use has been proposed?	X	
(g) Is the use manageable within available budget and staff?	X	
(h) Will this be manageable in the future within existing resources?	X	
(i) Does the use contribute to the public's understanding and appreciation of the refuge's natural or cultural resources, or is the use beneficial to the refuge's natural or cultural resources?	X	
(j) Can the use be accommodated without impairing existing wildlife-dependent recreational uses or reducing the potential to provide quality (see Section 1.6D, 603 FW 1, for description), compatible, wildlife-dependent recreation into the future?	X	

Where we do not have jurisdiction over the use [no to (a)], there is no need to evaluate it further as we cannot control the use. Uses that are illegal, inconsistent with existing policy, or unsafe [no to (b), (c), or (d)] may not be found appropriate. If the answer is "no" to any of the other questions above, we will generally not allow the use.

If indicated, the refuge manager has consulted with State fish and wildlife agencies. Yes _X_ No ___

When the refuge manager finds the use appropriate based on sound professional judgment, the refuge manager must justify the use in writing on an attached sheet and obtain the refuge supervisor's concurrence.

Based on an overall assessment of these factors, my summary conclusion is that the proposed use is:

        Not Appropriate _____   Appropriate_X_

Appendices

Approval of Appropriate Use Determinations

This signature page covers all of the above Findings of Appropriate Use considered within the Comprehensive Conservation Plan for Pocosin Lakes National Wildlife Refuge.

Refuge Manager: _____ Date: 8/24/07

If found to be **not appropriate** and the use is a "new use," the refuge supervisor does not need to sign concurrence.

If an existing use is found **not appropriate** outside the CCP process, the refuge supervisor must sign concurrence.

If the use is found **appropriate** use, the refuge supervisor must sign concurrence.

Refuge Supervisor: _____ Date: 9/20/07

A compatibility determination is required before the use may be allowed.

COMPATIBILITY DETERMINATIONS

Pocosin Lakes National Wildlife Refuge Compatibility Determination

Uses: The following uses were considered for compatibility determination reviews: 1) hunting; 2) fishing; 3) wildlife observation and photography; 4) environmental education and interpretation; 5) access for public uses; 6) trapping of selected furbearers and feral hogs for nuisance animal management; 7) refuge resource research studies; 8) cooperative farming program; 9) commercial photography; 10) commercial tours and guiding; 11) wood and reed gathering and cutting; and 12) meetings of non-service agencies and organizations. A description and the anticipated biological impacts for each use are addressed separately in this compatibility determination.

Refuge Name: Pocosin Lakes National Wildlife Refuge.

Date Established: 1963

Establishing and Acquisition Authorities: 16 U.S.C. Sec. 664 (Migratory Bird Conservation Act of 1929), 16 U.S.C. Sec 3901 (b) 100 Stat. 3583 (Emergency Wetland Resources Act of 1986), and 16 U.S.C. Sec 742f (a) (4) (Fish and Wildlife Act of 1956)

Refuge Purpose: The purpose of Pocosin Lakes National Wildlife Refuge, as reflected in the refuge's authorizing legislation, is to protect and conserve migratory birds, and other wildlife resources through the protection of wetlands, in accordance with the following laws:

> *...for use as an inviolate sanctuary, or for any other management purpose, for migratory birds...* 16 U.S.C. Sec. 664 (Migratory Bird Conservation Act of 1929);

> *...for the conservation of the wetlands of the Nation in order to maintain the public benefits they provide and to help fulfill international obligations contained in various migratory bird treaties and conventions...* 16 U.S.C. Sec 3901 (b) 100 Stat. 3583 (Emergency Wetland Resources Act of 1986);

> *...for the development, advancement, management, conservation, and protection of fish and wildlife resources...* 16 U.S.C. Sec 742f (a) (4) (Fish and Wildlife Act of 1956); *and*

> *...for the benefit of the United States Fish and Wildlife Service in performing its activities and services. Such acceptance may be subject to the terms of any restriction or affirmative covenant or condition of servitude...* 16 U.S.C. Sec 742f (a) (4) (Fish and Wildlife Act of 1956).

The refuge's purpose and importance to migratory birds, particularly waterfowl, is: *To conserve wintering habitat for waterfowl and wintering and production habitat for wood ducks to meet the habitat goals presented in the Ten-Year Waterfowl Habitat Acquisition Plan and the North American Waterfowl Management Plan.*

National Wildlife Refuge System Mission:

The mission of the System, as defined by the National Wildlife Refuge System Improvement Act of 1997, is:

> ... to administer a national network of lands and waters for the conservation, management, and where appropriate, restoration of the fish, wildlife and plant resources and their habitats within the United States for the benefit of present and future generations of Americans.

Other Applicable Laws, Regulations, and Policies:

Antiquities Act of 1906 (34 Stat. 225)
Migratory Bird Treaty Act of 1918 (15 U.S.C. 703-711; 40 Stat. 755)
Migratory Bird Conservation Act of 1929 (16 U.S.C. 715r; 45 Stat. 1222)
Migratory Bird Hunting Stamp Act of 1934 (16 U.S.C. 718-178h; 48 Stat. 451)
Criminal Code Provisions of 1940 (18 U.S.C. 41)
Bald and Golden Eagle Protection Act (16 U.S.C. 668-668d; 54 Stat. 250)
Refuge Trespass Act of June 25, 1948 (18 U.S.C. 41; 62 Stat. 686)
Fish and Wildlife Act of 1956 (16 U.S.C. 742a-742j; 70 Stat.1119)
Refuge Recreation Act of 1962 (16 U.S.C. 460k-460k-4; 76 Stat. 653)
Wilderness Act (16 U.S.C. 1131; 78 Stat. 890)
Land and Water Conservation Fund Act of 1965
National Historic Preservation Act of 1966, as amended (16 U.S.C. 470, et seq.; 80 Stat. 915)
National Wildlife Refuge System Administration Act of 1966 (16 U.S.C. 668dd, 668ee; 80 Stat. 927)
National Environmental Policy Act of 1969, NEPA (42 U.S.C. 4321, et seq; 83 Stat. 852)
Use of Off-Road Vehicles on Public Lands (Executive Order 11644, as amended by Executive Order 10989)
Endangered Species Act of 1973 (16 U.S.C. 1531 et seq; 87 Stat. 884)
Refuge Revenue Sharing Act of 1935, as amended in 1978 (16 U.S.C. 715s; 92 Stat. 1319)
National Wildlife Refuge Regulations for the Most Recent Fiscal Year (50 CFR Subchapter C; 43 CFR 3101.3-3)
Emergency Wetlands Resources Act of 1986 (S.B. 740)
North American Wetlands Conservation Act of 1990
Food Security Act (Farm Bill) of 1990 as amended (HR 2100)
Property Clause of the U.S. Constitution Article IV 3, Clause 2
Commerce Clause of the U.S. Constitution Article 1, Section 8
The National Wildlife Refuge System Improvement Act of 1997 (Public Law 105-57, USC668dd)
Executive Order 12996, Management and General Public Use of the National Wildlife Refuge System. March 25, 1996
Title 50, Code of Federal Regulations, Parts 25-33
Archaeological Resources Protection Act of 1979
Native American Graves Protection and Repatriation Act of 1990

Compatibility determinations for each use listed were considered separately. Although the preceding sections (from Uses through Other Applicable Laws, Regulations, and Policies) are only written once for brevity, they are part of each descriptive use and become part of that compatibility determination if considered separately.

Use: *Hunting*

Description of Use: The refuge is a mixture of pocosins (shrub wetlands), forest blocks of pine and hardwoods, marshes, managed wetlands (moist-soil areas), and interconnected streams and ditches. The pocosins have bay species (red bay, sweetbay, loblolly bay), gallberry, sweet gallberry, sweet pepperbush, fetterbush, river cane, and pond pine. The forests have a great variety of tree species that includes bald cypress, tupelo gum, oaks, black gum, elm, Carolina ash, and willow. This rich forested wetland provides good habitat for a number of game species, including white-tailed deer, black bear, squirrel, raccoon, woodcock, and waterfowl.

Many of the local residents enjoy an informal, rural lifestyle that includes frequent recreational use of the area's natural resources. Hunting and fishing have been, and continue to be, popular uses of refuge lands. The refuge has permitted hunting since 1970 on the Pungo Unit, when the Service first approved hunting on that part of the refuge. Hunting has been allowed on the Pocosin Lakes part of the refuge since 1991, soon after establishment. The administration, as well as special regulations for hunting, has changed over time but the majority of the program has remained unchanged.

This use includes the take of big game (deer), migratory birds (ducks, geese, tundra swans, mourning doves, woodcock, rails, and snipe) and upland game (quail, squirrel, rabbit, raccoon, opossum, fox, beaver, and nutria) in accordance with state and refuge regulations. Feral hogs, an invasive species like nutria, appear to be increasing in number. The hunting/take of feral hogs is also included in this use. All hunts will fall within the framework of the State's open seasons and follow State regulations (except for minor variances for special refuge permit-only hunts that are coordinated with the State). Refuge-specific regulations are more restrictive than State regulations to ensure compatibility. The staff reviews refuge-specific regulations annually and incorporates them into the refuge hunting brochure. The comprehensive conservation plan will increase law enforcement presence during hunting seasons; will evaluate the hunt program annually; and will modify seasons, hunt areas, or regulations, if necessary.

Availability of Resources: Based on a review of the refuge's budget allocated for this activity, there is adequate funding to ensure compatibility and to administer this use at its current level. A permanent, full-time law enforcement officer and public use specialist are needed to assist with the hunting program administration and visitor services.

Anticipated Impacts of the Use: The deer herd has expanded and increased substantially since the refuge was established. Prior to refuge establishment, this portion of Tyrell, Washington, and Hyde Counties was subject to heavy deer hunting pressure with pursuit hounds and moderate poaching activity that maintained the deer herd at low levels. Following refuge establishment and initiation of an effective wildlife law enforcement program, the deer herd has increased substantially in and around the refuge. The refuge's pocosin, marsh, and forest habitats, combined with commercially harvested forests and agricultural fields adjacent to the refuge, provide ideal habitat conditions for white-tailed deer.

Harvest management of big game (white-tailed deer) is the art of combining wildlife science and landowner objectives for the attainment of a specific management goal. Refuge hunt plan objectives should determine harvest management strategies. A complete analysis of biological data should determine the objectives. Specific harvest objectives allow the setting of hunting regulations. The refuge staff will thoroughly evaluate the results of each hunting season to ensure that the harvest management program remains dynamic and responsive to an evolving management environment (Bookhout 1994).

Harvest management of upland small game and furbearers (squirrel, rabbit, raccoon, opossum, and beaver) is considerably different from that of both big game and migratory birds. Current literature suggests that user take (<50 percent of total mortality) of most upland game is compensatory; that factors, such as immigration from adjacent areas and density-dependent production, operate in most upland game populations; and that hunting does not significantly impact populations. Hunting is substituted for natural mortality. Production of large, annual surpluses of young allows for lengthy seasons and generous bag limits with little concern for over-harvest and minimal chance of population impacts in most areas (Bookhout 1994).

Harvest management of migratory birds (ducks, woodcock) is more difficult to assess. Migratory bird regulations are established at the Federal level each year following a series of meetings involving both State and Federal biologists. Harvest guidelines are based on population survey data with regulations that are subject to change each year, including bag limits, season lengths, and framework dates (Bookhout 1994). Schmidt (1993) states, "In general, all studies have demonstrated a high degree of compensation of hunting mortality by other 'natural' mortality factors for harvest levels experienced to date." He also reports, "The proportion of waterfowl populations subject to hunting on refuges is very low, thus hunting is not likely to have an adverse impact on the status of any recognized waterfowl population in North America."

The refuge's great variety and abundance of high-quality wetland areas provide outstanding habitat for a variety of wading birds. Primary species include the great blue heron, little blue heron, green heron, cattle egret, snowy egret, great egret, American bittern, Virginia rail, and king rail. Similar to wading birds, the area's habitat for neotropical migratory birds is outstanding. Neotropical migratory birds use the interior hardwood forested areas and edges. Disturbance to these birds will be minimal and temporary as the staff will alter habitat slightly for the betterment of these species.

Based on available information, biologists have not documented any threatened or endangered species, other than the red-cockaded woodpecker, red wolf, and bald eagle, on Pocosin Lakes National Wildlife Refuge. It is anticipated that the current levels and expected future levels of hunting or other wildlife-dependent recreation activities will not directly, indirectly, or cumulatively impact any listed, proposed, or candidate species or designated/proposed critical habitat. Data gathered from future biological surveys regarding the importance or potential importance of the refuge to threatened or endangered species or critical habitat (or proposed threatened, endangered, or critical habitat) could result in changes to public use activities across time; however, these changes will have no effect on listed species.

Incidental taking of other wildlife species, either illegally or unintentionally, may occur with any consumptive use program. At current and anticipated public use levels, incidental take will be small and will not directly or cumulatively impact current or future populations of wildlife either on this refuge or in the surrounding areas. Implementation of an effective law enforcement program and development of site-specific refuge regulations and special conditions will eliminate most incidental take problems.

Public Review and Comment: Methods used to solicit public review and comment included posted notices at refuge headquarters and area locations; copies of the draft comprehensive conservation plan distributed to adjacent landowners, the public, and local, state, and federal agencies; public meetings; and news releases to area newspapers. The Scuppernong Reminder printed releases on July 20 and July 25, 2007, and the Coastland Times printed releases on July 19 and July 24, 2007. Appendix IV summarizes the public comments.

Determination (check one below):

_____ Use is Not Compatible

__X__ Use is Compatible with Following Stipulations

Stipulations Necessary to Ensure Compatibility: The refuge permits hunting in accordance with State of North Carolina regulations and licensing requirements. An Environmental Assessment is on file at the refuge headquarters as part of the Hunting Plan. Upon completion of the comprehensive conservation plan, the staff will update the Hunting Plan. The following stipulations are necessary to ensure the refuge hunting program is compatible with refuge purposes.

- Migratory bird hunting is prohibited on the Pungo Unit.
- No hunting disturbance is allowed on the Pungo Unit during the wintering waterfowl season.
- Vehicles are restricted to designated refuge roads and parking lots.
- Firearms, bows, and other weapons are prohibited except during designated hunting seasons.
- Hunting deer with dogs is not allowed on the refuge due to disturbance to non-target species.

All hunts are designed to provide quality user opportunities based upon known wildlife population levels and biological parameters. Hunt season dates and bag limits will be adjusted, as needed, to achieve balanced wildlife population levels within carrying capacities, regardless of impacts to user opportunities.

As the staff collects additional data and develops a long-range hunt plan, it could implement additional refuge-specific regulations. These regulations could include, but may not be limited to, season dates that differ from those in surrounding state zones, refuge permit requirements, and closed areas on a permanent or seasonal basis. The objectives of the regulations may be to reduce disturbance to specific wildlife species or habitats, such as bird rookeries, wintering waterfowl, or threatened and endangered species, to allow hunting when staff is available to administer the program, or to provide for public safety.

Justification: Hunting is compatible with the purposes for which the refuge was established and the mission of the National Wildlife Refuge System. It is one of the public use recreational activities that the 1997 National Wildlife Refuge System Improvement Act specifically identifies as a use to be allowed where possible on refuges. The refuge uses the hunting of deer and other species as management tools to protect the diverse ecosystem.

Mandatory 15-Year Re-evaluation Date: _____04/22/2023_____

Use: *Fishing*

Description of Use: Sport fishing is a common public use on the State waters, such as creeks, rivers, bays, and sounds. Fishing on the refuge includes fishing in these waters from the shorelines located on the Pocosin Lakes National Wildlife Refuge and in lakes, canals, and impoundments on the refuge. Fish creel limits, boating safety, and license requirements are in accordance with State of North Carolina regulations. The State maintains public boat ramps for small boats on streams adjacent to the refuge. Development of more public access to the water on and adjacent to the refuge will allow the public to utilize these important fishery resources. As identified in the comprehensive conservation plan, the refuge will provide additional access to the banks, conduct creel surveys, and perform water quality analyses in order to provide a quality fishing experience.

Availability of Resources: Based on a review of the refuge's budget allocated for this activity, there is adequate funding to ensure compatibility and to administer the use at its current level.

Anticipated Impacts of the Use: Recreational fishing should not adversely affect the fisheries resource, wildlife resource, endangered species, or any other natural resource of the refuge. There may be some limited disturbance to certain species of wildlife and some trampling of vegetation; however, this should be short-lived and relatively minor and will not negatively impact wetland values on the refuge. If the refuge identifies wildlife disturbance at these sites as a problem in future years, it will close the areas during sensitive seasons to eliminate this concern.

Improvement of access will create some disturbance to the natural environment during construction and lead to increased public use on the State and refuge waters. The refuge will carry out all construction activities with appropriate permits under Section 404 of the Clean Water Act and after State Historic Preservation Officer review of cultural resources. Engineers will incorporate soil stabilization features into the design of access points to minimize any future soil erosion potential and contractors would use sediment retention barriers during access improvement. Public use of the waters will increase as a result of improved access, but the level of use will not be expected to cause detrimental wildlife disturbance. Law enforcement activities will control the problems associated with littering and illegal take of fish. Providing information to refuge visitors about rules and regulations, along with increased law enforcement patrol, will keep these negative impacts to a minimum.

Public Review and Comment: Methods used to solicit public review and comment included posted notices at refuge headquarters and area locations; copies of the draft comprehensive conservation plan distributed to adjacent landowners, the public, and local, state, and federal agencies; public meetings; and news releases to area newspapers. The Scuppernong Reminder printed releases on July 20 and July 25, 2007, and the Coastland Times printed releases on July 19 and July 24, 2007. Appendix IV summarizes the public comments.

Determination (check one below):

_____ Use is Not Compatible

__X__ Use is Compatible with Following Stipulations

Stipulations Necessary to Ensure Compatibility: Conflicts between fishermen and hunters or other visitors using the refuge for non-consumptive wildlife recreation have not been a problem in the past and are not expected to be a problem in the future. A continued law enforcement presence can minimize associated violations, such as taking under-sized fish, open fires, and littering. Upon completion of the comprehensive conservation plan, the refuge staff will update the Fishing Plan. The following stipulations will help ensure the refuge fishing program is compatible with refuge purposes:

- All fishing tackle will have to be attended at all times.
- Leaving boats on the refuge overnight will be prohibited.
- Fishing will be allowed during daylight hours only.

Justification: Refuge regulations permit fishing of State and refuge waters under State regulations. The goal of recreational fishing is to provide a quality fishing experience on a sustainable basis. The 1997 National Wildlife Refuge System Improvement Act lists fishing as a priority public use activity that the Service should provide and expand where possible. Improved access facilities will reduce bank erosion and habitat disturbance, while providing additional quality fishing opportunities.

Mandatory 15-Year Re-evaluation Date: _____04/22/2023_____

Use: *Wildlife Observation and Photography*

Description of Use: Non-consumptive wildlife observation uses, such as bird watching, auto tour routes, hiking, and nature photography, are popular due to the area's abundant wildlife and proximity to the Tidewater Area of Virginia, the Outer Banks of North Carolina, and the availability of access and facilities. It is estimated that 27,000 visits per year are attributed to wildlife observation and related activities.

The refuge staff anticipates that an increase in non-consumptive wildlife-dependent uses will occur over the next few years as facilities and access are improved and especially as the public and conservation groups become more aware of the excellent birding and wildlife viewing opportunities on the refuge.

There are 80 miles of refuge roads minimally maintained for licensed public vehicle travel. The refuge maintains the 0.75-mile interpretive boardwalk trail for pedestrians on the east bank of the Scuppernong River, adjacent to the refuge office and visitor center. There is an observation platform on the south side of Pungo Lake. Additional infrastructure to support wildlife observation and photography is also planned, including additional trails, boardwalks, observation platforms, etc.

Availability of Resources: Based on a review of the refuge's budget allocated for this activity, there will be adequate funding to ensure compatibility and to administer the use at its current level.

Anticipated Impacts of the Use: Wildlife observation and photography activities could result in some disturbance to wildlife, especially if visitors venture too close to bald eagle nests, colonial nesting bird rookeries, or resting waterfowl during migration. The staff will prohibit visitors from traveling in areas around nests, rookeries, and managed wetlands at critical times for wildlife. The refuge will locate refuge road systems, foot trails, boardwalks, and wildlife observation platforms open to pedestrian use by the public to minimize disturbance that could occur in these sensitive areas. If the refuge identifies unacceptable levels of disturbance at any time, it will close sensitive sites to public entry. Some minimal trampling of vegetation could occur.

Construction of foot trails, boardwalks, observation platforms, and upgrading refuge roads will alter small portions of the natural environment. Proper planning prior to construction, sediment retention, and grade stabilization features will reduce negative impacts to wetlands, threatened and endangered species, and species of special concern. Impacts, such as trampling vegetation and wildlife disturbance by refuge visitors do occur, but are presently not significant. Upgrading refuge roads will reduce soil erosion associated with the current dirt roads and trails. Visitors cause other potential negative impacts by violating refuge regulations, such as littering or illegally taking plants or wildlife. Use of refuge roads by the public does result in added maintenance costs.

Public Review and Comment: Methods used to solicit public review and comment included posted notices at refuge headquarters and area locations; copies of the draft comprehensive conservation plan distributed to adjacent landowners, the public, and local, state, and federal agencies; public meetings; and news releases to area newspapers. The Scuppernong Reminder printed releases on July 20 and July 25, 2007, and the Coastland Times printed releases on July 19 and July 24, 2007. Appendix IV summarizes the public comments.

Determination (check one below):

_____ Use is Not Compatible

__X__ Use is Compatible with Following Stipulations

Stipulations Necessary to Ensure Compatibility: Prior to construction, the refuge staff will obtain permits from local, State and Federal regulatory agencies to reduce the possibility of negatively impacting wetlands, cultural resources, or protected species. Law enforcement patrol of public use areas will continue to minimize violations of refuge regulations. The staff will close refuge roads to the public during nesting seasons and migratory waterfowl seasons to minimize wildlife disturbance. The staff will monitor visitors participating in wildlife observation and photography to document any negative impacts. If any negative impacts become noticeable, the Service will take corrective action to reduce or eliminate the effects on wildlife.

Justification: Wildlife observation and photography are important and preferred public uses on Pocosin Lakes National Wildlife Refuge and the National Wildlife Refuge System. The 1997 National Wildlife Refuge System Improvement Act identified wildlife observation and photography as priority public recreational uses refuges should facilitate. It is through permitted, compatible public uses such as this, that the public becomes aware of and provides support for our national wildlife refuges.

Mandatory 15-Year Re-evaluation Date: _____04/22/2023_____

Use: *Environmental Education and Interpretation*

Description of Use: Environmental education and interpretation are those activities that seek to increase the public's knowledge and understanding of wildlife, national wildlife refuges, ecology and land management, as well as contribute to the conservation of natural resources. This use includes participating in programs provided by refuge staff, volunteers, and others and receiving information from panels and other static and interactive exhibits. Environmental education programs are presented at various locations, including the Visitor Center, Indoor Classroom, Outdoor Classroom, and Field Station. Interpretation is provided along the Scuppernong River Interpretive Boardwalk, at kiosks, and other sites.

The refuge's environmental education and interpretation activities have served thousands of users annually. Interpretive and outreach programs reach most of those individuals, but systematic education programs have been largely nonexistent. The refuge staff plans to develop this program with structured activities conducted by refuge staff or trained volunteers. Refuge staff will develop and provide curriculum and support materials to area teachers for use both on and off the refuge. They will also develop informational kiosks and interpretive panels at key refuge entrance points and along trails, and construct wildlife observation platforms as part of the environmental education and interpretation program. In addition, a small building to house special red wolf education activities, as well as to provide wolf health care activities, is also being developed.

Availability of Resources: Based on a review of the refuge's budget allocated for these activities, funding is adequate to ensure compatibility and to administer these uses at current levels.

Anticipated Impacts of the Use: Construction of facilities, such as board walks, kiosks and observation platforms, will alter small portions of the natural environment on the refuge. Proper planning and placement of facilities will ensure that wetlands, threatened or endangered species, or species of special concern are not negatively impacted. The refuge staff will obtain proper permits through the county, State and Federal regulatory agencies prior to construction to ensure resource protection. The use of on-site, hands-on, action-oriented activities to accomplish environmental education and interpretive tours may impose a low-level impact on the sites used for these activities. These low-level impacts may include trampling of vegetation and temporary disturbance to wildlife species in the immediate area. Educational activities held off of the refuge will not create any biological impacts on the resource.

Public Review and Comment: Methods used to solicit public review and comment included posted notices at refuge headquarters and area locations; copies of the draft comprehensive conservation plan distributed to adjacent landowners, the public, and local, state, and federal agencies; public meetings; and news releases to area newspapers. The Scuppernong Reminder printed releases on July 20 and July 25, 2007, and the Coastland Times printed releases on July 19 and July 24, 2007. Appendix IV summarizes the public comments.

Determination (check one below):

_____ Use is Not Compatible

__X__ Use is Compatible with Following Stipulations

Stipulations Necessary to Ensure Compatibility: Zoning of visitor activities by time and space, clustering public use facilities, proper monitoring, educating visitors, and enforcement will ensure compatibility with the purposes of the refuge and mission of the National Wildlife Refuge System. Through periodic evaluation of trails and visitor contact points, the visitor services program will assess resource impacts. If the refuge staff determines that human impacts are detrimental to important natural resources, the staff will take actions to reduce or eliminate those impacts. Major portions of the refuge will remain undeveloped, without public interpretive facilities.

Justification: The 1997 National Wildlife Refuge System Improvement Act identified environmental education and interpretation as activities that refuges should provide and expand. Educating and informing the public through structured environmental education courses, interpretive materials, and guided tours about migratory birds, endangered species, wildlife management, and ecosystems will lead to improved support of the Service's mission to protect our natural resources.

Mandatory 15-Year Re-evaluation Date: _____04/22/2023_____

Use: *Refuge Access for Public Uses*

Description of Use: The public gains access to the refuge in a number of ways to participate in the six priority public uses (hunting, fishing, wildlife observation, wildlife photography, and environmental education and interpretation) and compatible secondary uses. Most visitors utilize licensed four-wheeled motor vehicles and walk from their vehicles to off-road destinations. There are some visitors who utilize all-terrain vehicles, boats, bicycles, wheelchairs, and horses on refuge roads. The refuge allows access by all the means listed above with limitations on location and season of use.

Availability of Resources: Based on a review of the refuge's budget allocated for this activity, there will be adequate funding to ensure compatibility and to administer the use at its current level.

Anticipated Impacts of the Use: Providing access for public uses might result in some disturbance to wildlife, especially if visitors venture too close to bald eagle nests, colonial nesting bird rookeries, or resting waterfowl in migration. The staff will prohibit visitors from traveling in areas around nests, rookeries, and managed wetlands during critical periods for wildlife. The refuge will locate refuge road systems, all-terrain vehicle trails, boat ramps, foot trails, boardwalks, and wildlife observation platforms open to pedestrian use by the public to minimize disturbance that could occur in these sensitive areas. If the refuge identifies unacceptable levels of disturbance at any time, it will close sensitive sites to public entry. Some minimal trampling of vegetation could occur.

Construction of foot trails, boardwalks, observation platforms, and upgrading refuge roads will alter small portions of the natural environment. Proper planning prior to construction, sediment retention, and grade stabilization features will reduce negative impacts to wetlands, threatened and endangered species, and species of special concern. Impacts, such as trampling vegetation and wildlife disturbance by refuge visitors do occur, but are presently not significant. Upgrading refuge roads will reduce soil erosion associated with the current dirt roads and trails. Visitors cause other potential negative impacts by violating refuge regulations, such as littering or illegally taking plants or wildlife. Use of refuge roads by the public will incur added maintenance costs.

Public Review and Comment: Methods used to solicit public review and comment included posted notices at refuge headquarters and area locations; copies of the draft comprehensive conservation plan distributed to adjacent landowners, the public, and local, state, and federal agencies; public meetings; and news releases to area newspapers. The Scuppernong Reminder printed releases on July 20 and July 25, 2007, and the Coastland Times printed releases on July 19 and July 24, 2007. Appendix IV summarizes the public comments.

Determination (check one below):

____ Use is Not Compatible

_X_ Use is Compatible with Following Stipulations

Stipulations Necessary to Ensure Compatibility: Access should be limited to that necessary to facilitate priority and compatible secondary uses. Driving, ATV riding, boating, bicycling, horseback riding, etc., solely for recreational purposes (such as racing, water skiing, personal watercraft, air boats, etc.,) should be prohibited. Law enforcement patrol of public use areas will continue to minimize violations of refuge regulations. The staff will close refuge roads to the public during nesting seasons and migratory waterfowl seasons to minimize wildlife disturbance. The staff will monitor roads, trails, and heavily used pedestrian areas to document any negative impacts. If any negative impacts occur, the Service will take corrective action to reduce or eliminate the effects on wildlife. Prior to construction of boardwalks, foot trails, and wildlife observation platforms, the refuge staff will obtain permits from local, State, and Federal regulatory agencies to reduce the possibility of negatively impacting wetlands, cultural resources, or protected species.

There are specific stipulations that should apply to specific means of access:

- Limit all access when necessary to protect nesting bald eagles, colonial nesting birds, resting waterfowl from disturbance, or for other management purposes.
- Limit access by licensed motorized vehicles to the 80 miles of public use roads when gates are open.
- Limit access by wheelchair to the 250 miles of dirt roads, boardwalks, and trails that have been hardened to support wheelchair traffic.
- Limit access by bicycle to the 250 miles of dirt roads.
- Limit access by foot (walking or hiking) to anywhere on the refuge except areas that are closed for nesting bald eagles, colonial nesting birds, resting waterfowl, or other management purposes.
- Limit access by all-terrain vehicles to 27 miles of refuge dirt roads that are designated all-terrain vehicle trails during the hunting season to transport hunter and game and about 5 miles of road designated for disabled hunter access with a permit.
- Limit access by boat to New Lake from March 1 until October 31. No access should be allowed on New Lake from November 1 until February 28, or on Pungo Lake at any time. Small boats can be allowed in roadside canals year-round except for areas that are closed to prevent wildlife disturbance.
- Limit access for wildlife observation and wildlife photography by groups of one to six horseback riders to the 80 miles of public use roads, except for roads that are in areas open to big game hunting with firearms and for roads that are closed to prevent wildlife disturbance.

Appendices

- Limit access for wildlife observation and wildlife photography by groups of seven to thirty horseback riders to the 80 miles of public use roads when the gates are open. A group of seven to thirty horses should be considered a trail ride and require a special use permit. No trail rides should be allowed on the Pungo Unit during the wintering waterfowl season or in any areas open to big game hunting with firearms. Prohibit groups of horseback riders larger than 30 to prevent wildlife disturbance.
- Access by horse will not be permitted during hunting seasons for white-tailed deer or other large game or during special hunts on the refuge.

Justification: The public must have access to the refuge to participate in the public uses on Pocosin Lakes National Wildlife Refuge and the National Wildlife Refuge System. It is through permitted, compatible public uses that the public becomes aware of and provides support for our national wildlife refuges.

Mandatory 10-Year Re-evaluation Date: _____04/22/2018_____

Use: *Trapping of Selected Furbearers and Feral Hogs for Management*

Description of Use: This use includes the take of certain furbearers (raccoon, beaver, and nutria) and feral hogs by the use of traps. These species are at sufficiently high levels on the refuge to adversely affect ecosystem functions. Excessive numbers of raccoons can have negative effects on the reproduction of forest breeding birds and wood ducks. The nutria is an exotic animal that consumes great quantities of marsh grass and burrows into dikes of managed wetlands (moist-soil units). Feral hogs damage habitat by rutting the ground when grubbing for food. Beavers block culverts and water control structures, impairing wetland management operations and the drainage of adjacent landowners. Protection and management of habitat and improvements in game and nongame populations are central components of the comprehensive conservation plan. To this end, trapping and/or hunting remain the only viable methods to reduce population levels of raccoon, beaver, nutria, and feral hogs. The Service will issue special use permits to administer a trapping program consistent with sound biology, refuge purposes, and conservation of ecosystem functions.

Availability of Resources: Based on a review of the refuge's budget allocated for this activity, there is adequate funding to ensure compatibility and to administer the use at its current level.

Anticipated Impacts of the Use: Targeted removal of raccoon, beaver, nutria, and feral hogs from portions of the refuge will reduce the negative impacts these species are having on ecosystem functions. Regulated trapping of raccoon populations will reduce the nest predation this species causes to neotropical birds and wood ducks. Nutria and beaver management will protect marsh grass, dikes of managed wetlands (moist-soil units), roads, and drainage rights. Feral hog control will reduce habitat damage in pocosin habitat. However, no trapping program, regardless of how well it is designed, can prevent the possible take of other species. The refuge staff will require trappers to report the incidental take of other species. There will be a negligible impact on other wildlife species in both the short and long term.

Public Review and Comment: Methods used to solicit public review and comment included posted notices at refuge headquarters and area locations; copies of the draft comprehensive conservation plan distributed to adjacent landowners, the public, and local, state, and federal agencies; public meetings; and news releases to area newspapers. The <u>Scuppernong Reminder</u> printed releases on July 20 and July 25, 2007, and the <u>Coastland Times</u> printed releases on July 19 and July 24, 2007. Appendix IV summarizes the public comments.

Determination (check one below):

_____ Use is Not Compatible

__X__ Use is Compatible with Following Stipulations

Stipulations Necessary to Ensure Compatibility: The refuge staff should monitor the program closely to assess the potential adverse effects on other wildlife, as well as the benefits to game and nongame species and their habitats. The staff should modify the program as needed to maintain compatibility. Trappers should carry out all trapping activities under a refuge special use permit. The staff should limit trappers by number, area, and season in order to target problem areas and minimize any negative impacts. The staff should require each trapper to report the number and location of all traps and all wildlife taken. The implementation of a trapping program, under controlled conditions, should provide an essential population control management tool and is compatible with the purposes of the refuge.

Justification: The purposes of Pocosin Lakes National Wildlife Refuge emphasize conservation of wetlands and migratory birds. Trapping is a wildlife population management tool used to regulate the population of certain wildlife species when those species are disrupting ecosystem functions. There is documentation that raccoons cause negative impacts to forested wetlands and nesting birds. Nutria are exotic animals that cause negative impacts on marsh grass and the dikes of managed wetlands (moist-soil units). Beavers negatively impact water control structures and drainage. When these negative impacts become significant on the refuge, wildlife managers need trapping as a management tool to control the level of damage. Certainly, the native raccoons and beavers are important components of the ecosystem, but when their populations and negative impacts become significant, wildlife managers need a regulated trapping program to reduce their populations to acceptable levels.

Mandatory 10-Year Re-evaluation Date: _____04/22/2018_____

Use: *Refuge Resource Research Studies*

Description of Use: This activity involves university students and professors, non-governmental researchers, and governmental scientists access to the refuge's natural environment to conduct both short-term and long-term research projects. The outcome of this research should result in better knowledge of our natural resources and improved methods to manage, monitor, and protect refuge resources. The refuge will support Fish and Wildlife Service and U.S. Geological Survey research of neotropical migratory birds, waterfowl, bottomland hardwood restoration, amphibians and reptiles, forest bats, yellow-crowned night herons, and other studies. The refuge will make efforts to expand partnerships with North Carolina State University and other area universities to conduct research on the refuge associated with neotropical migratory songbirds.

Availability of Resources: The refuge needs no additional fiscal resources to conduct this use if it is the university or agency conducting the research. The existing staff could administer permits and monitor use as part of routine management duties. Research initiated by the refuge will require funding through the Refuge Operations Needs System (RONS), Flex Fund Grants, USGS Research Grants, or other sources.

Anticipated Impacts of the Use: There should be no significant negative impacts from scientific research on the refuge. The knowledge gained from the research will provide information to improve management techniques and better meet the needs of trust resource species. Impacts, such as trampling vegetation and temporary disturbance to wildlife, will occur, but should not be significant. Researchers may collect a small number of individual plants or animals for further study. These collections should have an insignificant effect on refuge plant and animal populations.

Public Review and Comment: Methods used to solicit public review and comment included posted notices at refuge headquarters and area locations; copies of the draft comprehensive conservation plan distributed to adjacent landowners, the public, and local, state, and federal agencies; public meetings; and news releases to area newspapers. The Scuppernong Reminder printed releases on July 20 and July 25, 2007, and the Coastland Times printed releases on July 19 and July 24, 2007. Appendix IV summarizes the public comments.

Determination (check one below):

_____ Use is Not Compatible

_X_ Use is Compatible with Following Stipulations

Stipulations Necessary to Ensure Compatibility: The refuge should examine each request for use of the refuge for research on its individual merit. It should ask questions of who, what, when, where, and why in order to determine if the requested research will contribute to the refuge purposes and if the researchers will conduct it on the refuge without significantly affecting the resources. If so, the refuge should issue a special use permit to the researcher, which will likely include special conditions necessary to ensure compatibility. The staff should monitor the progress and require the researcher to submit annual progress reports and copies of all publications derived from the research.

Justification: The benefits derived from sound research will provide a better understanding of species and the environmental communities present on the refuge. These benefits far outweigh any short-term disturbance or loss of individual plant and animals that could occur.

Mandatory 10-Year Re-evaluation Date: _____04/22/2018_____

Use: *Cooperative Farming Program*

Description of Use: Pocosin Lakes National Wildlife Refuge manages cropland to provide highly nutritious annual grain crops and browse for waterfowl, songbirds, and mammals. The crops provide grain for geese, swans, and black bear; wheat browse for geese and white-tailed deer; and food and cover for mammals and neotropical migratory songbirds from perennial grasslands.

The crops are produced by local farmers working on the refuge under a cooperative farming agreement. The farmers till, plant, and harvest the crops. In lieu of paying rent for use of the refuge land, the farmers leave a percentage of the crop in the field where it is available for use by refuge wildlife. The cooperative farming agreement specifies crops to be planted, dates of planting, crops to be left in the field unharvested, pesticides to be used, and pesticide application techniques to be used.

Availability of Resources: Based on a review of the refuge's budget allocated for this activity, there is adequate funding for the staff to administer the cooperative farming program.

Anticipated Impacts of the Use: It is anticipated that cropland management will supplement the natural habitats on the refuge (Ringelman 1990). The refuge will direct cooperative farming operations at providing the types of grain and the proper balance of grain to browse from crops that meet the food cover requirements of the wildlife species of concern. The staff will monitor cooperative farmers' compliance with the annual cooperative farming agreement.

The operations will include tillage and the applications of nutrients and pesticides that enhance crop production, but that could cause non-point source pollution. Tillage performed in accordance with a conservation plan developed by the USDA, Natural Resources Conservation Service, should not cause erosion that will result in sedimentation into aquatic ecosystems or carry nutrients or pesticides into those ecosystems. Nutrient management in accordance with soil test reports specifying the rates, timing, and formulations of nutrients should not cause runoff or percolation of nutrients. Pest management in accordance with an integrated pest management plan should result in scouting to assess pest problems and consideration of mechanical, cultural, and chemical techniques to control pests. Application of approved chemical pesticides in accordance with label directions should minimize the drift, runoff, and percolation of pesticides into the environment.

The minimum short-term impacts from cooperative farming operations will include soil disturbance by disking, and the loss of standing cover of weed species by mowing, disking, and herbicide application. The sown crops quickly cover the soil disturbed by tillage and produce grain and browse selected to supplement natural habitats. Rotating crops throughout the cropland acreage will minimize the need for fertilizer and pesticides and alternates the heavy residue-producing crops (e.g., corn) with poor residue-producing crops (e.g., soybeans).

Public Review and Comment: Methods used to solicit public review and comment included posted notices at refuge headquarters and area locations; copies of the draft comprehensive conservation plan distributed to adjacent landowners, the public, and local, state, and federal agencies; public meetings; and news releases to area newspapers. The Scuppernong Reminder printed releases on July 20 and July 25, 2007, and the Coastland Times printed releases on July 19 and July 24, 2007. Appendix IV summarizes the public comments.

Determination (check one below):

____ Use is Not Compatible

__X__ Use is Compatible with Following Stipulations

Stipulations Necessary to Ensure Compatibility: The refuge should carry out the cooperative farming program in accordance with national and regional policy and a management plan that specifies crops, crop rotation, tillage, nutrient management, and pest management. The refuge should direct cooperative farming operations at supplementing natural habitats found throughout the South Atlantic Coastal Plain. It should evaluate the impacts of the cropland, revise cropland management agreements, and carry out cropland management operations in a manner that would accomplish the refuge's cropland management objectives for migratory birds and resident wildlife.

Justification: The cooperative farming actions proposed in the comprehensive conservation plan for Pocosin Lakes National Wildlife Refuge are in accordance with Service guidelines for the protection, management, and enhancement of habitats for wildlife populations on the refuge. Adherence to the Cropland Management Plan supplements the natural habitats for both migratory birds and resident wildlife species; protects cultural resources; and provides opportunities for public recreation and environmental education.

Mandatory 10-Year Re-evaluation Date: _____04/22/2018_____

Use: *Commercial Photography*

Description of Use: Commercial photography includes capturing still photos and video for commercial gain. Commercial photography is a popular enterprise on the refuge due to the scenic natural habitats and abundant wildlife in an area. The area's proximity to the Tidewater Area of Virginia and the Outer Banks of North Carolina attracts several commercial photographers annually. Where commercial photography is beneficial because it expands public appreciation and understanding of wildlife, natural habitats, and the mission of the refuge system, it may involve vehicular and other access to areas that are otherwise closed. Infrastructure developed for visitors participating in recreational wildlife observation and photography could be used for commercial photography.

The refuge staff anticipates that an increase in commercial photography will occur over the next few years as the refuge gains visibility and areas of natural habitat in the area decrease.

Availability of Resources: Based on a review of the refuge's budget allocated for this activity, there is adequate funding to ensure compatibility and to administer the use.

Anticipated Impacts of the Use: Commercial wildlife photography activities could result in some disturbance to wildlife, especially if photographers venture too close to bald eagle nests, colonial nesting bird rookeries, or resting waterfowl in migration. The staff will prohibit photographers from traveling in areas around nests, rookeries, and managed wetlands during critical times for wildlife. The refuge will locate refuge road systems, foot trails, boardwalks and wildlife observation platforms open to use by photographers to minimize disturbance that could occur in these sensitive areas. If the refuge identifies unacceptable levels of disturbance at any time, it will close sensitive sites to

public entry. Some minimal trampling of vegetation could occur.
Construction of foot trails, boardwalks, observation platforms, and upgrading refuge roads will alter small portions of the natural environment. Proper planning prior to construction, sediment retention, and grade stabilization features will reduce negative impacts to wetlands, threatened and endangered species and species of special concern. Impacts, such as trampling vegetation and wildlife disturbance by refuge visitors, do occur, but are presently not significant. Upgrading refuge roads will reduce soil erosion associated with the current dirt roads and trails. Visitors could cause other potential negative impacts by violating refuge regulations, such as littering or illegally taking plants or wildlife. Use of refuge roads by photographers will incur added maintenance costs.

Public Review and Comment: Methods used to solicit public review and comment included posted notices at refuge headquarters and area locations; copies of the draft comprehensive conservation plan distributed to adjacent landowners, the public, and local, state, and federal agencies; public meetings; and news releases to area newspapers. The Scuppernong Reminder printed releases on July 20 and July 25, 2007, and the Coastland Times printed releases on July 19 and July 24, 2007. Appendix IV summarizes the public comments.

Determination (check one below):

_____ Use is Not Compatible

__X__ Use is Compatible with Following Stipulations

Stipulations Necessary to Ensure Compatibility: Law enforcement patrol of public use areas should continue to minimize violations of refuge regulations. The staff should close refuge roads to photographers during nesting seasons and migratory waterfowl seasons to minimize wildlife disturbance. The refuge should monitor use for commercial photography to document any negative impacts. If any negative impacts become noticeable, the refuge should take corrective action to reduce or eliminate the effects on wildlife. Specifically, commercial photography should be subject to the following stipulations:

- Manage commercial photography under special use permits that will stipulate the dates, times, and general locations that could be photographed and any special access that might be allowed.
- Consider requests for special use permits that include special access only if they demonstrate a means to enhance education, appreciation, and/or understanding of the natural resources and the Refuge System.
- Require commercial photographers to give proper credit to the refuge and the Fish and Wildlife Service in special use permits.

Justification: Commercial photography has the potential to inspire and educate the public about the Refuge System, natural habitats, and wildlife.

Mandatory 10-Year Re-evaluation Date: _____04/22/2018_____

Use: *Commercial Tours and Guiding*

Description of Use: Commercial tours and guiding include tours to observe and photograph wildlife, educate the public about wildlife, and guided fishing and hunting trips. As the visibility of the refuge increases and the amount of land in the area available for outdoor recreation and education decreases, there will be an increased demand for recreation and education on the refuge. The demand for visitor services may exceed the refuge staff's ability to provide them. Some individuals and groups may want services on a timetable that meets their schedule and does not necessarily match the availability of the staff.

The refuge will manage commercial tours and guides through the review and issuance of special use permits.

Availability of Resources: Based on a review of the refuge's budget allocated for this activity, there will be adequate funding to ensure compatibility and to administer the use. The existing management, biological, and public use staff will review, approve, and enforce conditions on special use permits.

Anticipated Impacts of the Use: Commercial tours and guided experiences could result in some disturbance to wildlife, especially if customers venture too close to bald eagle nests, colonial nesting bird rookeries, or resting waterfowl in migration. The staff will prohibit the commercial tours and guided hunters and anglers from traveling in areas around nests, rookeries, and managed wetlands during critical times for wildlife. The refuge will locate refuge road systems, foot trails, boardwalks, and wildlife observation platforms open to use by customers to minimize disturbance that could occur in these sensitive areas. If the staff identifies unacceptable levels of disturbance at any time, sensitive sites will be closed to public entry. Some minimal trampling of vegetation could occur.

Construction of foot trails, boardwalks, observation platforms, and upgrading refuge roads will alter small portions of the natural environment. Proper planning prior to construction, sediment retention, and grade stabilization features will reduce negative impacts to wetlands, threatened and endangered species, and species of special concern. Impacts, such as trampling vegetation and wildlife disturbance by refuge visitors, do occur, but are presently not significant. Upgrading refuge roads will reduce soil erosion associated with the current dirt roads and trails. Customers could cause other potential negative impacts by violating refuge regulations, such as littering or illegally taking plants or wildlife. Use of refuge roads by customers will result in added maintenance costs.

Public Review and Comment: Methods used to solicit public review and comment included posted notices at refuge headquarters and area locations; copies of the draft comprehensive conservation plan distributed to adjacent landowners, the public, and local, state, and federal agencies; public meetings; and news releases to area newspapers. The <u>Scuppernong Reminder</u> printed releases on July 20 and July 25, 2007, and the <u>Coastland Times</u> printed releases on July 19 and July 24, 2007. Appendix IV summarizes the public comments.

Determination (check one below):

_____ Use is Not Compatible

__X__ Use is Compatible with Following Stipulations

Stipulations Necessary to Ensure Compatibility: Law enforcement patrol of public use areas will continue to minimize violations of refuge regulations. The staff will close refuge roads to commercial tours and guided hunters and anglers during nesting seasons and migratory waterfowl seasons to minimize wildlife disturbance. The staff will monitor use for commercial tours and guided experiences to document any negative impacts. If any negative impacts become noticeable, the Service will take corrective action to reduce or eliminate the effects on wildlife. Prior to construction of trails, boardwalks, and observation platforms, the refuge will obtain permits from local, State, and Federal regulatory agencies to reduce the possibility of negatively impacting wetlands, cultural resources, or protected species. Specifically, commercial tours and guided experiences are subject to the following stipulations:

- Commercial tours and guided experiences should be managed under special use permits that stipulate the size of groups; type and number of vehicles or canoes and kayaks; frequency of tours; and the dates, times, and general locations that could be visited. At any one time, no more than one tour group, on one bus or three vans, should be allowed on the Pungo Unit during the wintering waterfowl season.
- Requests for special use permits should only be considered if they demonstrate a means to facilitate the priority public uses (hunting, fishing, wildlife observation, wildlife photography, and environmental education and interpretation) of the Refuge System.
- Commercial tour leaders and guides should be required to give proper credit to the refuge and the Fish and Wildlife Service in the special use permit.
- All guides should be required to possess valid State and Federal licenses, where applicable.
- Guide permit applicants that have serious criminal histories or a history of repeated local, State, or Federal fish or game violations should not be allowed.
- Guides should be required to maintain a minimum level of liability insurance adequate for local considerations, type of activity, etc. The insurance policy should have to contain an endorsement that the insurance company would notify the refuge before and upon cancellation of the policy.
- Guides should provide harvest information to the refuge, at least to the level of detail as reported by the public at harvest check stations.

Justification: Commercial tours and guides have the potential to facilitate the Refuge System's priority public uses beyond the ability of the refuge staff. They can also accommodate larger groups than the Service can handle and schedule tours and guided experiences to match the public's availability.

Mandatory 10-Year Re-evaluation Date: _____04/22/2018_____

Use: *Wood and Reed Gathering*

Description of Use: Wood and reed gathering includes the gathering of dead and blown down trees and cutting vegetation from roads, road shoulders, firebreaks, ditch and canal banks, and other areas where vegetation is periodically maintained. The public gathers wood for personal firewood, personal net stakes (for commercial and recreational fishing), personal hunting blinds, or other personal uses. The public cuts the stems of common reed (*Phragmites australis*) and other exotic species for personal hunting blind concealment material.

The refuge manages these uses through the review and issuance of special use permits and enforcement of the conditions on the permits.

Availability of Resources: Based on a review of the refuge's budget allocated for this activity, there is adequate funding to ensure compatibility and to administer the use. The existing management, biological, and law enforcement staff will review, approve, and enforce conditions on the special use permits.

Anticipated Impacts of the Use: Wood and reed gathering and cutting could result in some disturbance to wildlife, especially if permit holders venture too close to bald eagle nests, colonial nesting bird rookeries, or resting waterfowl in migration. The refuge will prohibit the permit holders from operating in areas around nests, rookeries, and managed wetlands during critical periods for wildlife. If the refuge identifies unacceptable levels of disturbance at any time, sensitive sites will be closed to public entry. Some minimal trampling of vegetation could occur.

Impacts, such as trampling vegetation and wildlife disturbance by permit holders, do occur, but are presently not significant. Upgrading refuge roads will reduce soil erosion associated with the current dirt roads and trails. Permit holders could cause other potential negative impacts by violating refuge regulations, such as littering or illegally taking plants or wildlife. Use of refuge roads by permit holders will result in added maintenance costs.

Gathering of dead wood will reduce the fuel available to wildfires that are a threat to the refuge habitat and the organic soil on which the habitat depends. The tendency of the wood and reed gatherers to collect wood and reeds along refuge roads will minimize the fuel available to be ignited by cigarettes thrown from vehicles. It also will reduce the workload on the staff that maintains roadsides.

Public Review and Comment: Methods used to solicit public review and comment included posted notices at refuge headquarters and area locations; copies of the draft comprehensive conservation plan distributed to adjacent landowners, the public, and local, state, and federal agencies; public meetings; and news releases to area newspapers. The Scuppernong Reminder printed releases on July 20 and July 25, 2007, and the Coastland Times printed releases on July 19 and July 24, 2007. Appendix IV summarizes the public comments.

Determination (check one below):

_____ Use is Not Compatible

__X__ Use is Compatible with Following Stipulations

Stipulations Necessary to Ensure Compatibility: Law enforcement patrol of public use areas should continue to ensure compliance with permit conditions. The staff should close refuge roads to wood and reed gatherers and cutters during nesting seasons and migratory waterfowl seasons to minimize wildlife disturbance. The staff should monitor wood and reed gathering and cutting to document any negative impacts. If any negative impacts were to occur, the Service should take corrective action to reduce or eliminate the effects on wildlife or habitats.

Specifically wood and reed cutters and gatherers should be subject to the following stipulations:

- Wood and reed gathering and cutting should be managed under special use permits that stipulate that the wood and reeds can be gathered for personal use only and give the dates and general locations where wood and reeds could be gathered and cut.
- Wood gathering and cutting should be limited to dead woody stems that are on the ground in natural habitat, or woody stems that are on the ground and leaning over roadsides, ditches, or canals.

- Wood gathering and cutting should not include any live trees or standing dead trees in natural habitat.
- Reed cutting should be limited to common reed (*Phragmites australis*).

Justification: Wood and reed cutting and gathering have the potential to reduce wildfire potential and maintenance on the refuge and reduce the refuge workload. Common reed is an exotic species the refuge wishes to control.

Mandatory 10-Year Re-evaluation Date: _____04/22/2018_____

Use: *Meetings of Non-Service Agencies and Organizations on the Refuge*

Description of Use: Meetings of non-Service agencies and organizations include the meetings of government agencies, such as the North Carolina Wildlife Resources Commission, North Carolina Division of Forest Resources, North Carolina Division of Parks and Recreation, and non-government organizations, such as the Partnership for the Sounds and the American Red Cross, that cooperate with the refuge in natural resource conservation, environmental education and interpretation, employee training, or other functions beneficial to the refuge. These meetings occur in the conference room, visitor center auditorium, indoor classroom, outdoor classroom, field station, and other facilities.

The refuge manages meetings through the review of requests for meeting purpose, scheduling facilities, and monitoring participants for compliance with requirements.

Availability of Resources: Based on a review of the refuge's budget allocated for this activity, there is adequate funding to ensure compatibility and to administer the use. The existing management, biological, and law enforcement staff will review, approve, and enforce conditions on special use permits.

Anticipated Impacts of the Use: Hosting meetings by non-Service agencies and organizations could result in utility bills slightly larger than normal in order to provide electricity and water required for the meetings. The meetings may also cause slightly more maintenance in the rooms utilized.

Hosting meetings will foster goodwill with our partners who support the refuge management program, provide education and interpretation opportunities, and train staff.

Public Review and Comment: Methods used to solicit public review and comment included posted notices at refuge headquarters and area locations; copies of the draft comprehensive conservation plan distributed to adjacent landowners, the public, and local, state, and federal agencies; public meetings; and news releases to area newspapers. The Scuppernong Reminder printed releases on July 20 and July 25, 2007, and the Coastland Times printed releases on July 19 and July 24, 2007. Appendix IV summarizes the public comments.

Determination (check one below):

_____ Use is Not Compatible

_X_ Use is Compatible with Following Stipulations

Stipulations Necessary to Ensure Compatibility: The use of refuge meeting space should be limited to meetings that contribute to the mission of the refuge, the Refuge System, and the Service or to the conservation of natural resources. The refuge should close areas of buildings and grounds not required for the meetings to minimize maintenance. The staff should monitor meeting rooms to document any negative impacts. If any negative impacts were to become noticeable, the Service should take corrective action to reduce or eliminate the effects on refuge buildings and grounds. Refuge staff should clearly articulate requirements for use and enforce compliance by monitoring meeting participants.

Justification: Hosting meetings by non-Service agencies and organizations will have no significant impact on refuge buildings or grounds and will foster goodwill with cooperating agencies and organizations.

Mandatory 10-Year Re-evaluation Date: _____04/22/2018_____

Literature Cited

Bookhout, T.A.. 1994. Research and management techniques for wildlife and habitats. Fifth edition. The Wildlife Society, Bethesda, MD 740pp.

Ringelman, J.K. 1990. Managing agricultural foods for waterfowl. In Laubhan, M.K., and D. Hamilton. Waterfowl Management Handbook. U.S. Fish and Wildlife Service, Fort Collins, CO

Schmidt, P.R. 1993. Memorandum - Information request regarding impacts of hunting on national wildlife refuges. U.S. Department of the Interior, Fish and Wildlife Service, Office of Migratory Bird Management, Washington, D.C. 7pp.

Approval of Compatibility Determination

The signature of approval is for all compatibility determinations considered within the comprehensive conservation plan. If one of the descriptive uses is considered for compatibility outside of the comprehensive conservation plan, the approval signature becomes part of that determination.

Refuge Manager: _____ 9/24/2007
(Signature/Date)

Regional Compatibility Coordinator: _____ 4/15/08
(Signature/Date)

Refuge Supervisor: Acting Brett E. Hunter 4/21/08
(Signature/Date)

Regional Chief, National Wildlife Refuge System, Southeast Region: _____ 4-22-08
(Signature/Date)

Appendix VI. Refuge Biota

ANIMALS
BIRDS
Total Species - 187, Breeding Species - 60
A = Abundant, C = Common, U = Uncommon, O = Occasional, R = Rare
*species with confirmed breeding records

SPECIES	SPRING	SUMMER	FALL	WINTER
ANIMALS				
BIRDS				
Avocet, American		R		
Bittern, American*	U	U	U	U
Bittern, Least*	U	U		
Blackbird, Brewer's				R
Blackbird, Red-winged*	A	A	A	A
Blackbird, Rusty				O
Bluebird, Eastern*	O	O	O	O
Bobolink	O		O	
Bobwhite, Northern*	A	A	A	A
Bufflehead			C	C
Bunting, Indigo*	U	U		
Bunting, Snow				R
Canvasback			O	O
Catbird, Gray*	C	C	C	U
Cardinal, Northern*	C	C	C	
Chat, Yellow-breasted	O	O	O	
Chickadee, Carolina*	C	C	C	C
Chuck-will's Widow		O	O	
Cormorant, Double-crested	C	U	C	C
Coot, American	C	O	C	A
Cowbird, Brown-headed*	C	C	C	C

Appendices

SPECIES	SPRING	SUMMER	FALL	WINTER
ANIMALS (continued)				
BIRDS (continued)				
Creeper, Brown			O	O
Crow, Common*	A	A	A	A
Crow, Fish*	C	C	C	C
Cuckoo, Black-billed	R		R	
Cuckoo, Yellow-billed*	U	U		
Dove, Ground			R	
Dove, Mourning*	C	C	C	C
Dove, Rock	O	O	O	O
Dowitcher, Long-billed	O		O	R
Dowitcher, Short-billed	R		R	R
Duck, American Black*	U	U	A	A
Duck, Ring-necked			C	C
Duck, Ruddy			C	C
Duck, Wood*	A	A	A	A
Dunlin	R			
Eagle, Bald (Threatened)	O	R	O	O
Eagle, Golden				R
Egret, Cattle	O	U	O	R
Egret, Great	U	U	U	U
Egret, Snowy	U	O	O	U
Falcon, Peregrine			O	O
Finch, House				U
Finch, Purple				U
Flicker, Common*	C	C	C	C
Flycatcher, Acadian*	U	U		
Flycatcher, Great Crested*	U	U		

SPECIES	SPRING	SUMMER	FALL	WINTER
ANIMALS (continued)				
BIRDS (continued)				
Gadwall	U		A	A
Gnatcatcher, Blue-gray*	O	O	O	O
Goldeneye, Common				R
Goldfinch, American			O	O
Goose, Canada*	U	U	C	C
Goose, Snow			A	A
Goose, White-fronted			R	R
Grackle, Boat-tailed	U	U	U	U
Grackle, Common*	A	A	A	A
Grebe, Pied-billed	U	U	C	C
Grosbeak, Evening			O	O
Gull, Bonaparte's				R
Gull, Great Black-backed		R		R
Gull, Herring	C	O	C	O
Gull, Laughing	C	O	O	R
Gull, Ring-billed	C	C	C	C
Harrier, Northern	O		C	C
Hawk, Broad-winged			O	
Hawk, Cooper's	O	O	O	O
Hawk, Red-tailed*	C	C	C	C
Hawk, Sharp-shinned*	C	U	C	C
Heron, Great Blue*	C	C	C	C
Heron, Little Blue	U	U	U	
Heron, Green-backed*	C	C	U	

Appendices

SPECIES	SPRING	SUMMER	FALL	WINTER
ANIMALS (continued)				
BIRDS (continued)				
Heron, Black-crowned Night	U	U	U	U
Heron, Tri-colored	O	O	O	
Heron, Yellow-crowned Night	R	R		
Hummingbird, Ruby-throated*		U	U	
Ibis, Glossy	O	O		
Ibis, White		O		
Jay, Blue*	U	U	U	U
Junco, Dark-eyed	U		U	C
Kestrel, American	C		C	C
Killdeer*	U	U	U	O
Kingbird, Eastern*	C	C	U	
Kingbird, Western			R	
Kingfisher, Belted	C	C	C	C
Kinglet, Golden-crowned			O	O
Kinglet, Ruby-crowned			O	O
Lark, Horned				R
Loon, Common	R			R
Mallard*	U	U	A	A
Martin, Purple*	C	C	O	
Meadowlark, Eastern*	A	A	C	A
Merganser, Hooded			O	O
Merganser, Red-breasted	R	R	U	U
Merlin	O		O	C
Mockingbird, Northern*	A	A	A	A
Moorhen, Common	U	U	R	R
Nighthawk, Common		U	U	

SPECIES	SPRING	SUMMER	FALL	WINTER
ANIMALS (continued)				
BIRDS (continued)				
Nuthatch, Brown-breasted*	U	U	U	U
Nuthatch, Red-breasted			R	R
Nuthatch, White-breasted*	U	U	U	R
Oldsquaw				R
Oriole, Northern	R			
Oriole, Orchard*	U			
Osprey*	O	O	O	
Ovenbird		O		
Owl, Barred*	U	U	U	U
Owl, Common Barn*	U	U	U	U
Owl, Eastern Screech*	U	U	U	U
Owl, Great Horned*	U	U	U	U
Owl, Long-eared				R
Owl, Saw Whet	R	R	R	R
Phoebe, Eastern	U	U	R	C
Pintail, Northern	U		A	A
Pipits, Water				U
Plover, Black-bellied	R		O	R
Plover, Golden			R	
Plover, Semipalmated	O		U	
Rail, Black	R		R	R
Rail, King*	U	U	U	U
Rail, Virginia*			U	U
Rail, Yellow				U
Redhead			O	O
Redstart, American		C	C	

Appendices

SPECIES	SPRING	SUMMER	FALL	WINTER
ANIMALS (continued)				
BIRDS (continued)				
Robin, American*	A	A	A	A
Sandpiper, Least	O		O	O
Sandpiper, Pectoral	R		R	
Sandpiper, Semipalmated	O		U	
Sandpiper, Solitary	R		R	
Sandpiper, Spotted	U	U	U	
Sandpiper, Upland			O	
Sandpiper, Western	R		U	
Sapsucker, Yellow-bellied	U		U	U
Scaup, Lesser			O	O
Shoveler, Northern	U		A	A
Shrike, Loggerhead	O	O	O	O
Siskin, Pine	U			U
Sora	O		O	O
Snipe, Common	U		U	U
Sparrow, Chipping	U	U	U	U
Sparrow, Clay-colored				R
Sparrow, Dark-eyed	U		U	C
Sparrow, Field	U	U	U	U
Sparrow, Fox	U		U	U
Sparrow, Grasshopper				O
Sparrow, House	R	R	R	R
Sparrow, Le Conte's				R
Sparrow, Lincoln's				U
Sparrow, Savannah	U		U	C
Sparrow, Seaside	?	?	?	?

SPECIES	SPRING	SUMMER	FALL	WINTER
ANIMALS (continued)				
BIRDS (continued)				
Sparrow, Sharp-tailed			R	R
Sparrow, Song	U		U	C
Sparrow, Swamp	U		U	C
Sparrow, Vesper				O
Sparrow, White-crowned			U	U
Sparrow, White-throated	U		C	C
Starling, European*	A	A	A	A
Stilt, Black-necked		R		
Swallow, Bank	O	O		
Swallow, Barn	U	U		
Swallow, Northern Rough-winged	U	U		
Swallow, Tree*	C	C	C	U
Swan, Tundra	R	R	A	A
Swift, Chimney		O	O	
Tanager, Summer	U	U		
Teal, American Green-winged	U		A	A
Teal, Blue-winged	U		U	U
Tern, Black	R		R	
Tern, Caspian	O		O	
Tern, Common		O		
Tern, Forster's	R		R	
Tern, Royal		R		
Thrasher, Brown*	C	C	C	C
Thrush, Hermit	U		U	U
Thrush, Swainson's	O		O	
Thrush, Wood*	C	C	U	

Appendices

SPECIES	SPRING	SUMMER	FALL	WINTER
ANIMALS (continued)				
BIRDS (continued)				
Titmouse, Tufted*	U	U	U	U
Towhee, Rufous-sided*	C	C	C	C
Vireo, Red-eyed*	U	U		
Vireo, Solitary				R
Vireo, White-eyed	U	U	U	
Vireo, Yellow-throated	R	U		
Vulture, Black*	U	U	U	U
Vulture, Turkey*	C	C	C	C
Warbler, Black-and-white	R	R		
Warbler, Hooded*	U	U		
Warbler, Magnolia	R			
Warbler, Northern Parula	O	O		
Warbler, Orange-crowned				R
Warbler, Palm			R	R
Warbler, Pine*	U	O	U	U
Warbler, Prairie*	U	U		
Warbler, Prothonotary*	U	U		
Warbler, Swainson's	O	O		
Warbler, Worm-eating	R			
Warbler, Yellow*	O	O		
Warbler, Yellow-rumped	C		A	A
Warbler, Yellow-throated*	U	U		
Waterthrush, Northern	R		R	
Waxwing, Cedar	O		O	O
Wigeon, American	U		A	A
Whip-poor-widow	O	O	O	O

SPECIES	SPRING	SUMMER	FALL	WINTER
ANIMALS (continued)				
BIRDS (continued)				
Willet	U		O	O
Woodcock, American	O	O	U	C
Woodpecker, Downy	U	U	U	U
Woodpecker, Hairy*	U	U	U	U
Woodpecker, Pileated*	U	U	U	U
Woodpecker, Red-bellied	U	U	U	U
Woodpecker, Red-cockaded*	U	U	U	U
Woodpecker, Red-headed*	O	O	O	O
Wood-pewee, Eastern	U	U	U	
Wren, Carolina*	U	U	C	C
Wren, House*	U	U	U	
Wren, Marsh*	U	U	U	U
Wren, Sedge			U	U
Wren, Winter				O
Yellow-throat, Common*	C	C	U	U
Yellowlegs, Greater	U	U		U
Yellowlegs, Lesser	O		O	O
ANIMALS (CONTINUED)				
MAMMALS				
Bat, Big Brown	*Eptesicus fuscus*			
Bat, Eastern Big-eared	*Corynorhinus rafinesquii*			
Bat, Evening	*Nycticelus numeralis*			
Bat, Hoary	*Lasiurus cinereus*			
Bat, Red	*Lasiurus borealis*			
Bat, Silver-haired	*Lasionycteris noctivagans*			
Bear, Black	*Ursus americana*			

Appendices

SPECIES		SPRING	SUMMER	FALL	WINTER
ANIMALS (CONTINUED)					
MAMMALS (CONTINUED)					
Beaver	*Castor canadensis*				
Bobcat	*Lynx rufus*				
Coyote	*Canis latrans*				
Deer, White-tailed	*Odocoileus virginianus*				
Fox, Gray	*Urocyon cinereoargenteus*				
Fox, Red	*Vulpes fulva*				
Mink	*Mustela vison*				
Mole, Eastern	*Scalopus aquaticus*				
Mole, Star-nosed	*Condylura cristata*				
Mouse, Cotton	*Peromyscus gossypinus*				
Mouse, Eastern Harvest	*Reithrodontomys humilis*				
Mouse, Golden	*Ochrotomys nuttalli*				
Mouse, House	*Mus musculus*				
Mouse, White-footed	*Peromyscus leucopus*				
Muskrat	*Ondatra zibethica*				
Myotis, Southeastern	*Myotis austroriparius*				
Nutria (Exotic)	*Myocastor coypus*				
Opossum	*Didelphis virginiana*				
Otter, River	*Lutra canadensis*				
Pipistrelle, Eastern	*Pipistrellus subflavus*				
Rabbit, Eastern Cottontail	*Sylvilagus floridanus*				
Rabbit, Marsh	*Sylvilagus palustris*				
Raccoon	*Procyon lotor*				
Rat, Hispid Cotton	*Sigmodon hispidus*				
Rat, Norway	*Rattus norvegicus*				
Rat, Rice	*Oryzomys palustris*				
Shrew, Carolina Short-tailed	*Blarina carolinensis*				

SPECIES	SPRING	SUMMER	FALL	WINTER
ANIMALS (CONTINUED)				
MAMMALS (CONTINUED)				
Shrew, Dismal Swamp Southeastern (Threatened)	*Sorex longorostris fisheri*			
Shrew, Least	*Crytotis parva*			
Shrew, Short-tailed	*Blarina brevicauda*			
Shrew, Southeastern	*Sorex longirostris*			
Squirrel, Gray	*Sciurus carolinensis*			
Squirrel, Southern Flying	*Glaucomys volans*			
Vole, Meadow	*Microtus pennsylvanicus*			
Weasel,, Long-tailed	*Mustela frenata*			
Woodchuck	*Marmota monax*			
Wolf, Red (Endangered)	*Canis rufus*			
FAUNA				
TURTLES				
Cooter, Florida	*Chrysemys floridana floridana*			
Mudturtle, Eastern	*Kinosternon subrubrum subrubrum*			
FAUNA A (continued)				
TURTLES A (continued)				
Turtle, Eastern Box	*Terrapeme carolina carolina*			
Turtle, Eastern Musk	*Sternotherus odoratus*			
Turtle, Eastern Painted	*Chrysemys picta picta*			
Turtle, Snapping	*Chelydra serpentina*			
Turtle, Spotted	*Clemmys guttata*			
Turtle, Yellow-bellied	*Chrysemys scripta scripta*			
FAUNA (continued)				
SNAKES				
Copperhead, Southern	*Agkistrodon contortrix*			
Cottonmouth, Eastern	*Agkistrodon piscivorus*			

SPECIES	SPRING	SUMMER	FALL	WINTER
FAUNA (continued)				
SNAKES (continued)				
Rattlesnake, Pygmy	*Sistrusus miliarius barbouri*			
Rattlesnake, Timber	*Crotalus horridus*			
Snake, Banded Water	*Nerodia fasciata fasciata*			
Snake, Black Rat	*Elaphe obsoleta obsoleta*			
Snake, Black Swamp	*Elaphe obseleta obselata*			
Snake, Brown	*Pseudonaja textilis*			
Snake, Brown Water	*Natrix taxispilota*			
Snake, Corn	*Elaphe guttata guttata*			
Snake, Eastern Garter	*Thamnophis sirtalis sirtalis*			
Snake, Eastern Hognose	*Heterdon platyrhinos*			
Snake, Eastern King	*Lampropeltis getulus getulus*			
Snake, Eastern Mud	*Farancia abacura abacura*			
Snake, Eastern Ribbon	*Thamnophis sauritus sauritus*			
Snake, Glossy Crayfish	*Regina rigida*			
Snake, Northern Brown	*Storeria dekayi dekayi*			
Snake, Northern Ringneck	*Diadophis punctatus edwardsii*			
Snake, Northern Water	*Natrix sipedon sipedon*			
Snake, Pine Woods	*Rhadinae flavilata*			
Snake, Rainbow	*Farancia erythrogram*			
Snake, Red-Bellied	*Storeria occipitomaculata*			
Snake, Red-Bellied Water	*Natrix erythrogaster erythrogaster*			
Snake, Rough Green	*Opheodrys aestivus*			
Snake, Southern Ringneck	*Diadophis punctatus punctatus*			
Snake, Worm	*Carphophis vermis*			
Snake, Yellow Rat	*Elaphe obsoleta quadrivittata*			

SPECIES	SPRING	SUMMER	FALL	WINTER
FAUNA (continued)				
SALAMANDERS				
Amphiuma, Two-toed	*Amphiuma means*			
Mudpuppy, Dwarf	*Necturus punctatus*			
Newt, Eastern	*Notophthalmus viridescens*			
Salamander, Dwarf	*Eurycea quadridigitata*			
Salamander, Eastern Mud	*Pseudotriton montanus montanus*			
Salamander, Mabee's	*Amybstema mabeei*			
Salamander, Many-Lined	*Stereochilus marginatus*			
Salamander, Marbled	*Ambystoma opacum*			
Salamander, Redback	*Plethodon cinereus*			
Salamander, Slimy	*Plethodone glutinosus glutinous*			
Salamander, Southern Dusky	*Desmognathus auriculatus*			
Salamander, Spotted	*Ambystoma muculatum*			
Salamander, Three-lined	*Eurycea quttolineata*			
Salamander, Two-lined	*Eurycea bislineata*			
Siren, Greater	*Siren lacertina*			
FAUNA (continued				
LIZARDS				
Anole, Green (Carolina Anole)	*Anolis carolinensis*			
Lizard, Eastern Fence	*Sceloporus undulatus hyacinthinus*			
Lizard, Eastern Glass	*Ophisaures ventralis*			
Lizard, Slender Glass	*Ophisaures attenuatus*			
Racerunner, Six-Lined	*Cnemidophorus sexlineatus*			
Skink, Broad-Headed	*Eumeces laticeps*			
Skink, Ground	*Leiolopisma laterale*			
Skink, Five-Lined	*Eumeces fasciatus*			
Skink, Southeastern Five-Lined	*Eumeces inexpectatus*			

Appendices

SPECIES	SPRING	SUMMER	FALL	WINTER
FAUNA (continued				
FROGS AND TOADS				
Bullfrog	*Rana catesbeiana*			
Frog, Brimley's Chorus	*Pseudarcris brimleyi*			
Frog, Carpenter	*Rana virgatipes*			
Frog, Gray Tree	*Hyla chrysoscelis (diploid form)*			
Frog, Green	*Rana clamitans melanota*			
Frog, Green Tree	*Hyla gratiosa*			
Frog, Little Grass	*Limnaoedus ocularis*			
Frog, Ornate Chorus	*Pseudacris ornata*			
Frog, Pickerel	*Rana palustris*			
Frog, Pine Woods Tree	*Hyla femoralis*			
Frog, Southern Chorus	*Pseudacris nigrita*			
Frog, Southern Cricket	*Acris gryllus gyrllus*			
Frog, Southern Leopard	*Rana utricularia*			
Frog, Squirrel Tree	*Hyla squirella*			
Peeper, Northern Spring	*Hyla cinera cinera*			
Spadefoot, Eastern	*Scaphiopus holbrooki holbrooki*			
Toad, Eastern Narrow-Mouthed	*Gastrophryne carolinensis*			
Toad, Fowler's	*Bufo woodhousei fowleri*			
Toad, Oak	*Bufo quercicus*			
Toad, Southern	*Bufo terrestris*			
FLORA				
TREES				
Ash, Carolina	*Fraxinus caroliniana*			
Ash, Green	*Fraxinus pennsylvanica*			
Bald cypress	*Taxodium distichum*			

SPECIES	SPRING	SUMMER	FALL	WINTER
FLORA (continued				
TREES (continued				
Bay, Loblolly	*Gordonia lasianthus*			
Bay, Sweet	*Magnolia virginiana*			
Birch, River	*Betula nigra*			
Cedar, Atlantic White	*Chamaecyparis thyoides*			
Cedar, Eastern Red	*Juniperus virginiana*			
Cherry, Black	*Prunus serotina*			
Dogwood, Flowering	*Cornus florida*			
Dogwood, Rough leaf	Cornus aspirifolia			
Dogwood, Swamp	*Cornus strictaCornus stricta*			
Elm, American	*Ulmus americana*			
Hickory, Mockernut	*Carya tomentosa*			
Hickory, Pignut	*Carya glabra*			
Hickory, Water	*Carya aquatica*			
Holly, American	*Ilex opaca*			
Locust, Black	*Robinia pseudo-acacia*			
Maple, Red	*Acer rubrum*			
Mulberry, Red	*Morus rubra*			
Oak, Cherrybark	*Quercus pagodafolia*			
Oak, Laurel	*Quercus laurifolia*			
Oak, Southern Red	*Quercus falcata*			
Oak, Water	*Quercus nigra*			
Oak, Willow	*Quercus phellos*			
Pecan	*Carya illinoensis*			
Persimmon, Common	*Diospyros virginiana*			
Pine, Loblolly	*Pinus taeda*			
Pine, Pond	*Pinus serotina*			

SPECIES	SPRING	SUMMER	FALL	WINTER
FLORA (continued				
TREES (continued				
Poplar, Yellow	*Liriodendron tulipifera*			
Sweetgum	*Liquidambar styraciflua*			
Sycamore	*Platanus occidentalis*			
Tree, Toothache	*Zanthoxylum clava-herculis*			
Tupelo, Swamp	*Nyssa sylvatica var. biflora*			
Tupelo, Water	*Nyssa aquatica*			
Walking stick, Devil's	*Aralia spinosa*			
Willow, Black	*Salix nigra*			
Wilow, Coastal Plain, Ward's, Swamp	*Salix caroliniana*			
Wilow, Sandbar	*Salix exigua*			
FLORA (continued				
SHRUBS				
Alder, Common	*Alnus serrulata*			
Bayberry, Northern	*Myrica pennsylvanica*			
Blackberry, Serrate Leaf	*Rubus argutus*			
Blackberry, Sand	*Rubus cuneifolius*			
Blueberry, Black Highbush	*Vaccinium atrococcum*			
Blueberry, Elliott's	*Vaccinium elliotti*			
Buttonbush	*Cephalanthus occidentalis*			
Dewberry, Prickly	*Rubus flagellaris*			
Dogwood, Silky	*Cornus amomum*			
Elder, Marsh	*Iva imbricata*			
Elderberry, American	*Sambucus canadensis*			
Fetterbush, Swamp	*Leucothoe racemosa*			
Gallberry, Sweet or Large	*Ilex coriacea*			
Groundsel Tree, High Tide Bush	*Baccharis halimifolia*			

SPECIES	SPRING	SUMMER	FALL	WINTER
FLORA (continued)				
SHRUBS (continued)				
Holly, Yaupon	*Ilex vomitoria*			
Huckleberry, Squaw	*Vaccinium stamineum*			
Inkberry, Bitter Gallberry	*Ilex glabra*			
Oak, Dwarf	*Quercus prinoides*			
Oak, Scrub	*Quercus marilandica*			
Pepperbush, Sweet	*Clethra alnofolia*			
Possumhaw	*Viburnum nudum*			
Redbay, Swamp	*Persea palustris*			
Pawpaw, Common	*Asimina triloba*			
Privet, Chinese (Exotic)	*Ligustrum chinense*			
Rose, Swamp	*Rosa palustris*			
Shadbush, Serviceberry	*Amelanchier candensis*			
Sumac, Winged	*Rhus copallina*			
Sweetspire, Virginia	*Itea virginica*			
Titi	*Cyrilla racemiflora*			
Waxmyrtle	*Myrica cerifera*			
FLORA (continued)				
WOODY VINES				
Creeper, Virginia	*Parthenocissus quinquefolia*			
Grape, Muscadine	*Vitis rotundifolia*			
Grape, Pigeon	*Vitis cinerea var. floridana*			
Greenbrier, Cat	*Smilax gluca*			
Greenbrier, Common	*Smilax rotundifolia*			
Greenbrier, Ear-leaf	*Smilax auriculata*			
Greenbrier, Laurel-Leaf	*Smilax laurifolia*			
Greenbrier, Saw	*Smilax bona-nox*			

SPECIES	SPRING	SUMMER	FALL	WINTER
FLORA (continued)				
WOODY VINES (continued)				
Honeysuckle, Coral	*Lonicera sempervirens*			
Honeysuckle, Japanese (Exotic)l	*Lonicera japonica*			
Ivy, Poison	*Rhus radicans*			
Trumpetcreeper	*Campsis radicans*			
Vine, Pepper	*Ampelopsis arborea*			
Wisteria (Exotic)	*Wisteria chinensis*			
FLORA				
FORBS (BROADLEAF HERBACEOUS PLANTS)				
Alligatorweed (Exotic)	*Alternanthera philoxeroides*			
Arrow Arum	*Peltandra virginica*			
Arrowhead, Awl-leaf	*Sagittaria subulata*			
Arrowhead, Broadleaf	*Sagittaria latifolia*			
Arrowhead, Bulltongue	*Sagittaria lancifolia*			
Aster, Bushy	*Aster dumosus*			
Bean, Trailing Wild	*Strophostyles helvola*			
Bedstraw, Catchweed	*Galium aparine*			
Beggarticks, Smooth	*Bidens laevis*			
Bladderwort	*Utricularia spp.*			
Buttercup, Celery-Leaf	*Ranunculus sceleratus*			
Buttonweed	*Diodia spp.*			
Cactus	*Opuntia compressa*			
Camphor Weed	*Pluchea purpurascens*			
Centella	*Centella asiatica*			
Cherry, Ground	*Physalis visocosa ssp. maritima*			
Chickweed, Mouse-Ear	*Cerastium vicosum*			
Clover, Crimson (Exotic)	*Trifolium incarnatum*			

SPECIES		SPRING	SUMMER	FALL	WINTER
FLORA (continued)					
FORBS (BROADLEAF HERBACEOUS PLANTS) (continued)					
Clover, White (Exotic)	*Trifolium repens*				
Cocklebur, Rough	*Xanthium strumarium*				
Coontail	*Ceratophyllum demersum*				
Cranesbill, Carolina	*Geranium carolinianum*				
Cress, Bitter	*Cardamine hairsuta*				
Cucumber, Creeping	*Melothria pendula*				
Cudweed, Narrow-Leaf	*Gnaphalium purpureum var. falcatum*				
Daisy Fleabane	*Erigeron canadensis*				
Daisy, False	*Eclipta alba*				
Dandelion, Dwarf	*Krigia virginica*				
Dock, Curly	*Rumex crispa*				
Dock, Water	*Rumex verticillatus*				
Dog Fennel, Small	*Eupatorium capillifolium*				
Dropwort, Water	*Oxypolis rigidior*				
Duckweed, Greater	*Spirodela polythiza*				
Duckweed, Minute	*Lemna perpusilla*				
Elephant's Foot	*Elephantopus nudatus*				
Feather, Parrot	*Myriophyllum brasiliense*				
Fimbry, Forked	*Fimbristylis dichotoma*				
Fleabane	*Pluchea pupurascens*				
Frogbit	*Limnobium spongia*				
Frogfruit	*Lippia lanceolata*				
Goldenrod, Anisescented	*Solidago odora*				
Goldenrod, Rough-leaved	*Solidago rugosa*				
Goldentop, Slender	*Euthamia tenuifolia*				
Goldenrod, Sweet	*Euthamia graminifolia*				

Appendices

SPECIES	SPRING	SUMMER	FALL	WINTER
FLORA (continued)				
FORBS (BROADLEAF HERBACEOUS PLANTS) (continued)				
Grasswort, Carolina	*Lilaeopsis carolinensis*			
Grasswort, Eastern	*Lilaeopsis chinensis*			
Grounsel, Wooly	*Senecio tomentosus*			
Hemlock, Poison	*Cicuta maculata*			
Hempweed, Climbing	*Mikania scandens*			
Horehound, Water	*Lycopus virginicus*			
Hyssop, Water	*Bacopa monnieri*			
Ironweed, Tall	*Vernonia gigantea*			
Jessamine, Yellow	*Gelsemium sempervirens*			
Jimsonweed (Exotic)	*Datura stramonium*			
Lespedeza, Sericea (Exotic)	*Lespedeza cuneata*			
Lettuce, Wild	*Lactuca canadensis*			
Lobelia, Downy	*Lobelia puberula*			
Loosestrife, False	*Ludwigia alternifolia*			
Mallow, Seashore	*Kosteletzkya virginica*			
Mallow, Swamp Rose	*Hibiscus moscheutos*			
Marigold, Nodding Bur	*Bidens cernua*			
Medic, Black (Exotic)	*Medicago lupalina*			
Milfoil, Eurasian (Exotic)	*Myriophyllum spicatum*			
Milfoil, Water	*Myriophyllum exalbescens*			
Monarda, Dotted	*Monarda punctata*			
Morningglory, Saltmarsh	*Ipomoea sagittata*			
Mudflower, Shade	*Micranthemum umbrosum*			
Mudwort, Awl-leaf	*Limosella subulata*			
Nettle, Horse	*Solanum carolinense*			
Niad	*Najas quadalupensis*			

SPECIES		SPRING	SUMMER	FALL	WINTER
FLORA (continued)					
FORBS (BROADLEAF HERBACEOUS PLANTS) (continued)					
Pea, Partridge	*Cassia fasciculata*				
Pearlwort, Trailing	*Sagina decumbens*				
Pennywort, Water	*Hydrocotyle umbellata*				
Pennywort, Floating	*Hydrocotyle ranunculoides*				
Pennywort, False	*Centella asiatica*				
Pickerelweed	*Pontederia cordata*				
Pimpernel, Water	*Samolus parviflorus*				
Pink, Sea	*Sabatia stellaris*				
Pinweed, Leggett's	*Lechea pulchella*				
Plantain, Pale Seed	*Plantago virginica*				
Pondweed, Leafy	*Potamogeton foliosus*				
Pondweed, Sago	*Potamogeton pectinatus*				
Pondweed, Clasping-Leaf	*Potamogeton perfoliatus*				
Pondweed, Bushy	*Najas flexilis*				
Pondweed, Horned	*Zannichellia palustris*				
Pondweeds	*Najas spp.*				
Primrose, Evening	*Oenothera humifusa*				
Purslane, Water	*Ludwigia palustris*				
Rabbit Tobacco	*Gnaphalium obtusifolium*				
Ragweed, Annual	*Ambrosia artemisiifolia*				
Redstem, Pink	*Ammania teres*				
Rocket, American Sea	*Cakile edentula*				
Rocket, Harper's Sea	*Cakile harperi*				
Salad, Corn	*Valerianella radiata*				
Sandmat, Seaside	*Chamaesyce polygonifolia*				
Skullcap, Hyssop	*Scutellaria integrifolia*				

Appendices

SPECIES	SPRING	SUMMER	FALL	WINTER
FLORA (continued)				
FORBS (BROADLEAF HERBACEOUS PLANTS) (continued)				
Smartweed, Dotted	*Polygonum punctatum*			
Sorrel, Sheep	*Rumex hastatulus*			
Soybean (Exotic)	*Glycine max*			
St. Andrews Cross	*Hypericum stragalum*			
Starwort, Water	*Callitriche heterophylla*			
Sweetclover, White	*Melilotus alba*			
Tea, Mexican	*Chenopodium ambrosioides*			
Thistle, Russian	*Salsola kali*			
Thistle, Yellow	*Cirsium horridulum*			
Thoroughwort, Late-flowering	*Eupatorium hyssopifolium*			
Toadflax	*Linaria canadensis*			
Tresses, Ladies	*Spiranthes vernalis*			
Violet, Bog White	*Viola lanceolata*			
Watercress	*Nasturtium officinale*			
Weed, Mermaid	*Proserpinaca palustris*			
Wild Sensitive Plant	*Cassia nictitans*			
Wintergreen, Spotted	*Chimaphila maculata*			
Wort, St. Johns	*Hypericum hypericoides*			
Yarrow, Common	*Achillea millefolium*			
FLORA (continued)				
GRASSES				
Bahiagrass (Exotic)	*Paspalum notatum*			
Barnyardgrass (Exotic)	*Echinochloa crusgalli*			
Bermudagrass (Exotic)	*Cynodon dactylon*			
Bluegrass, Annual	*Poa annua*			
Bluestem, Bushybeard	*Andropogon glomeratus*			

SPECIES	SPRING	SUMMER	FALL	WINTER
FLORA (continued)				
GRASSES (continued)				
Bluestem, Little	*Schizachyrium scoparium*			
Bluestem, Splitbeard	*Andropogon ternarius*			
Broomsedge	*Andropogon virginicus*			
Cordgrass, Big	*Spartina cynosuroides*			
Cordgrass, Saltmeadow	*Spartina patens*			
Cordgrass, Smooth	*Spartina alterniflora*			
Corn	*Zea mays*			
Crabgrass	*Digitaria spp.*			
Cutgrass, Giant	*Zizaniopsis mileacea*			
Cutgrass, Rice	*Leersia oryzoides*			
Dallisgrass (Exotic)	*Paspalum dilatatum*			
Deertongue	*Dichanthelium clandestinum*			
Eelgrass	*Vallisneria americana*			
Fescue, Tall (Exotic)l	*Lolium arundinaceum*			
Foxtail, Green	*Setaria virdis*			
Grass, American Cupscale	*Sacciolepis striata*			
Grass, Blue-eyed	*Sisyrinchium mucronatum*			
Grass, Widgeon	*Ruppia maritima*			
Grass, Yellow-eyed	*Xyris difformis*			
Grass, Yellow-eyed	*Xyris jupicai*			
Johnsongrass (Exotic)	*Sorghum halpense*			
Knotgrass	*Paspalum distichum*			
Maidencane	*Panicum hemitomom*			
Millet (Exotic)	*Setaria spp.*			
Orangegrass	*Hypericum gentianoides*			
Orchardgrass (Exotic)	*Dactylis glomerata*			

Appendices

SPECIES	SPRING	SUMMER	FALL	WINTER
FLORA (continued)				
GRASSES (continued)				
Panicgrass, Beaked	*Panicum anceps*			
Panicgrass, Velvet	*Dichanthelium scoparium*			
Panicum, Fall	*Panicum dichotomiflorum*			
Plumegrass, Sugarcane	*Saccharum giganteum*			
Purpletop	*Tridens flavus*			
Reed, Common (Exotic)	*Phragmites australis*			
Ryegrass, Annual (Exotic)	*Lolium multiflorum*			
Saltgrass, Seashore	*Distichlis spicata*			
Sawgrass	*Cladium jamaicense*			
Sorghum	*Sorghum bicolor*			
Switchgrass	*Panicum virgatum*			
Watergrass	*Hydrochloa spp.*			
Wheat (Exotic)	*Triticum aestivum*			
Woodoats, Slender	*Chasmanthium laxum*			
FLORA (continued)				
GRASSLIKE PLANTS				
Beakrush, Clustered	*Rhynchospora glomerata*			
Beakrush, Loosehead	*Rhynchospora chalorocephala*			
Bulrush, Softstem	*Scirpus validus*			
Cattail, Common	*Typha latifolia*			
Cattail, Narrow-leaf	*Typha angustifolia*			
Cattail, Southern	*Typha domingensis*			
Flatsedge, Slender	*Cyperus fillicinus*			
Flatsedge, Strawcolored	*Cyperus strigosus*			
Iris, Virginia	*Iris virginica*			
Iris, Yellow Water	*Iris pseudoacorus*			

SPECIES		SPRING	SUMMER	FALL	WINTER
FLORA (continued)					
GRASSLIKE PLANTS (continued)					
Rush, Canada	*Juncus canadensis*				
Rush, Turnflower	*Juncus biflorus*				
Rush, Black Needle	*Juncus roemerianus*				
Rush, Leathery	*Juncus coriaceus*				
Rush, Soft	*Juncus effusus*				
Sedge, Egg-bracted	*Carex ovalis*				
Spikerush, Blunt	*Eleocharis obtuse*				
Spikerush, Dwarf	*Eleocharis parvula*				
Spikerush, Foursquare	*Eleocharis quadrangulata*				
Spikerush, Small-Fruit	*Eleocharis microcarpa*				
Spikerush, Yellow	*Eleocharis flavescens*				
Threesquare, Common	*Scirpus pungens*				
Threesquare, Olney	*Scirpus olneyi*				
Woolgrass	*Scirpus cyperinus*				
FERN					
Fern, Cinnamon	*Osmunda cinnamomea*				
Fern, Netted Chain	*Woodwardia areolata*				
MOSS					
Moss, Spanish	*Tillandsia usneoides*				

Appendix VII. Priority Bird Species and Species Suites

Habitat	Extremely High Priority	High Priority
Pocosin –Grass Stage, Open Country	Bachman's Sparrow Henslow's Sparrow	Henslow's Sparrow Buff-breasted Sandpiper Bobolink Yellow Rail American Woodcock Short-eared Owl Sedge Wren
Pocosin – Shrub Stage	Bachman's Sparrow Henslow's Sparrow	Henslow's Sparrow American Woodcock Prairie Warbler Northern Bobwhite Field Sparrow
Pocosin-Conifer-Hardwood	Black-throated Green Warbler	Wood Thrush Northern Parula Hooded Warbler Worm-eating Warbler Yellow-throated Warbler
Tall Pocosin – Pond Pine, Forested Wetlands	Swainson's Warbler Red-cockaded Woodpecker	Brown-headed Nuthatch Prairie Warbler Northern Bobwhite Cerulean Warbler American Woodcock American Black Duck Prothonotary Warbler
Emergent Wetland - Moist Soil Units		Yellow Rail King Rail American Black Duck Virginia Rail
Mudflats (Drought Years, Water Management in Impoundments)		Stilt Sandpiper Solitary Sandpiper Buff-breasted Sandpiper

Appendices

Habitat	Moderate Priority	Local or Regional Interest
Pocosin –Grass Stage, Open Country	Grasshopper Sparrow Loggerhead Shrike Palm Warbler Northern Harrier Barn Owl	Eastern Kingbird Eastern Meadowlark Bald Eagle
Pocosin – Shrub Stage	Eastern Towhee Palm Warbler	White-eared Vireo Orchard Oriole Whip-poor-will
Pocosin – Conifer - Hardwood	Yellow-billed Cuckoo Carolina Chickadee	Acadian Flycatcher Yellow-throated Vireos Eastern Wood-peewee Black-and-white Warbler
Tall Pocosin - Pond Pine, Forested Wetlands	Rusty Blackbird Red-headed Woodpecker Chuck-will's-widow Pine Warbler	Louisiana Waterthrush Wood Duck Mississippi Kite Bald Eagle
Colonial Tree and/or Brush-nesting Waterbirds		Great Blue Heron Black-crowned Night Heron Great Egret Snowy Egret Little Blue Heron Yellow-crowned Night Heron
Emergent Wetland - Moist Soil Units	American Bittern Least Bittern Northern Harrier	Peregrine Falcon Bald Eagle
Mudflats (drought years, water management in impoundments)	Least Sandpiper Greater Yellowlegs, Pectoral Sandpiper	

Appendix VIII. Budget Requests

REFUGE OPERATION NEEDS SYSTEM (RONS) PROJECTS

Projects are ordered by the project number the first two digits of which stand for fiscal year the project was developed. The numbers are listed in the management alternatives.

Projects are listed as tier 1 projects that support approved critical mission or approved minimum staff or tier 2 projects that do not.

Project 97001 - Conduct Long-term Monitoring (2 half-time biological technicians)
Tier 2 Project
First Year Request $130,000, Recurring Request $69,000
Station Rank - 4

This project would provide the funding to hire two half-time GS-7 biological technicians to conduct long-term monitoring of wildlife populations and vegetative communities for the purposes of determining the effects of past management actions and to guide future management decisions. Key species to be monitored would include red-cockaded woodpeckers (endangered), black bear, American alligator, waterfowl, shorebirds, neotropical migratory birds, and other migratory birds. Key vegetative communities would include Atlantic white cedar stands (considered globally threatened) and intensively managed seasonally flooded wetlands within moist-soil units. Because of the dense shrub understory layer in the pocosin wetlands, red-cockaded woodpecker cavity tree surveys must be done with aircraft, followed by cutting trails in to the site for monitoring/management access. These technicians would also monitor the refuge's 200+ wood duck boxes for nesting success, as well as assist with waterfowl banding and other research efforts.

Project 97008 - Enhance Restoration and Management of Pocosin and Moist-soil Wetlands
Tier 2 Project
First Year Request $410,000, Recurring Request $20,000
Station Rank -12

This project would provide the funding to enhance restoration of 20,000 acres of pocosin wetlands and improve management of 700 acres of seasonally flooded wetlands (moist-soil units). Pocosin is a unique type of wetland that is rapidly disappearing worldwide. Atlantic white cedar stands are often found within pocosins and this species is considered globally threatened. Intensively managed moist-soil units have become very important to waterfowl, shorebirds, and other migratory species due to the overall loss of wetland habitat nationwide. Pocosin Lakes NWR protects vast expanses of pocosin and the Pungo Unit contains several important moist-soil units. Native trees, tree planting equipment, contract labor, a roller chopper, equipment transport vehicles, and other equipment are needed.

Project 97009 - Provide Essential Visitor and Resource Protection (Law Enforcement Officer)
Tier 2 Project
First Year Request $65,000, Recurring Request $71,000
Station Rank - 1

This project would provide the funding to hire a full-time GS-9 law enforcement officer to protect refuge visitors and resources on this 113,000-acre refuge, spanning portions of three counties. The majority of the refuge is open to hunting of several game species. Nearly six months of open hunting seasons attract over 8,000 hunters annually. Private hunt clubs surround the refuge. A new visitor center/environmental education center was opened in 2002, and visitation is expected to eventually exceed 400,000 visitors annually. An additional full-time officer is needed to combat increasing incidences of vandalism, timber and other trespass, dumping, incidents involving reintroduced endangered red wolves and other issues, such as suspected drug problems. The current law enforcement strength is one full-time officer shared with another refuge and a dual-function officer, a position that will be soon phased out as part of the conversion to a more professional law enforcement cadre.

Project 97013 - Develop a Cultural Resource Plan
Tier 2 Project
First Year Request $50,000, Recurring Request $0
Station Rank - 999

Develop a cultural resource plan and coordinate with the State Historic Preservation Officer. Identify various sites. The refuge is over 113,000 acres in size and has never had a cultural resource survey. Native Americans are known to have utilized the area, but no sites are identified.

Project 97021 - Develop a Public Use Plan (Resource Specialist)
Tier 2 Project
First Year Request $85,000, Recurring Request $59,000
Station Rank - 999

This project would provide the funding to hire a GS-7 park ranger to develop a public use plan that describes the needs and the direction of the refuge's public use program, in coordination with the Regional Office and planning teams. The plan must be developed to implement the Partnership for the Sounds in joint educational/outreach efforts. This is one of the largest partnerships on the east coast. The 113,000-acre refuge would have 450,000 visitors with no plan.

Project 99001 - Improve Waterfowl Monitoring Projects
Tier 2 Project
First Year Request $65,000, Recurring Request $30,000
Station Rank - 999

This project would provide the funding to hire two quarter-time GS-5 biological technicians to capture and band 400 wood ducks from July – September, and capture, neck collar, and band 250 tundra swans from December - March. The capture would be accomplished with nets propelled by rockets and/or swim in traps. New wood duck boxes would also be erected while old boxes would be checked and repaired. Moist-soil plants would be surveyed to determine food quality and abundance before waterfowl arrive in the fall. Water levels would be maintained throughout the year to provide optimum plant growth conditions, as well as standing water during winter waterfowl months. Two seasonal technicians would be needed to accomplish activities.

Project 99002 - Monitor Endangered Red-cockaded Woodpeckers
Tier 2 Project
First Year Request $30,000, Recurring Request $20,000
Station Rank - 5

This project would provide the funding to conduct aerial and ground surveys of the endangered red-cockaded woodpecker and manage its habitat in accordance with guidelines in the Service's Recovery and Management Plan for Red-cockaded Woodpeckers and their habitat. Because of the dense shrub understory layer in pocosin wetlands found in this area, red cockaded woodpecker cavity tree surveys must be conducted with aircraft followed by cutting trails in to the site for monitoring/management access.

Project 99009 - Purchase Boat, Motor, and Trailer
Tier 2 Project
First Year Request $20,000, Recurring Request $5,000
Station Rank - 999

This project would provide the funding to purchase a boat, which would be essential to management of several land tracts that have boat access only or to access portions of land tracks that have boat access only. Two partners' tracks - Buck Ridge and Roper Island - would require a boat for access as well as Frying Pan and a large portion of the refuge.

Project 99010 - Enhance Refuge Access for Protection, Management, and Public Use (Equipment Operator)
Tier 2 Project
First Year Request $65,000, Recurring Request $59,000
Station Rank - 12

This project would provide the funding to hire a WG-9 equipment operator to enhance refuge access for fire fighting, prescribed burning, law enforcement, and other management purposes, as well as public use activities through improved maintenance of over 100 miles of refuge roads and 25 miles of firebreaks. All refuge roads are dirt and require constant maintenance due to the soil type (high organic peat) of the region. Catastrophic wildfires have occurred in and around the refuge, and the risk of these fires remains high. Roads and firebreaks provide the access needed to control fires while they are small. In addition, over 10,000 hunters and thousands of other visitors use many of these roads each year to pursue their recreational activities, resulting in road damage and increased maintenance requirements. Additional manpower (an equipment operator) is needed to properly maintain refuge roads and firebreaks.

Project 99012 - Effectively Operate the Walter B. Jones, Sr., Center for the Sounds (Park Ranger, Office Assistant/Receptionist)
Tier 2 Project
First Year Request $140,000, Recurring Request $149,000
Station Rank - 2

This project would provide the funding to hire a GS-5 park ranger and GS-5 office assistant to provide environmental education and interpretation to a projected 400,000 visitors annually at the Walter B. Jones, Sr., Center for the Sounds and Pocosin Lakes NWR headquarters facility. Construction of this $1.9 million facility was completed in FY 01. It is located adjacent to a rest area on U.S. Highway 64, the main route to North Carolina's outer banks beaches. More than one million vehicles pass the site every year. Maintenance services are needed to keep this highly visible, award-winning facility clean and presentable to the public. Current refuge staffing is not adequate to perform this function and the building is already showing some signs of neglect. Brochures, cleaning supplies, utilities, and other materials are needed to properly operate the facility. Receptionists are needed to greet visitors in the Center and in the adjacent refuge administrative office. The Center is being operated in partnership with the non-profit Partnership for the Sounds, Inc.

Project 99013 - Survey Boundary (Resource Specialist – Surveyor))
Tier 2 Project
First Year Request $125,000, Recurring Request $72,000
Station Rank - 999

This project would provide the funding to hire a GS-11 resource specialist (surveyor) to survey several miles of refuge boundary. The refuge is seven years old without adequate surveys. Some areas have surveys from 1919. This project includes 8 properties and includes three Farm Service Agency tracts and several out parcels in swamp areas. During the hunting season (6 months), public hunters often encroach on adjoining land and cause a lot of trouble. A good survey would eliminate some of these problems.

Project 99014 - Enhance Fire Suppression Capabilities (Equipment)
Tier 2 Project
First Year Request $115,000, Recurring Request $10,000
Station Rank - 15

This project would provide the funding to purchase a third fire engine (pumper truck) and a second irrigation system to improve wildfire fighting and prescribed burning capabilities, and a second remote weather station in Columbia, North Carolina to help monitor fire weather conditions in the eastern half of the refuge that is over 40 miles from west to east. Most of Pocosin Lakes NWR's 113,000 acres consist of pocosin wetlands - southeastern shrub bog habitat that is highly susceptible to catastrophic wildfire. Attempts to drain much of the land prior to it becoming a refuge have artificially dried out thousands of acres increasing the potential for wildfires. Several catastrophic fires have occurred in and around the refuge in the past. Private structures adjacent to the refuge are at risk. The understory vegetation in pocosins will burn even after full green-up during the growing season and the high organic (peat) soil will also burn (called ground fire). Putting the ground fire out following the main fire often requires lots of water that is applied with pumper trucks and irrigation systems.

Project 99015 - Expand Hazardous Material Handling Capabilities
Tier 2 Project
First Year Request $43,000, Recurring Request $0
Station Rank - 999

This project would provide the funding to modify the storage building to contain fluid spills (if a spill should occur), according to new regulations. It would allow for the purchase of a dispensing system for oil and grease, and for the construction of a holding area for used oil and filters. It would also allow for the purchase of two self-contained oil houses for the Pungo maintenance site and new site in Columbia.

Project 00005 - Monitor and Control Phragmites and Other Invasive Species (Biological Technician)
Tier 2 Project
First Year Request $65,000, Recurring Request $59,000
Station Rank - 6

This project would provide the funding to hire a GS-7 biological technician to monitor and control invasive species on over 113,000 acres of refuge land. Giant reed (*Phragmites spp.*) forms extensive, dense monocultures in wetland areas displacing desirable vegetation used by waterfowl and other species managed on the refuge. Several hundred acres of Phragmites have become established on the refuge and our control efforts are not keeping pace with the spread of this plant. Other invasive species may also be present and this project would increase detection efforts for new threats by providing staff dedicated to invasive species management. The refuge is used by thousands of migrating swans, geese, ducks, and other birds annually, but the spread of Phragmites threatens the habitat these birds require. Local economically disadvantaged communities are promoting nature-based tourism for their economic development and depend on the resources managed by the refuge. A biological technician is needed to do the monitoring and treatment work.

Project 00006 - Restore Pocosin Wetlands (Assistant Refuge Manager)
Tier 1 Project
First Year Request $65,000, Recurring Request $63,000
Station Rank - 1

This project would provide the funding to hire a GS-9 assistant refuge manager to plan and coordinate the restoration of 20,000 acres of pocosin wetlands on the 113,700-acre refuge. Pocosin (a native American word meaning "upland swamp") habitat is associated with organic peat soils and is one of the most rapidly disappearing wetlands in the world. Only 10 percent of the original acreage is left, which is mostly on State and Federal land. This wetland type also supports Atlantic white cedar, whose population is threatened and reduced by 90 percent. Restoring these wetlands would provide much needed water control and flood control to resolve high water problems with 12 surrounding landowners. Water control structures will be placed in ditches; Atlantic white cedars would be planted; roads would be raised to allow higher water levels; and water levels would be monitored. An assistant refuge manager is needed to coordinate and supervise this restoration work.

Project 00008 - Improve Water Management Capabilities (Heavy Equipment Operator)
Tier 1 Project
First Year Request $65,000, Recurring Request $57,000
Station Rank - 3

This project would provide the funding to hire a WG-9 heavy equipment operator to replace existing dikes around two waterfowl impoundments and to maintain and repair an extensive dirt road (100 miles) system and canal/ditch (200 miles) system on the 113,700-acre refuge. The dikes on two waterfowl impoundments are not effective in manipulating water levels and need to be replaced. The replacement dikes are needed to allow controlled flooding of the waterfowl impoundments. The controlled flooding (or draining) of these impoundments on a seasonal basis creates prime growing conditions for various wetland plants. These wetland plants then provide a high-quality food source that is used by thousands of migrating waterfowl and shore birds. These trust species have food and water requirements that are not being met under current situations. The heavy equipment operator would use existing heavy equipment (e.g., bulldozers, excavators, and road graders) to maintain, repair, or replace dikes, canals, roads, and water control structures (20+) on the refuge, with an overall goal of restoring the natural hydrology on 19,000 acres of pocosin wetland habitat (upland swamp on predominantly organic peat soils).

Appendices

Project 00009 - Expand Endangered Species Management and Protection (Forester, 2 Biological Technicians)
Tier 2 Project
First Year Request $130,000, Recurring Request $190,000
Station Rank - 13

This project would provide the funding to hire a GS-11 forester and two GS-7 biological technicians to manage and protect over 30 clusters of endangered red cockaded woodpeckers on the Palmetto-Peartree Preserve, a 10,000-acre endangered species mitigation project being carried out by the Service, the Conservation Fund, and the North Carolina Department of Transportation. Our partners are currently increasing the number of clusters on this site through habitat improvements. Once the target (31 clusters) is reached (projected for 2007), the Service expects the Conservation Fund to turn over the area to the refuge for maintenance and management. Red-cockaded woodpecker management would include habitat management (prescribed burning, thinning, understory control, installation of artificial cavities, etc.), population monitoring, capture and relocation of birds, and maintenance of infrastructure (such as roads and trails) for access. A comprehensive public use and environmental education program, including a large hunting program, is also being planned for the area.

Project 00011 - Improve Biological Monitoring and Management (Wildlife Biologist)
Tier 1 Project
First Year Request $65,000, Recurring Request $63,000
Station Rank - 2

This project would provide the funding to hire a GS-9 wildlife biologist to conduct essential biological surveys and to coordinate other tasks in the refuge's biological program. Biological monitoring surveys are necessary to ensure sound management of the wildlife and plant resources on the 110,106-acre refuge. The wildlife biologist would help to accomplish refuge objectives mandated for endangered species (red wolf and red-cockaded woodpecker), Service trust species (waterfowl and songbirds), important resident species (black bear, white-tailed deer, and river otter), and invasive pest species (Phragmites and southern pine beetle), which adversely affect the habitat of the above listed animal categories. Monitoring surveys that would be conducted or coordinated by the wildlife biologist would include the following: carbon sequestration, endangered red-cockaded woodpecker, black bear, American alligator, Phragmites, and declining populations of Henslow's sparrow, songbirds, shorebirds, bats, and amphibians.

Project 00012 - Improve Mapping Capabilities to More Effectively Document Refuge Projects and Management Practices (Biologist)
Tier 2 Project
First Year Request $90,000, Recurring Request $59,000
Station Rank – 999

This project would provide the funding to hire a GS-7 biologist to improve mapping capabilities to more effectively document law enforcement reports, refuge biological projects and fire management programs. Aerial and infrared photographs will greatly aid habitat and fire management by identifying vegetation and landscape characteristics on the refuge, including limited accessible areas. GIS maps produced with Global Positioning Systems data and recent aerial photographs would directly benefit many refuge programs, such as endangered species, invasive species control, fire, Service trust species, pocosin habitat restoration, and Atlantic white cedar restoration. Benefits would include increasing accuracy and effectiveness of monitoring, reporting, and distributing critical data to other cooperative organizations and future mitigation projects.

Project 00013 - Improve Refuge Fire Equipment in Support of Wildfire and Prescribed Burning Operations
Tier 2 Project
First Year Request $54,000, Recurring Request $0
Station Rank - 999

This project would provide the funding to purchase tools and equipment for the maintenance and fire program. We have large amounts of heavy equipment and very few tools to handle the maintenance. Improvement of outdated and hazardous equipment will allow the refuge fire staff to more efficiently complete projects in support of ecosystem objectives. Safety codes are not met with current equipment, subjecting staff and the public to potential hazards.

Project 00014 - Enhance Fire Suppression Capabilities (Heavy Equipment Operator)
Tier 2 Project
First Year Request $65,000, Recurring Request $59,000
Station Rank - 11

This project would provide the funding to improve wildfire fighting and prescribed burning capabilities. Most of Pocosin Lakes NWR's 110,106 acres consist of pocosin wetlands - southeastern shrub bog habitat that is highly susceptible to catastrophic wildfire. Attempts to drain the land prior to it becoming a refuge have artificially dried out thousands of acres increasing the potential for wildfires. Several catastrophic fires have occurred in and around the refuge in the past. Private structures adjacent to the refuge are at risk. The understory vegetation in pocosins will burn even after full green-up during the growing season and the high organic (peat) soil will also burn. Increasing the number of firefighters will allow for faster, safer, and more efficient response to wildfire and more prescribed burning to reduce hazardous fuel loads (and enhance wildlife habitat). An additional WG-8 equipment operator is needed to strengthen the fire crew.

Project 00016 - Enhance Refuge Access for Protection, Management, and Public Use (Equipment)
Tier 2 Project
First Year Request $200,000, Recurring Request $10,000
Station Rank - 13

This project would provide the funding to enhance refuge access for fire fighting, prescribed burning, law enforcement, and other management purposes; hunting; fishing; wildlife observation; and other public use activities through improved maintenance of over 100 miles of refuge roads and 25 miles of firebreaks. All refuge roads are dirt and require constant maintenance due to the soil type (high organic peat) of the region. Catastrophic wildfires have occurred in and around the refuge, and the risk of these fires remains high. Roads and firebreaks provide the access needed to control fires while they are small. In addition, over 10,000 hunters and thousands of other visitors use many of these roads each year to pursue their recreational activities - usually resulting in road damage and increased maintenance requirements. Additional equipment (tractors with mowing and other implements) is needed to properly maintain refuge roads and firebreaks.

Project 00019 - Enhance Refuge Partnership Efforts
Tier 1 Project
First Year Request $33,000, Recurring Request $10,000
Station Rank - 4

This project would provide the funding to enhance partnership efforts with organizations such as Partnership for the Sounds, Red Wolf Coalition, Pocosin Arts, and Pettigrew State Park. The available budget for support activities with these important partnerships has been declining. This project would enhance these partnerships by providing matching funds. For example, the Partnership for the Sounds has already spent over five million dollars on projects that benefit five refuges in the area. Matching refuge funds would have improved these projects and garnered more partnership support. Properly funded, existing and future programs and projects of these refuge partners will reach over 400,000 people. Being able to partner with these groups financially will enhance the overall mission and programs of not only Pocosin Lakes NWR, but also other refuges (Alligator River, Mattamuskeet, and Roanoke River) in the immediate vicinity.

Project 01001 - Enhance Public Use Opportunities at Walter B. Jones, Sr., Center for the Sounds (Park Ranger)
Tier 2 Project
First Year Request $65,000, Recurring Request $59,000
Station Rank - 14

This project would provide the funding to hire a GS-7 park ranger to conduct interpretive and educational programs to visitors, including school groups, making full use of the new center and the environmental education classroom that have been constructed. It would provide additional public use opportunities in the recently completed Walter B. Jones, Sr., Center for the Sounds (refuge visitor center). Construction of this facility was completed in 2001 and over 400,000 visitors are expected annually (approximately 1.2 million cars pass the site each year). The project will provide recreational and educational opportunities that should foster a greater understanding and appreciation of the refuge, the area's natural resources, and the Refuge System's mission. The center will be operated in partnership with the non-profit Partnership for the Sounds.

Project 01002 Monitor and Control Phragmites and Other Invasive Species
Tier 2 Project
First Year Request $0, Recurring Request $50,000
Station Rank - 7

This project would provide the funding to monitor and control invasive species on over 113,000 acres of refuge land. Giant reed (*Phragmites spp.*) forms extensive, dense monocultures in wetland areas, displacing desirable vegetation used by waterfowl and other species managed on the refuge. Several hundred acres of Phragmites have become established on the refuge and our control efforts are not keeping pace with the spread of this plant. Other invasive species may also be present and this project will increase detection efforts for new threats by providing staff dedicated to invasive species management. The refuge is used by thousands of migrating swans, geese, ducks, and other birds annually, but the spread of Phragmites threatens the habitat these birds require. Local economically disadvantaged communities are promoting nature-based tourism for their economic development and depend on the resources managed by the refuge. This project provides the pesticides, pesticide application contracts, and aerial photography needed to complete the work described in Project No. 00005.

Project 02001- Monitor Fire Effects in Pocosins (Biological Technician/Firefighter)
Tier 2 Project
First Year Request $55,000, Recurring Request $69,000
Station Rank - 10

This project would provide the funding to hire a GS-9 biological technician/firefighter to conduct long-term monitoring of the effects of wild and prescribed fires on the refuge's pocosin wetlands. It is suspected that pocosin wetlands historically burned very infrequently, maybe once every 100 years. Unfortunately, due to the buildup of hazardous fuels over these time periods, the fires that occurred were normally catastrophic. If they occurred today, such fires would destroy property and take lives. More frequent controlled burns are needed today to reduce fuel loads, lessen the risk of catastrophic fire, and improve wildlife habitat. However, the effects of more frequent burning must be monitored in order to determine the optimum burning frequency that balances fire control and ecological health goals. The position is needed to monitor the effects of prescribed and wild fires on the pocosin wetlands and the variety of wildlife species, including threatened and endangered species that use them.

Project 03001 - Provide Adequate Visitor and Resource Protection (Law Enforcement Officer)
Tier 2 Project
First Year Request $65,000, Recurring Request $71,000
Station Rank - 3

This project would provide the funding to hire a GS-9 law enforcement officer for essential law enforcement protection to refuge visitors and resources. Basic law enforcement services are needed on this 110,106-acre refuge, spanning portions of three counties. The majority of the refuge is open to hunting of several game species. Nearly six months of open hunting seasons attract over 8,000 hunters annually. Private hunt clubs also surround the refuge. A new visitor center/environmental education center was opened in 2002, and is expected to eventually exceed 400,000 visitors annually. Vandalism, timber and other trespass, dumping, incidents involving reintroduced endangered red wolves, and other issues are increasing. Drug problems are suspected. This project will add a second GS-9 full-time law enforcement officer, thus providing adequate law enforcement protection for the refuge.

Pocosin Lakes NWR
Refuge Operation Needs System (RONS) Projects Listed by Project Number

Station Rank/ Tier	Project Number	Cost (First Year, Recurring)	Positions	Project Title
4/2	97001	$130,000 $69,000	1.0	Conduct Long-Term Monitoring (2 Half-Time Biological Technicians)
12/2	97008	$410,000 $20,000	0.0	Enhance Restoration and Management of Pocosin and Moist Soil Wetlands
½	97009	$65,000 $71,000	1.0	Provide Essential Visitor and Resource Protection (Law Enforcement Officer)
999/2	97013	$50,000 $0	0.0	Develop a Cultural Resource Plan
999/2	97021	$85,000 $59,000	1.0	Public Use Plan Development (Park Ranger)
999/2	99001	$65,000 $30,000	0.5	Improve Waterfowl Monitoring Projects (2 Quarter Time Biological Technicians)
5/2	99002	$30,000 $20,000	0.0	Monitor Endangered Red-cockaded Woodpeckers
999/2	99009	$20,000 $5,000	0.0	Purchase Boat, Motor, and Trailer
12/2	99010	$65,000 $59,000	1.0	Enhance Refuge Access for Protection, Management, and Public Use (Equipment Operator)
2/2	99012	$140,000 $149,000	2.0	Effectively Operate the Walter B. Jones, Sr., Center for the Sounds (Park Ranger, Office Assistant)
999/2	99013	$125,000 $72,000	1.0	Survey Boundary (Resource Specialist – Surveyor))
15/2	99014	$115,000 $10,000	0.0	Enhance Fire Suppression Capabilities (Equipment)
999/2	99015	$43,000 $0	0.0	Expand Hazardous Material Handling Capabilities
6/2	00005	$65,000 $59,000	1.0	Monitor and Control Phragmites and Other Invasive Species (Biological Technician)
1/1	00006	$65,000 $63,000	1.0	Restore Pocosin Wetlands (Assistant Refuge Manager)

Pocosin Lakes NWR
Refuge Operation Needs System (RONS) Projects Listed by Project Number

Station Rank/ Tier	Project Number	Cost (First Year, Recurring)	Positions	Project Title
3/1	00008	$65,000 $57,000	1.0	Improve Water Management Capabilities (Heavy Equipment Operator)
13/2	00009	$130,000 $190,000	3.0	Expand Endangered Species Management and Protection (Forester, 2 Biological Technicians)
2/1	00011	$65,000 $63,000	1.0	Improve Biological Monitoring and Management (Wildlife Biologist)
999/2	00012	$90,000 $59,000	1.0	Improve Mapping Capabilities to Document Refuge Projects and Management Practices (Biologist)
999/2	00013	$54,000 $0	0.0	Improve Refuge Fire Equipment In Support Of Wildfire And Prescribed Burning Operations
11/2	00014	$65,000 $59,000	1.0	Enhance Fire Suppression Capabilities (Heavy Equipment Operator)(Fire)
13/2	00016	$200,000 $10,000	0.0	Enhance Refuge Access for Protection, Management, and Public Use (Equipment)
4/1	00019	$33,000 $10,000	0.0	Enhance Refuge Partnership Efforts
14/2	01001	$65,000 $59,000	1.0	Enhance Public Use Opportunities at Walter B. Jones Center for the Sounds (Park Ranger)
7/2	01002	$0 $50,000	0.0	Monitor and Control Phragmites and Other Invasive Species
10/2	02001	$55,000 $69,000	1.0	Monitor Fire Effects in Pocosins (Biological Technician)(Fire)
3/2	03001	$65,000 $71,000	1.0	Provide Adequate Visitor & Resource Protection (Law Enforcement Officer)

\multicolumn{5}{c}{**Pocosin Lakes NWR**}
\multicolumn{5}{c}{**Refuge Operation Needs System (RONS) Projects Listed by Tier and Station Rank**}
Station Rank/	Project Number	Cost (First Year, Recurring)	Positions	Project Title
---	---	---	---	---
\multicolumn{5}{c}{**Tier 1**}
1	00006	$65,000 $63,000	1.0	Restore Pocosin Wetlands (Assistant Refuge Manager)
2	00011	$65,000 $63,000	1.0	Improve Biological Monitoring and Management (Wildlife Biologist)
3	00008	$65,000 $57,000	1.0	Improve Water Management Capabilities (Heavy Equipment Operator)
4	00019	$33,000 $10,000	0.0	Enhance Refuge Partnership Efforts
\multicolumn{5}{c}{**Tier 2**}
1	97009	$65,000 $71,000	1.0	Provide Essential Visitor & Resource Protection (Law Enforcement Officer)
2	99012	$140,000 $149,000	2.0	Effectively Operate the Walter B. Jones Center for the Sounds (Park Ranger, Office Assistant)
3	03001	$65,000 $71,000	1.0	Provide Adequate Visitor and Resource Protection (Law Enforcement Officer)
4	97001	$130,000 $69,000	1.0	Conduct Long Term Monitoring (2 Half-Time Biological Technicians)
5	99002	$30,000 $20,000	0.0	Monitor Endangered Red-cockaded Woodpeckers
6	00005	$65,000 $59,000	1.0	Monitor and Control Phragmites and Other Invasive Species (Biological Technician)
7	01002	$0 $50,000	0.0	Monitor and Control Phragmites and other Invasive Species
8	?	?	?	?
9	?	?	?	?
10	02001	$55,000 $69,000	1.0	Monitor Fire Effects in Pocosins (Biological Technician)(Fire)

Pocosin Lakes NWR
Refuge Operation Needs System (RONS) Projects Listed by Tier and Station Rank

Station Rank/	Project Number	Cost (First Year, Recurring)	Positions	Project Title
11	00014	$65,000 $59,000	1.0	Enhance Fire Suppression Capabilities (Heavy Equipment Operator)(Fire)
12	99010	$65,000 $59,000	1.0	Enhance Refuge Access for Protection, Management, and Public Use (Equipment Operator)
12	97008	$410,000 $20,000	0.0	Enhance Restoration and Management of Pocosin and Moist Soil Wetlands
13	00009	$130,000 $190,000	3.0	Expand Endangered Species Management and Protection (Forester, 2 Biological Technicians)
13	00016	$200,000 $10,000	0.0	Enhance Refuge Access for Protection, Management, and Public Use (Equipment)
14	01001	$65,000 $59,000	1.0	Enhance Public Use Opportunities at Walter B. Jones, Sr., Center for the Sounds (Park Ranger)
15	99014	$115,000 $10,000	0.0	Enhance Fire Suppression Capabilities (Equipment)
999	97013	$50,000 $0	0.0	Develop a Cultural Resource Plan
999	97021	$85,000 $59,000	1.0	Public Use Plan Development (Park Ranger)
999	99001	$65,000 $30,000	0.5	Improve Waterfowl Monitoring Projects (2 Quarter Time Biological Technicians)
999	99009	$20,000 $5,000	0.0	Purchase Boat, Motor, and Trailer
999	99013	$125,000 $72,000	1.0	Survey Boundary (Resource Specialist - Surveyor)
999	99015	$43,000 $0	0.0	Expand Hazardous Material Handling Capabilities
999	00012	$90,000 $59,000	1.0	Improve Mapping Capabilities to Document Refuge Projects and Management Practices (Biologist)

MAINTENANCE AND MANAGEMENT SYSTEM (MMS) PROJECTS
(Ordered by Project Number, Tables by Number and Rank Follow Descriptions)

MMS Projects Organized by Number			
Number	Description	Cost	Rank
92103184	Replace Grain Bin Blower	$26,000	5
93103203	Rehabilitate Office and Residence Interiors	$26,000	9
97110627	Construct Maintenance Facility Columbia	$1,044,000	2
98103198	Rehabilitate Boardwalk and Classroom	$26,000	6
98103193	Repair Bulkhead Material	$26,0007	7
99103188	Replace Tracks on Three D6 Dozers	$63,000	4
99103205	Replace Volume Lift Pumps	$50,000	26
99103202	Rehabilitate Flooring in Pole Shed and Shop	$32,000	14
99123340	Construct Storage Building and Water Facility for the Equipment Wash Rack	$24,000	4
99103210	Rehabilitate Parking Areas	$14,000	12
99103201	Rehabilitate Ditches	$63,000	8
99103195	Replace Water Control Structures	$94,000	3
99103192	Replace Front End Loader	$98,000	24
99103187	Replace Grapple Bucket	$17,000	16
00103211	Repair Road to the Observation Tower (FHA Route 118)	$113,000	22
00123336	Construct Red Wolf Education Center	$260,000	999
00103216	Replace Culverts and Risers	$125,000	4
00103214	Replace Creekside Lowboy Trailer	$66,000	22
00123337	Construct Interpretive Signs for Boardwalk and Outdoor Classroom	$38,000	999
00115271	Replace Case IH-780 Offset Disk Harrow	$19,000	36
01103219	Replace S.R. Boardwalk Signs and Repair Pungo Kiosk	$26,000	10
01103222	Replace Unimog Truck Tractor	$110,000	2
01103223	Replace Drop Neck Trailer	$63,000	45
01103225	Replace Three Slip on fire Fighting Pumper Units	$50,000	28
01103227	Replace Boom Ax Mower	$95,000	54
01103228	Rehabilitate Troop Carriers to Meet Fire Readiness Objectives	$16,000	27
01103229	Replace PL 5 Bombardier Fire Unit Track System	$16,000	25
01103230	Rehabilitate Fire Control Shop	$35,000	15

MMS Projects Organized by Number			
Number	Description	Cost	Rank
01103231	Replace Wajax Pacific Fire Pumper Unit	$27,000	53
01114833	Replace 1996 Dodge Ram Pickup	$31,000	61
01114836	Replace 1995 Ford Supercab Pickup	$31,000	19
01114839	Replace 2000 Ford Ranger	$31,000	62
01114843	Replace 1998 Dodge Pickup, Extended Cab	$31,000	63
01114845	Replace 1998 Dodge Service Truck	$31,000	64
01114846	Replace 1998 Dodge Pickup	$31,000	69
01114873	Replace 1996 Ford Bronco	$33,000	68
01114876	Replace 1992 Ford Truck	$53,000	50
01114879	Replace 1990 Dodge Ram Pickup	$31,000	999
01114892	Replace 1991 GM Service Truck	$37,000	12
01114894	Replace 1998 Ford Dump Truck	$115,000	68
01114901	Replace 1995 Ford Pickup	$31,000	41
01114903	Replace Fire Truck	$31,000	40
01114907	Replace 1993 Ford L9000 Truck Tractor	$95,000	67
01114910	Replace 1992 Ford Truck Tractor	$105,000	63
01114911	Replace 1984 IHC F-2574 Truck Tractor	$95,000	8
01114923	Replace 1992 Ford F800 Truck Tractor	$79,000	64
01114935	Replace 1994 Bombardier Fire Fighting Vehicle	$185,000	38
01115260	Replace 1998 John Deere 410E Backhoe	$80,000	74
01115262	Replace 1983 FMC Dragline	$211,000	60
01115254	Replace D6C Dozer	$215,000	59
01115265	Replace 1998 John Deere Excavator	$185,000	75
01115267	Replace Terra Torch Flame Thrower	$10,000	37
01117361	Replace Rome Offset Disk	$19,000	51
01117379	Replace John Deere 455 Riding Lawn Mowers (1 of 2)	$9,000	23
01117389	Replace John Deere 455 Riding Lawn Mowers (2 of 2)	$9,000	17
01117397	Replace 1987 Hester Fire Plow	$10,000	49
01117405	Replace Mathis Fire Plow	$10,000	48
01117412	Replace 1993 Hester 4000 Fire Plow (1 of 2)	$10,000	47
03124937	Replace Office—Field Station	$313,000	5
03124956	Construct, Plan, and Design Maintenance Facility	$307,000	1

MMS Projects Organized by Number			
Number	Description	Cost	Rank
03124975	Construct Addition to Walter B. Jones, Sr., Center for the Sounds	$1,044,000	3
03125602	Repair Northern Road, Public Use Road, FHA Route 127 (5.48 miles)	$1,348,000	11
03125604	Repair Nodwell Road, Public Use Road, FHA Route 126 (2.22 miles)	$546,000	13
03125609	Repair Middle Road, FHA Route 124 (4.58 miles)	$1,127,000	31
03125614	Repair Western Road, FHA Route 122 (6.12 miles)	$1,506,000	15
03125618	Repair Evans Road, Public Use Road, FHA Route 113 (1.27 miles)	$312,000	999
03125612	Repair Seagoing Road, Public Use Road, FHA Route 123 (6.43 miles)	$1,582,000	14
03125735	Replace Caterpillar 12G Motor Grader	$193,000	65
03125617	Repair Harvester Road, Public Use Road, FHA Route 114 (5.97 miles)	$1,200,000	16
03125743	Replace John Deere 772CH Motor Grader	$193,000	66
03125611	Repair DeHoog Road, Public Use Road, FHA Route 112 (7.66 miles)	$1,885,000	17
03125613	Repair Smith Wick Road, Public Use Road, FHA Route 129 (2.75 miles)	$677,000	35
03125616	Repair Clayton Road, Public Use Road, FHA Route 120 (3.07 miles)	$755,000	20
03125619	Repair Coulbourn Road, Public Use Road, FHA Route 121 (2.00 miles)	$492,000	21
03126523	Repair County Line Road, Public Use Road, FHA Route 110 (1.00 mile)	$246,000	19
03125626	Repair Boerma Road, Public Use Road, FHA Route 109 (6.09 miles)	$1,498,000	18
03125915	Convert the Allen Road Fire Tower to a Public Use Observation Tower	$94,000	6
03126065	Repair F2 Road, Public Use Road, FHA Route 106 (2.34 miles)	$576,000	23
03126067	Repair Phelps Road, Public Use Road, FHA Route 125 (1.22 miles)	$300,000	24
03130539	Repair Dike on Chinquapin Road North of Northern Road	$84,000	11
04134232	Replace John Deere Flex Wing Mower	$10,000	67

MMS Projects Organized by Number			
Number	Description	Cost	Rank
04134013	Replace 1994 Bombardier Fire Fighting Vehicle	$185,000	20
04134198	Replace Caterpillar D-5 Dozer	$150,000	999
04134200	Replace D5 Dozer	$190,000	76
04134201	Replace D6D Dozer	$215,000	47
04134207	Replace D3G Dozer	$100,000	70
04134209	Replace D6D Dozer	$215,000	61
04134216	Replace Forklift	$40,000	71
04134226	Replace Bush Whacker Flex Wing Mower	$10,000	83
04134228	Replace Toro Riding Mower	$8,000	29
04134234	Replace Gregory Roanoke Bush Axe Mower	$15,000	66
04134235	Replace John Deere Lift Type, 3 point Hitch Mower	$6,000	60
04134237	Replace Hyster 2 Disk Plow	$6,000	59
04134239	Replace Hyster 4 Disk Fire Plow	$7,000	58
04134507	Replace Three Slip-On Fire Fighting Pumper Units	$50,000	56
04134506	Replace Two Volume Lift (Gator) Pumps	$30,000	57
04134508	Replace Two Portable Fire Fighting Pumper Units	$40,000	55
04134510	Replace Irrigation Pump	$20,000	35
04134511	Replace 500 Gal Slip-on Fire Fighting Pumper Unit	$20,000	34
04134523	Replace Ford Tractor with Boom Mower	$60,000	69
04134525	Replace 1997 Ford New Holland Tractor	$50,000	72
04134528	Replace John Deere 7810 Tractor	$90,000	73
04134531	Replace Two Portable Bridge Trailers	$75,000	65
04134572	Replace 2004 Ford New Holland Tractor	$80,000	77
04134579	Replace Cargo Trailer	$6,000	71
04134583	Replace Fontaine Lowboy Trailer	$32,000	70
04134584	Replace Two Boaz Lowboy Trailers	$80,000	33
04134621	Replace Salem Travel Trailer	$20,000	79
04134624	Replace GMC 2-1/2 Ton Stake Dump Truck	$30,000	48
04134628	Replace 1978 GMC Dump Truck	$115,000	49
04134631	Replace 1996 Jeep	$30,000	42
04134632	Replace 2002 Ford Pickup	$25,000	84
04134637	Replace 2002 Ford Explorer	$25,000	73

| MMS Projects Organized by Number ||||
Number	Description	Cost	Rank
04134651	Replace 2002 Ford F150 Truck	$22,000	74
04134658	Replace 1999 Dodge Ram	$25,000	72
04134660	Replace 2003 Sterling Truck Tractor	$105,000	78
04134661	Replace 2004 Sterling Truck Tractor	$105,000	79
04134664	Replace 1995 US Military Full Track Troop Carrier	$230,000	43
04134665	Replace 1995 US Military Full Track Troop Carrier	$230,000	30
04134666	Replace 1992 Military Personnel Carrier	$230,000	31
04134669	Replace 1992 Weather Stations	$40,000	9
04134670	Replace Two 2002 Rockwell Travel Trailers	$20,000	80
04134672	Replace Geo-Boy Brush Cutter	$200,000	77
04134673	Replace 2004 GM Silverado Truck	$20,000	75
04134679	Replace Chevy Express Passenger Van	$25,000	76
04134682	Replace 18' Sea Ox Boat	$15,000	44
04134685	Replace Two Trailer Mounted Air Compressors	$20,000	45
04134686	Replace Canon Image Runner Copier	$8,000	46
04134689	Replace Dyna Packer	$30,000	80
04134691	Replace Transplanter	$20,000	78
04134890	Repair Pungo Lake Banding Site. Repairs include Replace Bulkhead Material.	$30,000	12
04134891	Repair Evans Pond Dike	$30,000	13
04134971	Repair Property Line Road, FHWA 103	$62,000	30
04134978	Repair West Lake Drive, Public Use Road, FHWA Route 104	$300,000	29
04134985	Repair South Lake Drive, Public Use Road, FHWA Route 105	$957,000	28
04134988	Repair Allen Road, Public Use Road, FHWA Route 108	$698,000	33
04134991	Repair Fields Road, Public Use Road, FHWA Route 115	$330,000	44
04134994	Repair Van Staalduinen Road, Public Use Road, FHWA Route 117	$244,000	26
04135001	Repair South Pungo Road, Public Use Road, FHWA Route 116	$659,000	25
04135005	Repair Hyde Park Road, Public Use Road, FHWA Route 119	$512,000	27
04135006	Repair Respess Road, Public Use Road, FHWA Route 102	$273,000	32

MMS Projects Organized by Number			
Number	Description	Cost	Rank
04135008	Repair D-Canal Road, Public Use Road, FHWA Route 101	$866,000	34
04136147	Repair Paved Parking Lot at HQ/VC	$44,000	999
04136160	Repair Gravel Parking Lot East of Ludington Drive	$25,000	41
04136165	Repair HQ/VC Overflow Parking Area No. 2	$21,000	42
04136173	Repair Field Station Parking Area No. 2	$10,000	10
04136215	Repair Field Station Parking Area and Drive	$38,000	40
04136218	Repair Pungo Observation Deck Parking Area	$18,000	43
04136221	Repair North Lake Drive Parking Area (south side of Respess)	$58,000	36
04136226	Repair North Lake Parking Area (North Side of Respess Road)	$5,000	37
04136227	Repair North Lake Drive Parking Area (West Side of Road	$3,000	38
04136242	Repair Parking Area at D Canal and North Pungo	$15,000	39
05137233	FY04 Storm Damage – Repair Trux Road	$1,016	999
05137251	FY04 Storm Damage – Repair Smartweed Impoundment Dike	$68,693	999
05137309	FY04 Storm Damage – Repair Hurricane Related Damage to Northwest Fork Road	$1,476,000	999
05138007	Replace refuge 40x60 tent	$15,000	999
05138009	Replace 2004 Dressta Dozer	$190,000	999
05138010	Replace 2005 Chevy Hybrid Truck	$30,000	81
05138011	Replace 2005 Ford Type 6 Wildland Fire Engine	$75,000	82
05138031	Repair Fire Control Building	$20,000	999
05138032	Clean Out of Hyde Park Canal	$20,000	999
05138033	Clean Out of Hyde Park Canal	$20,000	999
05138034	Replace Water Control Structure – Pungo Lake Outfall	$40,000	999
05138042	Clean Out of Farm Field Ditches	$12,363,000	999
05138043	Clean Out of Farm Field Ditches	$53,000	999
05138044	Repost 80 Miles of Refuge Boundary Line	$8,000	999
05138045	Rehabilitate Parking lot No. 2 at Office and Visitor Center	$21,000	7
05138046	Clean Silt Out of Allen Canal	$15,000	999
05138047	Clean Silt Out of Clayton Canal	$44,000	1
05138048	Replace Water Control Structures on North Lake and	$67,000	999

Appendices

MMS Projects Organized by Number			
Number	Description	Cost	Rank
05138049	Repair South Lake Drive Public Use Road FHWA	$20,000	999
05138050	Remove Vegetation from Shore Drive Fire Break	$20,000	999
05138051	Remove Vegetation from Evans Road Fire Break	$30,000	51
05138053	Repair Fire Control Building	$10,000	999
05138054	Clean Out of Hyde Park Canal	$20,000	999
05138055	Replace Water Control Structure – Pungo Lake Outfall	$40,000	5
05138056	Clean Out of Farm Field Ditches	$53,000	52
05138155	Clean Out of County Line Canal	$30,000	3
05138158	Clean Out of Farm Field Ditches	$4,000	999
05138159	Clean Out Boerma Canal	$46,000	6
05138160	Clean Out of Farm Field Ditches	$5,000	999
05138161	Clean Out Dehoog Canal	$58,000	2
05138162	Clean Out of Farm Field Ditches	$1,000	999
05138163	Clean Out of Farm Field Ditches	$7,000	53
05138164	Clean Out of Farm Field Ditches	$4,000	54
05138165	Replace Water Control Structure	$15,000	7
05138166	Clean Out of Farm Field Ditches	$2,000	55
05138168	Clean Out of Farm Field Ditches	$5,000	56
05138170	Clean Out of Farm Field Ditches	$1,000	57
05138174	Clean Out of Farm Field Ditches	$6,000	50
05138176	Clean Out of Farm Field Ditches	$14,000	58
05138178	Replace Water Control Structure	$15,000	8
05138180	Replace Water Control Structure on North Boundary	$15,000	9
05138181	Replace Water Control Structure on North Lake Road	$15,000	10

MMS Projects Organized by Rank			
Rank	Number	Description	Cost
1	00123337	Construct Interpretive Signs for Boardwalk and Outdoor Classroom	$38,000
1	03124956	Construct, Plan, and Design Maintenance Facility	$307,000
1	05138047	Clean Silt Out of Clayton Canal	$44,000
2	01103222	Replace Unimog Truck Tractor	$110,000
2	97110627	Construct Maintenance Facility	$1,044,000
2	05138161	Clean Out Dehoog Canal	$58,000
3	99103195	Replace Water Control Structures	$94,000
3	03124975	Construct Addition to Walter B. Jones, Sr., Center for the Sounds	$1,044,000
3	05138155	Clean Out County Line Canal	$30,000
4	99103188	Replace Tracks on Three D6 Dozers	$63,000
4	00103216	Replace Culverts and Risers	$125,000
4	99123340	Construct Storage Building and Water Facility for the Equipment Wash Rack	$24,000
5	92103184	Replace Grain Bin Blower	$26,000
5	05138055	Replace Water Control Structure – Pungo Lake Outfall	$40,000
6	98103198	Rehabilitate Boardwalk and Classroom	$26,000
6	03125915	Convert the Allen Road Fire Tower to a Public Use Observation Tower	$94,000
6	05138159	Clean Out Boerma Canal	$46,000
7	98103193	Repair Bulkhead Material	$26,000
7	02124937	Replace Office – Field Station	$313,000
7	05138045	Rehabilitate Parking lot No. 2 at Office and Visitor Center	$21,000
7	05138165	Replace Water Control Structure	$15,000
8	99103201	Rehabilitate Ditches	$63,000
8	01114911	Replace 1984 IHC F2574 Truck Tractor	$95,000
8	05138178	Replace Water Control Structure	$15,000
9	93103203	Rehabilitate Office and Residence Interiors	$26,000
9	04134669	Replace 1992 Weather Stations	$40,000
9	05138180	Replace Water Control Structure on North Boundary	$15,000
10	01103219	Replace S.R. Boardwalk Signs and Repair Pungo Kiosk	$26,000

MMS Projects Organized by Rank			
Rank	Number	Description	Cost
10	04136173	Repair Field Station Parking Area No. 2	$10,000
10	05138181	Replace Water Control Structure on North Lake Road	$15,000
11	03130539	Repair Dike Chinquapin Road North of Northern Road	$84,000
11	03125602	Repair Northern Road, Public Use Road, FHWA Route 127 (5.48 miles)	$1,348,000
12	04134890	Repair Pungo Lake Banding site. Repairs include Replace Bulkhead Material.	$30,000
12	01114892	Replace 1991 GM Service Truck	$37,000
12	99103210	Rehabilitate Parking Areas	$14,000
13	04134891	Repair Evans Pond Dike	$30,000
13	03125604	Repair Nodwell Road, Public Use Road, FHWA Route 126 (2.22 miles)	$546,000
14	99103202	Rehabilitate Flooring in Pole Shed and Shop	$32,000
14	03125612	Repair Seagoing Road, Public Use Road, FHWA Route 123 (6.43 miles)	$1,582,000
15	01103230	Rehabilitate Fire Control Shop	$35,000
15	03125614	Repair Western Road, FHWA Route 122 (6.12 miles)	$1,506,000
16	99103187	Replace Grapple Bucket	$17,000
16	03125617	Repair Harvester Road, Public Use Road, FHWA Route 114 (5.97 miles)	$1,200,000
17	01117389	Replace John Deere 455 Riding Lawn Mower (2 of 2)	$9,000
17	03125611	Repair DeHoog Road, Public Use Road, FHWA Route 112 (7.66 miles)	$1,885,000
18	03125626	Repair Boerma Road, Public Use Road, FHWA Route 109 (6.09 miles)	$1,498,000
19	01114836	Replace 1995 Ford Supercab Pickup	$31,000
19	03125623	Repair County Line Road, Public Use Road, FHWA Route 110 (1.00 mile)	$246,000
20	04134013	Replace 1994 Bombardier Fire Fighting Vehicle	$185,000
20	03125616	Repair Clayton Road, Public Use Road, FHWA Route 120 (3.07 miles)	$755,000
21	03125619	Repair Coulbourn Road, Public Use Road, FHWA Route 121 (2.00 miles)	$492,000
22	00103214	Replace Creekside Lowboy Trailer	$66,000

MMS Projects Organized by Rank			
Rank	Number	Description	Cost
22	00103211	Repair road to the observation tower FHWA Route 118	$113,000
23	01117379	Replace John Deere 455 Riding Lawn Mower (1 of 2)	$9,000
23	03126065	Repair F2 Road, Public Use Road, FHWA Route 106 (2.34 miles)	$576,000
24	99103192	Replace Front End Loader	$98,000
24	03126067	Repair Phelps Road, Public Use Road, FHWA Route 125 (1.22 miles)	$300,000
25	01103229	Replace PL 5 Bombardier Fire Unit Track System	$16,000
25	04135001	Repair South Pungo Road, Public Use Road, FHWA Route 116	$659,000
26	04134994	Repair Van Staalduinen Road, Public Use Road, FHWA Route 117	$244,000
26	99103205	Replace Volume Lift Pumps	$50,000
27	04135005	Repair Hyde Park Road, Public Use Road, FHWA Route 119	$512,000
27	01103228	Rehabilitate Troop Carriers to Meet Fire Readiness Objectives	$16,000
28	04134985	Repair South Lakes Drive, Public Use Road, FHWA Route 105	$957,000
28	01103225	Replace Three Slip-on Fire Fighting Pumper Units	$50,000
29	04134978	Repair West Lake Drive, Public Use Road, FHWA Route 104	$300,000
29	04134228	Replace Toro Riding Mower	$8,000
30	04134971	Repair Property Line Road, FHWA 103	$62,000
30	04134665	Replace 1995 U.S. Military Full Track Troop Carrier	$230,000
31	03125609	Repair Middle Road, FHA Route 124 (4.58miles)	$1,127,000
31	04134666	Replace 1992 Military Personnel Carrier	$230,000
32	04135006	Repair Respess Road, Public Use Road, FHWA Route 102	$273,000
33	04134988	Repair Allen Road, Public Use Road, FHWA Route 108	$698,000
33	04134584	Replace Two Boaz Lowboy Trailers	$80,000
34	04135008	Repair D-Canal Road, Public Use Road, FHWA Route 101	$866,000
34	04134511	Replace 500 Gallon Slip-on Fire Fighting Pumper Unit	$20,000
35	03125613	Repair Smith Wick Road, Public Use Road, FHWA Route 129 (2.75 miles)	$677,000
35	04134510	Replace Irrigation Pump	$20,000
36	00115271	Replace Case IH-780 Offset Disk Harrow	$19,000

Appendices

MMS Projects Organized by Rank			
Rank	Number	Description	Cost
36	04136221	Repair North Lake Drive Parking Area (S. Side Respess)	$58,000
37	01115267	Replace Terra Torch Flame Thrower	$10,000
37	04136226	Repair North Lake Drive Parking Area (N. Side Respess)	$5,000
38	01114935	Replace 1994 Bombardier Fire Fighting Vehicle	$185,000
38	04136227	Repair North Lake Drive Parking Area (W. Side Road)	$3,000
39	04136242	Repair Parking Area at D Canal and North Pungo	$15,000
40	01114903	Replace Fire Truck	$31,000
40	04136215	Repair Field Station Parking Area and Drive	$38,000
41	01114901	Replace 1995 Ford Pickup	$31,000
41	04136160	Repair Gravel Parking Lot East of Ludington Drive	$25,000
42	04134631	Replace 1996 Jeep	$30,000
42	04136165	Repair HQ/VC Overflow Parking Area No. 2	$21,000
43	04134664	Replace 1995 US Military Full Track Troop Carrier	$230,000
43	04136218	Repair Pungo Observation Deck Parking Area	$18,000
44	04134991	Repair Fields Road, Public Use Road, FHWA Route 115	$330,000
44	04134682	Replace 18' Sea Ox Boat	$15,000
45	01103223	Replace Drop Neck Trailer	$63,000
45	04134685	Replace Two Trailer Mounted Air Compressors	$20,000
46	04134686	Replace Canon Image Runner Copier	$8,000
47	04134201	Replace D6D Dozer	$215,000
47	01117412	Replace 1993 Hester 4000 Fire Plow (1 of 2)	$10,000
48	04134624	Replace GMC 2-1/2 Ton Stake Dump Truck	$30,000
48	01117405	Replace Mathis Fire Plow	$10,000
49	04134628	Replace 1978 GMC Dump Truck	$115,000
49	01117397	Replace 1987 Hester Fire Plow	$10,000
50	01114876	Replace 1992 Ford Truck	$53,000
50	05138174	Clean Out of Farm Field Ditches	$6,000
51	01117361	Replace Rome Offset Disk Plow	$19,000
51	05138051	Remove Vegetation from Evans Road Fire Break	$30,000
52	05138056	Clean Out of Farm Field Ditches	$53,000
53	01103231	Replace Wajax Pacific Fire Pumper Unit	$27,000
53	05138163	Cleanout of Farm Field Ditches	$7,000

\multicolumn{4}{c}{MMS Projects Organized by Rank}			
Rank	Number	Description	Cost
54	01103227	Replace Boom Ax Mower	$95,000
54	05138164	Clean Out of Farm Field Ditches	$4,000
55	04134508	Replace Two Portable Fire Fighting Pumper Units	$40,000
55	08138166	Clean Out of Farm Field Ditches	$2,000
56	04134507	Replace Three Slip-on Fire Fighting Pumper Units	$50,000
56	05138168	Clean Out of Farm Field Ditches	$5,000
57	04134506	Replace Two Volume Lift (Gator) Pumps	$30,000
57	05138170	Clean Out of Farm Field Ditches	$1,000
58	04134239	Replace Hyster 4 Disc Fire Plow	$7,000
58	05138176	Clean Out of Farm Field Ditches	$14,000
59	01115254	Replace D6C Dozer	$215,000
59	04134237	Replace Hyster 2 Disk Plow	$6,000
60	01115262	Replace 1983 FMC Dragline	$211,000
60	04134235	Replace John Deere Lift Type, 3 Point Hitch Mower	$6,000
61	04134209	Replace D6D Dozer	$215,000
61	01114833	Replace 1996 Dodge Ram Pickup	$31,000
62	01114839	Replace 2000 Ford Ranger	$31,000
63	01114910	Replace 1992 Ford Truck Tractor	$105,000
63	01114843	Replace 1998 Dodge Pickup, Extended Cab	$31,000
64	01114923	Replace 1992 Ford F800 Truck Tractor	$79,000
64	01114845	Replace 1998 Dodge Service Truck	$31,000
65	03125735	Replace Caterpillar 12G Motor Grader	$193,000
65	04134531	Replace Two Portable Bridge Trailers	$75,000
66	03125743	Replace John Deere 772CH Motor Grader	$193,000
66	04134234	Replace Gregory Roanoke Bush Axe Mower	$15,000
67	01114907	Replace 1993 Ford L9000 Truck Tractor	$95,000
67	04134232	Replace John Deere Flex Wing Mower	$10,000
68	01114894	Replace 1998 Ford Dump Truck	$115,000
68	01114873	Replace 1996 Ford Bronco	$33,000
69	04134523	Replace Ford Tractor with Boom Mower	$60,000
69	01114846	Replace 1998 Dodge Pickup Truck	$31,000
70	04134207	Replace D3G Dozer	$100,000

Appendices

MMS Projects Organized by Rank			
Rank	Number	Description	Cost
70	04134583	Replace Fontaine Lowboy Trailer	$32,000
71	04134216	Replace Forklift	$40,000
71	04134579	Replace Cargo Trailer	$6,000
72	04134525	Replace 1997 Ford New Holland Tractor	$50,000
72	04134658	Replace 1999 Dodge Ram Pickup Truck	$25,000
73	04134528	Replace John Deere 7810 Tractor	$90,000
73	04134637	Replace 2002 Ford Explorer	$25,000
74	01115260	Replace 1998 John Deere 410E Backhoe	$80,000
74	04134651	Replace 2002 Ford F150 Pickup Truck	$22,000
75	01115265	Replace 1998 John Deere Excavator	$185,000
75	04134673	Replace 2004 GM Silverado Pickup Truck	$20,000
76	04134200	Replace D5 Dozer	$190,000
76	04134679	Replace Chevy Express Passenger Van	$25,000
77	04134572	Replace 2004 Ford New Holland Tractor	$80,000
77	04134672	Replace Geo-Boy Brush Cutter	$200,000
78	04134660	Replace 2003 Sterling Truck Tractor	$105,000
78	04134691	Replace Transplanter	$20,000
79	04134661	Replace 2004 Sterling Truck Tractor	$105,000
79	04134621	Replace Salem Travel Trailer	$20,000
80	04134670	Replace Two 2002 Rockwell Travel Trailers	$20,000
80	04134689	Replace Dyna packer	$30,000
81	05138010	Replace 2005 Chevy Hybrid Truck	$30,000
82	05138011	Replace 2005 Ford Type 6 Wildland Fire Engine	$75,000
83	04134226	Replace Bush Whacker Flex Wing Mower	$10,000
84	04134632	Replace 2002 Ford Pickup Truck	$25,000
999	00123336	Construct Red Wolf Education Center	$260,000
999	97123339	Construct Visitor Information Kiosks	$44,000
999	03125618	Repair Evans Road, Public Use Road, FHWA Route 113 (1.27 miles)	$312,000
999	04134198	Replace Caterpillar D5 Dozer	$150,000
999	04136147	Repair Paved Parking Lot at HQ/VC	$44,000
999	05137233	FY04 Storm Damage – Repair Trux Road	$1,016

MMS Projects Organized by Rank			
Rank	Number	Description	Cost
999	05137251	FY04 Storm Damage – Repair Smartweed Impoundment Dike	$68,693
999	05137309	FY04 Storm Damage – Repair Hurricane Related Damage to Northwest Fork Road	$1,476,000
999	05138007	Replace Refuge 40x60 Tent	$15,000
999	05138009	Replace 2004 Dressta Dozer	$190,000
999	05138031	Repair Fire Control Building	$10,000
999	05138032	Clean Out of Hyde Park Canal	$20,000
999	05138034	Replace Water Control Structure – Pungo Lake Outfall	$40,000
999	05138042	Clean Out of Farm Field Ditches	$12,363,000
999	05138043	Clean Out of Farm Field Ditches	$53,000
999	05138044	Repost 80 Miles of Refuge Boundary Line	$8,000
999	05138046	Clean Silt Out of Allen Canal	$15,000
999	05138048	Replace Water Control Structure on North Lake	$67,000
999	05138049	Repair South Lake Drive Public Use Road FHWA R	$20,000
999	05138050	Remove Vegetation from Shore Drive Fire Break	$20,000
999	05138053	Repair Fire Control Building	$10,000
999	05138054	Clean Out of Hyde Park Canal	$20,000
999	05138158	Clean Out of Farm Field Ditches	$4,000
999	05138160	Clean Out of Farm Field Ditches	$5,000
999	05138033	Clean Out of Hyde Park Canal	$20,000
999	05138162	Clean Out of Farm Field Ditches	$1,000

Appendix IX. Wilderness Review

BACKGROUD

Wilderness reviews are a required component of the Fish and Wildlife Service comprehensive conservation planning process. The primary purpose of a wilderness review is to inventory the areas on refuges that might have wilderness character and identify each area as wilderness study area. A wilderness study area must be roadless and meet one of the following size criteria:

1. greater than 5,000 acres;
2. a roadless island of any size; or
3. less than 5,000 acres but of sufficient size to be practicably managed as wilderness.

A wilderness study area must also be natural and provide opportunities for solitude or primitive recreation. During the inventory phase of the wilderness review, the emphasis is on an assessment of wilderness character within the inventory unit. Sights and sounds originating from outside the unit, for example, those associated with military aircraft, cannot be used as justification to conclude that an area lacks wilderness character. Special values (e.g., ecological, geological, scenic, and historical) should be identified, but are not required. The determination to recommend (or not recommend) a wilderness study area to Congress for wilderness designation will be made through the comprehensive conservation plan decision-making process.

In May 2001, Fish and Wildlife Service staff met at Pocosin Lakes NWR to gather information and conduct field exams for the refuge's wilderness review. The review team from that meeting is listed in the table below.

Wilderness Review Team

Team Member	Title/Affiliation	Address	Phone
David Kitts	Acting Manager Pocosin Lakes NWR	P.O. Box 329 Columbia, NC 27925	252/796/3004
Wendy Stanton	Wildlife Biologist Pocosin Lakes NWR	P.O. Box 329 Columbia, NC 27925	252/796/3004
Michelle Chappell	Park Ranger Pocosin Lakes NWR	P.O. Box 329 Columbia, NC 27925	252/796/3004
Bob Glennon	Natural Resource Planner Ecosystem Planning Office	1106 West Queen Street Edenton, NC 27932	252/482-2364
D.A. Brown	Habitat Protection Biologist Ecosystem Planning Office	1106 West Queen Street Edenton, NC 27932	252/482-2364

Prior to the review, using database analysis of land status with a geographic information system, transportation system, and hydrographic information, ecosystem planning staff prepared a map of wilderness inventory units potentially meeting the wilderness study area criteria (Figure 8). These seven wilderness inventory units were evaluated over the course of the field exercise.

Figure 8. Wilderness inventory units of Pocosin Lakes NWR

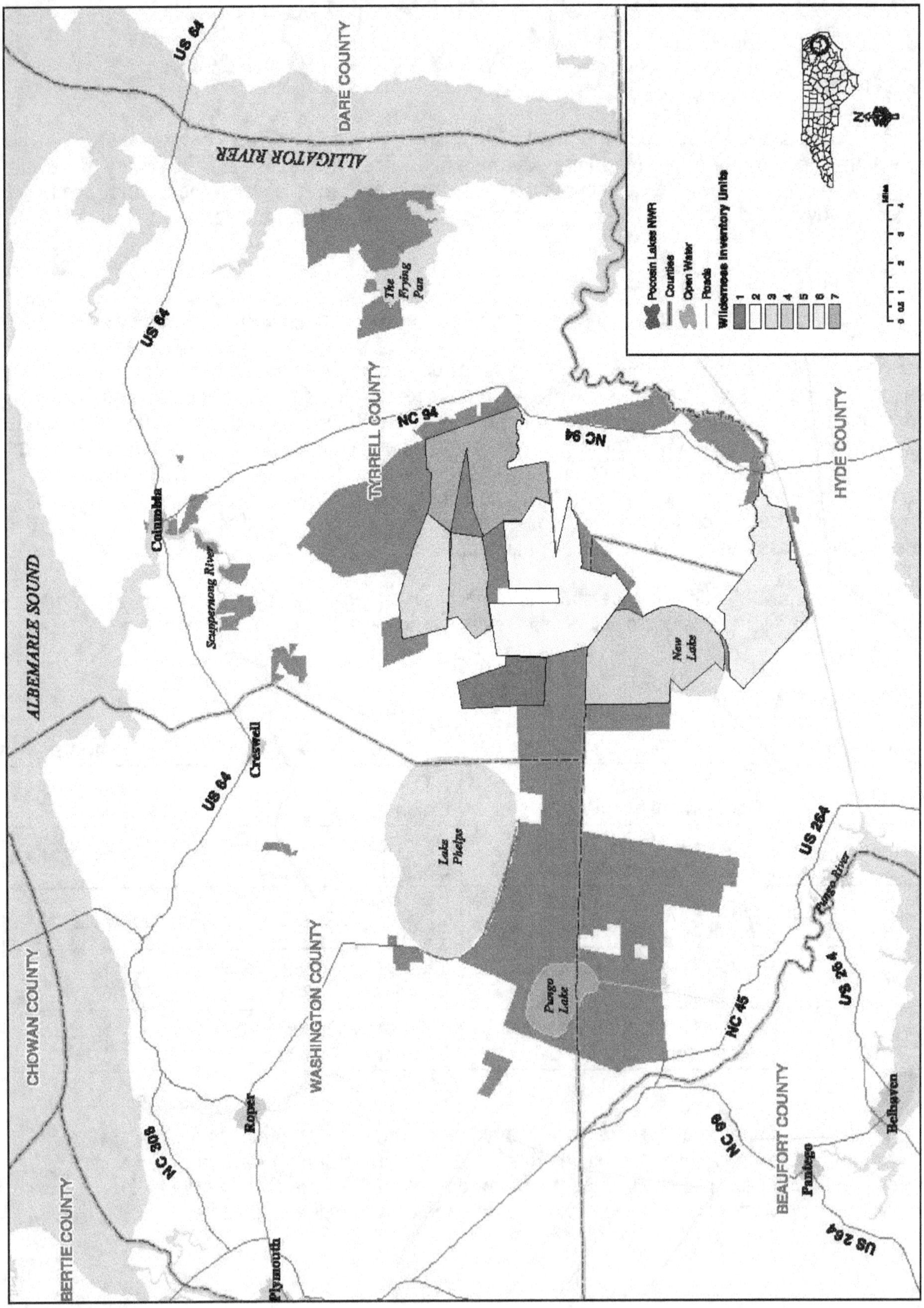

Wilderness inventory units - Pocosin Lakes NWR

Unit	Acreage	Habitat
1	2,762	Tall Pocosin
2	10,058	Tall Pocosin
3	3,770	Bottomland Hardwood Forest, Mixed Pine Hardwood Forest
4	2,778	Bottomland Hardwood Forest, Mixed Pine Hardwood Forest
5	8,292	Tall Pocosin
6	7,384	Freshwater Marsh, Cypress-Gum Swamp, and Tall Pocosin
7	7,562	Tall Pocosin, Mixed Pine Hardwood Forest

Participants also discussed the various steps, guidelines, and documentation requirements for conducting wilderness reviews; management goals, guidelines, and restrictions for designated wilderness; potential resource management issues associated with each inventory unit; and management alternatives for each unit that should be analyzed in the Draft CCP/EA for Pocosin Lakes NWR, which is a requirement of the National Environmental Policy Act.

DOCUMENTATION REQUIREMENTS

Photo documentation is required for each inventory unit to record existing wilderness character; any man-made features or "imprints of man's work" that affect the unit's naturalness; and condition of boundary roads. Photographs were taken during the field review; additional photographs were later taken from sounds and streams to give a complete impression of the inventory units. These photos will be keyed to text in the wilderness inventory evaluation reports and to maps.

WILDERNESS MANAGEMENT

The wilderness management policy and regulations allow motorized access and use of mechanized equipment for administrative purposes, provided such uses are the minimum necessary to accomplish wilderness objectives. For the purposes of analysis in the Draft CCP/EA, managers assumed that authorization of such uses would be temporary and rare in a wilderness area. If such restrictions would significantly limit Fish and Wildlife Service's ability to accomplish other resource management objectives, these impacts were fully described in the environmental consequences sections of the Draft CCP/EA and would have obviously been a factor for consideration in selecting a proposed alternative.

RESOURCE MANAGEMENT ISSUES

FIRE MANAGEMENT. A major concern is the need for controlled burning in areas where accumulated fuels could contribute to catastrophic wildfires, threatening the urban interface. The current smoke management guidelines have limited prescribed burns to 1,000 acres, so a burn on an entire 5,000-acre tract without firebreaks is not possible.

NAVIGABLE WATERS. Navigable waters (e.g., sounds, lakes, rivers, and creeks) bound most of the inventory units on Pocosin Lakes NWR. These waters are under the jurisdiction of the State of North Carolina. The Fish and Wildlife Service has limited authority to restrict activities, such as motorized boating, on navigable bodies of water.

RED-COCKADED WOODPECKER. The federally listed red-cockaded woodpecker inhabits mature loblolly pine trees in mixed pine and hardwood forests and requires relatively open old-growth pine stands for nesting and feeding. The aggregate of nesting cavity trees is called a cluster and may include one to twenty or more cavity trees on three to sixty acres. There are clusters on the Pocosin Lakes River NWR with a possibility for more clusters. The Red-cockaded Woodpecker Recovery Plan designated the Pocosin Lakes clusters as a support population rather than a recovery population. The staff will develop a Red-cockaded Woodpecker Management Plan for Pocosin Lakes NWR after the National Recovery Plan is completed. Current management activities on the refuge consist of clearing trails to the cavity trees by using machetes and a brush saw, paint marking and numbering trees, notation of locations with a geographic positioning system, and monitoring of nesting activity.

SOUTHERN PINE BEETLE. The Southern pine beetle attacks all species of pines, including the pond pine found on Pocosin Lakes NWR. The infestations are of concern because of the potential for killing red-cockaded woodpecker nest trees. On Alligator River NWR in Dare County, immediately east of Pocosin Lakes NWR, control measures have typically consisted of felling a buffer strip of green, uninfested trees at the spreading edge or front of the active infestation using a tracked feller-buncher. The width of the buffer strip is as wide as the average height of the trees.

MANAGEMENT SITUATIONS SUMMARY

A management situation summary will be prepared for each identified wilderness study area. The summary includes information regarding other important resource values and uses, which do not relate specifically to the key wilderness inventory criteria. It will be used primarily in evaluating alternatives and making management decisions during the study phase and in responding to questions from the public. Much of this information is required for the comprehensive conservation plan and can be summarized and the planning record referenced for more detail.

Maps of the area will be prepared showing roads, ditches, and special values, such as anadromous fish spawning areas, primary and secondary nurseries, outstanding resource waters, state natural heritage areas, and location of Federal and State listed threatened and endangered species. Surface disturbances would also be documented. Fish and Wildlife Service staff indicated that some roads and ditches might be abandoned at some point in the future, following a road review.

The following types of information should be included in a management situation summary:

- national wildlife refuge purposes;
- historic and existing public uses;
- historic and existing national wildlife refuge management activities;
- status of current step-down management plans (e.g., provisions of the fire management plan that relate to a specific wilderness study area);
- existing or proposed management practices requiring motorized access or equipment and/or mechanized transport;
- compatibility determinations;
- special use permits;
- military uses and memorandums of understanding;
- research uses; and
- commercial uses.

SUMMARY OF WILDERNESS REVIEW FINDINGS

The review team identified two wilderness study areas at the refuge in the table below and in Figure 9.

Wilderness study areas - Pocosin Lakes NWR

Unit Number	Suggested Name of WSA	Access	Acreage
2	Harvester Road Wilderness Study Area	Visual from Perimeter	10,058
6	Intracoastal Waterway Wilderness Study Area	Visual from Perimeter	7,384
Total			17,342

The findings for each of the inventory units, including the wilderness study areas, are summarized below.

Unit 1 (2,762 acres) was inventoried as a small tract of tall pocosin with the potential to be added to Unit 2, if the road and ditch that separates the two units could be abandoned. The refuge staff indicates that the road and ditch are important for refuge management and hydrology restoration and cannot be abandoned.

Unit 2 (10,058 acres) meets the criteria for a wilderness study area. The unit is larger than 5,000 acres, apparently natural, and provides outstanding opportunities for solitude. It is a tall pocosin named by the North Carolina Natural Heritage Program as the Harvester Road Tall Pocosin. The roads and ditches on the perimeter of the unit are important to refuge management and hydrology restoration. There are no roads or ditches within the unit. Access for pedestrians within the wilderness study area is not safe because the deep organic soil will not support the weight of visitors' bodies. Visitors may view the wilderness study area from the roads on the perimeter.

Unit 3 (3,770 acres) was inventoried as a small tract of bottomland hardwood forest and mixed pine hardwood forest with the potential to be added to Unit 4 and/or 7 if the roads and ditches that separate the units could be abandoned. The refuge staff indicates that the roads and ditches are important for refuge management and hydrology restoration and cannot be abandoned. Farmers who own the adjacent land have the rights to maintain the ditches to ensure drainage of their land.

Unit 4 (2,778 acres) was inventoried as a small tract with the potential to be added to Unit 3 and/or 7 if the roads and ditches that separate the units could be abandoned. The refuge staff indicates that the roads and ditches are important for refuge management and hydrology restoration and cannot be abandoned. Farmers who own the adjacent land have the rights to maintain the ditches to ensure drainage of their land.

Unit 5 (8,292 acres) meets the criteria for a wilderness study area, but will be burned by prescription more frequently than the natural frequency in pocosins to meet wildlife management needs.

Unit 6 (7,384 acres) meets the criteria for a wilderness study area. The unit is larger than 5,000 acres, apparently natural, and provides outstanding opportunities for solitude. The vegetation in the unit is freshwater marsh, cypress-gum swamp, and tall pocosin. The unit is too wet to be burned by prescription. Access for pedestrians within the wilderness study area is not safe because the deep organic soil will not support the weight of visitors' bodies. Visitors may view the wilderness study area from the roads on the perimeter.

Figure 9. Potential wilderness study areas of the Pocosin Lakes NWR

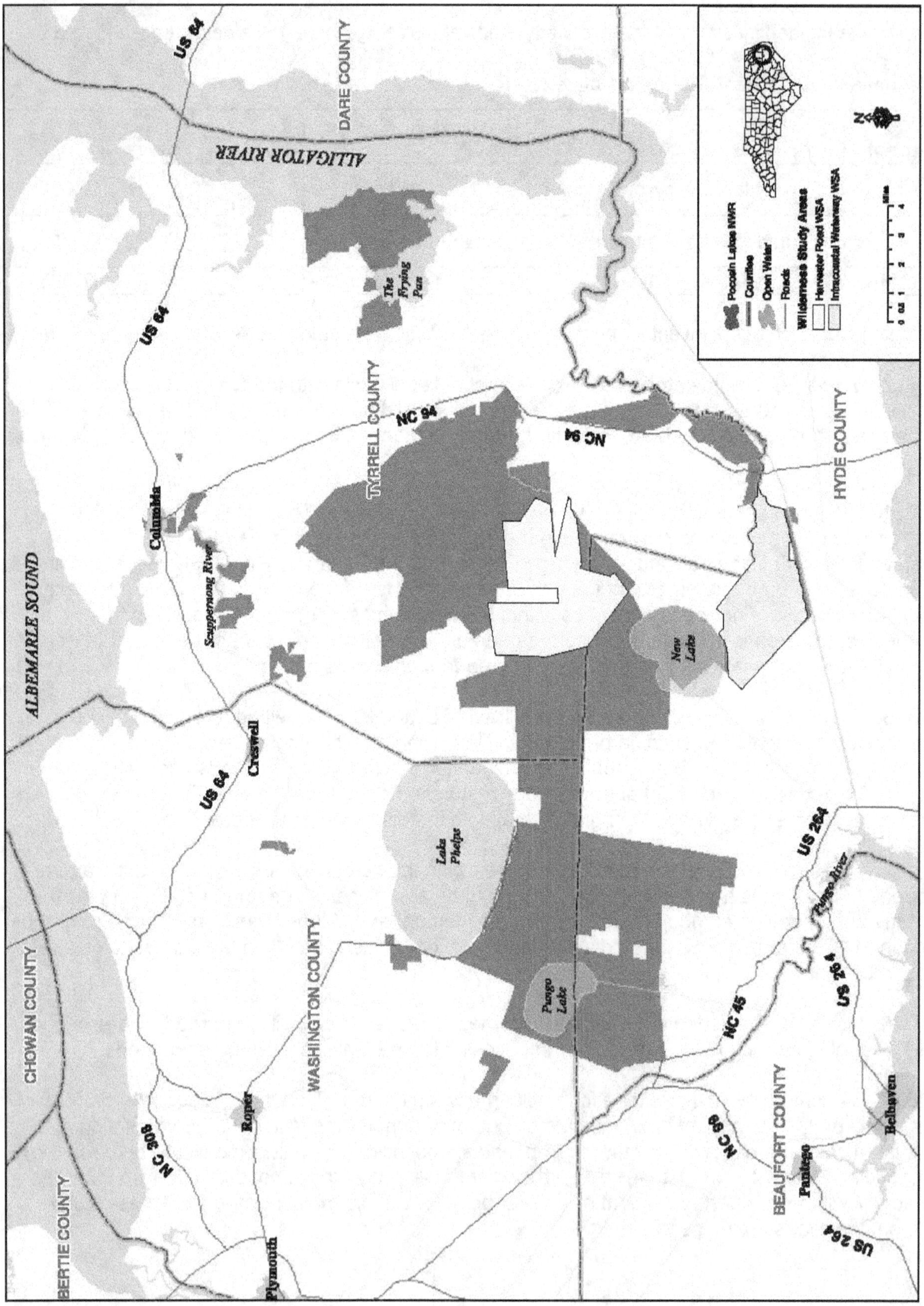

Pocosin Lakes National Wildlife Refuge

Unit 7 (7,562 acres) meets the criteria for a wilderness study area. The unit is larger than 5,000 acres, apparently natural, and provides outstanding opportunities for solitude. However, it will require intensive management to restore the Atlantic white cedar forest that once occupied the unit. The Atlantic white cedar was harvested decades ago and the site was not disturbed sufficiently to ensure regeneration of the stand. Other species now dominate the site. The unit will need intensive mechanical disturbance, herbicide application, and artificial regeneration.

The management needs that preclude consideration as a wilderness study area are summarized below.

Management needs and other considerations in wilderness inventory units not considered wilderness study areas

Unit Number	Management Needs	Other Considerations	Acreage
1	Hydrology Restoration	Small Tract, Ditch Cannot be Filled to Join Other Units	2,762
3	Hydrology Restoration	Small Tract, Ditch Cannot be Filled to Join Unit 4 or 7, Neighbors Depend on Drainage	3,770
4	Hydrology Restoration	Small Tract, Ditch Cannot be Filled to Join Unit 3 or 7, Neighbors Depend on Drainage	2,778
5	Prescribed Burning More Frequent Than Natural Frequency	None	8,292
7	Intensive Mechanical Disturbance, Herbicide Application, Artificial Regeneration for Atlantic White Cedar	None	7,562

Appendix X. Consultation and Coordination

The Service formed a planning core team composed of representatives from various Service divisions to prepare the Draft CCP/EA. Initially, the team focused on identifying the issues and concerns pertinent to refuge management. The team met on several occasions from December 2000 to June 2002. A biological review team met on the refuge four times between December 1999 and December 2000 to assess the habitats on the refuge and the needs of wildlife species in the ecosystem, and to make recommendations on land management and acquisition needs. The core team also sought the contributions of experts from various fields.

This appendix summarizes the consultation and coordination that occurred in the processes of identifying the issues, alternatives, and proposed alternative, which were presented in the Draft CCP/EA; during the period of time while the Draft CCP/EA was being prepared and distributed; and during the period of public review and comment on the Draft CCP/EA.

Pocosin Lakes NWR comprehensive conservation plan core planning team members

Name and Title	Station, Refuge, Location
Howard Phillips, Refuge Manager David Kitts, Assistant Manager Wendy Stanton, Wildlife Biologist Vince Carver, Fire Management Officer Susan Russo, former Park Ranger Michelle Chappell, former Park Ranger	Pocosin Lakes National Wildlife Refuge U.S. Fish and Wildlife Service Columbia, North Carolina
Robert Glennon, former Natural Resource Planner David Brown, former Habitat Protection Biologist	Ecosystem Planning Office U.S. Fish and Wildlife Service Edenton, North Carolina

Pocosin Lakes National Wildlife Refuge comprehensive conservation plan biological review team members

Name, Title	Affiliation, Location
Bob Noffsinger, former Supervisory Wildlife Management Biologist	Migratory Bird Field Office U.S. Fish and Wildlife Service Manteo, North Carolina
Frank Bowers, former Migratory Bird Coordinator	Southeast Regional Office U.S. Fish and Wildlife Service Atlanta, Georgia
Chuck Hunter, former Nongame Migratory Bird Coordinator	Southeast Regional Office U.S. Fish and Wildlife Service Atlanta, Georgia
Ronnie Smith, Fisheries Biologist	Fisheries Assistance Office U.S. Fish and Wildlife Service Edenton, North Carolina
John Stanton, former Wildlife Biologist	Mattamuskeet National Wildlife Refuge U.S. Fish and Wildlife Service Swan Quarter, North Carolina
Wendy Stanton, Wildlife Biologist	Pocosin Lakes National Wildlife Refuge U.S. Fish and Wildlife Service Columbia, North Carolina
Dennis Stewart, Wildlife Biologist	Alligator River National Wildlife Refuge U.S. Fish and Wildlife Service Manteo, North Carolina
Ralph Keel, former Wildlife Biologist	Great Dismal Swamp National Wildlife Refuge U.S. Fish and Wildlife Service Suffolk, Virginia
John Gallegos, Wildlife Biologist	Back Bay National Wildlife Refuge U.S. Fish and Wildlife Service Virginia Beach, Virginia
David Allen, Nongame Wildlife Biologist	North Carolina Wildlife Resources Commission New Bern, North Carolina

Expert contributors to the Pocosin Lakes NWR comprehensive conservation plan and their area(s) of expertise

Name, Title, Affiliation, Location	Area of Expertise
Bill Grabill, former Refuge Supervisor U.S. Fish and Wildlife Service Atlanta, Georgia	Refuge Management
Rufus Croom, District Conservationist USDA, Natural Resources Conservation Service Plymouth, North Carolina	Soil and Water Conservation Federal Land Conservation Programs
John Gagnon, Soil Scientist USDA, Natural Resources Conservation Service Edenton, North Carolina	Soil Science
Kevin Moody, former NEPA Specialist U.S. Fish and Wildlife Service Atlanta, Georgia	National Environmental Policy Act
John Ann Shearer, Private Lands Biologist U.S. Fish and Wildlife Service Raleigh, North Carolina	Wetland Management, Partners for Fish and Wildlife Program
Richard Kanaski, Regional Archaeologist U.S. Fish and Wildlife Service Savannah, Georgia	Cultural Resources

To expand the range of issues and to generate potential alternatives, the core planning team met in January 2001. Shortly thereafter, on February 15, 16, 20, 22, and 23, in Washington, Swan Quarter, Plymouth, Columbia, and Manns Harbor, North Carolina, the planning team held public meetings to gain the insights of local citizens and their perceptions of the issues and concerns facing the refuge.

The issues and alternatives generated from these meetings, coupled with the input of the planning team, were summarized in Chapters I and III of the environmental assessment, which was Section B of the Draft CCP for Pocosin Lakes NWR. After the team developed the alternatives, it held public meetings on April 25 and 28, 2005, in Plymouth and Columbia, North Carolina, to garner public reaction on the alternatives.

The Draft CCP/EA for Pocosin Lakes NWR was released for public review and comment in July 2007. A news release and flyers were sent announcing the deadline for accepting public comments as August 15, 2007. In addition, two open house meetings were held on Wednesday, July 25, at the Vernon James Center in Washington County and on Thursday, July 26, at the Walter B. Jones, Sr., Center for the Sounds in Tyrrell County. Comments were compliled and responses were developed. Some changes were incorporated into this final CCP.

Appendix XI. Finding of No Significant Impact

Pocosin Lakes National Wildlife Refuge
Comprehensive Conservation Plan
Tyrrell, Washington, and Hyde Counties, North Carolina

Introduction
The U.S. Fish and Wildlife Service proposes to protect and manage certain fish and wildlife resources in Tyrrell, Washington, and Hyde Counties, North Carolina, through the Pocosin Lakes National Wildlife Refuge. An Environmental Assessment was prepared to inform the public of the possible environmental consequences of implementing the Comprehensive Conservation Plan for Pocosin Lakes National Wildlife Refuge. A description of the alternatives, the rationale for selecting the preferred alternative, the environmental effects of the preferred alternative, the potential adverse effects of the action, and a declaration concerning the factors determining the significance of effects, in compliance with the National Environmental Policy Act of 1969, are outlined below. The supporting information can be found in the Environmental Assessment, which was Section B of the Draft Comprehensive Conservation Plan.

Alternatives
In developing the Comprehensive Conservation Plan (CCP) for Pocosin Lakes National Wildlife Refuge, the Fish and Wildlife Service evaluated four alternatives: Alternatives 1, 2, 3, and 4.

The Service adopted Alternative 2 as the preferred alternative for guiding the direction of the refuge over the next 15 years. The overriding concern reflected in this CCP is that wildlife conservation assumes first priority in refuge management and wildlife-dependent recreational uses are allowed if they are compatible with wildlife conservation. Wildlife-dependent recreation uses (e.g., hunting, fishing, wildlife observation, wildlife photography, and environmental education and interpretation) will be emphasized and encouraged.

Alternative 1. Current Management
Alternative 1 represents no change from current management of the refuge. Under this alternative, 110,106 acres of refuge lands would be protected, maintained, restored, and enhanced for waterfowl, neotropical migratory birds, threatened and endangered species, and resident wildlife. Refuge management programs would continue to be developed and implemented with baseline biological information only on waterbird populations and moist-soil vegetation. All refuge management actions would be directed toward achieving the refuge's primary purposes (i.e., conserving wintering habitat for waterfowl, providing production habitat for wood ducks, and helping to meet the habitat conservation goals of the North American Waterfowl Management Plan), while contributing to other national, regional, and State goals to protect and restore migratory bird populations. Cooperative farming would continue to be used to manage and maintain approximately 1,250 acres of cropland; the refuge would manage 443 acres of moist-soil habitats. The refuge would manage marshes and pine forests with prescribed fire. The current level of wildlife-dependent recreation (e.g., hunting, fishing, wildlife observation, wildlife photography, and environmental education and interpretation) opportunities would be maintained to serve 242,000 visitors. Outreach efforts would target a population of 4 million. There would be a modest volunteer program to support refuge programs. Under this alternative, the refuge would continue to seek acquisition of all willing-seller properties within the present acquisition boundary.

Alternative 2. Preferred Alternative
The preferred alternative, Alternative 2, represents management of the highest priority habitats and wildlife species on the refuge. Under this alternative, 110,106 acres of refuge lands would be protected, maintained, restored, and enhanced for waterfowl, neotropical migratory birds, threatened and endangered species and resident wildlife. Refuge management programs would continue to be developed and implemented with baseline biological information on high-priority habitats and wildlife species. All refuge management actions would be directed toward achieving the refuge's primary purposes (i.e., conserving wintering habitat for waterfowl, providing production habitat for wood ducks, and helping to meet the habitat conservation goals of the North American Waterfowl Management Plan), while contributing to other national, regional, and State goals to protect and restore migratory bird populations. Cooperative farming would continue to be used to manage and maintain approximately 1,410 acres of cropland; the refuge would manage 593 acres of moist-soil habitats. The refuge would manage marshes and pine forests with prescribed fire, and selected habitats with thinning and timber harvest. The level of wildlife-dependent recreation (e.g., hunting, fishing, wildlife observation, wildlife photography, and environmental education and interpretation) opportunities would be increased to serve 467,000 visitors. Outreach efforts would target a population of 16 million. There would be an extensive volunteer program to support refuge programs. Under this alternative, the refuge would continue to seek acquisition of all willing-seller properties within the present acquisition boundary. The refuge would add more staff, equipment, and facilities in order to survey wildlife and habitat, manage habitat, and provide public use opportunities.

Alternative 3
Alternative 3 represents management of all habitats and wildlife species on the refuge. Under this alternative, 110,106 acres of refuge lands would be protected, maintained, restored, and enhanced for waterfowl, neotropical migratory birds, threatened and endangered species and resident wildlife. Refuge management programs would continue to be developed and implemented with baseline biological information on all habitats and wildlife species. All refuge management actions would be directed toward achieving the refuge's primary purposes (i.e., conserving wintering habitat for waterfowl, providing production habitat for wood ducks, and helping to meet the habitat conservation goals of the North American Waterfowl Management Plan), while contributing to other national, regional, and State goals to protect and restore migratory bird populations. Cooperative farming would continue to be used to manage and maintain approximately 1,710 acres of cropland; the refuge would manage 743 acres of moist-soil habitats. The refuge would manage marshes and pine forests with prescribed fire, and all habitats with thinning and timber harvest. The level of wildlife-dependent recreation (e.g., hunting, fishing, wildlife observation, wildlife photography, and environmental education and interpretation) opportunities would be increased to serve 722,000 visitors. Outreach efforts would target a population of 25 million. There would be an extensive volunteer program to support refuge programs. Under this alternative, the refuge would continue to seek acquisition of all willing-seller properties within the present acquisition boundary. The refuge would add more staff, equipment, and facilities in order to survey wildlife and habitat, manage habitat, and provide public use opportunities.

Alternative 4
Alternative 4 represents minimal management of habitats and wildlife species on the refuge as staff retires or transfers and is not replaced. Under this alternative, 110,106 acres of refuge lands would be protected, maintained, restored, and enhanced for waterfowl, neotropical migratory birds, threatened and endangered species, and resident wildlife. Refuge management programs would continue to be developed and implemented with baseline biological information only on waterfowl populations and moist-soil vegetation. All refuge management actions would be directed toward achieving the refuge's primary purposes (i.e., conserving wintering habitat for waterfowl, providing production habitat for wood ducks, and helping to meet the habitat conservation goals of the North

American Waterfowl Management Plan), while contributing to other national, regional, and State goals to protect and restore migratory bird populations. Cooperative farming would continue to be used to manage and maintain approximately 1,250 acres of cropland; the refuge would manage 443 acres of moist-soil habitats. The refuge would manage marshes and pine forests with prescribed fire. The level of wildlife-dependent recreation (e.g., hunting, fishing, wildlife observation, wildlife photography, and environmental education and interpretation) opportunities would be decreased to serve 84,000 visitors. Outreach efforts would target a population of 10,000. There would be a modest volunteer program to support refuge programs. Under this alternative, the refuge would continue to seek acquisition of all willing-seller properties within the present acquisition boundary. The refuge would lose staff to retirements and transfers and not replace them. It would replace equipment and facilities as they break down or are beyond repair. Road access for the public would be limited access on roads that lead to wildlife observation platforms.

Selection Rationale
Alternative 2 is selected for implementation because it directs the development of programs to best achieve the refuge purposes and goals; emphasizes the management of high-priority habitats; collects data on selected habitats and wildlife species; and ensures long-term achievement of refuge and Service objectives. At the same time, these management actions provide balanced levels of compatible public use opportunities consistent with existing laws, Service policies, and sound biological principles. It provides the best mix of program elements to achieve desired long-term conditions.

Under Alternative 2, a land protection plan will be developed and lands outside the boundary will be prioritized for land protection to best achieve national, ecosystem, and refuge-specific goals and objectives within anticipated funding and staffing levels. In addition, the action positively addresses significant issues and concerns expressed by the public.

Environmental Effects
Implementation of the Service's management action is expected to result in environmental, social, and economic effects as outlined in the CCP. Habitat management, population management, land conservation, and visitor service management activities on Pocosin Lakes NWR would result in increased migratory bird utilization and production; increased protection for threatened and endangered species; enhanced wildlife populations; improved habitat conditions; and enhanced opportunities for wildlife-dependent recreation and environmental education. These effects are detailed as follows:

1. Waterfowl, marsh bird and wading bird use of the refuge would improve as intensive water management efforts would provide dependable flooded habitats with high-quality food to match the migration chronologies of these species. Forest breeding birds would benefit from forest management actions. Woodcock population numbers and habitat use would be monitored and managed and woodcock use of the refuge would be expected to increase.

2. Migratory bird production would increase by enhancing forest habitat quality for neotropical migratory birds, habitat and food availability for wintering waterfowl, and through forest management. Forest management practices, such as prescribed burning, thinning, selective harvests, and conservation of mature stand components, would benefit nesting and feeding habitat for neotropical migratory birds.

3. Refuge land acquisition, habitat management, and habitat and wildlife protection would benefit the recovery of threatened and endangered species. Bald eagles may have historically nested on the refuge. Red-cockaded woodpeckers nest in the pine forests. Red wolves inhabit the entire refuge.

4. The refuge's habitat mix of cropland, moist soil, marsh, and pine and hardwood forest, as well as habitat management, would improve food and cover for resident wildlife species and enhance wetland communities within the refuge.

5. Habitat management, along with a focus on accessibility and facility developments, would result in improved wildlife-dependent recreational opportunities. While public use would result in some minimal, short-term adverse effects on wildlife, and user conflicts may occur at certain times of the year, these effects are minimized by site design, time zoning, and implementing refuge regulations. Anticipated long-term impacts to wildlife and wildlife habitats of implementing the management action are positive. In the long-run, wildlife habitat and increased opportunities for wildlife-dependent recreation opportunities could result in an increase in economic benefits to the local community.

6. Implementing the comprehensive CCP is not expected to have any significant adverse effects on wetlands and floodplains, pursuant to Executive Orders 11990 and 11988, as actions would not result in development of buildings and/or structures within floodplain areas, nor would they result in irrevocable, long-term adverse impacts. In fact, a major thrust of the management action is to implement forest and marsh management within the wildlife communities of the refuge that has been severely impacted by actions of previous landowners. Implementing the management action would result in substantial enhancement of forest and herbaceous wetland communities and net increases to the Nation's habitat and quality.

Potential Adverse Effects and Mitigation Measures
Wildlife Disturbance

Disturbance to wildlife at some level is an unavoidable consequence of any public use program, regardless of the activity involved. Obviously, some activities innately have the potential to be more disturbing than others. The management actions to be implemented have been carefully planned to avoid unacceptable levels of impact.

As currently proposed, the known and anticipated levels of disturbance of the management action are considered minimal and well within the tolerance level of known wildlife species and populations present in the area. Implementation of the public use program would take place through carefully controlled time and space zoning such as establishment of protection zones around key sites, rookeries and eagle nests (if necessary), and routing of roads and trails to avoid direct contact with sensitive areas, such as nesting bird habitat. All hunting activities (season lengths, bag limits, number of hunters) would be conducted within the constraints of sound biological principles and refuge-specific regulations established to restrict illegal or non-conforming activities. Monitoring activities through wildlife inventories and assessments of public use levels and activities would be utilized, and public use programs would be adjusted as needed to limit disturbance.

User Group Conflicts

As public use levels expand across time, some conflicts between user groups may occur. Programs would be adjusted, as needed, to eliminate or minimize these problems and provide quality wildlife-dependent recreational opportunities. Experience has proven that time and space zonings, such as establishment of separate use areas, use periods, and restricting numbers of users, are effective tools in eliminating conflicts between user groups.

Effects on Adjacent Landowners

Implementation of the management action should not substantially impact adjacent or in-holding landowners. Some minor impacts would be off-set by benefits to the adjacent landowners. Essential access to private property would be allowed through issuance of special use permits. Future land acquisition would occur on a willing-seller basis only, at fair market values within the approved acquisition boundary. Lands are acquired through a combination of fee title purchases and/or donations and less-than-fee title interests (e.g., conservation easements, cooperative agreements) from willing sellers. Funds for the acquisition of lands within the approved acquisition boundary would likely come from the Land and Water Conservation Fund or the Migratory Bird Conservation Act.

Land Ownership and Site Development

Land ownership by the Service precludes any future economic development by the private sector; however, the presence of the refuge provides opportunities for ecotourism and therefore potential for nature-based tourism economic development in local communities. Proposed acquisition efforts by the Service would result in changes in land and recreational use patterns, since all uses on national wildlife refuges must meet compatibility standards. Potential development of access roads, dikes, water control structures, and visitor parking areas could lead to minor short-term negative impacts on plants, soil, and some wildlife species. When site development activities are proposed, each activity will be given the appropriate National Environmental Policy Act consideration during pre-construction planning. At that time, any required mitigation activities will be incorporated into the specific project to reduce the level of impacts to the human environment and to protect fish and wildlife and their habitats.

As indicated earlier, one of the direct effects of site development is increased public use; this increased use may lead to littering, noise, and vehicle traffic. While funding and personnel resources will be allocated to minimize these effects, such allocations make these resources unavailable for other programs.

The management action is not expected to have significant adverse effects on wetlands and floodplains, pursuant to Executive Orders 11990 and 11988.

Coordination

The management action has been thoroughly coordinated with all interested and/or affected parties. Parties contacted include:

All affected landowners
Congressional representatives
Governor of North Carolina
North Carolina Wildlife Resources Commission
North Carolina State Historic Preservation Officer
North Carolina Department of Environment and Natural Resources,
Division of Coastal Management
Local community officials
Interested citizens
Conservation organizations

Findings

It is my determination that the management action does not constitute a major federal action significantly affecting the quality of the human environment under the meaning of Section 102(2)(c) of the National Environmental Policy Act of 1969 (as amended). As such, an environmental impact statement is not required. This determination is based on the following factors (40 C.F.R. 1508.27), as addressed in the Environmental Assessment, which was Section B of the Draft Comprehensive Conservation Plan for the Pocosin Lakes National Wildlife Refuge:

1. Both beneficial and adverse effects have been considered and this action will not have a significant effect on the human environment. (Environmental Assessment, pages 141-152).

2. The actions will not have a significant effect on public health and safety. (Environmental Assessment, pages 141-152).

3. The project will not significantly affect any unique characteristics of the geographic area such as proximity to historical or cultural resources, wild and scenic rivers, or ecologically critical areas. (Environmental Assessment, pages 141-152).

4. The effects on the quality of the human environment are not likely to be highly controversial. (Environmental Assessment, pages 141-152).

5. The actions do not involve highly uncertain, unique, or unknown environmental risks to the human environment. (Environmental Assessment, pages 141-152).

6. The actions will not establish a precedent for future actions with significant effects nor do they represent a decision in principle about a future consideration. (Environmental Assessment, pages 141-152).

7. There will be no cumulatively significant impacts on the environment. Cumulative impacts have been analyzed with consideration of other similar activities on adjacent lands, in past action, and in foreseeable future actions. (Environmental Assessment, pages 141-152).

8. The actions will not significantly affect any site listed in, or eligible for listing in, the National Register of Historic Places, nor will they cause loss or destruction of significant scientific, cultural, or historic resources. (Environmental Assessment, pages 141-152).

9. The actions are not likely to adversely affect threatened or endangered species, or their habitats. (Environmental Assessment, pages 141-152; Appendix V).

10. The actions will not lead to a violation of federal, state, or local laws imposed for the protection of the environment. (Environmental Assessment, pages 141-152).

Supporting References

Fish and Wildlife Service. 2007. Draft Comprehensive Conservation Plan and Environmental Assessment for Pocosin Lakes National Wildlife Refuge, Tyrrell, Washington, and Hyde Counties, North Carolina. U.S. Department of the Interior, Fish and Wildlife Service, Southeast Region.

Document Availability

The Environmental Assessment was Section B of the Draft Comprehensive Conservation Plan for Pocosin Lakes National Wildlife Refuge and was made available in July 2007. Additional copies are available by writing: U.S. Fish and Wildlife Service, 1875 Century Boulevard, Atlanta, GA 30345 or download from www.fws.gov/southeast/planning/draftDocs.htm..

_____   _____9/28/07_____
Sam D. Hamilton   Date
Regional Director

www.ingramcontent.com/pod-product-compliance
Lightning Source LLC
Chambersburg PA
CBHW081058290526
45795CB00006B/1908